State Responses to International Law

Do countries keep their promises to the international community? When they sign treaties or learn about new expectations, do they take them seriously and implement them? Since we already know intuitively that not all countries do, the next question – and the topic of this book – is: who complies? By considering a wide range of different rules – each precise enough to allow one to measure state compliance – and a variety of methods, we hope to answer this question once and for all.

Including a systematic analysis of eight different countries selected for the variety of regime type, international engagement, and economic development they represent, the work caps a five-year research program. Stiles highlights the importance of systematic study of compliance in order to move further towards solving truly global issues, such as terrorism, human trafficking, air pollution, and collective goods provision. With international laws generally designed to improve the human condition and current levels of compliance inconsistent at best, it is vital to gain a better understanding of who complies and why.

This detailed study will be of interest to students of Politics, International Law, and International Relations.

Kendall Stiles is Professor of Political Science at Brigham Young University, Utah, USA. He teaches International Relations with an emphasis on law and institutions.

Routledge advances in international relations and global politics

1 **Foreign Policy and Discourse Analysis**
France, Britain and Europe
Henrik Larsen

2 **Agency, Structure and International Politics**
From ontology to empirical enquiry
Gil Friedman and Harvey Starr

3 **The Political Economy of Regional Co-operation in the Middle East**
Ali Carkoglu, Mine Eder and Kemal Kirisci

4 **Peace Maintenance**
The evolution of international political authority
Jarat Chopra

5 **International Relations and Historical Sociology**
Breaking down boundaries
Stephen Hobden

6 **Equivalence in Comparative Politics**
Edited by Jan W. van Deth

7 **The Politics of Central Banks**
Robert Elgie and Helen Thompson

8 **Politics and Globalisation**
Knowledge, ethics and agency
Martin Shaw

9 **History and International Relations**
Thomas W. Smith

10 **Idealism and Realism in International Relations**
Robert M. A. Crawford

11 **National and International Conflicts, 1945–1995**
New empirical and theoretical approaches
Frank Pfetsch and Christoph Rohloff

12 **Party Systems and Voter Alignments Revisited**
Edited by Lauri Karvonen and Stein Kuhnle

13 **Ethics, Justice and International Relations**
Constructing an international community
Peter Sutch

14 **Capturing Globalization**
Edited by James H. Mittelman and Norani Othman

15 **Uncertain Europe**
Building a new European security order?
Edited by Martin A. Smith and Graham Timmins

16 **Power, Postcolonialism and International Relations**
Reading race, gender and class
Edited by Geeta Chowdhry and Sheila Nair

17 **Constituting Human Rights**
Global civil society and the society of democratic states
Mervyn Frost

18 **US Economic Statecraft for Survival 1933–1991**
Of sanctions, embargoes and economic warfare
Alan P. Dobson

19 **The EU and NATO Enlargement**
Richard McAllister and Roland Dannreuther

20 **Spatializing International Politics**
Analysing activism on the internet
Jayne Rodgers

21 **Ethnonationalism in the Contemporary World**
Walker Connor and the study of nationalism
Edited by Daniele Conversi

22 **Meaning and International Relations**
Edited by Peter Mandaville and Andrew Williams

23 **Political Loyalty and the Nation-State**
Edited by Michael Waller and Andrew Linklater

24 **Russian Foreign Policy and the CIS**
Theories, debates and actions
Nicole J. Jackson

25 **Asia and Europe**
Development and different dimensions of ASEM
Yeo Lay Hwee

26 **Global Instability and Strategic Crisis**
Neville Brown

27 **Africa in International Politics**
External involvement on the continent
Edited by Ian Taylor and Paul Williams

28 **Global Governmentality**
Governing international spaces
Edited by Wendy Larner and William Walters

29 **Political Learning and Citizenship Education Under Conflict**
The political socialization of Israeli and Palestinian youngsters
Orit Ichilov

30 **Gender and Civil Society**
Transcending boundaries
Edited by Jude Howell and Diane Mulligan

31 **State Crises, Globalisation and National Movements in North-East Africa**
The Horn's dilemma
Edited by Asafa Jalata

32 Diplomacy and Developing Nations
Post-cold war foreign policy-making structures and processes
Edited by Justin Robertson and Maurice A. East

33 Autonomy, Self-governance and Conflict Resolution
Innovative approaches to institutional design in divided societies
Edited by Marc Weller and Stefan Wolff

34 Mediating International Crises
Jonathan Wilkenfeld, Kathleen J. Young, David M. Quinn and Victor Asal

35 Postcolonial Politics, the Internet and Everyday Life
Pacific traversals online
M. I. Franklin

36 Reconstituting the Global Liberal Order
Legitimacy and regulation
Kanishka Jayasuriya

37 International Relations, Security and Jeremy Bentham
Gunhild Hoogensen

38 Interregionalism and International Relations
Edited by Heiner Hänggi, Ralf Roloff and Jürgen Rüland

39 The International Criminal Court
A global civil society achievement
Marlies Glasius

40 A Human Security Doctrine for Europe
Project, principles, practicalities
Edited by Marlies Glasius and Mary Kaldor

41 The History and Politics of UN Security Council Reform
Dimitris Bourantonis

42 Russia and NATO Since 1991
From cold war through cold peace to partnership?
Martin A. Smith

43 The Politics of Protection
Sites of insecurity and political agency
Edited by Jef Huysmans, Andrew Dobson and Raia Prokhovnik

44 International Relations in Europe
Traditions, perspectives and destinations
Edited by Knud Erik Jørgensen and Tonny Brems Knudsen

45 The Empire of Security and the Safety of the People
Edited by William Bain

46 Globalization and Religious Nationalism in India
The search for ontological security
Catrina Kinnvall

47 Culture and International Relations
Narratives, natives and tourists
Julie Reeves

48 Global Civil Society
Contested futures
Edited by Gideon Baker and David Chandler

49 Rethinking Ethical Foreign Policy
Pitfalls, possibilities and paradoxes
Edited by David Chandler and Volker Heins

50 International Cooperation and Arctic Governance
Regime effectiveness and northern region building
Edited by Olav Schram Stokke and Geir Hønneland

51 Human Security
Concepts and implications
Shahrbanou Tadjbakhsh and Anuradha Chenoy

52 International Relations and Security in the Digital Age
Edited by Johan Eriksson and Giampiero Giacomello

53 State-Building
Theory and practice
Edited by Aidan Hehir and Neil Robinson

54 Violence and Non-Violence in Africa
Edited by Pal Ahluwalia, Louise Bethlehem and Ruth Ginio

55 Developing Countries and Global Trade Negotiations
Edited by Larry Crump and S. Javed Maswood

56 Civil Society, Religion and Global Governance
Paradigms of power and persuasion
Edited by Helen James

57 War, Peace and Hegemony in a Globalized World
The changing balance of power in the twenty-first century
Edited by Chandra Chari

58 Economic Globalisation as Religious War
Tragic convergence
Michael McKinley

59 Globalization, Prostitution and Sex-trafficking
Corporeal politics
Elina Penttinen

60 Peacebuilding
Women in international perspective
Elisabeth Porter

61 Ethics, Liberalism and Realism in International Relations
Mark D. Gismondi

62 Law and Legalization in Transnational Relations
Edited by Christian Brütsch and Dirk Lehmkuhl

63 Fighting Terrorism and Drugs
Europe and international police cooperation
Jörg Friedrichs

64 Identity Politics in the Age of Genocide
The holocaust and historical representation
David B. MacDonald

65 Globalisation, Public Opinion and the State
Western Europe and East and Southeast Asia
Edited by Takashi Inoguchi and Ian Marsh

66 **Urbicide**
The politics of urban destruction
Martin Coward

67 **Transnational Activism in the UN and the EU**
A comparative study
Jutta Joachim and Birgit Locher

68 **Gender Inclusive**
Essays on violence, men and feminist international relations
Adam Jones

69 **Capitalism, Democracy and the Prevention of War and Poverty**
Edited by Peter Graeff and Guido Mehlkop

70 **Environmental Change and Foreign Policy**
Theory and practice
Edited by Paul G. Harris

71 **Climate Change and Foreign Policy**
Case studies from East to West
Edited by Paul G. Harris

72 **Securitizations of Citizenship**
Edited by Peter Nyers

73 **The Power of Ideology**
From the Roman Empire to Al-Qaeda
Alex Roberto Hybel

74 **The Securitization of Humanitarian Migration**
Digging moats and sinking boats
Scott D. Watson

75 **Mediation in the Asia-Pacific Region**
Transforming conflicts and building peace
Edited by Dale Bagshaw and Elisabeth Porter

76 **United Nations Reform**
Heading North or South?
Spencer Zifcak

77 **New Norms and Knowledge in World Politics**
Protecting people, intellectual property and the environment
Preslava Stoeva

78 **Power, Resistance and Conflict in the Contemporary World**
Social movements, networks and hierarchies
Athina Karatzogianni and Andrew Robinson

79 **World-Regional Social Policy and Global Governance**
New research and policy agendas in Africa, Asia, Europe and Latin America
Edited by Bob Deacon, Maria Cristina Macovei, Luk Van Langenhove and Nicola Yeates

80 **International Relations Theory and Philosophy**
Interpretive dialogues
Edited by Cerwyn Moore and Chris Farrands

81 **Superpower Rivalry and Conflict**
The long shadow of the Cold War on the twenty-first century
Edited by Chandra Chari

82 **Coping and Conformity in World Politics**
Hugh C. Dyer

83 **Defining and Defying Organized Crime**
Discourse, perception and reality
Edited by Felia Allum, Francesca Longo, Daniela Irrera and Panos A. Kostakos

84 **Federalism in Asia**
India, Pakistan and Malaysia
Harihar Bhattacharyya

85 **The World Bank and HIV/AIDS**
Setting a global agenda
Sophie Harman

86 **The "War on Terror" and the Growth of Executive Power?**
A comparative analysis
Edited by John E. Owens and Riccardo Pelizzo

87 **The Contested Politics of Mobility**
Borderzones and irregularity
Edited by Vicki Squires

88 **Human Security, Law and the Prevention of Terrorism**
Andrej Zwitter

89 **Multilayered Migration Governance**
The promise of partnership
Edited by Rahel Kunz, Sandra Lavenex and Marion Panizzon

90 **Role Theory in International Relations**
Approaches and analyses
Edited by Sebastian Harnisch, Cornelia Frank and Hanns W. Maull

91 **Issue Salience in International Relations**
Edited by Kai Oppermann and Henrike Viehrig

92 **Corporate Risk and National Security Redefined**
Karen Lund Petersen

93 **Interrogating Democracy in World Politics**
Edited by Joe Hoover, Meera Sabaratnam and Laust Schouenborg

94 **Globalizing Resistance against War**
Theories of resistance and the new anti-war movement
Tiina Seppälä

95 **The Politics of Self-Determination**
Beyond the decolonisation process
Kristina Roepstorff

96 **Sovereignty and the Responsibility to Protect**
The power of norms and the norms of the powerful
Theresa Reinold

97 **Anglo-American Relations**
Contemporary perspectives
Edited by Alan P. Dobson and Steve Marsh

98 **The Emerging Politics of Antarctica**
Edited by Anne-Marie Brady

99 **Genocide, Ethnonationalism, and the United Nations**
Exploring the causes of mass killing since 1945
Hannibal Travis

100 **Caribbean Sovereignty, Development and Democracy in an Age of Globalization**
Edited by Linden Lewis

101 **Rethinking Foreign Policy**
Edited by Fredrik Bynander and Stefano Guzzini

102 The Promise and Perils of Transnationalization
NGO activism and the socialization of women's human rights in Egypt and Iran
Benjamin Stachursky

103 Peacebuilding and International Administration
The cases of Bosnia and Herzegovina and Kosovo
Niels van Willigen

104 The Politics of the Globalization of Law
Getting from rights to justice
Edited by Alison Brysk

105 The Arctic in International Politics
Coming in from the cold
Peter Hough

106 Understanding Transatlantic Relations
Whither the West?
Serena Simoni

107 India in South Asia
Domestic identity politics and foreign policy from Nehru to the BJP
Sinderpal Singh

108 A Strategic Understanding of UN Economic Sanctions
International relations, law and development
Golnoosh Hakimdavar

109 Politics and the Bomb
The role of experts in the creation of cooperative nuclear non-proliferation agreements
Sara Z. Kutchesfahani

110 Interpreting Global Security
Mark Bevir, Oliver Daddow and Ian Hall

111 Foreign Policy, Domestic Politics and International Relations
The case of Italy
Elisabetta Brighi

112 The Scourge of Genocide
Essays and reflections
Adam Jones

113 Authority, Ascendancy, and Supremacy
China, Russia, and the United States' pursuit of relevancy and power
Gregory O. Hall

114 The Politics of Arctic Sovereignty
Oil, ice and Inuit governance
Jessica M. Shadian

115 Small States and International Security
Europe and beyond
Edited by Clive Archer, Alyson J. K. Bailes and Anders Wivel

116 Networked Governance and Transatlantic Relations
Building bridges through science diplomacy
Gabriella Paár-Jákli

117 The Role, Position and Agency of Cusp States in International Relations
Edited by Marc Herzog and Philip Robins

118 The Politics of Conflict Economies
Miners, merchants and warriors in the African borderland
Morten Bøås

119 Exercising Human Rights
Gender, agency, and practice
Robin Redhead

120 State Responses to International Law
Kendall Stiles

State Responses to International Law

Kendall Stiles

Routledge
Taylor & Francis Group
LONDON AND NEW YORK

First published 2015
by Routledge
2 Park Square, Milton Park, Abingdon, Oxfordshire OX14 4RN

and by Routledge
711 Third Avenue, New York, NY 10017

First issued in paperback 2016

Routledge is an imprint of the Taylor & Francis Group, an informa business

British Library Cataloguing in Publication Data
A catalogue record for this book is available from the British Library

Library of Congress Cataloging in Publication Data
Stiles, Kendall W., author.
State responses to international law/Kendall Stiles.
pages cm. – (Routledge advances in international relations and global politics; 120)
Includes bibliographical references and index.
1. International law. 2. International obligations. 3. Human rights.
I. Title.
KZ3410.S75 2015
341–dc23 2014016221

ISBN: 978-0-415-79109-0 (pbk)
ISBN: 978-1-138-79079-7 (hbk)

Typeset in Times New Roman
by Wearset Ltd, Boldon, Tyne and Wear

Contents

Figures

Tables

Part I

Quantitative analysis

1 Explaining compliance with international law

Why we need to know who complies

This projects starts with the observation that there is considerable variation in the degree to which states comply with international law. Further, this variation seems to cut across issue areas. Canada almost always complies with almost every rule, while North Korea rarely complies with any rule. While most of the literature on international law compliance focuses on the nature of the rules and their broader context, this opening observation warrants further scrutiny. Put simply: are there certain national characteristics that increase the likelihood that a country will comply with international rules? The purpose of this study is to answer this question.

This book is an effort to cut through some of these theoretical difficulties by focusing on a range of issues for which very specific rules have been articulated – rules that have been acknowledged as valid and vital by essentially the entire community of states. Further, these rules call for specific actions by states, such that it is possible for outsiders to monitor and assess compliance. Not only that, in some cases the assessment of compliance has already been carried out by relatively impartial observers. By measuring compliance with a variety of rules across a variety of issues and an even wider variety of countries, we can begin to answer our central question: who complies?

We explore a wide range of possible explanations. At this point, we should say that none is entirely satisfactory, and so this work is not an apology for a particular theory. Nor is it an exposition of a single, simple explanation that supplants all the rest. Such an approach could not be carried out and still be intellectually honest because the reality around us is simply too complex and contingent. We are favorable to a qualified rationalism and reject as simplistic some of the dominant theories, namely legitimacy theory, managerialism, liberalism, and realism. Rationalism is only a starting point, however, as one must go beyond myopic materialism to understand that national aims derive from a combination of preferences held by state elites, the international system, and the domestic system. Depending in particular on domestic political institutions, the personal attitudes of heads of state, and the degree to which international norms have insinuated themselves into the national discourse, state policies may comply more or less with international norms. Furthermore, much depends on the issue at hand, as decisions to comply with regulatory law, human rights law, and law relating to national sovereignty are arrived at in different ways and the basis of different principles and interests.

We will argue that while rationalism is a fair starting point, one must not rely on myopic materialism to explain all compliance since we find so many instances in which states opt to sacrifice short-term material gain for the sake of other objectives. In particular, we are convinced that much depends on the type of reputation state elites hope to establish – both vis-à-vis the international community and their national counterparts as well as in relation to the domestic society. A desire for a reputation for "playing by the rules" will both direct and constrain state behavior. However, if compliance risks provoking discontent at home, what seems to matter most is the head of state's "executive tenacity." Naturally, autocrats can act with far more freedom than democratically elected leaders, but this means they will always ignore public opinion. Conversely, if the state elites are more interested in developing a reputation for irascibility, this must be weighed against domestic expectations and it is possible that the politically vulnerable leader will opt to comply in the face of public support for the rule despite his initial inclinations. All of this occurs against a backdrop of economic incentives and governing capacity, of course.

What others have said about who complies

Before discussing the methodology of this study and the plan of the book, it is necessary to consider what others have said with respect to our central question. Theories of compliance tend to focus on one of two things: the characteristics of the rules that enhance compliance and the characteristics of the countries that enhance compliance. As indicated earlier, we choose – somewhat arbitrarily – to focus only on the second question. We will nonetheless provide some historical background and legal exposition on each of the rules we will study, but the book will not focus on this. With respect to the second question, theories can generally be categorized into three different groups or "theoretical clusters." First are theories that assume states are strategic utility maximers. Governments weigh whether to comply with a rule primarily in terms of costs and benefits. These costs and benefits may be economic or political, international or domestic, short term or long term. But ultimately the question is not whether complying is the right thing to do, but whether it is the shrewd thing to do. Second are theories that assume the opposite – that states worry most about their reputations and whether what they are doing is appropriate – or at least whether it will be seen by their friends and neighbors as appropriate. These theories predict that much will depend on how closely tied a country is to the rest of the world – or at least its neighborhood. They also predict that much will depend on whether the rule appears legitimate and fair, and whether the government wants to have a reputation for complying with these types of rules. Finally, another school – not entirely distinct from the two previously mentioned – stresses domestic processes, including domestic political and legal institutions, decision-making processes, domestic pressure groups and public opinion, and so forth. From this perspective, much depends on regime type and societal structures. Democracies will behave differently from autocracies and countries with highly educated, post-modernist societies will behave differently from those with feudalistic, traditional societies.

As we will see throughout the book, while separating these theories conceptually is not especially difficult, it is very difficult to sort out which theoretical cluster actually explains real-world developments most accurately. It is the central argument of this book that almost all theories of compliance make an important contribution to solving the puzzle of compliance, and that only a synthetic approach can provide a complete explanation. As we proceed through the theoretical and empirical material, a synthetic theory will become clear and will be elaborated in the concluding chapter.

Rationalism and realism[1]

Scholars of the realist and rationalist traditions generally agree that states will do what they think is necessary and prudent to achieve their objectives, and questions of legality are weighed against the importance of the objectives. Primary among these national aims is security, although economic gains may at times take precedence – especially where security can be taken for granted (Krasner 1999; Glennon 2001). States may even pursue the "politics of prestige" from time to time (Morgenthau 1978, 77–91). As pointed out by Goldsmith and Posner (2005), states will cooperate only when the expected advantages outweigh the costs: "International law emerges from states' pursuit of self-interested policies on the international stage. International law is, in this sense, endogenous to state interests. It is not a check on state self-interest; it is a product of state self-interest" (Goldsmith and Posner 2005, 13).

Compliance with international rules is seen as instrumental and theorists predict it will end as soon as it is no longer advantageous (Hathaway 2002; Glennon 2004/2005). This is the case even where institutions may lower transaction costs and raise the price of breach of promises, especially where promises are seen as of marginal salience (Guzman 2002). This said, the most powerful states will generally shape international rules and provide incentives and sanctions to induce compliance when the stakes warrant it (Drezner 2007, 5). One should not be surprised by a degree of cynicism as well. Vreeland finds, for example, that dictators seem to be willing to sign international human rights agreements in order to temporarily dull opposition and make it easier to increase repression later on (Vreeland 2008). Some have gone so far as to say that international law is dominated by – if not cynical and duplicitous – at least "cheap" talk wherein states commit only to carry on activities in which they are already engaged (Downs *et al.* 1996).

Even post-modernist constructivists will agree that policy flows from a general perception of the interests of the state, with interests defined in a particular historical and normative context (Sterling-Folker 2002). The simplest version of this theory holds that states will generally do what they've been doing already. As put by Jacobson and Weiss:

> One very important factor shaping how well a country does is what it has traditionally done in the past with respect to the issue in question, including what legislation and regulation it already had in place at the time it became party to the treaty.
>
> (Jacobson and Weiss 1995, 140)

Raustiala refers to the level of past compliance with rules as a good predictor of future compliance (2000, 393).

Note that this approach is agnostic with regard to the source of state interests – it only predicts that state interests will be consistent as a result of pre-existing conditions and the "entangling alliances" states subsequently enter into. That said, it has been noted that exogenous shocks have sometimes produced shifts in a state's foreign policy orientation. The most obvious, of course, is when a state has been attacked. There is broad consensus that the "day of infamy" contributed directly to the shift of US policy from relative isolation to international engagement (LaFeber 1989, 386; Jones 2001, 188). Others refer to the biological metaphor of "punctuated equilibrium" to explain how some global cataclysms may alter dramatically the foreign policies of many states at once. Consider, for example, how revelations about the Holocaust affected state policies regarding genocide and the protection of civilians, or how the collapse of the Soviet Union allowed states in Eastern Europe to realign their foreign policies. Taken together, then, these theories point toward predicting state behavior from a range of habits, commitments, and exogenous shocks, regardless of motivation. Although we will emphasize this in the next section, it is worth noting that many rationalists anticipate that actors will seek a reputation for honoring agreements and working well with others – if only for instrumental reasons rather than any sense of propriety or altruism (Tomz 2007).

The great struggle of foreign policy-making consists of the competition between various state interests: guns vs. butter, engagement vs. isolation, confrontation vs. accommodation (Abbott 1999). Even where only two objectives are in play, there is an infinite number of points on the Pareto-optimal curve (Krasner 1991). Much may depend on which priorities are most urgent, with the result that important objectives – such as having the long-term reputation for keeping international promises – may be set aside in a crisis. Much also depends on the nature of the objective and whether it can be achieved unilaterally (Downs and Jones 2002). Collective goods often require close collaboration, although this can vary dramatically across different types of collective goods (Sandler 2004). In some cases, securing other states' compliance may be unimportant (international research efforts to find an AIDS vaccine, for instance, may require only one lucky researcher) while in other cases, 100 percent compliance is essential (a non-proliferation regime may be unraveled by one lunatic dictator).

Much also depends on the time horizon of international negotiation and law. Where interactions are expected to be short-lived or sporadic, states may be more willing to adopt erratic strategies, including deception, capriciousness, or inconsistency. They may also seek short-term gains without regard to the damage that might be caused to the relationship (Axelrod 1984; Keohane 1984). But where interactions are expected to be repeated over many years, or where issues are linked or reputations earned through word of mouth, we should expect to see greater concern for reliability on the part of negotiators – which should translate into an effort to at least appear to comply with past commitments (Mercer 1996, 7; Goldsmith and Posner 2005, 103; Tomz 2007). Of course, states may sometimes seek a reputation for being unpredictable or even reckless, or may seek to appear compliant with respect to certain rules and not others, so rational choice scholars hesitate to put too much stock in this argument (Keohane 1997; Downs and Jones 2002).

Others – realists in particular – focus on the relative power of states and their capacity to insulate themselves from external pressures. Paradoxically, theories that address this question offer conflicting predictions. To begin, it is generally understood that states that are extremely powerful are more inclined to "go it alone" with respect to international law. This is particularly apparent where the United States is concerned (Daalder and Lindsay 2003; Chomsky 2006). Such states may attempt to shape international rules and press others into compliance, but find it possible to insulate themselves from foreign pressure when their behavior is found wanting. Weakness is a virtue, in this situation, since it requires states to care about their reputations (Milgrom *et al.* 1990).

The sanctions literature makes it clear that only states that are relatively weak can be expected to submit to coercion (Pape 1997). Peter Haas puts it well:

> Institutional analysis is insufficient on its own to account for patterns of national compliance. Even holding institutional factors constant, one encounters wide variation in national enforcement with the same regulations. States vary in terms of their vulnerability to institutional inducements. Not all states are vulnerable to external influence, although with increasing globalization this number is probably declining.
>
> (Haas 2000, 59)

Powerful states usually work to ensure international institutions make it easier to "discipline" weak states (Drezner 2007, 5). And where their contribution to the collective good is essential, great powers make even may great sacrifices in the short run (Kindleberger 1973). But generally, strong states will protect their interests by ensuring weak enforcement where vital interests are at stake (Murphy 2004).

While vulnerability makes a state more inclined to submit to international pressure, it is possible to be too weak to comply with international law. After all, most international rules require some form of positive effort (Duruigbo 2001). With respect to our case of the war on terror, it is easy to appreciate that compliance requires the capacity to draft and pass new laws in the short term, and in the long term the ability to guard borders, investigate crimes, arrest, detain and try suspects, and so forth. In the United States, such efforts have resulted in an entirely new government ministry and the expenditure of roughly $68 billion from September 11th to the end of 2003 (White House 2003).

A lack of capacity is the key impediment to rule compliance according to the "managerial school," exemplified by the work of Abram and Antonia Chayes (Chayes and Chayes 1995). The same has been noted by Jacobson and Weiss and Haas (Jacobson and Weiss 1995; Haas 2000). This implies that wealthier states should be expected to comply more fully – especially with respect to rules that require administrative capacity such as regulatory and criminal laws.

Testing rationalism requires considerable information. Much needs to be known about the country's preferences, circumstances, resources, commitments, and so forth, not to mention the various interests of key domestic groups (Börzel *et al.* 2010). It is also important to know to what degree states are willing to delay gratification or link disparate issues. For that matter, we should know something about the major interest groups, political parties, and political institutions to know better how costs and benefits are calculated within states (Sterling-Folker 2002). Ultimately it may be very difficult to sort out whether a state is motivated by greed or principle. If it calculates that "honesty is the best policy" in the long run, it may be willing to make considerable sacrifices in the short run, similar to a government that seeks to simply do the right thing, whatever the cost. Likewise, if acquiring a reputation for trust-worthiness is deemed the best means of achieving material goals, a purely rationalist government's actions will likely parallel those of a principled government most of the time.

Sociological approaches

Contrary to the rationalist approach, the theories we will consider in this section assume that interests are not endogenous, but may in fact arise from a process of discourse and argument, which in turn will be affected by the overall place of the state's elites in the international community. States, it is argued, are "social actors, who respond to imagined or real social pressures to formally assimilate with other states in their reference group" (Avdeyeva 2007, 878). States therefore fear ostracism and seek ways to communicate to other states their willingness to comply with the prevailing norms.

The international system – made up of states, international organizations, and non-governmental organizations – is an important source of state preference, contrary to the expectations of interest-driven theory (Finnemore 1996). "States are socialized to want certain things by the international society in which they and the people in them live." Put another way, "states may not always know what they want and are receptive to teaching about what are appropriate and useful actions to take" (Finnemore 1996, 1, 4).

The key message that the international system communicates to states is not only what objectives are reasonable and will curry favor, but what means are appropriate to achieve those aims. As put by Hasenclever: "Political actors associate specific actions with specific situations by rules of appropriateness. What is appropriate for a particular person in a particular situation is defined by political or social institutions and transmitted through socialization" (Hasenclever *et al.* 1997, 156).

Although the international system has a variety of ways of signaling its preferences and states have a variety of ways of signaling their commitment to those values, international treaties provide a uniquely unambiguous and public opportunity to do both. For society-driven theory, public commitment to norms has value on several levels. It communicates to foreign and domestic audiences what state officials intend to do, thus providing predictability and where criminal law is concerned putting on notice those who will be expected to alter their conduct. It also serves to provide endorsement to a global norm the state expects other states to likewise support, thereby serving a diplomatic function. Fundamentally, a state stakes its reputation when making public commitments, which relates to and in turn shapes its social relations with other states (Finnemore 1996; Checkel 2001). Not only do states have a vested interest in maintaining a reputation for compliance, according to this perspective, but state elites will also seek approval on a more personal level – to the point that they might be expected to internalize global and regional norms. The more closely linked the state to the world community, the greater state leaders will value inclusion and acceptance.

At the same time, it invites the international community to hold it accountable for compliance (Moravcsik 2000), which explains why states are often reluctant to enter into binding agreements where compliance is unlikely (Downs *et al.* 1996; Victor *et al.* 1998, 661). It also serves to provide endorsement to a global norm the state expects other states to likewise support, thereby serving a diplomatic function. As explained by Raustiala,

> Governments may desire a reputation for law-abiding generally, or they may be concerned with reputation with regard to particular legal commitments only. Where the credibility of commitments is important to governments, compliance with existing commitments may be understood as a means to enhance and signal current and future credibility.
>
> (2000, 402)

Ultimately, states may find themselves "trapped" by their own promises and will be subjected to considerable peer pressure to honor those commitments (Hafner-Burton and Tsutsui 2005; Avdeyeva 2007). This may stem in part from the rather abstract (and often violated) international legal principle that once states have given their consent to a treaty it is binding unless superseded by a higher duty or some mitigating factor (*pacta sunt servanda*). But it also may flow from the social interactions between diplomats and their fear of losing face with their peers. There is intriguing empirical evidence that states that are more open to the international community are in fact more likely to comply with legal commitments, regardless of their material interests or capacities (Gray *et al.* 2006).

More importantly, those governments who sincerely feel that the rule in question is legitimate, in that it was arrived at fairly and its substance is fair, are far more likely to comply with it (Franck 1990). This is sometimes expressed in terms of the desire for a reputation for cooperation and compliance, but it flows more from shared values rather than a strategic calculation to obtain the benefits such a reputation can provide. English School authors attempt to thread this theoretical needle with their emphasis on membership in a "society" (Bull 2002; Booth and Wheeler 2007).

A country's foreign policy orientation involves a web of commitments and a history of statements and actions that both reveal preferences and constrain future behavior. Membership in regional groups – even those without clear policy agendas – is often in itself a good predictor of state policy (Nye 1971; Chayes and Chayes 1995). For that matter, even mere contiguity can be enough to pressure a state to mimic the policies of its neighbors through a combination of socialization and threat assessment (Simmons 2000). While research is still preliminary on this question, it is possible that relations of mutual dependence between neighboring states contributes to a policy of imitation – or at least a decision to minimize the distance between one's policies and those of one's neighbors (Hawkins *et al.* 2006). Likewise, close ties as expressed through trade agreements, mutual defense pacts, military collaboration, and so forth may tell us a great deal about a state's overall priorities on the world stage since these bonds are often difficult to break. It is difficult to imagine, for example, a dramatic rupture of the US–UK "special relationship" or the withdrawal of the Netherlands from European institutions.

More cynically, some have argued that public commitment to international norms should not be expected to correlate with compliance since there is no inherent causal dynamic between good rules and good conduct (Keohane 1997, 494). Krasner has famously argued that international agreements appear to have been meant to be broken, especially when the stakes are high (1999). And others have found considerable evidence that hypocrisy is rampant in many areas of international life – particularly those involving internal reforms as opposed to reciprocal exchanges (Hathaway 2002). But overall states seem to understand that actions with respect to past agreements carry reputational consequences which will enhance or diminish the quality of future transactions (Tomz 2007).

Still others argue that law compliance has intrinsic value for certain cultures. Britain, France, the United States and even India, Russia, and Argentina pride themselves on a long and distinguished legal tradition. Even when behaving badly, these and other states go to great lengths to find legal justifications and rationales for their conduct. In some cases, it is thought that legalism itself might become a cultural trait (Stiles and Wells 2007). Conversely, some cultures are thought to be ambivalent or even hostile to law, whether for religious or political reasons. Clearly, local culture can influence attitudes toward specific types of law, as we see in the case of women's or minority rights (Gray *et al.* 2006).

Anticipating an argument of the liberal school, they point out that making legal commitments mobilizes legally oriented interest and advocacy groups and legitimizes their participation in domestic decision-making. It also expands the role of legal bureaucracies within foreign offices and other government agencies. Finally, so long as domestic actors understand legal agreements to be serious undertakings, it will modify their plans and actions in reliance on such commitments, increasing the audience costs of violations (Abbott and Snidal 2000, 428).

One problem with this approach is that it tells us little about the overall direction of international law and fails to explain much about its substance. Rather it implies that the international community – and regions within it – rise and fall together. Thus the approach might just as easily predict the collapse of the international system of law as it would its resilience. There is evidence that norms don't just grow stronger and spread but also grow weaker and die (Risse *et al.* 1990; Glennon 2004/2005). Just as it is difficult to tell whether a particular market "correction" on Wall Street is the first stage of a collapse, it is difficult to tell whether a particular state's defiance of an international rule is the beginning of the end of the rule itself or merely a pause in its growth.

Likewise, the theory does not help us sort out utility maximers who want a reputation for compliance but who are not genuinely committed to the norm. It might be possible to look more closely at states under stress that find themselves forced to choose between compliance and some other good (Stiles 2000). But even this only takes us so far since most international rules have built-in escape clauses that permit just this sort of behavior.

Liberal culture and institutions

Liberal theory stresses the constraining power of governance, with its attachment to law, proper procedures and comity, incorporates normative elements to which we will turn later. For now it is enough to say that it argues Kant was right in predicting that liberal democracies will be far more inclined to keep international promises and support international economic liberalism as well (Ruggie 1982; Slaughter 1993). Democratic regimes intuitively understand the place of law and good governance as public trusts invested in governments. Law percolates up from a society committed to liberal ideals of tolerance and due process while law also trickles down from elites committed to rule-making and rule-enforcement (what Koh calls "internalization" – 1997). New democratic regimes are among the most enthusiastic supporters of international rules since they want to establish their bona fides to the international community and "lock in" progressive policies by entangling themselves in multiple international commitments. Eager to please, their compliance is generally high (Moravcsik 2000; Simmons 2009).

Political openness creates entrees for international and domestic pressures not available in autocratic regimes (Koh 1996; Keohane 1997; Victor 1999; Simmons 2000). Democracy tends to shape a country's approach to rule-compliance for ideological and cultural reasons. Democratic states have demonstrated an interest in establishing the rule of law – both at home and abroad – and establishing a reputation for supporting international legal institutions and rules (Guzman 2002; Murphy 2004). Beth Simmons has argued persuasively that a country's legal culture is a strong predictor of its willingness to comply with international law – the stronger the principle of submission to law at home, the greater the willingness to comply with law abroad (Simmons 2000). Specifically, where civil society organizations are able to mobilize to pressure their own governments to comply with international commitments – most evident in transitional democracies – policy change is likely to be strong (Simmons 2009). Democracies are also more receptive to law-based persuasion, including, for example, a tendency for domestic judges to consider opinions of foreign courts in their rulings (Slaughter 2003). Taken together, liberal states are therefore more likely to be responsive to prevailing international norms, commit to them, and comply with them (Ku and Diehl 2006, 172–175).

A corollary to the mainstream political view of liberalism is the notion that free polities will also be free economies. They will engage the world economy, respect private property rights, promote equity and fairness in market transactions, and thereby generate economic growth and a cosmopolitan culture. This is the most affirmative view of "globalization" (Kant 1897[1795]; Friedman 2007). For economic liberals, political and economic freedom are mutually reinforcing and to a degree mutually defining (Friedman 1992; Sen 2001). Many conservative think-tanks in Washington D.C. promote this view, and the Heritage Foundation specifically measures economic freedom around the world on a regular basis (Heritage Foundation 2010). Note that economic liberals argue that there should be no need for exploitation or enslavement under a truly free economic system, and therefore disagree strongly with the radical view of capitalism.

Liberal theories also disaggregate the state, separating the institutions involved in committing to international norms from those that must implement the commitment. In an argument compatible with the managerial school (Chayes and Chayes 1995), authors point out that a key impediment to implementing international agreements is the inability of state elites to issue effective commands (Chayes *et al.* 2000). This can stem from an inability to communicate these commands in meaningful ways and to resistance by regulatory agencies and law enforcement officials, which in turn can be the product of poverty, lack of technology, competing interests, and corruption (Naim 2005, 277–278). What promotes compliance more than anything are inducements, capacity-building, and persuasion. This approach assumes that almost all states want to comply with almost all the commitments they make (Chayes and Chayes 1995). Whether it is to secure the material benefits of compliance, enhance their reputations, or deflect domestic protest, governments seek to bring their domestic policies in conformity with the international commitments they've made (Koh 1997, 2636).

From this perspective, states come into compliance with norms through a six-step process: IOs and states monitor behavior, assess it in relation to the norm, identify deficiencies and failings, determine the feasibility of compliance in terms of state capacity, provide assistance to bridge the gap between existing and necessary capacity, and, in some cases, alter the rules themselves so that they fall within the range of what states can realistically do (Koh 1997, 2637). This typically requires some third party that is widely trusted to interpret rules impartially – something many IOs, as we have seen, are in a position to do (Lazarev 1991, 20). It is up to IO staff members to forge ties with their counterparts within national governments and to promote cross-national links between comparable state officials (Chayes and Chayes 1995, 279–281). Nurturing these government networks can reap substantial results: "Overall, by harnessing hard power, building compliance capacity, and diffusing ideas and technologies around the world, government networks are likely to strengthen the rule of international law in ways long demanded and expected of traditional international institutions" (Slaughter 2004, 303–304).

Where this fails, bureaucratic inefficiency, whether inadvertent or deliberate, further intensifies pressure to grease the wheels, leading to complicity between the bribe-giver and bribe-taker (Rose-Ackerman 1997, 37). The result of bribery and other forms of corruption is typically a covert redirection of public resources toward other ends – ends that usually do not serve the broader public interest but instead reinforce social cleavages. The net effect of dysfunctions in administration can be the "privatization of public policy," especially where bureaucrats have high levels of authority and discretion with little oversight and accountability (Kaufmann 2005). None of this prevents states from endorsing international norms, passing laws to implement them, and even allocating resources for their enforcement. What it means is that one must take care how one measures compliance and stress end results rather than just processes.

This said, democracies are also unable to move as quickly as autocratic regimes can. Where legislation requires the support of an opposition party, delays in ratification or implementation may occur and result in incomplete internalization of the rule (Koh 1997; Weiss 1999). Democratic regimes may be somewhat less consistent than their authoritarian counterparts as changes in public opinion and party preference can lead to changes in the majority party, which have been found to have significant effects on compliance with certain types of rules (Grieco *et al.* 2009). Further, as conduits for domestic pressures, democratic regimes may give voice and influence to attitudes that run counter to international rules. The WTO, for example, ruled against the EU on the issue of genetically modified foods but accomplished almost nothing since the policy was non-negotiable in Europe given popular opposition (Esserman and Howse 2003). Likewise, the US Senate has refused to ratify most human rights treaties on the grounds that they may interfere with national sovereignty aims. Xenophobia, religious intolerance, and protectionism often stem from deep-seated attitudes that prevent democratic regimes from committing to or complying with international rules.

In general, liberal regimes can be expected to comply with international rules because of their natural attraction to legalized remedies to public problems, their capacity to include a variety of domestic and international actors in decision-making, their generally more honest and transparent bureaucracies, and their willingness to keep promises (as mentioned in the previous section). On the other hand, democracies may become paralyzed or even dysfunctional when it comes to international law compliance since they are sensitive to shifts in public opinion and often require multiple layers of approval by competing sub-national actors to make policy. To predict what a liberal regime will do therefore requires some understanding of its particular decision-making procedures, the public's preferences, and the government's interest in its reputation. These questions lead us back to both the rationalist theory and the sociological theories discussed previously.

Pointing toward theoretical integration

Each of these theories offers explanations for compliance that are intuitively appealing. It seems eminently reasonable to think that states pick and choose among rules and move forward in those areas where the benefits outweigh the costs. This seems to be what both a dictator and a democrat would do – one to please himself and the other to please his constituents. And there is plenty of evidence – especially in the area of international trade negotiations – that governments make careful calculations before signing an agreement. Even in such areas as human rights or environmental protection, principle often gives way to pragmatism and states seek to insulate themselves from pain while maximizing benefits. On the other hand, both the sociological and liberal approaches seem to address a broader, more sweeping trend in world law (Sandholtz and Stiles 2009), namely that law is not static, nor is it merely strictly contractual. Rather it seems to be moving toward some loftier vision of human dignity and planetary health, such that each new rule fits into a broader set of ideals. This is consistent with the notion that ordinary people are pressing their democratic governments (which have proliferated in recent decades) to adopt laws that spread liberal principles and environmental protection – in addition to better trade bargains. Of course, neither theory can tell us whether this trend will continue since all such normative changes are contingent on people's attitudes. But for now there seems to be an impetus for both political liberalization and environmental protection across a wide range of issues (keeping in mind these trends may be mutually exclusive at some level).

This review of the existing literature also highlights a weakness in each approach. Namely, none of the three can put forward general explanations that are easily testable. It is only possible to know whether a state is following rationalist and/or realist impulses when it breaks international law – not when it complies with it. And even then it is possible that breaking a rule is the first step to crafting a new one. Just as one does not know the motives of the bride and groom on their wedding day (love? money? status?), it is difficult to sort out motives when all are behaving themselves. Further, it is not always possible to determine whether the government is responding to domestic public opinion (particularly when this is split) or rather to international pressures and principles.

It is not uncommon for all of the competing theories to predict the self-same behavior under similar circumstances.

Happily, this project will focus as much on failures to comply as on compliance itself, and so some of these empirical difficulties will be avoided. But it is important to acknowledge that these difficulties will not go away where compliance is high over time.

Another implication is that each theory seems to go only so far before it runs into a conceptual roadblock. Part of the reason for the emergence of the sociological approach was to answer the question implicitly raised by rationalism: whence preferences? But by arguing that preferences are endogenous, the sociological approach raises yet another question: why these preferences? Liberalism only partly answers the question by saying that they come from the people, but this raises one final question: which people and why? Given the co-existence of multiple mutually contradictory attitudes in any society at any time (and sometimes within one individual's mind) one can be forgiven for asking why certain attitudes held by certain people (foreign and/or domestic) seem determinative and whether it is possible to predict this.

Although theoretical synthesis has been proposed and rejected many times in the field of international relations, what is needed in the area of law compliance is more properly described as "theoretical integration" (Andreatta and Koenig-Archibugi 2010). Integration more properly describes the process of combining common insights and reconciling theoretical contradictions in order to develop a more coherent whole – albeit something that is not just the sum of the parts.

To illustrate, we will show that many of the different theoretical approaches supplement the other in important ways, such that only in combination can they offer a more general explanation. Rationalism of a simplistic variety – short term and materialistic – accounts for much of what we see, but needs to be supplemented by notions of reputation and legitimacy to more fully explain state interests. Political liberalism only takes us so far, as we have already seen, unless domestic interest groups, the culture within which they operate, and state capacity to enforce law are factored into the equation. Finally, the capacity of a state to resist pressure from within and without is an important prerequisite to understanding its willingness and ability to comply with a wide range of rules.

Consider, for example, a strong democratic regime that aspires to extend additional civil rights to women. Knowing this intent may allow us to predict that women's rights will expand, but only if we also know whether the society's culture is traditional and patriarchal. We also need to know the political and social status of those who would oppose expanding women's rights, as well as the status of those who would support it. While a highly motivated, strong regime might be able to mobilize the resources to overcome opposition, those resources may simply be lacking in some cases where poverty, corruption, or even geography get in the way. Finally, we should know the degree to which the international community is willing to support the effort, which leads us to ask about the state's alliance partners, its overall foreign policy orientation, and even its economic strength or vulnerability. The implication is that, while at the aggregate level we may find that democracy, state capacity, foreign policy orientation, and culture all correlate in some way with increased rights for women, we may not have a grasp on the actual causal dynamic without exploring the linkages between various factors.

While the democratic-autocratic scale is commonly used to measure executive powers and executive interests, there seems to be another dimension that warrants exploration, even though it also defies quantification. Even in democratic governments, the executive head often seeks to remain in office as long as possible. We refer to this as "executive tenacity." Note that this cannot always be measured in terms of autocracy or even length of tenure since it refers to intention. This desire to remain in office influences many other decisions and colors the overall approach of the regime to international law. For one thing, where retaining office is legal and feasible, it influences whether the executive commits to long-term policy change. The "shadow of the future" looms large for one who hopes to live out his or her life as the president. This could lead to a very slow commitment process, but it may also produce extremely stable and predictable behavior in the future. Such a negotiating partner may be very attractive as a result. On the other hand, where retaining office for an extended period of time is either illegal or politically infeasible, difficulties will likely arise. To begin, such an individual may be tempted to bend the procedural or constitutional rules to eliminate term limits, reduce threats from political opponents, and minimize public participation. The result may be the violation of important international norms related to civil rights. While such a leader may therefore be able to commit to technical or market-related norms, s/he cannot commit to human rights norms. In the worst-case scenario, where legal and political obstacles are insurmountable, executive tenacity may lead to upheaval, unrest, and even civil war – all of which will dramatically impinge upon the state's willingness and ability to comply with a wide range of international commitments. Sadly, it is not always easy to predict how tenacious an executive is likely to be until a crisis erupts, but understanding his or her intention is nonetheless central to predicting compliance.

Plan of the book

This book has ten chapters organized into two parts. The first part consists of a description of eight different international rules along with global compliance patterns. The eight rules in question are: anti-terror law emerging from 9/11; anti-trafficking law developed in 2000; rules on combating maritime piracy; rules on ship safety; rules on airliner safety; laws against ozone depletion; anti-slavery law; and rules regarding the basic rights of women. These rules have several things in common. To begin, they are essentially universal. They are also largely uncontroversial at this point in history. They all involve outcomes that are measurable and that have been measured. And they all address pressing concerns. On the other hand, they span the scope of international rules in that some deal with the territorial integrity of states, some deal with regulating the market, and some deal with human rights. Some are ancient and some are of recent vintage – although all claim to be rooted in fundamental international legal principles.

By way of explanation, these rules were selected primarily because compliance is clearly measurable. Many international rules are extremely vague by design. Even where laws provide very specific goals, such as the requirement that all pilots and crews on international flights be properly trained, they do not always spell out how they are to be accomplished. In some cases, even basic definitions are still under debate.

Another problem stems from the fact that international rules do not exist in a vacuum. Laws are ranked and nested, such that some take precedence over others. The call for states to eliminate slavery is enhanced, on the one hand, by numerous rules involving the equality of citizens, the need for fair pay for work, and the right to leave one's job. On the other hand, it is constrained by the rule that all governments are sovereign within their own territories, and therefore have considerable latitude with respect to how they treat their own citizens. Even when it comes to regulating international transactions, international law cannot force countries to do what they have not agreed to. On the other hand, once a rule becomes "custom," all states are obligated to comply or face penalties. The implication is that complying with one rule may require breaking another, leaving the observer uncertain how to score things.

Chapter 5 provides a more systematic statistical analysis of compliance across the rules. We initially compare compliance rates across the rules to determine whether there is such a thing as a "universal complier." From there we move to a systematic test of the various theories covered in Chapter 1 – first with correlation analysis and then with regressions. The statistical methods are kept relatively simple primarily because the goal is to sort out which theories offer the strongest explanation for the outcomes – something which can be done with multivariate regression. Much of the work in Chapter 5 involves an exercise in variable elimination. In addition, the data lend themselves to straightforward methods since the best we can do is a snapshot of behavior. We do not have longitudinal data for panel, time-series, or Bayesian tests. Modeling also seemed inappropriate given the range of possible independent variables.

Part II of the book involves a systematic look at eight different countries and why they do or do not comply with international rules. The countries were selected for their variety on several dimensions, namely regime type, international engagement, and economic development. By selecting these particular cases, we should be able to do two things. On the one hand, we will be able to see more clearly which of these different factors explains the decision to comply. On the other, we will be able to see the dynamic interaction of these factors more clearly than is generally possible with statistical analysis. The cases will allow us to look at decision-making over time in order to see when certain factors play a more significant part, for example.

Chapter 10 provides a summary and synthesis of the findings, along with theoretical conclusions and recommendations for future policy and research.

Note

1 The following material includes excerpts from the following: Kendall Stiles and Adam Thayne, "Compliance with International Law: International Law on Terrorism at the United Nations," *Cooperation and Conflict* 41(2) (July 2006): 153–176; Kendall Stiles, "Who Is Keeping the Sea Safe? Testing Theories of International Law Compliance," *Cooperation and Conflict* 45(2) (June 2010): 139–161; and "International Organization and Respect for International Law," in Robert Denemark, general editor, *The International Studies Encyclopedia*, London: Wiley-Blackwell, 2010, 4352–4374.

References

Abbott, Kenneth W. (1999) "International Relations Theory, International Law, and the Regime Governing Atrocities in International Conflicts," *American Journal of International Law* 93(2): 361–379.

Abbott, Kenneth W. and Duncan Snidal (2000) "Hard and Soft Law in International Governance," *International Organization* 54(3): 421–456.

Andreatta, Filippo and Mathias Koenig-Archibugi (2010) "Which Synthesis? Strategies of Theoretical Integration and the Neorealist-Neoliberal Debate," *International Political Science Review* 31 (March): 207–227.

Avdeyeva, Olga (2007) "When Do States Comply with International Treaties? Policies on Violence against Women in Post-Communist Countries," *International Studies Quarterly* 51 (December): 877–900.

Axelrod, Robert (1984) *The Evolution of Cooperation*. New York: Basic Books.

Booth, Ken and Nicholas Wheeler (2007) *Security Dilemma: Fear, Cooperation, and Trust in World Politics*. New York: Palgrave Macmillan.

Börzel, Tobias Hofmann, Diana Panke, and Carina Sprungk (2010) "Obstinate and Inefficient: Why Member States Do Not Comply with European Law," *Comparative Political Studies* 43 (November): 1363–1390.

Bull, Hedley (2002) *The Anarchical Society: A Study of Order in World Politics*. New York: Columbia University Press.

Chayes, Abraham and A.H. Chayes (1995) *The New Sovereignty: Compliance with International Regulatory Agreements*. Cambridge: Harvard University Press.

Chayes, Abraham, Antonia Handler Chayes, and Ronald B. Mitchell (2000) "Managing Compliance: A Comparative Perspective," in Edith Brown Weiss and Harold Jacobson, eds., *Engaging Countries: Strengthening Compliance with International Environmental Accords*. Cambridge, MA: MIT Press, pp. 39–62.

Checkel, Jeffrey (2001) "Why Comply? Social Learning and European Identity Change," *International Organization* 55 (Summer): 553–588.

Chomsky, Noam (2006) *Rogue States: The Rule of Force in World Affairs*. New Delhi: India Research Press.

Daalder, Ivo and James Lindsay (2003) *America Unbound: The Bush Revolution in Foreign Policy*. Washington D.C.: Brookings Institution.

Downs, George W. and Michael A. Jones (2002) "Reputation, Compliance, and International Law," *Journal of Legal Studies* 31(1) (January): S95–S114.

Downs, George W., David M. Rocke, and Peter N. Barsoom (1996) "Is the Good News about Compliance Good News about Cooperation?" *International Organization* 50(3): 379–406.

Drezner, Daniel (2007) *All Politics Is Global: Explaining International Regulatory Regimes*. Princeton: Princeton University Press.

Duruigbo, Emeka (2001) "International Relations, Economics and Compliance with International Law: Harnessing Common Resources to Protect the Environment and Solve Global Problems," *California Western International Law Journal* 31 (Spring): 177–213.

Esserman, S. and R. Howse (2003) "The WTO on Trial," *Foreign Affairs* 82(1): 130–140.

Finnemore, Martha (1996) *National Interests in International Society*. Ithaca: Cornell University Press.

Franck, Thomas (1990) *The Power of Legitimacy Among Nations*. New York: Oxford University Press.

Friedman, Milton (1992) *Economic Freedom, Human Freedom, Political Freedom*. Hayward: California State University.

Friedman, Thomas (2007) *The World Is Flat, 3.0: A Brief History of the Twenty-first Century*. New York: Picador.

Glennon, Michael J. (2001) *Limits of Law, Prerogatives of Power: Interventionism after Kosovo*. New York: Palgrave Macmillan.

Glennon, Michael J. (2004/2005) "How International Rules Die," *Georgia Law Journal* 93: 939–991.

Goldsmith, J.L. and E.A. Posner (2005) *The Limits of International Law*. London: Oxford University Press.

Gray, Mark M., Miki Caul Kittilson, and Wayne Sandholtz (2006) "Women and Globalization: A Study of 180 Countries, 1975–2000," *International Organization* 60 (Spring): 293–333.

Grieco, Joseph M., Christopher F. Gelpi, and T. Camber Warren (2009) "When Preferences and Commitments Collide: The Effect of Relative Partisan Shifts on International Treaty Compliance," *International Organization* 63 (Spring): 341–355.

Guzman, Andrew T. (2002) "A Compliance-based Theory of International Law," *California Law Review* 90: 1826–1887.

Haas, Peter (2000) "Choosing to Comply: Theorizing from International Relations and Comparative Politics," in Dinah Shelton, ed., *Commitment and Compliance: The Role of Non-Binding Norms in the International Legal System*. Oxford: Oxford University Press, pp. 43–64.

Hafner-Burton, Emilie and Kiyoteru Tsutsui (2005) "Human Rights in a Globalizing World: The Paradox of Empty Promises," *American Journal of Sociology* 110: 1373–1411.

Hasenclever, Andreas, Peter Mayer, and Volker Rittberger (1997) *Theories of International Regimes*. New York: Cambridge University Press.

Hathaway, Oona (2002) "Do Human Rights Treaties Make a Difference?" *Yale Law Journal* 111: 1935–2041.

Hawkins, Darren G., David A. Lake, Daniel L. Nielson, and Mark J. Tierney (2006) "Delegating Under Anarchy: States, International Organizations, and Principal-agent Theory," in D.G. Hawkins, D.A. Lake, D.L. Nielson, and M.J. Tierney, eds., *Delegation and Agency in International Organizations*. Cambridge: Cambridge University Press.

Heritage Foundation (2010) Index of Economic Freedom. Available at www.heritage.org/index/. Accessed December 8, 2010.

Jacobson, Harold and Edith Brown Weiss (1995) "Strengthening Compliance with International Environmental Accords: Preliminary Observations from a Collaborative Project," *Global Governance* 1(2) (May-August): 119–148.

Jones, Howard (2001) *Crucible of Power: A History of American Foreign Relations from 1897*. Wilmington, DE: Scholarly Resources.

Kant, Immanuel (1897[1795]) *Perpetual Peace: A Philosophic Essay*. Trans. Benjamin Trueblood. Washington D.C.: American Peace Society.
Kaufmann, Daniel (2005) "Ten Myths on Governance and Corruption," *Finance and Development* 43(2) (September). Available at www.imf.org/external/pubs/ft/fandd/2005/09/basics.htm. Accessed December 20, 2010.
Keohane, Robert O. (1984) *After Hegemony: Cooperation and Discord in the World Political Economy*. Princeton: Princeton University Press.
Keohane, Robert O. (1997) "International Relations and International Law: Two Optics," *Harvard Journal of International Law* 38(2) (Spring): 487–502.
Kindleberger, Charles (1973) *The World in Depression: 1929–1939*. Berkeley: University of California Press.
Koh, Harold Hongju (1996) "Transnational Legal Process," *Nebraska Law Review* 75: 181–207.
Koh, Harold Hongju (1997) "Why Do Nations Obey International Law?" *Yale Law Journal* 106(6): 2599–2659.
Krasner, Stephen (1991) "Global Communications and National Power: Life on the Pareto-optimal Frontier," *World Politics* 43(3): 336–366.
Krasner, Stephen (1999) *Sovereignty: Organized Hypocrisy*. Princeton: Princeton University Press.
Ku, Charlotte and Paul F. Diehl (2006) "Filling In the Gaps: Extrasystemic Mechanisms for Addressing Imbalances Between the International Legal Operating System and the Normative System," *Global Governance* 12 (April–June): 165–185.
LaFeber, Walter (1989) *The American Age: United States Foreign Policy at Home and Abroad since 1750*. New York: W.W. Norton.
Lazarev, M.I. (1991) "On a Theoretical Concept of Control over the Fulfillment of International Obligations of States," in W.E. Butler, ed., *Control over Compliance with International Law*. London: Martinus Nijhoff, pp. 17–22.
Mercer, Jonathan (1996) *Reputation and International Politics*. Ithaca: Cornell University Press.
Milgrom, Paul R, Douglass C. North, and Barry R. Weingast (1990) "The Role of Institutions in the Revival of Trade: The Medieval Law Merchant, Private Judges, and Champagne Fairs," *Economics and Politics* 2(1) (March): 1–23.
Moravcsik, Andrew (2000) "The Origins of Human Rights Regimes: Democratic Delegation in Postwar Europe," *International Organization* 54(2) (Spring): 217–252.
Morgenthau, Hans J. (1978) *Politics Among Nations: The Struggle for Power and Peace*, 5th edn., revised. New York: Alfred A. Knopf.
Murphy, J. (2004) *The United States and the Rule of Law in International Affairs*. Cambridge: Cambridge University Press.
Naim, Moises (2005) *Illicit: How Smugglers, Traffickers and Copycats are Hijacking the Global Economy*. New York: Doubleday.
Nye, Joseph S. (1971). *Peace in Parts*. Boston: Little, Brown.
Pape, Robert A. (1997) "Why Economic Sanctions Do Not Work," *International Security* 22(2): 90–136.
Raustiala, Kal (2000) "Compliance and Effectiveness in International Regulatory Cooperation," *Case Western Reserve Journal of International Law* 32(3): 387–440.
Risse, Thomas, Steven Ropp, and Kathryn Sikkink (1999) *The Power of Human Rights: International Norms and Domestic Change*. New York: Cambridge University Press.
Rose-Ackerman, Susan (1997) "The Political Economy of Corruption," in Kimberly Ann Elliott, ed., *Corruption and the Global Political Economy*. Washington D.C.: Institute for International Economics, pp. 31–60.

Ruggie, John Gerard (1982) "International Regimes, Transactions, and Change: Embedded Liberalism in the Postwar Economic Order," *International Organization* 36(2) (Spring): 379–415.

Sandholtz, Wayne and Kendall Stiles (2009) *International Norms and Cycles of Change*. New York: Oxford University Press.

Sandler, Todd (2004) *Global Collective Action*. Cambridge: Cambridge University Press.

Sen, Amartya (2001) *Development as Freedom*. London: Oxford University Press.

Simmons, Beth A. (2000) "International Law and State Behavior: Commitment and Compliance in International Monetary Affairs," *American Political Science Review* 94(4): 819–835.

Simmons, Beth A. (2009) *Mobilizing for Human Rights: International Law in Domestic Politics*. New York: Cambridge University Press.

Slaughter (Burley), Anne-Marie (1993) "International Law and International Relations Theory: A Dual Agenda," *American Journal of International Law* 87(4): 205–239.

Slaughter, Anne-Marie (2003) "A Global Community of Courts," *Harvard Journal of International Law* 44(1): 191–219.

Slaughter, Anne-Marie (2004) "Sovereignty and Power in a Networked World Order," *Stanford Journal of International Law* 40(3): 283–327.

Sterling-Folker, Jennifer (2002) *Theories of International Cooperation and the Primacy of Anarchy: Explaining U.S. International Monetary Policy-Making After Bretton Woods*. Albany: SUNY Press.

Stiles, Kendall (2000) "US Responses to Defeat in International Courts: A Contingent Model of Decision-making," *Political Research Quarterly* 53(2) (June): 401–425.

Stiles, Kendall with Deborah Wells (2007) "On the Crossing of Rubicons: Norm Dissemination and Policy Idiosyncrasy in the UK," *Political Science Quarterly* 3(122) (Fall): 461–480.

Tomz, Michael (2007) *Reputation and International Cooperation: Sovereign Debt across Three Centuries*. Princeton: Princeton University Press.

Victor, David (1999) "International Environmental Agreements: Compliance and Enforcement: Enforcing International Law: Implications for an Effective Global Warming Regime," *Duke Environmental Law & Policy Forum* 10 (Fall): 147–184.

Victor, D.G., K. Raustiala, and E.B. Skolnikoff, eds. (1998) *The Implementation and Effectiveness of International Environmental Commitments: Theory and Practice*. Cambridge: MIT Press.

Vreeland, James Raymond (2008) "Political Institutions and Human Rights: Why Dictatorships Enter into the United Nations Convention Against Torture," *International Organization* 62 (Winter): 65–101.

Weiss, Edith Brown (1999) "Understanding Compliance with International Environmental Agreements: The Baker's Dozen Myth," *University of Richmond Law Review* 32 (January): 1555–1589.

White House (2003) "Securing the Homeland, Strengthening the Nation: 2003 Budget Request to Congress for Homeland Security," Washington D.C.: General Printing Office.

2 Rules governing territorial defense

Anti-terrorism, anti-piracy, and anti-trafficking

State sovereignty, claimed as a unique right since the 1600s, has never been as firmly established as some have asserted (Krasner 1999). Not only have other states denied each other the full range of sovereign prerogatives, but non-states actors have continually challenged the right and ability of states to govern their own territories. Threats have come from internal and external actors, ranging from narcotics traffickers to internet gaming sites. But in recent years considerable attention has been given to three sets of threats: transnational terrorists, maritime pirates, and human traffickers. The threats are both new and old and represent a challenge to state authorities to govern their territory. They exploit weaknesses that emerge from lack of resources and administrative capacity as well as the tolerance of liberal societies for free trade and migration.

We will begin with a review of multilateral efforts to combat transnational terrorism, particularly in the wake of the September 11, 2001 attacks in the United States. We will then review current anti-piracy law and anti-trafficking law. In doing so, we will explore the degree of global commitment to the current language both with reference to the negotiation process as well as implementation.

Anti-terror law[1]

Terrorism is a particularly serious threat to all states because it represents a challenge – at least in the short term – to the right of a state to govern its territory. This is particularly true with respect to transnational terrorism which does not aim to seize power from a regime but rather to create an alternative type of political entity (Wilkinson 2000; Romaniuk 2010). It is perhaps not surprising that most states have agreed to develop multilateral rules to ward off terrorists since all can agree that preserving sovereignty is a fundamental good. At the same time, since sovereignty is at stake in enforcing anti-terror law, it is perhaps not surprising that states have resisted surrendering too much information or control in the process (Romaniuk 2010).

Terrorism, until the 1960s, was widely regarded as a domestic matter. Most terrorists functioned locally and sought either independence for their nation or ethnic group or seizure of power of the state. During the Cold War, both superpowers and their allies aided and abetted certain types of terrorism when it suited their strategic purposes, a policy that was not officially repudiated until the mid-1980s (Luck 2004, 90). Particularly with respect to liberation movements targeted at the European powers (or against Israel), international law was remarkably tolerant of irregular violence (Murphy 1978, 312; McWhinney 1987, 138). The Organization of the Islamic Conference (OIC) and the African Union (AU) adopted local anti-terror rules that specifically exempted such acts, and efforts by the Western powers to eliminate this "political exception" went nowhere (Kerstetter 1978, 537). For that matter, even some European states took into account the political motives of terrorists, as when France refused to extradite Basques separatists to Spain or Ireland refused to extradite Irish Republican Army members to Britain (Wilkinson 2000, 120).

There was no generally recognized definition of terrorism during the Cold War. The predominant approach was to ban certain specific acts, including attacks on diplomats, airplane hijacking, and bombing – usually in direct response to a particularly horrific act (Murphy 1978, 279; Maogoto 2005, 280). It was not until the 1980s that Western states began to agree on the need to treat all terrorists as criminals, regardless of political motivation. This seems to have stemmed not only from an increase in attacks but also in the leadership provided by the Reagan administration in the United States (Bhoumik 2005, 294). The end of the Cold War and the dramatic shift in foreign policy in Russia accelerated the trend. Interpol was freed to treat terrorists as criminals, which enhanced information-sharing among its members, and removed the political exception from the European Terrorism Convention in 1996 (Wilkinson 2000, 191, 121). The Group of Seven created the Financial Action Task Force and urged member-states to create domestic "financial intelligence units" that would track the flow of money to terrorist organizations (G7/P8 1996; Alexander 2002, 367).

The rest of the world cautiously responded to this shift in focus. In 1985, for example, the UN General Assembly passed a resolution condemning terrorism, but also condemning imperialism, apartheid, and other global ills that were listed as proximate causes (McWhinney 1987, 143; Maogoto 2005, 257). Eastern European and former Soviet republics generally adopted the Western norms in the early 1990s, as did newly democratic regimes in Latin America. The OIC and AU remained skeptical and generally resisted criminalizing all terrorism. But even OIC members approved the strong language of the Convention on Financing Terrorism in 1999 (perhaps in error, given their subsequent efforts to amend it – Hafner 2003, 157). The Convention not only provided no political exception, but also instituted a "prosecute or extradite" provision that required signatories to either arrest and prosecute terror suspects or turn them over to a country that will (Witten 1998, 777). Even the Security Council was on record that a collective military response to terrorist attacks might be permissible (see resolutions 1054, 1267, 1333, and 1363). Thus the stage was set in 2001 for a substantial multilateral response to the 9/11 attacks.

The response of the international community was immediate, passionate, and firm. Led by the United States, the General Assembly and Security Council each condemned the attack and urged states to take necessary measures to collaborate to punish the perpetrators and prevent future attacks. Some UN diplomats, personally affected by the tragedy, urged their governments to adopt the strongest language possible (Interviews 2001).

The US engaged in active capital-to-capital diplomacy to build an anti-terrorism coalition, beginning with the four other permanent members and Japan, Germany, Saudi Arabia, and Pakistan. Once the evidence pointed to Al Qaeda and Osama Bin Laden, the US began orchestrating a military response, but not without approaching the Security Council for approval.

American and British delegates cosponsored a resolution on September 27th designed to dramatically improve international efforts to combat terrorism.

The Security Council…

1 *Decides* that all States shall:
 a Prevent and suppress the financing of terrorist acts;
 b Criminalize the willful provision or collection … of funds by their nationals or in their territories with the intention that the funds should be used … to carry out terrorist acts;…
 d Prohibit their nationals or any persons and entities within their territories from making any funds, financial assets or economic resources or financial or other related services available, directly or indirectly, for the benefit of persons who commit or attempt to commit or facilitate or participate in the commission of terrorist acts;…
2 *Decides also* that all States shall:…
 e Ensure that any person who participates in the financing, planning, preparation or perpetration of terrorist acts or in supporting terrorist acts is brought to justice and ensure that … such terrorist acts are established as serious criminal offences in domestic laws and regulations and that the punishment duly reflects the seriousness of such terrorist acts;…
 g Prevent the movement of terrorists or terrorist groups by effective border controls

It also called upon all states to sign and ratify all twelve existing anti-terror conventions. The proposed rules would be mandatory, based on Chapter VII and Article 25 of the Charter, and compliance was to be monitored by an ad-hoc committee that would collect reports from every UN member-state attesting to their efforts to strengthen domestic legislation and practices. Resolution 1373 was adopted almost immediately by unanimous vote and with almost no alterations to the very strong wording of the original draft (Interviews 2002).

It was a very rare instance of the Security Council requiring compliance on the part of all member-states to a new rule without them having the opportunity to assist in its drafting directly. In doing so, the Council placed itself at odds with the General Assembly to some extent. In part to address this concern, the General Assembly called a special session on terrorism in early October. Well over 100 member-states spoke out against terror, in sympathy for the US, and in support of 1373.

In order to make it clear that 1373 was not a fleeting, emotional response to a crisis, the Security Council immediately set about creating its enforcement structures. The Counter-Terrorism Committee (CTC) was tasked with collecting anti-terror plans from each UN member-state. Its members generated guidelines for states, established a strict time-table for submission and review, and hired experts to assist in evaluating the plans. Five Security Council members were assigned to each of three committees, along with a few experts, and began to allocate review of the copious volume of national plans. By the end of 2001, 112 states had submitted reports. Thirty more had done so by mid-March 2002 (UNSC 2002). To the surprise of Security Council members, the greatest obstacle to submitting reports on the part of those who had not complied was finding the professional staff in the capitals to draft a summary of the country's statutes regarding terror-related crimes. The committee therefore re-oriented its focus in the direction of technical assistance and capacity-building (Interviews 2002).

When the resolution was passed, for example, only four states had ratified the convention on financing or terror, although forty-six more had signed it and all have endorsed it in the General Assembly. The USA Patriot Act and the Anti-Terrorism Act (2001) of the UK were both passed in part to comply with 1373 and to provide a model for other states. Taken together, the tone of the meetings taking place between CTC staff and UN member-states to review the national plans have taken on a collaborative, non-confrontational character.

The overwhelming majority of states have submitted initial reports on the status of their anti-terror legislation and resources. The second phase involves providing evidence that laws and enforcement capacity have been strengthened, and the upcoming third phase will involve an assessment of implementation and performance (Cortright and Lopez, 2004). From the beginning, the CTC has opted not to make use of the latent enforcement powers at its disposal, but instead to approach the report-writing process in a non-confrontational, collaborative spirit (UN CTC 2004, SC Res. 1526 [2004]). In 2004, the CTC's institutional status was upgraded with the creation of the "CTED" (Counter-Terrorism Committee Executive Directorate) with a larger budget and more permanent status. In 2006, the powers of the CTED would be circumscribed as states objected to the strict application of the Resolution (Romaniuk 2010). We therefore use the material generated by the CTC prior to this change in approach to generate our scores.

Our scoring seeks to measure the degree of compliance on the part of states with UN Security Council Resolution 1373 and the Counter Terrorism Committee (CTC). The five-point scale is constructed in dichotomous fashion; each of the criteria that comprise the scale is worth either one point or zero points. The cumulative point total for all seven criteria produces a score between zero and seven (labeled TERSCORE). A score of seven reflects virtually perfect compliance while a zero score reflects little compliance. The criteria are inspired by the Counter Terrorism Committee's stated and implied expectations for UN member-states, as evidenced in the committee's briefings, comments on individual country reports, *notes verbales*, and interviews with CTC members. This said, it should be emphasized that the scoring is ours.

A 1 point – First report turned in on time (although the official deadline was December 27, 2001, the point is earned if the date of document circulation was on or before December 31, 2001).
B 1 point – Following CTC's recommended structure for the reports (first report).
C 1 point – Some sort of new domestic law has been created or an existing law has been improved to criminalize terrorist activity in general.
D 1 point – Some sort of new domestic law has been created or an existing law has been improved to criminalize collection of funds for terrorism purposes.
E 1 point – Has the CTC specifically asked about extradition or border control efforts in the most recent report? If no, the point is earned.

Criterion "A" asks whether or not the first report was turned in to the CTC by the committee's target date. The deadline for the first report was December 27, 2001. However, in order to compensate for circulation and paperwork delays, we have extended the criterion deadline to December 31, 2001. In other words, if a state turned in its first report on or before the end of 2001, it earns the point in this category. The logic of this criterion is simple: states that are eager (or at least willing) to comply with the resolution deliver their reports by the expected date. Failing to turn in the report on time indicates a careless attitude towards compliance that could perhaps be interpreted as reluctance or even an unwillingness to follow the committee's instructions.

Criterion "B" establishes whether or not states followed the Committee's recommended report structure in the first report. Because the format proposed by the CTC is actually a series of questions regarding implementation, failure to follow the format has substantive implications. According to a briefing for member-states (dated April 4, 2002), following the structure of the resolution allows the committee "to immediately put the comments of the report in the context of one of the 18 sub-paragraphs which constitute operative paragraphs 1 to 3 of the resolution" (UN CTC 2002). The CTC directly criticized those reports that fail to conform to the CTC's report structure, arguing that such reports "lack substance" (UN CTC 2002). The CTC clearly wants the requested information in the suggested format, and criterion "B" awards one point to those states that follow the committee's recommended report structure.

Criterion "C" gauges whether or not states have enacted domestic legislation to criminalize terrorist activity in general. States earn this point if they have criminalized any terrorist activity (besides the collection of funds for terrorism) or enhanced an existing terrorism law since the adoption of Resolution 1373. This standard is based on the Resolution's stated expectations. According to Resolution 1373, states are to "criminalize active and passive assistance for terrorism in domestic laws and bring violators of these laws to justice" (UN CTC 2002). The priority of this criterion is reflected in the states' reports; the committee persistently asks each member-state about the status of domestic terrorism legislation. Those states that have fulfilled this requirement, as outlined in their reports, receive one point.

Criterion "D" is comparable to the preceding requirement. Resolution 1373 insists that states "deny all forms of financial support for terrorist groups" (UN CTC 2004). In harmony with that request, this criterion measures whether or not states have passed legislation that makes it illegal to provide financial backing to terrorist groups. States earn this point if they have enacted or improved legislation to criminalize the collection of funds for terrorist purposes. Moreover, in order to accommodate different types of action, the point is also awarded if states have frozen terrorist funds by executive order (although, admittedly, the CTC is most interested in seeing domestic legislation).

Criterion "E" seeks to gauge states' efforts at inhibiting terrorists' movements. As with the previous criteria, this standard is rooted in Resolution 1373 and the Committee's expectations. According to the resolution, states are to "suppress the provision of safe haven ... for terrorists" as well as "co-operate with other governments in the investigation, detection, arrest and prosecution of those involved in [terrorist] acts" (UN CTC 2004). In order to measure these requirements, we have appealed to each state's most recent report. If the committee has asked about extradition or border control efforts in the most recent report, the point goes unearned. Conversely, if the CTC has not asked about efforts in either of these categories (in the most recent report), the state earns the point. Our logic stems from this premise: the committee questions states primarily in "trouble areas." Therefore, if the committee is reasonably pleased with a particular state's efforts in this area, it will not ask the state to account for its actions.

We also add two additional questions related to whether the nation has ratified at least half of the twelve general anti-terror conventions currently available, and specifically whether the country has ratified the convention banning the financing of terror. We use both the seven-point and five-point scales in this work (Stiles and Thayne 2006).

Compliance varies dramatically across cases. Further, it is apparent that relatively few states were able to comply fully with even these preliminary measures within a few years of their promulgation. Only eleven out of 181 states in the data set received a score of five, while more than half received scores of two or lower. A closer look at the scores shows that many countries that received a five are closely tied to Great Britain, both as a current ally and as part of its Empire. On the other hand, states that scored a zero seem to share either poverty or smallness, indicating that lack of resources may in fact play a larger role than initially anticipated.

Figure 2.1 presents compliance data with reference to geography in the hope of bringing to light regional patterns. Africa clearly has more non-compliant states, as does Central Asia, but this does not mean that one can safely predict how a particular country in those regions will behave. Note that some neighboring countries have widely different policies with respect to UNSC Res 1373 (Stiles and Thayne 2006). Because no obvious pattern emerges from the map or table, we move to a more systematic statistical test, the results of which are reported in Chapter 5.

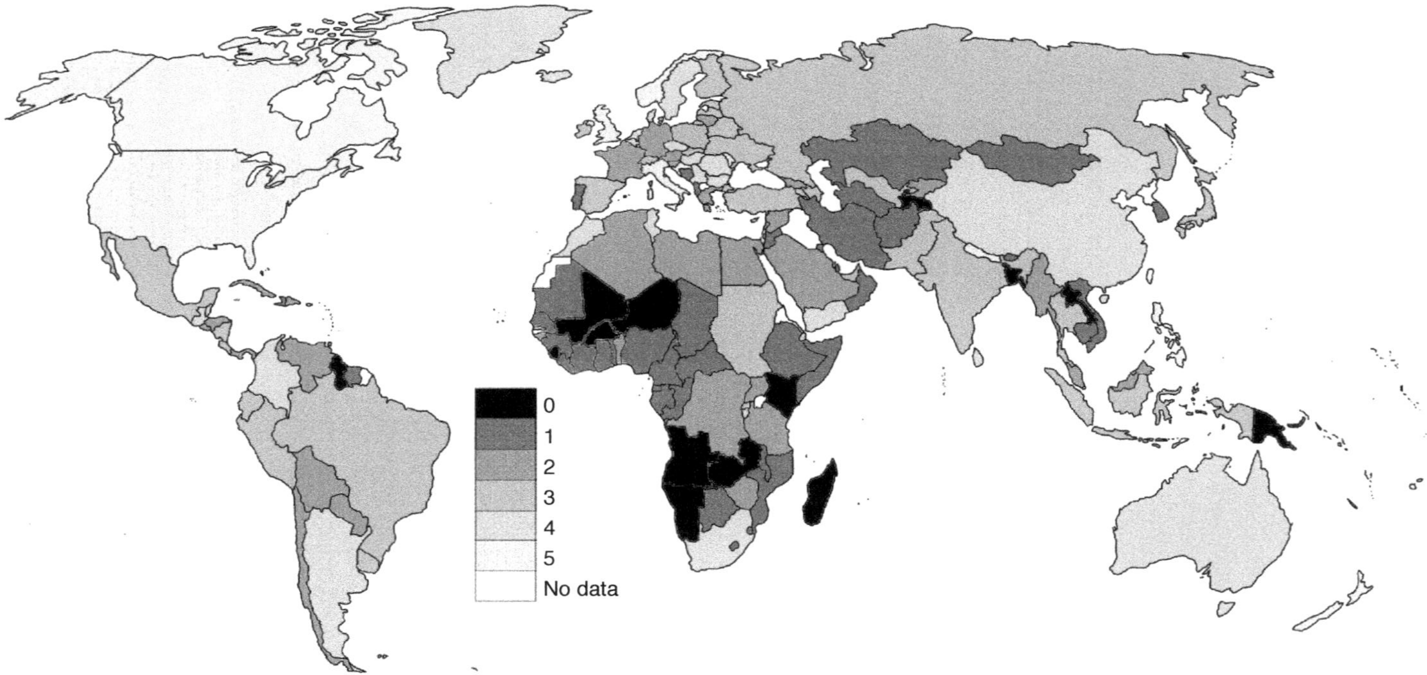

Figure 2.1 World map of degrees of compliance with UNSC Res. 1373: 2004 (source: Adapted from UN Counter-Terrorism Committee, various reports).

Anti-piracy[2]

Contemporary law on piracy flows from debates on how states should treat irregular naval forces. For many years, states lacked the resources to deploy large navies and relied on naval mercenaries (privateers) to wage naval war and patrol the oceans. Once their services were no longer needed, privateers often turned their skills and ships to other money-making activities – legal or otherwise (Risso 2001, 294; Starkey 2001, 69). Pirates showed little loyalty to their former employers, and by the beginning of the eighteenth century were considered a serious threat to the international system. At a minimum, they deprived states of the seamen and ships they needed and at worst they attacked the very states that helped sustain them. States gradually came to the conclusion that they would be far better off severing ties to these irregular navies – something that became easier as nation-states consolidated their power in Europe (Thomson 1990) and as ship construction moved from the relatively cheaper and more fragile wood to the more expensive and durable steel (Winslow 1988, 245).

In 1856, the major powers outlawed privateering, leaving no space for irregular navies. Pirates were viewed as threats against not only states but also commerce and humanity generally. The United Kingdom in particular carried out a war against pirates on these grounds, claiming jurisdiction over all the high seas and the territorial seas of less developed countries, such as China or Brazil (Rubin 1988, 249; White 1989). The crime of piracy could be prosecuted under the principle of universal jurisdiction: any state was permitted to arrest and try any pirate for attacks anywhere against anyone (Garmon 2002, 260). In practice, states have not invoked this right, preferring instead to act on the basis of the less controversial basis of territoriality principle (acting against crimes committed in the state's territorial seas – currently extending twelve nautical miles), nationality principle (the crime was committed by a citizen of the state), or the passive personality principle (the crime was committed against a national) (Buhler 1999, 76). Some have argued the universal principle of jurisdiction is mostly hypothetical and falls under the category of international custom (Randall 1988, 791).

Under the first and third Conventions on the Law of the Sea, piracy is limited to acts on the high seas – beyond the twelve-mile limit (Garmon 2002, 262). Presumably, anything taking place within the twelve-mile limit (territorial waters) falls within the national jurisdiction and therefore need not be addressed by international law. But in recent years, the International Maritime Organization and the International Maritime Bureau have addressed what has become a plague of pirate attacks in territorial waters. Roughly half of all pirate attacks since 1990 have occurred in the Straits of Malacca (consistent with the fact that roughly half of all international commercial shipping travels here), almost all of which is within the territorial seas of Malaysia or Indonesia. Many pirate attacks are perpetrated by dock workers in collaboration with customs and port officials (Chalk 1998, 3).

The IMO stresses states' duties to police their own waters and to collaborate with neighboring states to ensure that maritime jurisdictional issues are addressed (Goodman 1999, 158; IMO 2000). It has also enjoined states to more vigorously pursue pirates who attack ships in port and within territorial waters (IMO 1983). States, however, have resisted efforts to make these measures legally obligatory where attacks on the high seas are concerned. The provision in the LOS regarding enforcement of anti-piracy law on the high seas has ambiguous wording by design. On the one hand, it requires states to pursue and apprehend pirates and grants them universal jurisdiction to try them; on the other hand, a false arrest generates liability (articles 100, 105, 106). In addition, the IMO has published numerous circulars and codes of conduct (which are not technically binding) that clarify these obligations. All IMO members are expected to implement them (Barchue 2006, 6; Kachel 2006, 21–51).

Piracy has been defined as an act of depredation for "private" ends. Politically motivated violence at sea was treated separately. This "political exclusion" was codified in the various Conventions on the Law of the Sea, but was sorely tested after the attack on the *Achille Lauro* in 1985 made it clear that the law did not prohibit terrorism at sea (Balkin 2006, 7). Within a few years, governments signed the 1988 Convention on the Suppression of Unlawful Acts against the Safety of Maritime Navigation (SUA) to fill the legal gap. Overall, a consensus has emerged that attacks on civilians, whether for political or private ends, and whether within territorial waters or on the high seas, are unlawful and ought to be both prevented and punished. This has been reinforced by UN Security Council resolutions authorizing more aggressive actions with respect to Somali pirates, although the sanctity of the twelve-mile limit has been reaffirmed (Fink and Galvin 2009).

This does not mean that states feel a legal obligation to act on these beliefs. Arrest and prosecution of pirates – even those acting within territorial waters – is rare. Despite the urging of the IMO, states have been reluctant to invoke universal jurisdiction or pursue suspects into another country's territorial waters (IMO 1983). When given the opportunity, IMO member-states have tended to limit the Organization's enforcement and monitoring powers, leaving such activities to the IMB – a creation of the International Chamber of Commerce. Piracy was excluded from the list of crimes that could be prosecuted by the International Criminal Court and the IMO was barred from demanding public accountability for pursuing or prosecuting pirates (Marisec 2004, 5, 17). This, however, has not stopped the IMO from partnering with the IMB in "naming and shaming" states that fail to protect international shipping from pirates.

The naming and shaming takes the indirect form of publicly available, detailed reports of every incident involving violence at sea – including attacks within territorial waters and even at port. The reports detail not only the time and place of each attack, but also the flag of the ship that was victimized and the extent of the theft or violence that occurred. When available, the reports also provide a sketch of the pirates, including their numbers, the vessel they used, their means of accessing the ship, and their weaponry. Finally, and perhaps most damning, each report provides a detailed account of the response of the responsible state, ranging from ignoring distress calls to offering vague advice, to dispatching an investigatory team, to arresting and prosecuting the attackers (IMB website). Since these records have been stored for more than a decade, they provide a trove of information that can be used to measure the degree to which a government responds to pirate attacks within its jurisdiction. We choose to use this data to rate compliance with anti-piracy norms.

For the purposes of this study, we have measured state compliance with this rule by logging states' responses to over 1,440 pirate attacks between 2001 and 2007 – a period of great pirate activity. Because it is nearly impossible to prove a negative, we do not address whether states have successfully deterred attacks, but rather whether they have carried out their minimal legal obligation to pursue pirates after the fact. The IMB "attaches" each attack to a particular country; a relatively simple task since almost all attacks occur in close proximity to a particular country's coastline. Furthermore, the record of the incident shows which country was first contacted by the victims of the attack. Therefore it is easy to determine which state is primarily responsible for taking action, although it is possible that other states join in the effort, as we have seen in the case of Somali pirates. Finally, the specific actions taken by that state are logged. We use the data on state response to generate a "responsiveness" score. A state scores a point each time it replies to a distress call, even if this consists merely of expressing sympathy to the victims of the attack. States that had not even manned the emergency station when the call arrived have a point deducted. If a state dispatches police or coastguard forces to investigate the crime by interviewing the captain or crew, it receives another point. If these forces also make an arrest, the state receives still another point. Thus the score each state receives for each incident ranges from +3 to –1. The scores for every incident in a given year are averaged for the "average responsiveness rate."

We chose to annualize the data set, averaging most figures for each state for each year in order to allow for comparisons across states, which are my unit of analysis. This means that Indonesia's response rate is treated with equal weight to that of The Netherlands, even though the former experienced nearly 500 attacks during the period and the latter experienced none. The result is naturally that some information is lost. For example, we do not include data on the locations of pirate attacks (high seas, territorial seas, ports), since averaging such data by country would not make sense.

Only six countries out of the sixty-five countries where pirates have attacked have responded in some fashion in every instance. More than one-third of the countries (24/65) received a zero – meaning that they likely never responded to any distress calls. On the other hand, roughly the same number received a responsiveness score between seven and thirty-one, while another ten scored between one-third and three-fourths. These figures are disconcerting and indicate that most states do not respond effectively to piracy. Keeping in mind that most of the attacks occur within the territorial waters, it demonstrates a profound inability and/or unwillingness to protect basic sovereignty.

So who does act against pirates? The countries that earned a perfect score – Benin, Georgia, Greece, Morocco, the United Arab Emirates, and the United

States – seem to have very little in common. Even including the next category (Cuba, the Solomons, Sri Lanka, Brazil, Ghana, Bulgaria, Colombia, Panama, Papua New Guinea, and Sierra Leone) does not reveal any patterns.

Figure 2.2 offers a somewhat different picture of compliance with anti-piracy norms. To begin, it is clear that piracy, while a global problem, is not universal. Although there is no statistical correlation between the size of a country's navy and the number of attacks, it appears that pirates avoid the waters around developed countries. Next, it is clear that where pirates have attacked, they are least likely to have been pursued off the coast of Africa, although some Central American countries have poor response rates as well. Again, however, there are considerable regional variations, as we find between Myanmar and Thailand or Tanzania and Mozambique.

In a few cases, we know that relations between neighboring countries help explain the response rate, as in the Malacca Straits where, for the first half of the decade, Malaysia and Indonesia undercut efforts to patrol or protect international shipping on the grounds that incursions into territorial waters would be seen as a challenge to sovereignty (Chalk 1998, 21; Becker 2005, 134). Conditions deteriorated to the point that Lloyds of London rated it as a virtual war-zone and raised premiums on ships plying the Straits, which appears to have prompted states in the region to increase collaboration.

At any rate, it appears that while compliance is generally low, it is especially so in the world's poorest regions. This means that the managerial or rationalist schools may yet offer the strongest explanation, something we address directly in Chapter 5.

Anti-trafficking

At the beginning of the twentieth century, in response to reports of European women being trafficked for prostitution, states approved a ban on the so-called "white slave trade" in 1919 and merged them with bans on the slave trade in 1949 and as part of the Supplemental Convention (Coote 1909; Weissbrodt and Anti-Slavery International 2002, 18). For the next forty years, human trafficking was a relatively minor issue on the international stage, however. The fall of the Berlin Wall seems to have created new opportunities for unscrupulous individuals to dupe people – especially young women – to migrate to the West and to cities in the developing world. The International Organization for Migration estimated hundreds of thousands being trafficking by the mid-1990s (Skrobanek *et al.* 1997, 99).

The upsurge in activity prompted a number of initiatives. The United States undertook special investigations into the way law enforcement treated trafficked persons, which in turn led to a new statute in 2000 that created, among other things, a new visa for trafficked persons that allowed them to remain in the country (Gallagher 2001, 983; Abramson 2003, 477). The Group of Eight declared trafficking a priority at its 1998 summit, and by 1999 several countries had offered language for new legal instruments at the United Nations (Koslowski 2001, 337, 346).

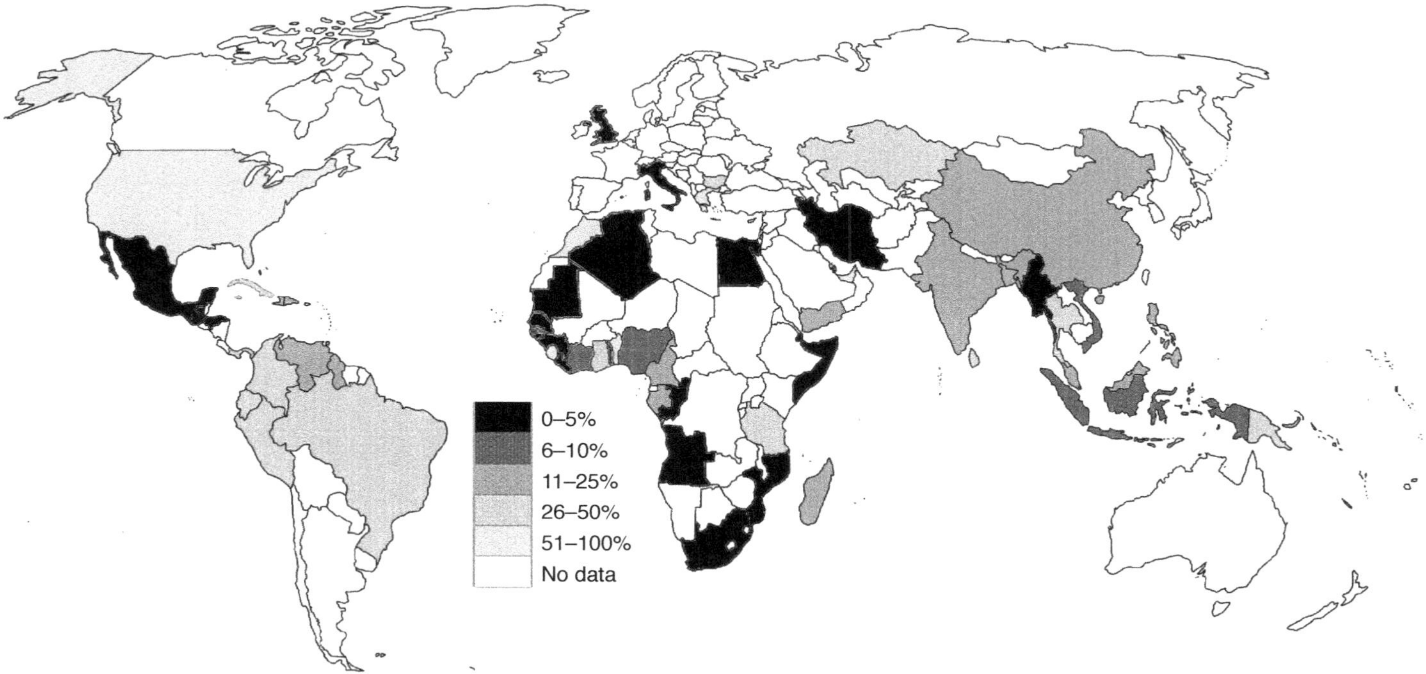

Figure 2.2 World map of rates of responsiveness to pirate attacks, 2001–2007 (source: IMO annual report, various issues).

Ultimately, agreement was reached on the negotiation of a protocol on trafficking to supplement the UN's Convention against Transnational Organized Crime. Negotiations quickly arrived at a definition of trafficking: any international movement of persons "for the purpose of exploitation" by means involving "the threat or use of force or other forms of coercion, of abduction, of fraud, of deception, of the abuse of power or of a position of vulnerability" (article 3). There was considerable disagreement, however, on whether it was possible that a woman could choose to be trafficked – especially into a life of prostitution. Western government disagreed since some had legalized prostitution while other had not (Leuchtag 2003, 13). Ultimately the language was left somewhat vague on the question (Gallagher 2001, 985).

A number of states, IGOs, and NGOs have attempted to measure trafficking. The International Labour Organization puts the number of individuals in forced labor at 12.3 million (ILO 2005) while others argue for a figure closer to 200,000 (Van der Anker 2004, 18). The International Organization for Migration has published collections of studies that demonstrate the lack of agreement (estimates for the number of women trafficked annually through Bangladesh range from 2,400 to 180,000, for example – Ali 2005, 143). The US Central Intelligence Agency dropped its estimates of trafficked persons into the US from as much as 50,000 a year in 1999 to as little as 14,500 in 2004 (Gozdziak and Collett 2005, 108).

Another set of measures assess government efforts to curb slavery and trafficking. The US State Department has developed the most authoritative measure through the Congressionally mandated Trafficking in Persons Report. Following an assessment of a state's trafficking levels, an analysis of its anti-trafficking statutes, its expenditures on trafficking interdiction and public education, and other factors, the State Department provides an annual score on a three-point scale, with one being the best and three placing the country on a black list subject to sanctions. A fourth point was added later to allow the government to fine-tune the distinction between the second and third tier and giving it additional leverage on reluctant but redeemable states. The US called this the second tier "watch list" for states that were in danger of slipping into the third tier (Interview 2007; Miller 2007). In order to avoid being ranked at the third tier, states must adopt laws to outlaw trafficking and exploitation as defined in the Protocol and take minimal steps to eliminate the problem. States must enforce the laws, provide services to assist victims, prosecute any public officials found to be complicit with traffickers, and work with other governments to coordinate strategies – including extraditing suspects as called for (section 108 of Trafficking Victims Protection Act of 2000).

The UN Office on Drugs and Crime has ranked every country in the world on a five-point scale in terms of how many individuals are reported to have left, arrived in or transited through it, based on official and other sources (UNODC 2006, 35–36). And Kevin Bales has rated every country's slavery levels and policies and trafficking levels and measures on a five-point scale (Bales 2005).

One might expect that different measures of state performance in the areas of slavery and trafficking should correlate with each other. After all, it seems reasonable to expect that states with strong anti-trafficking and anti-slavery measures would have low levels of each, and vice-versa. The first is a measure of Kevin Bales' slavery levels (using the mid-point in the estimated ranges) for each country as a percentage of total population. Next are Bales' trafficking scores, followed by the State Department's TIP scores (with tier-two watch-list valued at 2.5) and finally the cumulative UNODC score that combines each country's three scores (origin, destination, and transit). All figures are for 2005 or 2006. Table 2.1 shows the results of the correlations. Only the Bales and UN trafficking scores correlate as expected. This probably stems from the fact that the TIP score measures policy, while the UN and Bales scores attempt to measure outcomes.

The selection of a valid indicator of compliance with anti-trafficking rules is problematic. Because the most promising indicators appear to conflict, the choice must be based primarily on theory and intuition. Given the fact that the TIP is intended primarily to measure policy initiatives, it seems to be more consistent with the spirit of this study as a study of efforts at compliance. The TIP scores are generally well-respected and match up very well with the WomanStats trafficking measure. One the other hand, politics may taint the measure. Some have charged that Japan has benefited from such favoritism (Calundruccio 2005, 269; Lee 2005, 187). In fact, the list of tier three countries in recent years reads like a rogues' gallery with very few friends of America. We therefore choose to use this measure, but with a grain of salt. Figure 2.3 shows the geographic pattern of compliance.

The list of countries with low TIP scores reads like the OECD membership roster. Conversely, countries in the third tier include some of the United States' worst enemies. Otherwise, the scores are not especially predictable. Asian countries generally fare worse, but many African states are solidly in the middle ranks, along with Latin American and Middle Eastern countries. The implication is that capacity seems to be just one factor, but not the determining one, as ties to the US seem also to play a significant part. Precisely to what degree these factors interact will be determined in Chapter 5.

Table 2.1 Correlation matrix of trafficking measures

	TIP score	*UN trafficking score*	*Bales' trafficking score*
TIP score	x	–0.058	0.056
UN trafficking score		x	0.327*
Bales' trafficking score			x

Note
*= $p<0.05$.

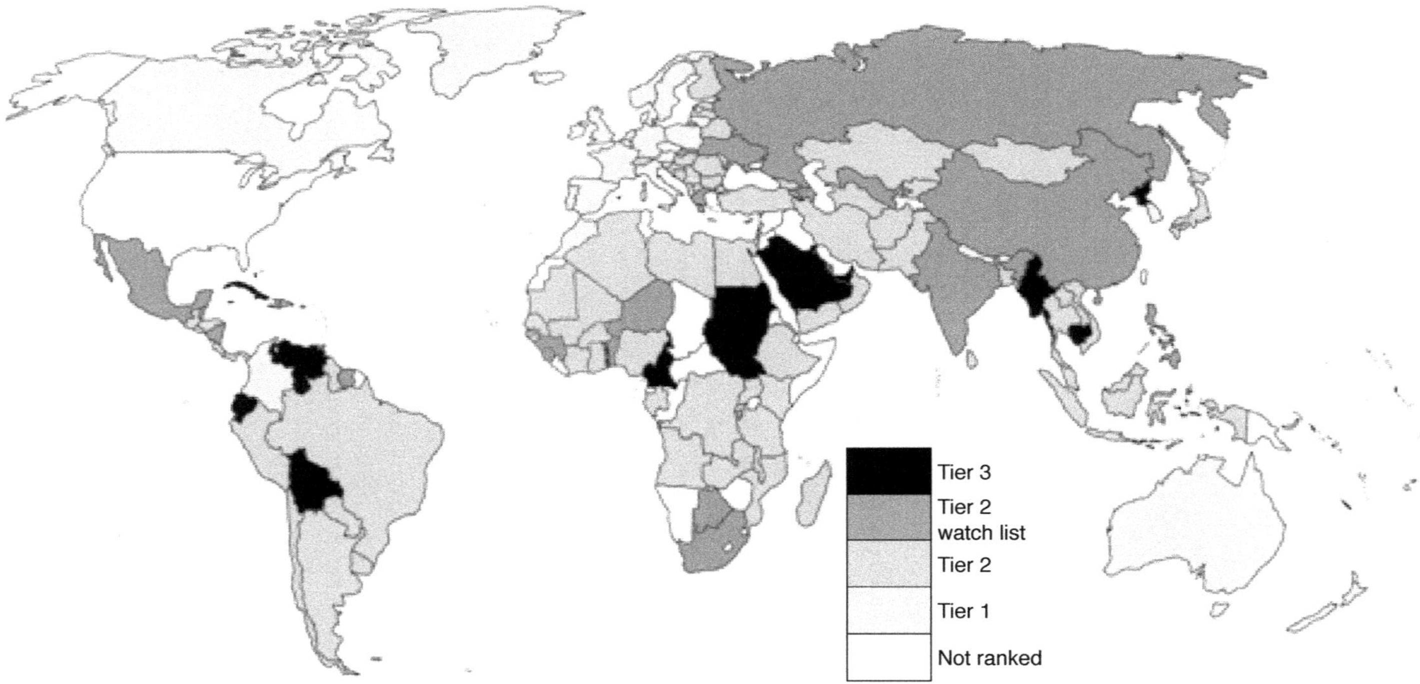

Figure 2.3 Trafficking in persons rankings, 2005 (source: US State Dept. TIP Report).

Conclusions

Taken together, the material on these three sets of rules does not point toward one single theory of compliance. That said, the premises of the managerial school, realism, liberalism, and rationalism seem have been specifically supported by some of the data. In particular, economically developed democracies seem to generally implement the various rules discussed in this chapter, although there are exceptions. This is consistent with the evidence that states with more effective administrative structures are better able to defend the territory against criminal non-state actors. It is not always clear, however, whether the states have a specific financial incentive to do so, or whether they simply value territorial integrity. At any rate, since the public officials in these types of countries tend to eschew complicity with criminal organizations, they are better able to act in the national interest.

There is not enough evidence at this point to sort out which of the theories has the strongest claim and so we will turn in Chapter 5 to a more systematic side-by-side comparison of the cases.

Notes

1 Much of the discussion of anti-terror law compliance is adapted from Kendall Stiles and Adam Thayne, "Compliance with International Law: International Law on Terrorism at the United Nations," *Cooperation and Conflict* 4(2) (July 2006): 153–176.
2 Much of the material on compliance with anti-piracy measures comes from Kendall Stiles, "Who Is Keeping the Sea Safe? Testing Theories of International Law Compliance," *Cooperation and Conflict* 45(2) (June 2010): 139–161.

References

Abramson, Kara (2003) "Beyond Consent: Toward Safeguarding Human Rights – Implementing the United Nations Trafficking Protocol," *Harvard International Law Journal* 44 (Summer): 473–502.

Alexander, Yonah (2002) *Combating Terrorism: Strategies of Ten Countries*. Ann Arbor: University of Michigan Press.

Ali, A.K.M. Masud (2005) "Trading Along a Treacherous Trail: Research on Trafficking in Persons in South Asia," in Frank Laczko and Elzbieta Gozdziak, eds., *Data and Research on Human Trafficking: A Global Survey*. Geneva Switzerland: IOM, pp. 141–164.

Bales, Kevin (2005) *Understanding Slavery: A Reader*. Berkeley: University of California Press.

Balkin, Rosalie (2006) "The International Maritime Organization and Maritime Security," *Tulane Maritime Law Journal* 30 (Winter/Summer): 1–35.

Barchue, L.D. (2006) *Making the Case for the Voluntary IMO Member State Audit Scheme*. London: IMO Headquarters.

Becker, Michael A. (2005) "The Shifting Public Order of the Oceans: Freedom of Navigation and the Interdiction of Ships at Sea," *Harvard International Law Journal* 46 (Winter): 131–229.

Bhoumik, Arunabha (2005) "Democratic Responses to Terrorism: A Comparative Study of the United States, Israel, and India," *Denver Journal of International Law and Policy* 33 (Spring): 285–345.

Buhler, Phillip A. (1999) "New Struggle with an Old Menace: Towards a Revised Definition of Maritime Policy," *Currents: International Trade Law Journal* 8 (Winter): 61–70.

Calandruccio, Giuseppe (2005) "A Review of Recent Research on Human Trafficking in the Middle East," in Frank Laczko and Elzbieta Gozdziak, eds., *Data and Research on Human Trafficking: A Global Survey*. Geneva: IOM, pp. 267–300.

Chalk, Peter (1998) "Low-Intensity Conflict in Southeast Asia: Piracy, Drug Trafficking and Political Terrorism," *Conflict Studies* 305/306 (January/February): 1–38.

Coote, William A. (1909) "The Suppression of the White Slave Traffic," in Ernest A. Bell, ed., *War on the White Slave Trade*. Chicago: Charles Thompson, pp. 29–46.

Cortright, David and George Lopez (2004) "Containing Iraq: Sanctions Worked," *Foreign Affairs* 83(4) (July/August): 1–14.

Fink, Martin and Richard Galvin (2009) "Combating Pirates off the Coast of Somalia: Current Legal Challenges," *Netherlands International Law Review* 55: 367–395.

G7/P8 (1996) "Ministerial Conference on Terrorism." Paris, July 30.

Gallagher, Anne (2001) "Human Rights and the New UN Protocols on Trafficking and Migrant Smuggling: A Preliminary Analysis," *Human Rights Quarterly* 23(4) (Winter): 975–1004.

Garmon, Tina (2002) "International Law of the Sea: Reconciling the Law of Piracy and Terrorism in the Wake of September 11th," *The Maritime Lawyer* 27 (Winter): 257–275.

Goodman, Timothy H. (1999) " 'Leaving the Corsair's Name to Other Times': How to Enforce the Law of Sea: Piracy in the 21st Century Through Regional Agreements," *Case Western Reserve Journal of International Law* 31 (Winter): 139–168.

Gozdziak, Elzbieta M. and Elizabeth A. Collett (2005) "Research on Human Trafficking in North America: A Review of the Literature," in Frank Laczko and Elzbieta Gozdziak, eds., *Data and Research on Human Trafficking: A Global Survey*. Geneva: IOM, pp. 99–128.

Hafner, Gerhard (2003) "Certain Issues of the Work of the Sixth Committee at the 56th General Assembly," *American Journal of International Law* 97 (January): 147–162.

International Labour Organization (2005) "A Global Alliance Against Forced Labour," Director-General's Global Report under the Follow-up to the ILO Declaration on Fundamental Principles and Rights at Work 2005, Report I (B), International Labour Conference 93rd Session, Geneva.

International Maritime Organization (1983) "Measures to Prevent Acts of Piracy and Armed Robbery against Ships," IMO Resolution A.545 (13).

International Maritime Organization (2000) "Piracy and Armed Robbery: Focus on IMO," January.

Interviews (2001) Author interviews with UN staff and members of member-state permanent missions, October 23–26.

Interviews (2002) Author interviews with UN staff and members of member-state permanent missions, March 14–18.

Interview (2007) Author interview with Senior Staff member, US House of Representatives, April 26, 2007, Washington D.C.

Kachel, Markus (2006) "Competencies of International Maritime Organizations to Establish Rules and Standards," in Peter Ehlers and Rainer Lagoni, eds., *International*

Maritime Organizations and their Contributions towards a Sustainable Marine Development. Hamburg: LIT, pp. 21–51.

Kerstetter, Wayne A. (1978) "Practical Problems of Law Enforcement," in Alona Evans and John F. Murphy, eds., *Legal Aspects of International Terrorism*. Lexington, MA: Lexington Books, pp. 535–551.

Koslowski, Rey (2001). "Economic Globalization, Human Smuggling, and Global Governance," in David Kyle and Rey Koslowski, eds., *Global Human Smuggling: Comparative Perspectives*. Baltimore: John Hopkins University Press, pp. 257–293.

Krasner, Stephen (1999) *Sovereignty: Organized Hypocrisy*. Princeton: Princeton University Press.

Lee, June J.H. (2005) "Human Trafficking in East Asia: Current Trends, Data Collection and Knowledge," in Frank Laczko and Elzbieta Gozdziak, eds., *Data and Research on Human Trafficking: A Global Survey*. Geneva: IOM, pp. 165–202.

Leuchtag, Alice (2003). "Human Rights, Sex Trafficking, and Prostitution," *The Humanist* 63 (January/February): 10–16.

Luck, Edward (2004) "Tackling Terrorism," in David Malone, ed., *The UN Security Council: From the Cold War to the 21st Century*. Boulder, CO: Lynne Rienner, pp. 85–100.

Maogoto, Jackson Nyamuya (2005) "Countering Terrorism: From Wigged Judges to Helmeted Soldiers – Legal Perspectives on America's Counter-Terrorism Responses," *San Diego International Law Journal* 6 (Spring): 243–294.

Marisec (2004) *Pirates and Armed Robbers: Guidelines on Prevention for Masters and Ship Security Officers*, rev. ed. London: International Chamber of Shippers/International Shipping Federation.

McWhinney, Edward (1987) *Aerial Piracy and International Terrorism: The Illegal Diversion of Aircraft and International Law*. Dordrecht, NE: Martinus Nijhoff Pubs.

Miller, John (2007) Former Ambassador at Large for Trafficking, Interview with the Author, April 10, 2007, Washington D.C.

Murphy, John (1978) "Protected Persons and Diplomatic Facilities," in Alona Evans and John F. Murphy, eds., *Legal Aspects of International Terrorism*. Lexington, MA: Lexington Books, pp. 277–339.

Randall, Kenneth C. (1988) "Universal Jurisdiction Under International Law," *Texas Law Review* 66 (March): 785–841.

Risso, Patricia (2001) "Cross-Cultural Perceptions of Piracy: Maritime Violence in the Western Indian Ocean and Persian Gulf Region during a Long Eighteenth Century," *Journal of World History* 12(2) (Fall): 293–320.

Romaniuk, Peter (2010) *Multilateral Counter-terrorism: The Global Politics of Cooperation and Contestation*. London: Routledge.

Rubin, Alfred P. (1988). *The Law of Piracy*. Newport, RI: Naval War College Press.

Skrobanek, Siriporn, Nattaya Boonpakdi, and Chutima Janthakeero (1997) *The Traffic in Women: Human Realities of the International Sex Trade*. London: Zed Books.

Starkey, David J. (2001) "The Origins and Regulation of Eighteenth-Century British Privateering," in C.R. Pennell, ed. *Bandits at Sea: A Pirates Reader*. New York: New York University Press, pp. 69–81.

Stiles, Kendall (2010) "Who Is Keeping the Sea Safe? Testing Theories of International Law Compliance," *Cooperation & Conflict* 45(2) (June): 139–161.

Stiles, Kendall and Adam Thayne (2006) "Compliance with International Law: International Law on Terrorism at the United Nations," *Cooperation and Conflict* 41(2) (July): 153–176.

Thomson, Janice E. (1990) "State Practices, International Norms, and the Decline of Mercenarism," *International Studies Quarterly* 34(1) (March): 23–47.

UN Counter-Terrorism Committee (2002) Note by the Chairman, February 8.

UN Counter-Terrorism Committee (2004) Minutes of 4688th Meeting: High Level Meeting of the Security Council: Combating Terrorism [S/PV.4688].

United Nations Office on Drugs and Crime (2006) "Trafficking in Persons: Global Patterns," Vienna, Austria. Downloaded from www.unodc.org/pdf/traffickinginpersons_report_2006ver2.pdf. Accessed February 21, 2007.

UNSC (2002) Counter-Terrorism Committee pursuant to SC Resolution 1373 (2001), Note by the Chairman, February 8.

Van der Anker, Christien (2004) "Contemporary Slavery, Global Justice and Globalization," in Christien Van der Anker, ed., *The Political Economy of New Slavery*. London: Palgrave, pp. 15–36.

Weissbrodt, David and Anti-Slavery International (2002) *Abolishing Slavery and its Contemporary Forms*. New York: UNHCHR.

White, G. Edwards (1989) "The United States Constitution in the Third Century: Foreign Affairs History: The Marshall Court and International Law: The Piracy Cases," *American Journal of International Law* 83 (October): 727–735.

Wilkinson, Paul (2000) *Terrorism Versus Democracy: The Liberal State Response*. London: Frank Cass.

Winslow, Peter E. (1988) *"Wealth and Honour": Portsmouth During the Golden Age of Privateering, 1775–1815*. Portsmouth, ME: Peter Randall.

Witten, Samuel (1998) "The International Convention for the Suppression of Terrorist Bombings," *American Journal of International Law* 92 (October): 769–789.

3 Rules designed to regulate the market

Shipping and airline regulation and CFC control

While states naturally seek to survive as political entities, they also recognize that they operate in a broader environment made up of private actors, some of which enjoy considerable power. Foremost among these are businesses – particularly those large firms that wield tremendous economic power. States have attempted to harness these actors for public ends, usually through unilateral regulation or nationalization. But from time to time multilateral agreements are forged, typically because states determine that unilateral approaches have proven ineffective.

In this chapter, we will look at two different types of regulations. First, we will consider rules governing international transportation – specifically airlines and shipping companies. The principal concern in these regulations is to ensure the safe movement of goods and passengers. Next, we will consider a global effort to protect the Earth's ozone layer through the regulation of chlorofluorocarbon usage.

Ship safety[1]

The rules governing safe ship operation and safe command of vessels emerged during the late 1800s. The International Convention for the Safety of Life at Sea (SOLAS) was originally drafted in 1913 following the *Titanic* disaster. It has been revised and amended a number of times and has had two protocols added to it. The revisions have strengthened the rules – something most states were eager to do. As put by Zacher: "Damage control is the one general shipping issue where it is easiest to make the case that the regulatory regime is regarded as serving the interests of virtually all states" (Zacher 1996, 50). Muted opposition came from states that did not have the resources to enforce stricter standards or that hoped to attract overseas companies to register under their "flags of convenience." The tension between these states and those advanced industrialized states that sought tougher standards was resolved in the 1970s by making most standards voluntary and flexible (DeSombre 2006, chapter 4).

Following a string of maritime disasters, developed states demanded stricter compliance with safety standards for both ships flagged in developing countries and developing country ports (Rodriguez and Hubbard 2005). In 1989, IMO members adopted the International Safety Management (ISM) Code that required states to supervise the refitting of ocean-going vessels to ensure they would conform to a long list of safety standards. Some of the standards included proper navigational equipment (including a programme for global positioning system [GPS] satellite communication), thorough training of officers and crews, carefully designed security plans to deal with emergencies, state-of-the-art communications systems, and provisions for proper documentation of ship and cargo. Compliant ships would receive a certificate that could be displayed in foreign ports. The International Ship and Port Facility Security (ISPS) code was adopted in 2002, and made mandatory for all 148 SOLAS signatories. It requires all states to ensure that ships carrying their flags obtain the ISM certificate, and authorized port authorities to bar, detain, or expel non-compliant vessels (IMO 2003).

To ensure standardized monitoring of compliance with these rules, states have drawn up memoranda of understanding (MOU) and established expert bodies to draft guidelines, train port officials, and collect inspection data for general consumption. The most sophisticated of these MOUs involve states in Europe and the North Atlantic (the Paris MOU) and East Asia and the North Pacific (the Tokyo MOU). Port officials inspect vessels and evaluate conditions, disseminate their findings to other MOU members, and decide whether to permit the ship to continue (Paris MOU 2008).

As explained by DeSombre:

> As a result of the inspection process, a ship can be found to be "clean," or it can have some number of recorded deficiencies. If there are enough deficiencies or they are serious enough, the ship can be detained in port until the most egregious ones are corrected.... If a ship is detained, the port state must notify the flag state...
>
> (2006, 93)

The MOUs rate the overall performance not only of ships and shipping companies, but also of the flag states themselves. It is this rating of flag states that interests us here. Although governments cannot always control the quality of ships that carry their flag, they are still ultimately responsible for them and are routinely held accountable by port states, insurers, and creditors (DeSombre 2006, 93). Flag states that wish to improve their reputations have several options: put pressure on the private companies they have hired to register ships for them to improve their standards, nationalize this work in-house through a government agency, urge ship captains and ship owners to raise their standards through incentives, or remove sub-standard ships from the flag. Note that all are costly in terms of the expense of additional inspections and/or lost revenues from exclusions.

The Paris and Tokyo MOUs have uploaded complete inspection records, and so we use their reports on nearly 200,000 ship inspections conducted between 2003 and 2007 as my source material. In 2006, the most common problems that prompted a citation included inadequate fire safety measures, problems with the compass and steering mechanisms, and engine and propulsion problems (Paris MOU 2006). The most common types of infractions that prompted a detention, as reported by the Paris MOU in April 2008, include inadequate maintenance (rust, breakage), broken or missing fire extinguishers and dampers, inadequate lifeboats and lifeboat access, missing paperwork (activity logs, certificates), faulty engines, and other deficiencies in emergency equipment and training (Paris MOU 2007). In almost every case, ships were cited for several deficiencies, and so it is difficult to determine which infraction was decisive. In at least one case a ship was detained simply for excess filth and vermin (the Egypt-registered *Ikhnaton* on April 3 in Trieste). In the overwhelming majority of cases, it was the ship's own crew that was protected by the inspections, since the most common infraction was related to on-board safety. It is also worth noting that in almost every case the problems were rectified very quickly and the ship was allowed to proceed.

We measure compliance with ship safety rules by logging the number of times the commercial ships of a particular flag state are prohibited from entering a state's port or proceeding to the next port of call (i.e., detained) relative to the total number of inspections its ships are subjected to. The more detentions per inspection, the less compliant the flag state. Based on a survey of the Paris and Tokyo MOUs covering 2003–2007, compliance rates are relatively high. Out of 192,439 inspections carried out by the Paris and Tokyo MOU port states, there have been only 9,759 detentions of ships on safety grounds and almost all of the ships in question were allowed to go on their way once repairs were completed. This is not to say that every ship that was not detained was in full compliance (51 percent had at least one deficiency). And it is worth noting that inspections are not random. Port states specifically target ships sailing under flags that have bad reputations and ignore the rest (Güner-Özbek 2006, 105–134). Since the other 80,000 ships were not inspected at all (given the 70 percent overall inspection rate) and were obviously allowed to proceed without incident, basic compliance with the ship regulations can be inferred to hover around 96.5 percent (or perhaps a bit less).

Which states might be most likely to comply? Unlike the rules covered in Chapter 2, this and other rules covered in this chapter have more to do with regulating corporate activity and the market than promoting state sovereignty. One implication of this is that one might expect that states with stronger material incentives will comply. Of course, benefits should be weighed against costs, according to rationalist thinking, which means that states most likely to comply should be those for whom the cost-benefit calculus is most advantageous. In this case, this implies that states that are especially dependent on international shipping will be most compliant, with the possible exception of "flag of convenience" states that might use their more lenient inspection regime as an inducement for shipping companies seeking to lower operating costs.

Countries that received perfect detention scores (zero) include industrialized maritime states (Australia, Chile, Iceland, South Africa), less developed island states (Solomon Islands, Trinidad and Tobago, Mauritius, Cuba), and still others that appear to have little in common. Of these, Equatorial Guinea and Mauritius are flag of convenience states. On the other extreme, the states with the worst detention rates (over one-fifth) include Argentina and Mexico – both advanced and heavily shipping dependent – as well as poor and isolated Democratic Republic of Korea. Other nations in this portion of the list appear to have little in common, although four poor African countries round out the bottom of the list. None is a flag of convenience state.

Beyond these observations, it is interesting to note that most industrialized states appear on the high compliance end of the scale, with detention rates below 5 percent, while most of the states with relatively higher detention rates are poorer. The world map in Figure 3.1 helps to show some regional patterns. Western Europe, North America, and Oceania appear especially compliant, while the rest of the world shows no clear pattern. This is consistent with the notion that wealth correlates with compliance, perhaps because of capacity or because of a favorable cost-benefit calculus. This and the other observations indicate that the managerial school's emphasis on capacity to administer regulations is probably validated, along with rationalism's approach. Beyond that, more information is needed to determine which theory holds the most promise.

Airline safety

Beginning almost as soon as transnational flights were technically possible, governments gathered to establish multilateral agreements to govern safety, jurisdiction, security, and so forth. Inspired heavily by international maritime law, they signed the Paris Convention in 1919 and the Chicago Convention (Convention on International Civil Aviation) in 1944, shortly after Paris was liberated (Huang 2009, 10). An American initiative, the signatories agreed to adopt and abide by regulations "in order that international civil aviation may be developed in a safe and orderly manner … on the basis of equality of opportunity" (Preamble, Chicago Convention). In the process, they created the International Civil Aviation Organization, recognizing that international standards would need to be supervised by a single entity to prevent chaos and danger. They further endowed the organization with the power to establish specific regulations – with the approval of member-states. The development of global regulations has been the principal activity of the ICAO since its inception. Most of these are promulgated as amendments to the Chicago Convention's eighteen Annexes (standards), although they may also take the form of advisory statements (recommended practices) on the one, or may involve the adoption of a new universally applicable legal instrument (there have been nearly thirty substantive international instruments governing civil aviation since the Chicago Convention) or other more narrow agreement. At the same time, it is important to note that the signatories (especially the US) were careful not to give the ICAO enforcement powers (Nayar 1995).

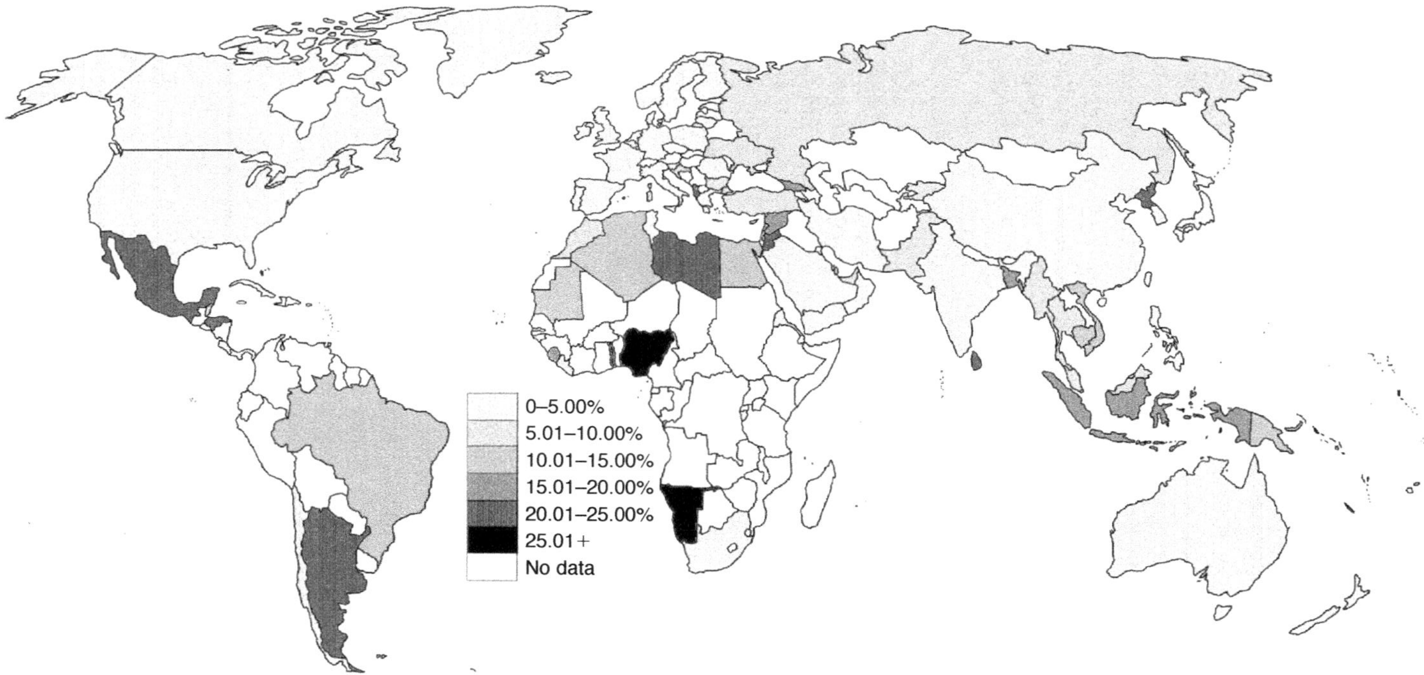

Figure 3.1 Map of ship detention rates from 2003 to 2007 (source: Paris MOU, Tokyo MOU, various years).

The bulk of the agreements and regulations surrounding aviation safety involve standards that governments are expected to implement. They involve the mechanisms, laws, and procedures each government is expected to adopt and manage, as well as the specific operational and technical specifications of aircraft, navigation systems and rules, airport operation and safety, and staff training (both on the ground and in the air). Regulations are first proposed by ICAO staff, signatory states, or other international organizations, at which point the Air Navigation Committee (ANC) – composed of fifteen technical experts nominated and approved by signatory states – offers a preliminary opinion, following which the proposal is generally taken up by one of several staff offices for more detailed analysis and revision. Once this process is complete, a more formal proposal is submitted to the ANC for formal action. This consists generally of a recommendation to the thirty-six-member ICAO Council – the diplomatic body tasked with day-to-day supervision of the organization where states with large aviation sectors are well represented (OECD countries make up roughly one-third of the membership). This is not to say that the Council can disregard these recommendations. As pointed out by Huang, "experience … demonstrates that when a subordinate technical body presents a package for consideration by the superior policy body, it is practically not easy for the latter to overturn the package and reinvent the wheel" (Huang 2009, 56). Proposals must receive a two-thirds vote for approval, meaning that many developing countries must sign off. At this point, the draft regulation is promulgated and signatories have roughly four months to log their disapproval. Should more than half do so (a very unlikely event), the regulation can be blocked. Generally, drafts are approved and become binding law (in the case of standards), and states that are non-compliant are required to articulate their deficiencies, which are then publicly reported (ICAO 2004). Thus far, very few states have indicated an inability to implement ICAO standards – but at least respect for state sovereignty is respected (Huang 2009, 69; MacKenzie 2010, 397).

The standards have multiplied over the years, reaching close to one thousand. In practice, these standards are not always especially strong since it is generally understood that they should be affordable and within the capacity of weaker members (Huang 2009, 50). States also were careful when reviewing expert panel recommendations since they knew they would be expected to implement them (MacKenzie 2010, 194). Whether the standards promulgated by the ICAO are mandatory is under debate. Some have argued that they need only be implemented if doing so is feasible, while other argue that they must be implemented unless doing so is not feasible (Huang 2009, 61). ICAO has traditionally honored the notion of state sovereignty over airspace, with the implication that it has denied itself any supranational authority and instead operates on the basis of persuasion (MacKenzie 2010, 193).

In the late 1990s, concerns about implementation of standards – especially in the United States and Europe with respect to developing countries – led the Assembly (the universal body in which every signatory has one vote) to adopt a more assertive approach. The United States had already measured compliance with ICAO standards through its International Aviation Safety Assessment program in the early 1990s and found that roughly two-thirds of countries of those who chose to participate failed (Button *et al.* 2004, 255). In 1999, the Universal Safety Oversight Audit Programme came into being, through which ICAO technical experts visited more than one hundred ICAO member-states with the goal of assessing the regulatory framework of each state. Specifically, they hoped to learn whether ICAO standards for regulations, administration, procedures, training, and so forth were being implemented by the national government (Annex 1, 6, and 8 – later expanded – Huang 2009, 70). Note that this did not typically involve inspecting aircraft per se, but rather looking through government documentation, interviewing senior staff in national aviation administrative offices, and comparing their findings to ICAO standards, on the understanding that there exists a high correlation between administration and airline safety (Shyur 2008). This was done once in the late 1990s and then again a few years later (in the hope that performance would have improved) (ICAO 2009). We use scores from the follow-up inspections to measure compliance since they are the most recent such systematic effort by the ICAO.

The degree of non-compliance, even after several consultations, makes it clear that many states do not regard ICAO standards as binding in the full sense, but instead see them as goals to be sought when the resources are available (Huang 2009, 70). On the other hand, all members have been willing to sign a memorandum of understanding authorizing the ICAO staff to inspect confidential national reports, indicating an acceptance of a strong ICAO role in principle. This also implies that they agree that the standards are legally binding and that they should be held accountable for non-compliance. This was especially apparent when members agreed to have the results of their audits posted on the organization's website in 2008, where "naming and shaming" could occur (MacKenzie 2010, 389).

We now turn to the country-by-country measures of ICAO compliance, as reported in Figure 3.2. There is considerable variance across our cases, with a few countries recording no infractions at all and a few others failing roughly half of the test – or more in the case of Laos. The average rate of infraction was 12.8 percent – roughly the failure rate of the United Kingdom. Most OECD states have infraction scores below 10 percent while a dozen Sub-Saharan African countries have scores above 20 percent (with many African countries not submitting to the inspections which are nominally voluntary). The map in Figure 3.2 seems to indicate that compliance is related to wealth, but there are many exceptions. Portugal, Britain, and Belgium are outliers among developed countries with relatively high rates of infraction on the one hand, while Kenya, Cuba, and Tanzania appear to be exceeding expectations. Clearly, none of these countries has close airline ties with the US, so something else must be driving the policies. We will undertake a more formal analysis in Chapter 5.

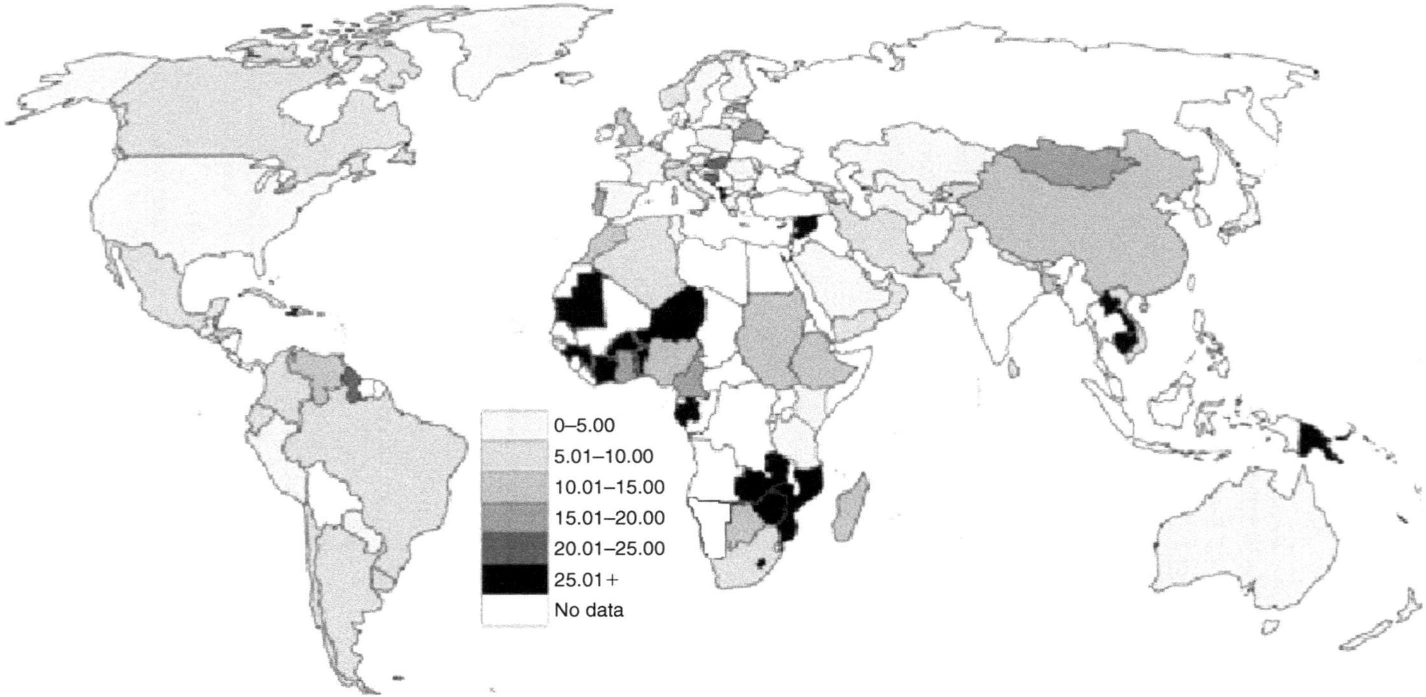

Figure 3.2 ICAO airline safety scores, 2004 follow-up inspection (source: ICAO 2004).

CFC ban

Beginning in the mid-1970s, atmospheric scientists began to draw connections between chlorofluorocarbon (CFC) emissions from aerosols, Styrofoam containers, Freon in refrigerator condensers and the like, and the destruction of ozone in the upper atmosphere which has the ability to deflect some of the Sun's ultraviolet radiation (Haas 1992). They projected that at current rates of emission the ozone layer would begin to thin, thereby exposing humans and animals to unhealthy levels of radiation, leading to increased incidence of skin cancer and other ailments (Braithwaite and Drahos 2000, 264). The United States took the lead in 1977 by mandating the gradual elimination of CFC production in the US. Dow Chemical moved quickly to develop substitutes and became a key player in the subsequent American effort to create international rules against CFC production (Sprinz and Vaahtoranta 1994). The pressure they exerted, along with the UN Environmental Program (UNEP) and a variety of environmental NGOs, led to the Vienna Convention for the Protection of the Ozone Layer in 1985 and then to a Protocol on CFCs in 1987. During the negotiations, a debate emerged between the United States, Canada, and several Nordic states on the one hand and most Continental European states and the United Kingdom on the other. The former sought stricter targets, a broader range of chemicals to be banned, and more legalistic language and enforcement mechanisms. The US proposed automatic sanctions against violators, as determined by an independent body of experts. Even the Nordics parted ways with the US on this point once it was apparent there could be no consensus on the matter, and so the issue was set aside for future negotiation (Ehrmann 2002, 392).

In the Meetings of the Parties (MOP) from 1989 to 1992 negotiators elaborated an enforcement scheme that reflected a managerial approach rather than the punitive approach favored by the United States (Boyle 1999, 910). In other words, while the MOP was empowered to identify rule violators, doing so was intended to initiate a series of cooperative and supportive measures, including the provision of technical advice, financial support for CFC-reducing projects, and quiet diplomacy (Victor *et al.* 1998, 141). The negotiators created an Implementation Committee (IC) made up of ten geographically representative states to be elected by the MOP that would oversee the parties' compliance. The IC could initiate reviews of each party's annual reports and identify deficiencies – including the failure to provide reports itself as well as gaps between progress toward elimination of CFCs and other ozone-depleting substances and the various targets the parties had accepted. In addition, the IC could receive complaints from any party regarding any other party's performance – including self-recriminating statements by parties regarding their own records (UNEP 1998, see especially Articles 2, 4, and 7). The IC meets roughly twice a year to present its conclusions to the MOP and forward its recommendations for action – almost all of which are adopted pro-forma.

Overall, the Montreal Protocol has been remarkably effective with respect to limiting large-scale production and consumption of ozone-depleting substances.

Not only have almost all countries ceased production and sale of CFCs, but global production of a wide range of listed chemicals has declined since 1987 and many are on the verge of elimination (Greene 1998, 90). This is not to say that there has been no illicit production of or traffic in CFCs. The US, for example, continues to prosecute firms that have purchased contraband CFC-12, a crime punishable with jail time, as was the case of a senior officer of a refrigeration firm convicted of importing eight million pounds of CFC-12 in the late 1990s (EPA 2007).

Some of this stems from the fact that the Protocol is a flexible instrument that has been repeated, amended, and expanded as new scientific information trickles in (Boyle 1999). But much of the credit goes to the IC's operation which incorporates in practice both a managerial approach as well as a sanctions approach. The IC, for example, serves as a certifier of compliance to those administering the Protocol's Multilateral Fund as well as the World Bank's Global Environmental Facility's ozone projects, both of which provide considerable financial and technical support to developing countries and economies in transition as they wean themselves from CFCs (Greene 1998). This places it at the center of a network of international agencies that have real clout. In addition, the IC can recommend that a party's privileges under the Protocol be temporary suspended, although this comes short of the type of sanctioning originally envisioned by the US.

In practice, the IC only gradually asserted its prerogatives. It began by identifying the more than fifty states that had failed to submit baseline figures on CFC production and consumption circa 1995 with the result that a flood of new reports were submitted over the next years. Reporting continues to be a problem for many countries – especially less developed parties to the Protocol – and the IC routinely includes a list of states whose reports are derelict in the minutes of its semi-annual meetings. The IC also began in 1997 to recommend and supervise implementation of programs designed to ensure full compliance on the part of states. In particular, Russia and a variety of former Soviet allies and states were placed under fairly strict regimens to improve their woeful records. In most cases the problems stemmed from a lack of administrative capacity which was remedied through training and increased budgets for environmental law enforcement. In others the problems stemmed from lack of political will, which was addressed mostly through threats of sanctions and "naming and shaming," with the support of an array of international bodies (Greene 1998).

By the early 2000s, most developing countries were no longer grandfathered under the Protocol's Article 5 provisions allowing them a ten-year grace period for implementation of chemical bans, and so the IC began to turn its attention to demanding stricter compliance from them. In addition to identifying general problems of lack of compliance, the IC singles out particular countries in its semi-annual reports, both to recommend new programs and to praise or chastise performance with respect to existing programs. The reports have the tone of a caring guardian and are remarkably frank. In order to avoid loss of face, some countries have taken rather drastic and sudden steps immediately following a negative IC report in order to dissuade the MOP from endorsing it, such as was the case of Mauritania which was threatened with withdrawal of Article 5 protection for failure to provide baseline data in 1994 by supplying everything that was called for (Victor *et al.* 1998, 151). Taken together, the IC mechanism has gradually acquired many of the characteristics of an international judicial body (Boyle 1999).

The dependent variable will be the frequency of negative comments against a state by the Implementation Committee of the Montreal Protocol. As discussed above, states violate the Montreal Protocol by failing to submit required reports in a timely fashion (most deadlines have a de facto two-year grace period), by committing new violations requiring new programs of action, and by failing to abide by the terms of an existing program of action. One hundred and six of the 191 Montreal Protocol's parties have been cited for one of the three types of violations since January 2002. Of these 106, forty-seven were cited for late reports, fifty-eight for breaches of the Protocol, and sixty-three for breaches of a remedial program for a total of 305 separate infractions or an average of about fifty-one per year. For the purposes of this study, we will weigh these violations in terms of their seriousness. Late reports will be scored as a one, new violations as a two, and failures to fulfill previous programs as a three. These weighted Protocol compliance scores will serve as the dependent variable in the regressions. Note that a low score indicates strong compliance.

Because geography may well play a more important role than is usually the case, we will consider Figure 3.3. While it appears that industrialized democracies in higher latitudes in fact have relatively strong compliance scores, it appears they are far from alone. We see strong compliance across Africa, Asia, and Latin America, even in countries that are tropical, poor, and autocratic. On the other hand, the countries with the poorest compliance records can be found scattered across the globe and across the latitudes.

Compliance levels are remarkably high overall. Nearly half of all countries received either one or zero negative comments from the compliance committee and only a small number (twenty-one) received ten or more criticisms. What this most likely indicates is that the demands on states are relatively modest and few countries are unable to complete the reports and show reductions in CFC emissions. Also, most developing countries were granted considerable latitude and time to make the deeper sacrifices called for. It is interesting to note that some of the states with the worst scores are industrialized, but have industrial facilities that are outdated (note that eight of the twenty-one are former Warsaw Pact members). These states face a steep climb to achieve environmentally friendly production.

Conclusions

The story of international regulatory law is a story of a glass half-full. To begin, it is worth noting that the standards being set to regulate maritime and airliner safety and protect the ozone layer are not so weak as to be meaningless. The fact of the matter is that all three areas are among the most orderly and successful in world affairs. States and firms have been pushed in directions they would not

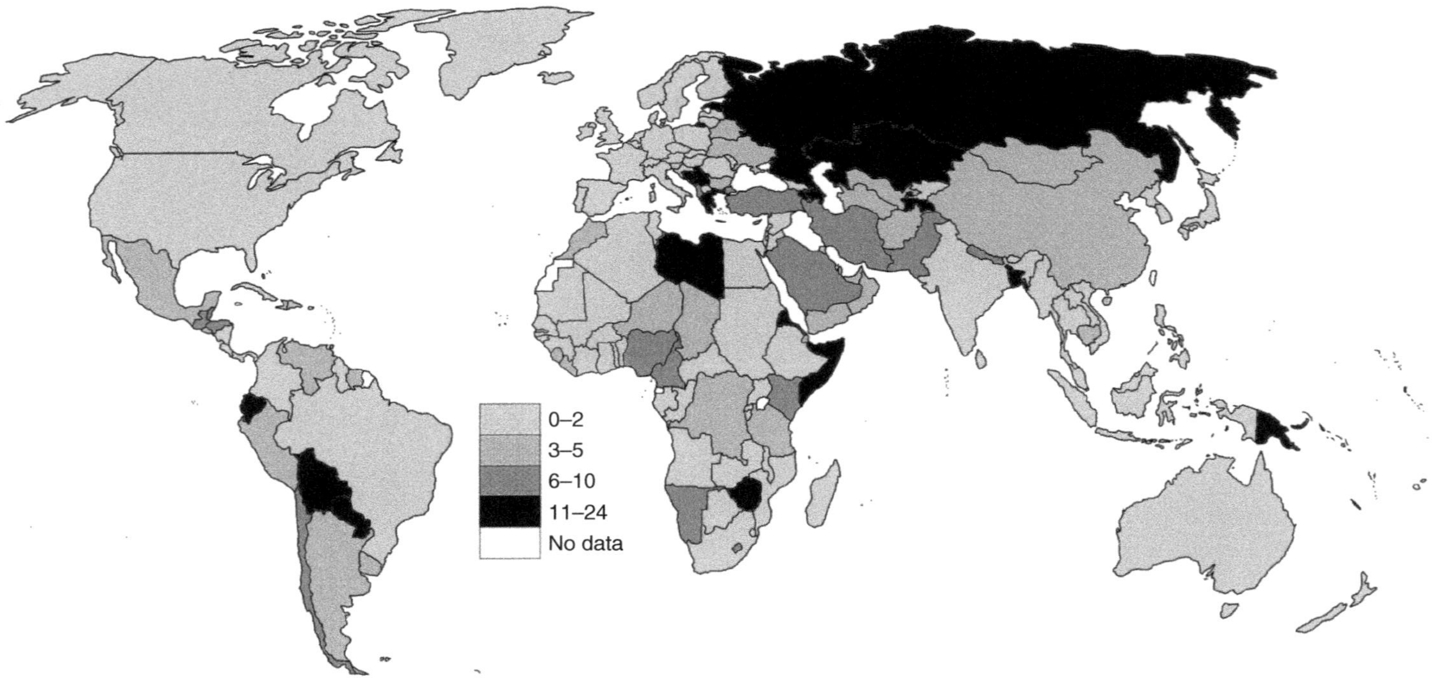

Figure 3.3 Cumulative Montreal Protocol compliance scores, 2002–2008 (source: Ozone Commission annual reports, various years).

have otherwise gone to minimize risk and protect the global environment. Ships and aircraft are safer than ever, and the ozone hole has stopped expanding and is beginning to close (IPCC 2005).

That said, many states are not in compliance with these regulations, although the reasons for this are not entirely clear from the discussion in this chapter. There appears to be evidence that states are hoping to avoid paying the cost of compliance, perhaps by free-riding on others (Montreal Protocol) or hoping their conduct will be ignored (airlines). Still others are hoping to make short-term gains by exploiting weak enforcement. Rational economic calculations seem to be at work in all three areas. At the same time, the data indicate that states with advanced economies and mature democratic institutions – and close ties to the US and its economy – are generally more prone to comply with the rules – or at least make a concerted effort to do so. In some cases this can be attributed to direct action by the US (airlines) while in others the pressure may be more indirect. There is also evidence that a legitimation dynamic is at work – particularly with respect to airline and ship safety where states are consciously surrendering sovereignty in favor of public international audits.

As indicated in the introduction, multiple theories of compliance appear to work together to explain the processes and outcomes at issue. And as mentioned before, sorting out which theories are most promising will require more systematic quantitative and qualitative analysis, to which we turn in Chapter 5 and subsequent chapters.

Note

1 Much of the material on ship safety rules and compliance comes from Kendall Stiles, "Who Is Keeping the Sea Safe? Testing Theories of International Law Compliance," *Cooperation and Conflict* 45(2) (June 2010): 139–161.

References

Boyle, Alan E. (1999) "Some Reflections on the Relationship of Treaties and Soft Law," *The International and Comparative Law Quarterly* 48(4) (October): 901–913.

Braithwaite, John and Peter Drahos (2000) *Global Business Regulation*. New York: Cambridge University Press.

Button, Kenneth, Audrey Clarke, Ginta Palubinskas, Roger Stough, and Marc Thibault (2004) "Conforming with ICAO Safety Oversight Standards," *Journal of Air Transport Management* 10(4) (July): 249–255.

DeSombre, Elizabeth (2006) *Flagging Standards: Globalization and Environmental, Safety, and Labor Regulations at Sea*. Cambridge, MA: MIT Press.

Ehrmann, Markus (2002) "Procedures of Compliance Control in International Environmental Treaties," *Colorado Journal of International Environmental Law* 13 (Summer): 377–429.

EPA (2007) "Black Market CFCs/HCFCs and You." From Environmental Protection Agency, Ozone Layer Depletion – Regulatory Programs. Available at www.epa.gov/ozone/enforce/blackmkt.html#cases. Accessed December 10, 2007.

Greene, Owen (1998) "The System for Implementation Review of the Ozone Regime," in David G. Victor, Kal Raustiala, and Eugene B. Skolinkoff, eds., *The Implementation and Effectiveness of International Environmental Commitments: Theory and Practice*. Cambridge, MA: MIT Press, pp. 89–136.
Güner-Özbek, Meltem Deniz (2006) "Paris Memorandum of Understanding; An Example of International Co-operation and its Perspectives," in Peter Ehlers and Rainer Lagoni, eds., *International Maritime Organizations and Their Contribution Towards a Sustainable Marine Development*. Hamburg: LIT, pp. 105–134.
Haas, Peter (1992) "Banning Chlorofluorocarbons: Epistemic Community Efforts to Protect Stratospheric Ozone," *International Organization* 46(1) (Winter): 187–224.
Huang, Jiefang (2009) *Aviation Safety Through the Rule of Law: ICAO's Mechanisms and Practices*. The Netherlands: Wolters Kluwer Law & Business.
ICAO (2004) "Making an ICAO Standard." Available at www.icao.int/en/anb/mais/index.html. Accessed August 6, 2010.
ICAO (2009) "Flight Safety Information Exchange." Available at www.icao.int/fsix/auditRep1.cfm. Accessed August 6, 2010.
IMO (2003) ISPS Code, "International Ship and Port Facility Security Code and SOLAS Amendments Adopted on 12 December 2002."
IPCC (2005) "Summary for Policymakers." *IPCC/TEAP Special Report on Safeguarding the Ozone Layer and the Global Climate System: Issues Related to Hydrofluorocarbons and Perfluorocarbons*. Cambridge: Intergovernmental Panel on Climate Change/Cambridge University Press. Available at www.ipcc.ch/pdf/special-reports/sroc/sroc_spm.pdf. Accessed August 6, 2010.
MacKenzie, David (2010) *ICAO: A History of the International Civil Aviation Organization*. Toronto: University of Toronto Press.
Nayar, Baldev Raj. 1995. "Regimes, Power, and International Aviation," *International Organization* 49(1) (Winter): 139–170.
Paris MOU (2006) *Annual Report 2006*. Paris: Paris MOU on Port State Control.
Paris MOU (2007) *Target Lists 2005–2007*. Available at www.parismou.org/upload/pdf/PMoU%Target%20lists%202005–2007.pdf. Accessed on October 21, 2008.
Paris MOU (2008) *Detentions List, April 2008*. Paris: Paris MOU on Port State Control.
Rodriguez, Anthonio and Mary Campbell Hubbard (2005) "The International Safety Management (ISM) Code: A New Level of Uniformity," New Orleans, Louisiana, May 23. Available at www.frc-law.com/files/pub_ISM.pdf. Accessed July 20, 2009.
Shyur, Huan-Jyh (2008) "A Quantitative Model for Aviation Safety Risk Assessment," *Computers and Industrial Engineering* 54(1) (February): 33–44.
Sprinz, Detlef and Tapani Vaatoranta (1994) "The Interest-Based Explanation of International Environmental Policy," *International Organization* 48(1) (Winter): 77–105.
Stiles, Kendall (2010) "Who Is Keeping the Sea Safe? Testing Theories of International Law Compliance," *Cooperation & Conflict* 45(2) (June): 139–161.
UNEP (1998) Non-Compliance Procedure. Annex II of the Report of the Tenth Meeting of the Parties. Accessed at http://ozone.unep.org/Publications/MP_Handbook/Section_3.5_Annexes_Non-Compliance_Procedure. Accessed August 6, 2010
Victor, David G., Kal Raustiala, and Eugene B. Skolinkoff, eds. (1998) *The Implementation and Effectiveness of International Environmental Commitments: Theory and Practice*. Cambridge, MA: MIT Press.
Zacher, Mark (1996) *Governing Global Networks: International Regimes for Transportation and Communications* (with Brent A. Sutton). New York: Cambridge University Press.

4 Laws on human rights promotion

Anti-slavery law and protection of women

Historically, states have been far more interested first in their survival and second in regulating the market than promoting the rights of their citizens. But especially since World War II, states have demanded higher standards with respect to the way states treat their own citizens. Perhaps the first time states began to put pressure on each other was in the early nineteenth century when Britain and others outlawed first the international trade in slaves and then slavery itself. In more recent times, states have attempted to outlaw legal discrimination against women. These two sets of rules will be the focus of this chapter.

Anti-slavery law

Slavery is generally defined as the ownership of one human being by another. More properly conceived as chattel slavery, the practice is as old as civilization (Meltzer 1993, 12–15). For thousands of years it was considered natural – especially with respect to the treatment of conquered peoples – and what few rules existed dealt primarily with restrictions on abuse rather than ownership. Then beginning in the mid-eighteenth century opinion and policies shifted dramatically (D'Anjou 1996, 194). The shift stemmed from a combination of economic, political, religious, and institutional changes. The British government adopted laws against slave trading in the decade of the nineteenth century in large part because of public pressure from evangelical Protestants and liberally minded intellectuals, but also because the slave trade was no longer essential to most British plantation owners in the Americas (they had enough slaves in place that the population could be sustained through reproduction) (Porter 1970, 136; Oldfield 1992, 338; Jennings 1997, 134; Kaufman and Pape 1999, 654).

In the 1820s, British abolitionists set their sights on abolishing slavery in the colonies through negotiations with local governors (Mathieson 1967, 139). As put by MP Foxwell Buxton in 1823:

> The object at which we aim, is the extinction of slavery – in nothing less than the whole of the British dominions – not, however the rapid termination of that state – not the sudden emancipation of the negro – but such preparatory steps, such measure of precaution, as, by slow degrees, and in a

> course of years, first fitting and qualifying the slave for the enjoyment of freedom, shall gently conduct us to the annihilation of slavery.... We are far from meaning to attempt to cut down slavery in the full majority of its vigour. We rather shall leave it gently to decay – slowly, silently, almost imperceptibly, to die away and to be forgotten.
>
> (Williams 1970, 94)

The strategy proved unworkable, however, as the local governors refused to consider emancipation. By 1834, the new Whig majority had enough votes to pass an outright ban and by 1840 legal slavery ceased to exist in the British Empire (Mathieson 1967, 231).

Other countries followed suit, each for its own reasons. France, Spain, Portugal, and later Turkey elevated relatively liberal regimes to power, while the United States experienced a devastating civil war. The net result was that by the turn of the twentieth century, legalized chattel slavery was fading into history (Sandholtz and Stiles 2009).

This is not to say that slave-like practices did not persist. In Haiti, and in French and Portuguese colonies, slaves were often re-classified as indentured servants with euphemistic names (Lloyd 1968, 201; Temperley 2000, 4). The newly emancipated slaves lacked the education, social ties, and organizational structures to combat the new arrangements and in some cases found themselves with lives that were even more insecure than under chattel slavery (Haraksingh 1995, 227).

For this reason, Great Britain and a few other states began to press for multilateral standards that would clearly delineate what would be considered unacceptable. But in order to secure widespread acceptance of new instruments, the language was watered down and nothing other than chattel slavery, defined as "the status or condition of a person over whom any or all of the powers attaching to the right of ownership are exercised," was explicitly outlawed, although most of the parties to the talks understood that slave-like practices were inappropriate but not necessarily illegal (Meirs 2003, 113, 130). The 1926 Slavery Convention called for the gradual elimination of chattel slavery – something that was already largely accomplished except in some parts of the Middle East and Africa. Further, the Convention stipulated only that governments keep each other and the League of Nations informed of legal reforms as they emerged (Sawyer 1986, 219). In spite of the weaknesses of the agreement, some countries delayed ratification for decades.

Several more specific agreements were negotiated at the International Labour Organization to outlaw forced labor in the private sector and other practices. After World War II, new efforts were made to broaden the definition of slavery, although even Great Britain resisted banning slavery in colonies. The 1956 Supplemental Convention on the Abolishment of Slavery, the Slave Trade, and Institutions and Practices Similar to Slavery broadened the definition a bit farther. The 1956 Convention represents the state of the art and continues to provide the basis for current work on slavery at the United Nations (Herzfeld 2000, 1).

By this point, the ban on slavery has developed to the level of a peremptory norm in international law – a rule that supersedes other law (Redman 1994, 764; Van der Anker 2004, 15).

How then is it then that more than twenty-five million are enslaved today (Reinhardt 2001, 52; Re 2002, 33; Bales 2004, 8)? Almost all states have adopted statutes that ban slavery and slave trading, as well as debt peonage, indentured servitude, serfdom, and private forced labor. Most states have further reinforced this broader view in a variety of more recent instruments including a major 1956 Supplemental Convention and by expressing support for the definitions proffered by the United Nations Working Group on Contemporary Forms of Slavery (UNHCHR 2004). But there are still incentives to shirk these rules or enforce them weakly. In particular, women and children have been recruited into labor-intensive industries to lower costs in many countries around the world. Mauritania's slave population may number in the millions and nearly 100,000 have been forced into slavery in the Sudan, according to credible reports (Rassam 1999, 322; Teyeb 2000, 52; Jok 2001; Re 2002, 33). Unlike slaves in the eighteenth century, slaves today are not considered an investment by their owners but rather are seen as a disposable resource to be used up and discarded (Bales 2004, 15).

What would the various theories of international compliance predict with respect to compliance with anti-slavery rules? To begin, rationalist theories would predict that countries that have a surplus of labor and an abundance of labor-intensive industries (which is to say much of the least developed world) would benefit from lax enforcement of anti-slavery rules – although they would need to be concerned about doing so flagrantly and running the risk of international sanctions. Very poor states with relatively low trade flows might therefore emerge as candidates. Liberal theory would naturally point to a society's government and overall commitment to liberal norms, anti-slavery being preeminent among them. This might also be reflected in the willingness to endorse anti-slavery instruments. One should expect that all states that tolerate slavery are naturally authoritarian and deeply traditional. Since the US has long advocated an end to slavery, realist theory might predict that American allies and states dependent on the US would be least likely to tolerate slavery. Finally, the managerial school would predict that states with higher enforcement capacity would be able to minimize slavery – assuming that all states seek to bring it to an end.

Kevin Bales of Free the Slaves has undertaken a systematic effort to count the world's slaves. Relying primarily on local reports by NGOs, advocacy groups, and police departments, he has provided an estimated count of slave populations of more than one hundred states by providing a high and low estimate. To date this is the only such data set. He has also rated each country's efforts to combat slavery, but since the law in question is so mature, we believe it is more reasonable to measure anti-slavery law compliance with the estimate of the slave population. We take the mid-point of his estimate and calculate the percentage of the total population the figure represents.

Out of 102 countries rated, only seven have slave populations above one-half of 1 percent. On the other extreme, seven countries have no slaves at all. Of the rest, the majority have what might be considered negligible levels of enslavement (below 0.05 percent). Of course, several of these countries have very large populations to start with (namely China, Russia, the US), and so even a tiny percentage translates into very large numbers of slaves. Particularly worrisome, however, is India's percentage of slaves, which is nearly 2 percent of a population of well over one billion. When one recalls that the ban on slavery is a peremptory norm of considerable age, anything less than perfect compliance seems indicative of a failure to fully internalize the rule.

Figure 4.1 proves fairly useful in that regional patterns are more readily apparent. In particular, South Asia emerges as a region particularly prone to high levels of slavery, while the rest of Asia appears to have taken steps to minimize enslavement. Africa and Europe have more mixed records, although Europe – both East and West – appears to have the problem in hand. Taken together, it appears that what we may be witnessing is a regional effect in South Asia, which implies that local cultural factors (perhaps the caste system?) may increase the tolerance for slavery today.

CEDAW

The rights of women have historically been considered less important than the rights of slaves, racial minorities, or foreigners for most countries, and this was reflected in the sequence of international law creation. The League of Nations and the International Labour Organization began addressing some women's issues, albeit tentatively, during the 1930s (Berkovitch 1999, 170). Generally, however, the thought of separate rights for women was alien to even democratic governments in that they generally saw them as subsumed under broader human rights and democratic principles. Women's organizations nonetheless succeeded in pressuring state negotiators at various post-war conferences to make room for women's issues. But although the Commission on the Status of Women (CSW) was created as a sub-committee of the Economic and Social Council of the UN (ECOSOC) in 1947, it was given next to no powers (Galey 1984, 464). It nonetheless managed to promote several narrow international agreements dealing with marriage and women's rights during the 1950s and 1960s.

In 1963, the General Assembly, urged on by Western women's advocacy groups, approved resolution 1921, "in which it requested the Economic and Social Council to invite the CSW to prepare a draft declaration that would combine in a single instrument international standards articulating the equal rights of men and women" (CEDAW 2010). This initial effort ultimately produced a GA resolution in 1967 that declared the equality of men and women under the law, including in marriage and in the workplace – both controversial issues. In particular, the resolution called for the ending of cultural traditions that produced gender discrimination, implying that culture itself, and with it gender roles, can be altered – a position that continues to be controversial among states and scholars (Merry 2003).

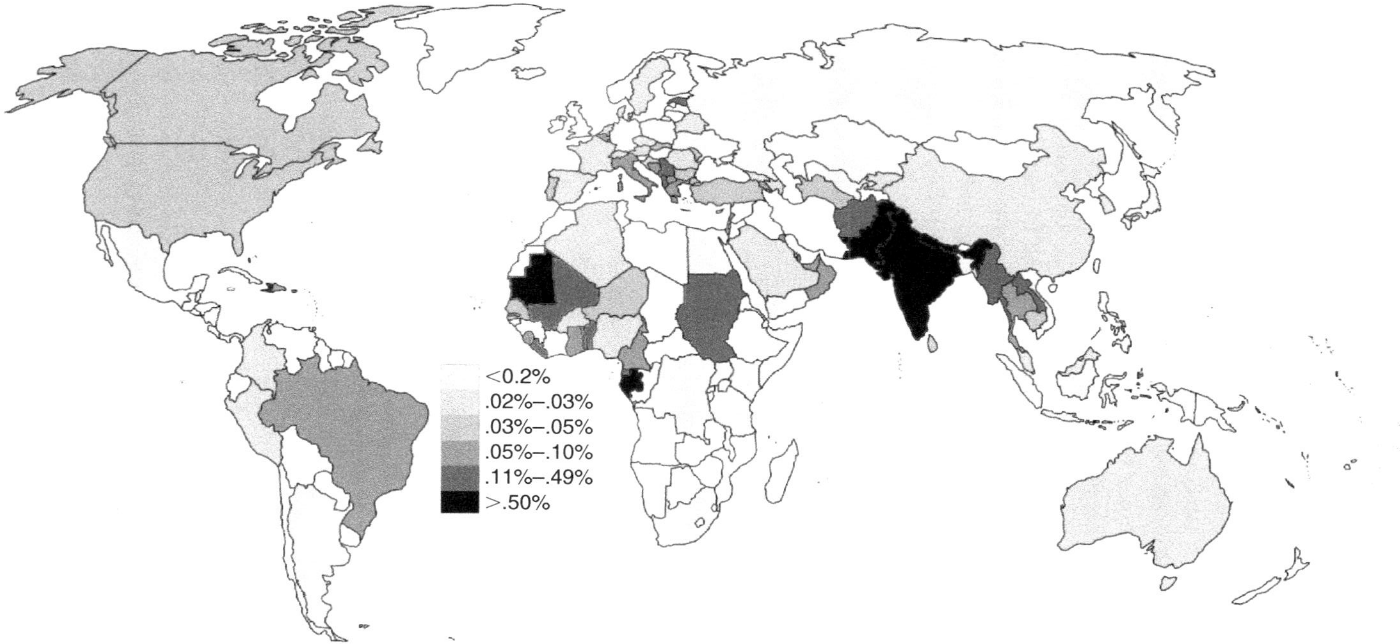

Figure 4.1 Estimates of the percentage of the population in slavery, 2003 (source: Adapted from Bales 2004).

The emergence of a binding legal instrument on women's legal equality would take several more years. The process was aided by the adoption of rules governing the status of women in the International Convention on Civil and Political Rights and other universal human rights agreements (Galey 1984, 465; Elson 2006, 13). It moved gradually through the traditional stages of working groups, committees, and so forth during the 1970s, but received a strong push from the 1975 Mexico City World Conference of the International Women's Year (Rehof 1993, 11; Berkovitch 1999, 171). The conference not only launched the UN Decade for Women but also produced a statement calling for the conclusion of the negotiations on a treaty. Furthermore, 1980 was an important benchmark and target since this was the year of the Copenhagen World Conference to assess progress at the mid-point of the UN Decade for Women (CEDAW 2010). In 1979, the GA approved the Convention on the Elimination of All Forms of Discrimination Against Women (CEDAW) by a vote of 130 to zero with ten abstentions and twelve not voting. In addition to several small island states, those abstaining and not voting included six predominantly Arab nations as well as Mexico, Brazil, and South Africa. Iraq and Morocco also lodged reservations to their affirmative vote. The treaty came into effect in 1981 after twenty states ratified it. The treaty was ratified quickly by a large number of states and had 186 states parties as of August 2010. Only Iran, Somalia, the United States, and a few small island states have not ratified it.

The treaty requires states to ensure that their constitutions and legislation embody equality between men and women, punish discrimination, abolish or modify laws that still discriminate, and ensure that the penal code does not discriminate against women (article 2; Ngaba 1995, 84). In addition it requires states to provide equal access to women to political institutions (article 7) and obligates states to adopt laws and policies that advance women's issues (Elson 2006, 31). ECOSOC and the CEDAW Committee also encouraged governments to create specialized agencies within their national government to supervise implementation of pro-woman policies – something that was almost universally done by the mid-1990s (Berkovitch 1999, 163).

Promoting the advancement of women and ensuring their equal treatment continues to be controversial among societies that support patriarchal systems and governments routinely defend their failure to alter laws and policies on the grounds that doing so violates deep-seated traditions (Merry 2003). Many feminists argue that CEDAW does not go far enough. In particular, nothing in the original document specifically banned violence against women – especially when the violence is perpetrated by family members and neighbors (Tang 2000, 68).

The treaty created a mechanism for on-going interpretation through the reporting system. The CEDAW Committee, made up of experts (most of whom actually worked for the governments that nominated them in the early years – Galey 1984, 477) receives reports from states parties – one within the first year of ratification and others at three-year intervals. While countries have generally dragged their feet at submitting timely and thorough reports, the process of commenting on them has allowed the Committee to clarify the Convention's meaning. The Committee began asking governments to report on violence against women in the late 1980s and in "1989 the committee adopted general recommendation 12, recommending consideration of the issue and requiring statistics on gender violence. General recommendation 19 in 1992 developed the issue further, defining gender-based violence as a form of discrimination" that directly threatens the purposes of the Convention (O'Hare 1999, 372; Merry 2003, 951).

In 1993, the Vienna World Conference addressed a variety of human rights issues, including women's rights. It produced a Declaration on the Elimination of Violence Against Women (DEVAW) which was ultimately adopted by the UN General Assembly. The statement first helps to break down

> the public/private divide by refusing to permit states to rely on their own "private" conceptions of culture in the maintenance of women's oppression. Second, DEVAW stresses the importance of the Women's Convention as a mechanism to address violence against women. Hence, states are asked to consider ratifying the Convention where they have not already done so, or to withdraw any existing reservations where they have.
>
> (O'Hare 1999, 377; see also Berkovitch 1999, 174)

Since 1993, then, a ban on violence against women is an integral part of CEDAW, both with respect to how CEDAW officials interpret the Convention as well as how states have been taught to understand it. This message has been further articulated through a variety of country reviews connected to the new right of individual petition – something that also emerged from the Vienna meetings. At this point, individuals, NGOs and IGOs may submit materials regarding a government's persistent and widespread abuse of women's rights. The Optional Protocol (adopted in 1999) that allows this has only been ratified by relatively few states, however, and governments have a number of procedural mechanisms at their disposal to limit their exposure (Tang 2000, 69).

CEDAW lacks punitive powers. Seventy-eight percent of states parties were delinquent in their report submissions as of 2000 (Merry 2003, 851). The consequences of failure to report, let alone respond to criticism, are minimal. This reflects the preferences of states, by and large, that generally tend to minimize the capacity of international organizations to enforce human rights law (Merry 2003, 942).

Despite this, scholars have found that a state's commitment to CEDAW seems to correlate with stronger health, safety, literacy, and political status for women in those countries (Gray *et al.* 2006). While it is always difficult to sort out cause and effect, it seems reasonable to think that such a pattern would hold. In our study, we choose to measure compliance with CEDAW in terms of violence against women. As put by O'Hare:

> Occurring both within the public and private spheres, violence against women is the most brutal manifestation of women's oppression. It violates a

> woman's right to bodily integrity and liberty; to be free from torture, inhuman, and degrading treatment; and in its most acute form, it violates a woman's right to life.
>
> (O'Hare 1999, 364–365)

Because the meaning of the Convention is clear, it seems reasonable to begin asking whether actions are being taken to at a minimum ensure that the most basic need – freedom from violence – is being met as a way of measuring compliance with CEDAW generally. As it happens, a project that has been underway for several years has reached fruition, allowing us to systematically measure the physical security of women in nearly all the countries of the world. The WomanStats project measures this with a:

> 5-point ordinal scale attempts to capture the degree of physical threat experienced by women generally within the society. The scale focuses in particular on the level of violence against women, including the prevalence of domestic violence, rape, marital rape, and murder of women in the nation. These subcomponents are examined in terms of custom, practice, law, and statistics related to these four forms of violence against women.
>
> (Hudson *et al.* 2008/2009, 37)

The measure has the advantage of not only tracking outcomes, but also legal and political processes. It errs on the side of the government having good intentions, even if the results have not yet materialized. This is consistent with the spirit of this project which asks whether states are complying in good faith with their international obligations.

With respect to our theories of compliance, one might ask which type of country would be most likely to have laws and practices in place to protect the rights of women. Clearly a liberal argument can be made that women's rights are a spillover of human rights generally. Most governments have made the argument that there is no need for special protections for women since they are covered under the umbrella of human rights. After all, where all adults can vote, women can also vote. And where all adults can run for office, women can run for office. And where women can get elected, they can attempt to influence women's policy. But scholars who focus on cultural factors point out that even in liberal societies women are often oppressed. Consider the number of democratic Christian countries where women are considered second class citizens. It is no coincidence that in the United States black men received the vote (*de jure*) decades before women, according to this approach. The key issue is whether ordinary citizens are personally committed to gender equality. Also key is whether women are organized and mobilized (Tang 2000, 71).

Still others have argued that much depends on the linkages of a state to the outside world. Gray *et al.* (2006) have concluded that the greater the levels of transnational economic ties, the better off the women. This could also dovetail with the view that states with strong ties to the West might be especially inclined to at least make gestures in favor of protecting women's rights. So once again, each theory has a plausible story to explain compliance to CEDAW.

We once again present the basic data on compliance in graphic form. The countries with scores of one or two – the most progressive on the issue – read like a list of OECD members. Nine of the eleven countries to score a one and half of those scoring a two are OECD members. Only two – Mexico and Turkey – received a four. On the other hand, forty-seven out of the fifty-five countries to score a four were not fully democratic (as defined by Freedom House).

The map in Figure 4.2 is perhaps the most patterned of any we have seen in the project thus far. A swath of black from Peru to Indonesia by way of the Middle East seems to indicate that neighboring states tend to treat women much the same. With a few exceptions, women are far better protected in the West (broadly defined) than the rest of the world. Because many variables overlap in this case – trade activity, culture, democracy, development, women's NGO activity – it is not possible to sort out which theory best explains the pattern. We will pursue this question in Chapter 5.

Conclusions

The rules governing slavery and women's rights are in many ways typical of international human rights law generally. The language is lofty and broad, and somewhat vague – although recent interpretations have clarified their meaning. Monitoring and enforcement are constrained by a need to protect state sovereignty. Penalties for non-compliance are few and far between, and implementation is mixed. Slavery and women's rights also crosses the public/private divide as we see in the case of other human rights areas, such as the treatment of racial minorities and the disabled. Compliance requires states to enter the workplace and the home to a great degree.

Which states seem most committed to implementing these rules? Although the pattern seems somewhat clear with respect to women's rights, it is far less so in the case of slavery. South Asia scores poorly in both counts, perhaps because of cultural traditions that tolerate marked class and gender stratification. OECD members seem to generally show deeper commitment, although for various reasons some of them also tolerate violations at the level of private actors and within the home. It appears, then, that local culture and legal traditions have a bearing on outcomes. At the same time, economic calculations of cost and benefit may be a factor since ignoring the rights of slaves and women has considerable economic benefit. The United States plays a somewhat ambiguous role in both areas – as is often the case with respect to international human rights law – making the realist model somewhat more difficult to test. On the other hand, Western states generally promote the norms and might be able to exert some pressure to comply. Finally, states with greater economic and administrative capacity seem better able to promote women's rights, although it is not so clear that they do a better job of eliminating slavery.

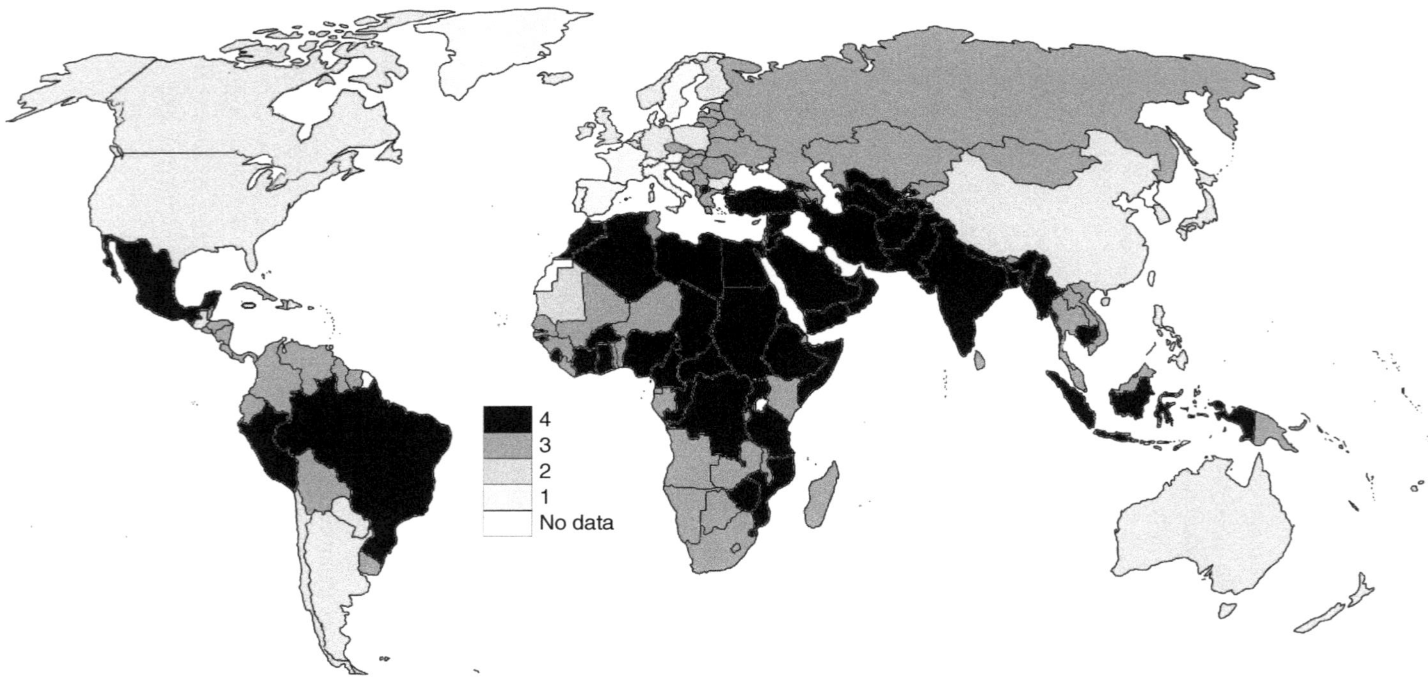

Figure 4.2 WomanStat physical security of women index, 2007 (source: www.WomanStats.org).

As we have seen in the two previous chapters, the record is a mixed one. It appears that several theories capture at least part of the causal dynamic with respect to compliance with international law. We therefore now turn to a more systematic analysis in Chapter 5 in order to establish more definitively which theories explain more of the outcomes.

References

Bales, Kevin (2004) *Disposable People: New Slavery in the Global Economy*, rev. ed. Berkeley: University of California Press.

Berkovitch, Nitza (1999) *From Motherhood to Citizenship: Women's Rights and International Organizations*. Baltimore: Johns Hopkins University Press.

CEDAW (2010) "A Short History of CEDAW Convention." Available at www.un.org/womenwatch/daw/cedaw/history.htm. Accessed July 13, 2010.

D'Anjou, Leo (1996) *Social Movements and Cultural Change: The First Abolition Campaign Revisited*. New York: Aldine de Gruyter.

Elson, Diane (2006) *Budgeting for Women's Rights: Monitoring Government Budgets for Compliance with CEDAW*. New York: UNIFEM.

Galey, Margaret E. (1984) "International Enforcement of Women's Rights," *Human Rights Quarterly* 6(4) (November): 463–490.

Gray, Mark M., Miki Caul Kittilson, and Wayne Sandholtz (2006) "Women and Globalization: A Study of 180 Countries, 1975–2000," *International Organization* 60(2) (Spring): 293–333.

Haraksingh, Kusha (1995) "The Worker and the Wage in a Plantation Economy: Trinidad in the late-Nineteenth Century," in Mary Turner, ed., *From Chattel Slaves to Wage Slaves: The Dynamics of Labour Bargaining in the Americas*, Kingston: Ian Rand, pp. 224–239.

Herzfeld, Beth (2000) "Campaigning Against Bonded Labour," *IFWEA Journal* (December): 1.

Hudson, Valerie M., Mary Caprioli, and Bonnie Ballif-Spanvill (2008/2009) "The Heart of the Matter: The Security of Women and the Security of States," *International Security* 33(3) (Winter): 7–45.

Jennings, Judith. (1997) *The Business of Abolishing the British Slave Trade, 1783–1807*. London: Frank Cass.

Jok, Jok Madut (2001). *War and Slavery in Sudan*. Philadelphia: University of Pennsylvania University Press.

Kaufman, Chaim D. and Robert A. Pape (1999). "Explaining Costly International Moral Action: Britain's Fifty-year Campaign Against the Atlantic Slave Trade," *International Organization* 53(4) (Autumn): 631–668.

Lloyd, Christopher (1968) *The Navy and the Slave Trade: The Suppression of the African Slave Trade in the Nineteenth Century*. London: Frank Cass.

Mathieson, William Law (1967) *British Slave Emancipation, 1838–1849*. New York: Octagan Books.

Meirs, Suzanne (2003) *Slavery in the Twentieth Century: The Evolution of a Global Problem*. Lanham, MD: Alta Mira Press.

Meltzer, Milton (1993) *Slavery: A World History*, updated ed. New York: Da Capo Press.

Merry, Sally Engle (2003) "Constructing a Global Law-Violence against Women and the Human Rights," *Law & Social Inquiry* 28(4) (Autumn): 941–977.

Ngaba, Sindiso (1995) "CEDAW: Eliminating Discrimination against Women," Agenda, No. 27, Reproductive Rights, pp. 81–89.
O'Hare, Ursula A. (1999) "Realizing Human Rights for Women," *Human Rights Quarterly* 21(2) (May): 364–402.
Oldfield, J.R. (1992) "The London Committee and Mobilization of Public Opinion against the Slave Trade," *The Historical Journal* 35(2) (June): 331–343.
Porter, Dale H. (1970) *The Abolition of the Slave Trade in England, 1784–1807*. New York: Archon Books.
Rassam, A. Yasmine (1999) "Contemporary Forms of Slavery and the Evolution of the Prohibition of Slavery and the Slave Trade Under Customary International Law," *Virginia Journal of International Law* 39 (Winter): 303–352.
Re, Richard (2002) "A Persistent Evil: The Global Problem of Slavery," *Harvard International Review* 23 (Winter): 32–36.
Redman, Renee Colette (1994) "Beyond the United States: The League of Nations and the Right to be Free from Enslavement – The First Human Right to be Recognized as Customary International Law," *Chicago-Kent Law Review* 70 (January): 759–800.
Rehof, Lars Adam (1993) *Guide to the Travaux Préparatories of the United Nations Convention on the Elimination of All Forms of Discrimination against Women*. Dordrecht, Netherlands: Martinus Nijhoff.
Reinhardt, Emma Dorothy (2001) "Modern-day Slavery in America," *World & I* 16 (February): 52.
Sandholtz, Wayne and Kendall Stiles (2009) *International Norms and Cycles of Change*. London: Oxford University Press.
Sawyer, Roger (1986) *Slavery in the Twentieth Century*. London: Routledge & Kegan Paul.
Tang, Kwong-Leung (2000) "The Leadership Role of International Law in Enforcing Women's Rights: The Optional Protocol to the Women's Convention," *Gender and Development* 8(3) (November): 65–73.
Temperley, Howard (2000) "Introduction," in Howard Temperley, ed., *After Slavery: Emancipation and its Discontents*. London: Frank Cass, pp. 1–10.
Teyeb, Moctar (2000) "Slavery in Mauritania is a Serious Problem," *Tikkum* 15 (July): 10.
UNHCHR (2004) *Report of the Working Group on Contemporary Forms of Slavery* [E/CN.4/Sub.2/2004/L.11], August 12. New York: UN.
Van der Anker, Christien (2004) "Contemporary Slavery, Global Justice and Globalization," in Christien Van der Anker, ed., *The Political Economy of New Slavery*. London: Palgrave, pp. 15–36.
Williams, Eric (1970) *The British West Indies at Westminster, 1789–1823: Extracts from the Debates in Parliament*. Westport, CT: Negro University Press.

5 Cross-national analysis of compliance

The three previous chapters discuss the rules that are used in this study to measure and explain international compliance with international law. These rules were chosen in part because of their relative clarity and precision, as well as the somewhat greater ease of measuring compliance. Those measures were also discussed along with preliminary indications of overall state compliance.

We now turn to a more systematic exploration of why certain countries comply. We will consider compliance with all the various rules discussed thus far in order to ascertain whether any of the characteristics described by the competing theories discussed in Chapter 1 hold promise.

The analysis will begin with exploring whether compliance with one rule increases the likelihood of compliance with the others and why or why not. Next we will consider several sets of variables in order to determine whether they explain compliance with each of the rules, both separately and in combination. The chapter will conclude with analysis and interpretation, pointing to the need for the country studies that will conclude this project.

A key observation we will be able to make is that all of the theories seem to explain some of the patterns of compliance we see. For that matter, compliance itself seems to correlate with compliance for the most part. At the same time, none of the theories stands up to regression analysis for more than a few of the rules. This points, as we will see, to a need for integrative theorizing as well as for non-quantitative research methods.

Patterns of compliance

As we discussed in Chapter 1, many theories of international law compliance begin with the premise that certain types of countries are more likely to obey laws in general. In particular, the liberal school argues that democratic countries are generally disposed to respect international law – including international custom. And the managerial school argues that states with greater administrative capacity and wealth will be better able to adhere to a wide range of rules. Realists argue that relations with the hegemon have a great bearing on compliance, while interest-driven theory argues that states care about their reputations across a wide range of issues.

We will explore whether these general propositions are borne out. If compliance is a general tendency, we should see a pattern of compliance across a range of issues. To test this we begin with a simple correlation matrix across the measures of compliance discussed in Chapters 2 through 4. If countries comply for the same reasons, we should expect to see high degrees of correlation across most factors. The results can be found in Table 5.1 and Figure 5.1.[1]

Nearly all the variables are correlated with at least one other variable, and several are linked to more than one. Only compliance with anti-piracy is an outlier. Further, none of the variables are correlated in an unexpected direction. The variables that are correlated do not seem to display any logical connection, which strengthens the point that there might be cross-topical factors to explain compliance. For example, there does not seem to be any obvious reason why states that have safer airlines would have fewer slaves. Likewise, taking steps to limit chlorofluorocarbon emissions and otherwise comply with provisions of the Montreal Protocol does not seem logically related to improving the treatment of women or fighting terrorism. The fact that many of these variables seem to move together points to some general factors that explain rule-compliance.

Taken as a whole, however, out of twenty-eight dyads, we see correlations in only nine cases, or just under one-third of the total. It is particularly interesting to note that there seems to be no pattern within somewhat similar types of rules. Although compliance with anti-terror and anti-trafficking measures are strongly correlated, neither correlates with anti-piracy measures, as might be expected given their structural similarity. Likewise, while airline safety and ship safety correlate, neither correlates with ozone protection, as might be expected since they all involve regulation of corporations.

Testing theories of compliance

The story at this point is at best mixed, although the burden of proof is clearly on theories that argue in favor of cross-issue consistency. We now turn to a rule-by-rule comparison of the strength of various factors that might explain compliance,

Table 5.1 Correlation matrix on compliance variables

	Ship safety	*CEDAW*	*Terror*	*TIP*	*Slaves*	*Piracy*	*Airliner*	*Ozone*
Ship safety	x	0.079	0.088	0.044	−0.20	0.027	0.325**	−0.037
	CEDAW	x	0.365**	0.479**	0.165	−0.026	0.163	0.183*
		Terror	x	0.322**	0.097	0.131	0.429**	0.196**
			TIP	x	0.020	−0.041	0.190	0.231**
				Slaves	x	0.144	0.352**	−0.055
					Piracy	x	0.101	−0.042
						Airliner	x	−0.044
							Ozone	x

Notes
$* = p < 0.05$.
$** = p < 0.01$.

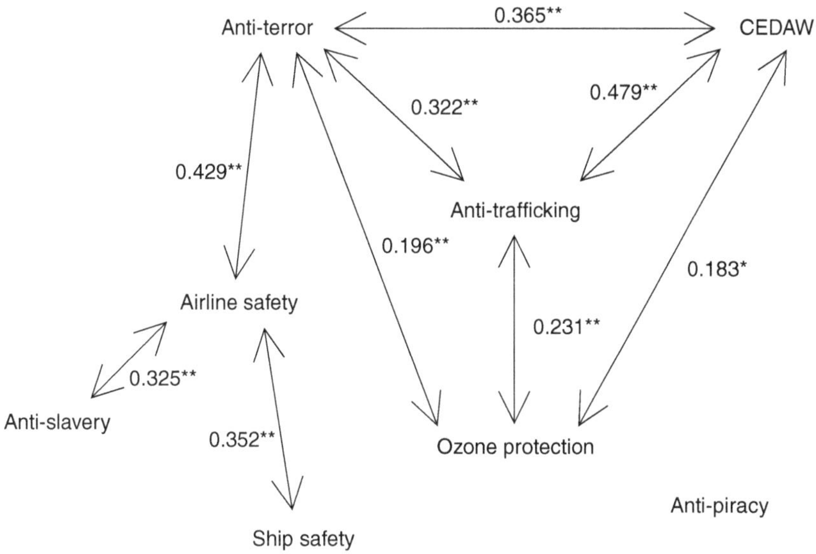

Figure 5.1 Compliance variable correlations.

Notes
$* = p < .05$.
$** = p < .01$.

relying on indicators that can be drawn from the major theoretical approaches. We will move systematically through a variety of factors, beginning with simple correlation analysis and culminating in regression. The goal is to ensure that each theoretical approach is being given the fairest possible treatment. Ultimately, however, it will become clear that certain approaches offer little promise in explaining compliance.

Rationalism and Realism – Interest-driven theory explores the nature of reputation, among other things. It argues that even where states have the power to violate international commitments, they generally choose not to. Those that violate rules will likely violate rules across the board since they care less about their reputations. A useful way to measure the importance of reputation to a state is to consider its treatment of foreign bond-holders and creditors. As sovereign entities, states have the power to renege on these financial commitments with relatively little short-term damage. Doing so naturally causes potential creditors to report their sad experience to the rest of the financial world, with the result that credit-rating agencies will downgrade these countries. Countries with very low credit ratings are apparently less concerned about their reputations for honoring commitments and complying with international expectations – an attitude that should be reflected across issues.

We use three different measures of credit-worthiness. The first is the familiar Moody's bond-rating, taken in 2005 (or as close to it as possible). Unfortunately, Moody's only rates roughly half the world's states. The sixteen-point scale rewards good credit risks with higher numbers. *Institutional Investor* also issues regular ratings of nearly every state. Each is ranked on the basis of credit-worthiness. Finally, the Political Research Service organization scores countries on the basis of its record of foreign debt payment and exposure.

The variables are remarkably strong at the bivariate level (Table 5.2). Moody's and *Institutional Investor* measures correlate strongly with compliance with CEDAW, anti-terror rules, anti-trafficking rules, airliner safety, and the Montreal Protocol. Further, PRS measures correlate with CEDAW, anti-terror measures, and airliner safety. This implies that knowing a country's credit rating may be as useful in predicting compliance as knowing that it is an established democracy.

Several theories indicate that a country's overall economic strength can go far to explain compliance with a wide range of rules. To begin, compliance with most rules requires financial resources. Money, being fungible, can be converted to a wide range of uses, including the hiring and training of police and military forces, government inspectors, and judges and jailers. More indirectly, wealthy states generally have the ability to create rules they want and block those they dislike – and they can often bribe or sanction poorer states to ensure their adoption. They therefore not only have the resources to comply, they generally have incentives to do so. Wealthy states should therefore be more compliant.

We measure wealth with a variety of indicators. Gross national product measures the total resources of a state, while dividing it by the population gives some sense of the resources available to its citizens. Total military spending and total government revenue offer a more precise measure of the resources available to governments themselves which must take the necessary steps to comply or not comply with international rules. And finally, to gauge a state's economic autonomy, we use its level of aid dependence and its debt exposure.

The story of these findings, as reported in Table 5.3, confirms that wealth – and economic liberalism – generally correlate with compliance. The only surprise is the fact that countries with higher foreign debt over export ratios are actually more likely to respond when ships near their shores are attacked by pirates. In general, the pattern that has begun to emerge, namely that ship detention rates and enslavement levels are not easily explained, holds.

Table 5.2 Credit rating and law compliance

	Ship safety	*CEDAW*	*Terror*	*TIP*	*Slaves*	*Piracy*	*Airliner*	*Ozone*
Moody's	0.046	0.519**	0.327**	0.545**	0.177	0.114	0.330**	0.398**
Credit Risk II	0.021	0.605**	0.490**	0.514**	0.151	0.186	0.481**	0.163**
For Debt PRS	0.084	0.252**	0.278**	0.142	–0.049	0.030	0.272**	–0.119

Notes
* = $p<0.05$.
** = $p<0.01$.

Table 5.3 Wealth and law compliance

	Ship safety	*CEDAW*	*Terror*	*TIP*	*Slaves*	*Piracy*	*Airliner*	*Ozone*
GNP	0.054	0.237**	0.242**	0.275**	−0.044	0.305*	0.145	0.078
GNP/cap	0.116	0.619**	0.420**	0.521**	−0.094	0.182	0.348**	0.234**
Mil spend	0.044	0.152	0.208*	0.247**	−0.030	0.333*	0.108	0.043
Gov revenue	0.311	0.456**	0.146	0.454**	−0.147	−0.328	0.175	0.143
ODA over GDP	−0.018	−0.110	−0.027	−0.083	0.029	0.033	−0.071	−0.023
Debt over exports	0.041	−0.123	0.108	−0.003	0.043	0.388*	0.153	0.069
Econ. freedom	0.062	0.501**	0.360**	0.434**	0.024	0.063	0.252**	0.177*

Notes
* = $p<0.05$.
** = $p<0.01$.

To test more precisely the managerial school's claims that what matters most is the governing capacity of a state, we look at three of the World Bank's indicators. Governing effectiveness refers to a state's ability to enforce its laws, broadly speaking, while regulatory quality focuses on its ability to govern the private sector. The anti-corruption measure addresses the degree to which states strive to root out most forms of corruption – in particular graft and bribery. As we can see in Table 5.4, the results are generally consistent with the measures of aggregate national wealth.

Realists argue that compliance with international law, as with essentially all developments in world affairs, can be explained with reference to power relations between states. Neorealists emphasize global structures and polarity. Both agree that the closer a state's political ties to the world's hegemon, the more likely it is to imitate its policies. With respect to our cases, we should expect to see higher levels of compliance across the board, since the US has endorsed each of these rules (although the US has yet to ratify CEDAW, it nonetheless endorses and complies with nearly all of its provisions).

We use a wide range of measures of the strength of each country's ties to the United States. To begin, we use three measures of overall commitment generated by the Correlates of War study. The indicators compile various indicators such as alliance membership, military aid, and so forth. The measures are scored as an s-score (both clean and weighted) and tau-b. This allows us to skirt the

Table 5.4 Governing capacity and law compliance

	Ship safety	*CEDAW*	*Terror*	*TIP*	*Slaves*	*Piracy*	*Airliner*	*Ozone*
Gov effect	0.003	0.646**	0.456**	0.527**	0.073	0.132	0.375**	0.264**
Reg quality	0.043	0.629**	0.461**	0.544**	0.072	0.201	0.324**	0.246**
Anti-corrupt	0.073	0.598**	0.415**	0.537**	0.072	0.160	0.369**	0.284**

Notes
* = $p<0.05$.
** = $p<0.01$.

controversy surrounding the statistics. We also use our own measures of military relations – namely whether the country in question hosts an American military base, whether the country was part of the "coalition of the willing" in the 2003 Iraq War, and whether the country has formal association with or membership in the North Atlantic Treaty Organization. We expect that the COW measures and the measures of alliance should largely replicate each other. Finally, we also use various measures of economic dependence on the US, which should indicate closer political ties (exports to the US, foreign direct investment from the US, and official development assistance from the US).

With a few exceptions, a familiar pattern appears in Table 5.5, namely that most of the indicators correlate with most of the dependent variables. The various measures of alliance with the US are generally consistent with each other. However, measures of economic dependence are more inconsistent and generally less useful in predicting compliance.

Sociological Approaches – Still other theories emphasize the degree to which a state is engaged in the international community. Socialization in the "society of states" should cause governments to comply more readily with international rules. To measure this, we take a simple measure of the number of embassies hosted by the country. Although this also serves as an indicator of international prominence, it is a useful way to gauge the degree to which a government seeks relations with its counterparts. The next measure provides a total of signatures affixed to multilateral treaties since 1960. Again, this is designed to offer a window into the international engagement of a country. Finally, the Swiss Federal Institute of Technology (Zurich) has compiled its own index of political globalization by including a range of measures.

Once again, we see that internationalization is a strong predictor of compliance with many rules, consistent with what has become a pattern across a wide range of indicators (Table 5.6).

To provide a more specific measure of internationalization, we consider the argument that even if states don't necessarily imitate global patterns, they tend to imitate their neighbors. We will consider state membership in a variety of regions as well as regional international organizations. In particular, we explore whether Western states are more inclined to comply with international law than Muslim and/or Arab states (Table 5.7).

The findings confirm that countries tend to behave similarly to their neighbors. They also confirm that Western countries generally comply with international law while Arab, Muslim, and poor countries do not. The findings are far too mixed to generalize this conclusion, however.

Dovetailing with this approach, some theories argue that the characteristics of a nation's citizens are predominant in determining international law compliance patterns. In particular, conservative societies are expected to generally resist international norms, while post-modern societies embrace internationalism. While it is not easy to measure a country's culture, we expect that the percentage of Muslims in the society, combined with the degree of opposition to divorce, should serve as relatively valid indicators of social conservatism. We also have

Table 5.5 Ties to the US and law compliance

	Ship safety	*CEDAW*	*Terror*	*TIP*	*Slaves*	*Piracy*	*Airliner*	*Ozone*
COW s-score wtd	0.072	0.437**	0.270**	0.363**	0.078	–0.029	0.150	0.118
COW tau	0.078	0.417**	0.267**	0.209*	0.119	–0.001	0.247**	0.031
COW s-score	0.060	0.418**	0.254**	0.184*	0.155	–0.011	0.250**	0.099
US base	0.102	342**	0.192**	0.370**	0.079	–0.090	0.251**	0.129
Coalition willing	0.086	0.175*	0.214*	0.264**	0.120	0.164	0.195*	0.101
NATO plus	0.115	0.394**	0.398**	0.506**	0.064	0.098	0.298**	0.213**
Export to US	–0.026	0.190*	0.233**	0.153	0.057	–0.160	0.135	0.085
US FDI	0.070	0.236	0.330*	0.331*	0.030	–0.282	0.027	0.182
US aid	0.026	–0.106	0.056	–0.024	0.024	–0.079	–0.015	0.011

Notes
* = $p < 0.05$.
** = $p < 0.01$.

Table 5.6 Internationalization and law compliance

	Ship safety	*CEDAW*	*Terror*	*TIP*	*Slaves*	*Piracy*	*Airliner*	*Ozone*
For. Embassies	–0.028	0.291**	0.337**	0.378**	0.115	–0.123	0.336**	0.136
All Treaties	0.099	0.603**	0.417**	0.559**	0.063	0.046	0.232*	0.193*
Globalization	–0.020	0.625**	0.489**	0.477**	0.175	0.166	0.466**	0.162

Notes
* = $p < 0.05$.
** = $p < 0.01$.

available data on the degree to which the population fears global warming – an attitude that is generally indicative of a society that has acknowledged the risks of industrialization.

Conservative public attitudes do seem to correlate with non-compliance, as predicted, although the pattern does not hold for all sets of rules. On the other hand, attitudes about global warming show no predict power whatever.

The last set of variables is intended to test the liberal proposition that democratic states generally comply with international rules. We use a variety of measures to accomplish this, beginning with the data from Polity IV, a large-scale scoring of regimes based on their openness to public participation and democratic institutions. The scale gives a minus-ten to the most autocratic regimes and a plus-ten to the most democratic. The World Bank has also scored each country's commitment to the rule of law based on a compilation of various opinion surveys, mostly involving foreign corporate respondents. Finally, we also use the Freedom House scores, which rank countries along the lines of political rights and civil liberties, each on a seven-point scale (1 is most free). As we can see in Table 5.8, each of these measures of democracy is correlated with some of the dependent variables. In particular, each correlates with compliance with CEDAW, anti-terror law, and anti-trafficking rules. Further, the rule of law measure also correlates with airliner safety and anti-ozone compliance. None correlates with ship safety, anti-slavery and anti-piracy measures.

Table 5.7 Regionalism and law compliance

	Ship safety	*CEDAW*	*Terror*	*TIP*	*Slaves*	*Piracy*	*Airliner*	*Ozone*
Europe	0.115	0.495**	0.354**	0.438**	0.108	0.196	0.181	0.076
OECD	0.103	0.615**	0.370**	0.578**	0.074	0.162	0.203*	0.178*
OIC	0.035	–0.380**	–0.067	–0.119	0.001	0.083	0.153	–0.049
Sub-Saharan Africa	–0.026	–0.298**	–0.351**	–0.181*	–0.186	–0.223	–0.494**	0.056
Arab League	0.018	–0.327**	–0.015	–0.135	–0.240*	0.014	0.012	–0.027
GCC	0.033	–0.199*	–0.074	–0.229*	0.026	0.161	0.150	0.000

Notes
* = $p < 0.05$.
** = $p < 0.01$.

Table 5.8 Culture and law compliance

	Ship safety	*CEDAW*	*Terror*	*TIP*	*Slaves*	*Piracy*	*Airliner*	*Ozone*
Percent Muslim	−0.113	−0.537**	−0.279**	−0.215**	−0.185	−0.041	−0.062	−0.172*
Anti-divorce	−0.409**	−0.559**	−0.284*	−0.400**	−0.252	−0.078	−0.070	−0.226
Anti-global warming	0.122	0.101	−0.267	−0.026	0.145	−0.019	0.086	−0.139

Notes
* = $p < 0.05$.
** = $p < 0.01$.

Liberalism – To further clarify the dynamic in question, we have also modified the measure of democracy to inject a dynamic element. As we have seen, some have argued that countries that experience democratization have a unique commitment to "locking in" adherence to international norms. Specifically, we look at the range of Polity scores from 1989 to 2004 in five-year increments, taking the two most extreme scores. By so doing, we hope to capture post-Cold War changes in regime type as well as regime volatility. We also measure the overall change in regime type from 1989 to 2004 by using the figures for those two years. And finally, since there is reason to believe that regimes that are in the mid-range of the scale are particularly eager to demonstrate their legal bona fides, we calculated the additive inverse of the square of the Polity score ($x = -x^2$).

The findings complicate the picture, rather than clarify it. Considering the overall volatility of the Polity scores, the greater range, the less compliance we can expect in the areas of human trafficking and airline safety. The longitudinal change of regime from 1989 to 2004 correlates with none of the dependent variables, and belonging to the mid-range of the Polity scores decreases the chances a country will comply with international law in almost all cases.

A clear implication is that democracy appears to be a two-edged sword with respect to compliance. Clearly, based on Polity, rule of law, and Freedom House measures, democracies are more likely to comply with many international rules. However, transitioning to democracy, or sitting in the mid-range of political systems, seems to make compliance less likely. This finding supports one key claim of the liberal school – that "democracies do law," but undermines the "lock-in hypothesis." Taken together, this implies that only established democracies can be expected to comply more readily. Democratization should not be expected to increase compliance in the short term. Specifically, nations that are experiencing a democratic transition and that lie at the mid-point of democracy are not likely to comply better than other states, contrary to recent research (see Chapter 1) – at least where a wide range of rules are considered (Table 5.9).

Taken together, it is easy to understand the theoretical heterodoxy we find in the literature. There is after all a great deal of evidence to support each approach. Particularly with respect to CEDAW, anti-terror law, anti-trafficking law, airliner

Table 5.9 Democracy and law compliance

	Ship safety	*CEDAW*	*Terror*	*TIP*	*Slaves*	*Piracy*	*Airliner*	*Ozone*
Polity	0.042	0.563**	0.310**	0.428**	0.182	0.112	0.119	0.146
WB rule of law	0.040	0.616**	0.396**	0.550**	0.086	0.194	0.359**	0.275**
Freedom House	–0.103	–0.639**	–0.343**	–0.538**	–0.104	–0.228	–0.179	–0.212**
Polity range	0.054	–0.155	–0.236**	–0.065	0.026	–0.058	–0.223*	–0.044
Polity change	0.065	–0.112	–0.172	–0.030	0.031	0.063	–0.185	0.017
Inverted Polity U	–0.268*	–0.544**	–0.393**	–0.379**	–0.118	–0.179	–0.354**	–0.176*

Notes
* = $p < 0.05$.
** = $p < 0.01$.

safety, and the Montreal Protocol, compliance can be explained by indicators of nearly every theory. Except for measures of democratic transitions, most theories can consider themselves vindicated. What is therefore needed now is further analysis to discriminate between explanations. We therefore turn to a more systematic review of each set of rules, focusing on the five rules for which many candidates exist.

Regressions on compliance indicators

In this section, we will focus on five compliance indicators – CEDAW, anti-terror and anti-trafficking rules, airliner safety, and the Montreal Protocol. We select independent variables as representatives of the various theoretical approaches, recognizing that other candidates might be offered. The variables were chosen primarily because of the strength of the correlation and the size of the coefficient. Again, the hope is to provide each theory with its best representative (a "champion" as it were) as it takes on the other theories head-to-head.

Regression is designed to allow researchers to compare the relative explanatory power of multiple factors. In this case, we use linear regression, although given the presence of a dummy variable (OECD), probit could also be used. In the regressions, we will report standardized coefficients in order to more clearly compare the variables' explanatory power, as well as the full value for the significance of the relationship, recognizing that even where the correlation falls outside the 90 percent level, there may still be useful information to be gleaned.

The independent variables chosen are as follows. To begin, we measure democratic levels with Polity 2004 figures. The measure had the strongest coefficients with most of the variables and is generally considered the most rigorous measure of regime type. It also has almost total coverage. The next measure, of credit-worthiness, is the *Institutional Investor* scoring. This is chosen primarily because of coverage, although it is also clear that its results are consistent with those of Moody's. GNP per capita is used to measure a nation's wealth since it best reflects the resources available to a state through taxation, corporate activity, development levels, and so forth. Again, we have figures on nearly all states.

Next, we measure specific government capacity with the government effectiveness score produced by the World Bank. The fact of the matter is that all of the six measures of government capacity developed by the Bank are very closely correlated with each other, and so the choice was somewhat arbitrary. Based on the description of the measure, however, the Bank appears to have attempted to describe precisely the type of phenomena of particular interest to the managerial school. Of the indicators of ties to the US, we find that the COW weighted s-score is the more complete and reliable, although we recognize that the choice might be controversial. It also is available for nearly all countries and at any correlates very highly with most of the other indicators in the set.

Two more measures complete the model. The first is multilateral treaty signing as an indicator of internationalism. It correlated strongly with all five dependent variables with very high coefficients, and seems to embody an important dimension of international socialization. Finally, we include OECD membership due to its inclusion of all Western, developed countries (including several Asian countries with close ties to the West). The correlations were strong with many variables and coefficients were high. We will address cultural variables in a subsequent phase of the analysis.

We begin with CEDAW as the rule and the physical security of women as the indicator of compliance, as discussed earlier. Table 5.10 displays the results of the model. The first observation should be that only one variable is significant at the 95 percent level: Polity. Put another way, we are nearly certain that, controlling for all the other factors, countries with stronger democratic institutions and procedures are more likely to comply with the provisions of CEDAW.

This clearly supports the overall tenets of the liberal theory and comes as no surprise. One should expect that, even controlling for wealth, ties to the US, government capacity (which has the reverse sign than was expected), and so forth, democratic states take more steps to protect the life and safety of women. This may stem in part from policies allowing more women to vote or serve in public office – something we can measure. It may also be that progressive cultural forces are dominant in democracies (both as a cause and an effect). To control

Table 5.10 First regression on CEDAW

Independent variables	*Standardized coefficients*	*Significance*
Polity	0.277	0.002
Credit-worthiness	0.184	0.190
GNP per capita	0.243	0.096
Government effectiveness	–0.047	0.269
COW weighted s-score	0.023	0.787
Multilateral treaty signing	0.052	0.684
OECD membership	0.167	0.183
Constant		0.000
R^2	0.533	
N	120	

for this, we use the percentage of Muslims in a country. Finally, it is possible that democratic states signed CEDAW in greater numbers and simply took their commitments more seriously (a view that stems from the legitimacy school).

At the merely bivariate level, it is worth noting that the numbers of years since women received the vote at the national level and the number of women serving in parliament both correlate with a lessening of violence against women (0.490** and 0.534** respectively). Also, the degree of commitment to CEDAW itself (signature without ratification vs. signature with ratification) correlates with a reduction in violence against women (0.253**) as found in Gray *et al.* (2006). Finally, Muslim population size correlates at –0.537**. All the new variables are highly correlated with the dependent variable and have high coefficients in the expected directions. We will now regress these variables to identify the strongest factors.

Table 5.11 provides the results of the second model. We note at the outset that contrary to what was promised, credit-worthiness had to be deleted from the model because of collinearity (meaning that it too closely duplicated other variables in the model and was distorting the findings). The variable was not significant at any rate. In the adjusted model, then, we are able to compare the power of general and CEDAW-specific variables. Once again, as with the first model, one variable emerges as significant, all things being equal. Even allowing for wealth, democracy, women in parliament, and legal commitment to CEDAW, the factor that best explains the treatment of women (as an indicator of compliance with CEDAW) is the proportion of the population that is Muslim. We hasten to add that this measure is designed as a proxy for social conservatism rather than religiosity or doctrinal belief system.

The finding is both heartening and rather troubling. What this implies is that when it comes to the treatment of women, governments are very constrained by the domestic culture – especially the traditional roles of men and women. This also raises questions about the nature of compliance when what is required is a grass-roots effort to change the habits and attitudes of ordinary people.

Table 5.11 Second regression on CEDAW

Independent variables	*Standardized coefficients*	*Significance*
Polity	0.087	0.320
Credit-worthiness	0.163	0.095
GNP per capita	0.173	0.146
COW weighted s-score	–0.029	0.726
Multilateral treaty signing	0.088	0.467
OECD membership	0.139	0.252
Years since women got the vote	0.081	0.289
Percentage of women in parliament	0.059	0.465
Percentage of population that is Muslim	–0.284	0.001
Constant		0.000
$R^2=0.613$		
$N=134$		

We now turn to compliance with international norms against terrorism. We begin with the same set of independent variables as found in Table 5.10. We also use the UNSC Res. 1373 compliance score as our indicator. The results can be found in Table 5.12.

Again, only one of the indicators remains highly significant in the regression model. In this case, however, it is not Polity (which fades to almost perfect randomness) but rather credit-worthiness. This is consistent with the view that states care about their reputations as law-abiding citizens of the international system. But there are several factors that are specific to anti-terror law that might better explain compliance than these general indicators. To begin, it is reasonable to ask whether ratifying anti-terror conventions increases a state's level of compliance. Since there are twelve universal anti-terror conventions, each of relatively similar significance (in that they each address only a fairly narrow aspect of terrorism), we have chosen to simply count how many of the twelve each country has ratified. We also surmise that states that are directly affected by political violence at home might have a greater incentive to combat terrorism globally. We use the TERRATIT measures of terrorism to gauge the level of threat within each country.

At the biraviate level, compliance with anti-terror measures correlates strongly with the number of universal anti-terror conventions ratified by the state (0.470**), although there is no connection to compliance and the degree of political violence or terrorist attacks within the country. We therefore include anti-terror convention ratification in the model to produce what is found in Table 5.13.

The revised model shows the robustness of the role of credit-worthiness rankings in explaining anti-terror law compliance, but it is also clear that the greater the number of treaties signed, the greater the likelihood that a country will receive higher marks on compliance. Note especially the increase in the overall R^2 score from the first model to the second (0.236 to 0.319), indicating that we

Table 5.12 Regression on anti-terror law

DV: Anti-terror compliance		
Independent variables	*Standardized coefficients*	*Significance*
Polity	0.002	0.989
Credit-worthiness	0.497	0.005
GNP per capita	0.002	0.992
Government effectiveness	–0.037	0.864
COW weighted s-score	–0.010	0.929
Multilateral treaty signing	0.163	0.315
OECD membership	–0.102	0.516
Constant		0.000
R^2	0.263	
N	134	

Table 5.13 Second regression on anti-terror law

Independent variables	*Standardized coefficients*	*Significance*
Polity	0.032	0.765
Credit rating	0.363	0.038
GNP per capita	0.091	0.607
Government effectiveness	–0.034	0.871
COW weighted s-score	0.019	0.860
Multilateral treaty signing	0.017	0.916
OECD membership	–0.138	0.364
Anti-terror treaties ratified	0.300	0.002
Constant		0.564
$R^2=0.319$		
$N=134$		

have explained far more of the variance overall. Even though these factors appear to emerge from two very different theoretical traditions (rationalism and legitimacy theory), there is a common thread between the two – namely that states that care about reputations and make public commitments to a particular international norm are likely to comply to a greater extent than either countries that care little about their reputations (for compliance, that is) or countries that do not publicly commit to the rule. This points us towards the possibility that certain variables have a multiplier effect on each other, something we will address more systematically in the case study material in Chapters 6 through 9.

To what extent to the general indicators explain compliance with anti-trafficking law? Table 5.14 presents the results of our next regression on the State Department anti-trafficking score.

The model shows, once again, that one independent variable is highly significant. In this case, it is the government's administrative capacity that explains much of its degree of compliance. This stands to reason, since fighting trafficking

Table 5.14 Regression on anti-trafficking law

DV: Anti-trafficking compliance		
Independent variables	*Standardized coefficients*	*Significance*
Polity	–0.001	0.990
Credit-worthiness	–0.288	0.063
GNP per capita	–0.242	0.138
Government effectiveness	0.698	0.000
COW weighted s-score	0.085	0.385
Multilateral treaty signing	0.144	0.327
OECD membership	0.306	0.327
Constant		0.000
R^2	0.433	
N	134	

involves a wide range of administrative skills, from border control to passport control to monitoring irregular labor and red light districts. Where it is easy to slip across a porous border and then mingle with citizens in lightly patrolled urban areas, trafficking can be expected to be high. This perspective is consistent with the managerial school.

This begs the question whether there are factors unique to trafficking that should be considered in the model. Again, let us look at whether states have made a commitment to the rule in a concrete and visible way. In this case, the task is relatively simple since there exists a UN Protocol on Trafficking (2000) that describes the rules precisely and narrowly. We will consider whether a state has ratified the Protocol. With respect to government capacity, it is worth considering some items of special significance to trafficking, namely the strength of border controls and the ability of the police to arrest suspects. We choose a simple formula for the former, namely the size of a country's military in relation to its land border. For the latter, we choose the arrest rate of murder suspects – on the assumption that states will do their best to catch murderers.

Compliance with anti-trafficking norms correlates with whether a state has ratified the 2000 Protocol (0.174*) and military spending divided by the land frontier (0.301**). It does not correlate with the country's overall record for arresting murder suspects. We therefore fold the first two variables into the model, the results of which are presented in Table 5.15.

Adding the two trafficking-specific variables did not alter the overall lessons of the model, namely that a country's regulatory capacity is the best predictor of its compliance with anti-trafficking norms.

Airline safety compliance, as measured by the deficiencies logged by ICAO inspectors during the second round of airline inspections in the mid-2000s, was also regressed against the general variables. The findings are reported in Table 5.16.

Table 5.15 Second regression on anti-trafficking law

Independent variables	*Standardized coefficients*	*Significance*
Polity	–0.014	0.903
Credit-worthiness	–0.273	0.133
GNP per capita	–0.233	0.244
Government effectiveness	0.684	0.002
COW weighted s-score	0.113	0.322
Multilateral treaty signings	0.038	0.839
OECD membership	0.323	0.089
Ratified Trafficking Protocol	0.051	0.556
Military spending/land border	0.090	0.331
Constant		0.001
R^2=0.428		
N=134		

Table 5.16 Regression on airline safety law

Independent variables	*Standardized coefficients*	*Significance*
Polity	–0.072	0.584
Credit-worthiness	0.767	0.000
GNP per capita	0.216	0.343
Government effectiveness	–0.193	0.429
COW weighted s-score	–0.037	0.780
Multilateral treaty signing	0.070	0.727
OECD membership	–0.405	0.033
Constant		0.000
R^2	0.294	
N	134	

In this case, credit-worthiness again emerges as the most significant factor in explaining compliance. OECD membership is also important, although less so. What is intriguing, however, is that the sign of the coefficient is reversed in the regression (note that this is not due to collinearity of other statistical anomalies since the reversal occurs in other models with fewer variables). This implies that, when other factors are considered, OECD membership seems to increase the chances of less compliance.

To more precisely measure a country's interest in complying with international aviation safety norms, we count the number of countries that send and receive flights to and from the state in question. These are designated "air partners" (Piermartini and Rousova 2009). We find that there exists a highly significant correlation (0.298**). Likewise, to measure the commitment to air safety norms, we count the number of international conventions sponsored by the ICAO that the state has ratified (something which the ICAO makes readily available on its website). Again, we find a strong correlation (0.299**). We add these variables to the model, as reported in Table 5.17.

Table 5.17 Second regression on airline safety

Independent variables	*Standardized coefficients*	*Significance*
Polity	–0.043	0.752
Credit-worthiness	0.729	0.001
GNP per capita	0.263	0.251
Governing effectiveness	–0.245	0.339
COW weighted s-score	–0.036	0.741
Multilateral treaty signings	0.012	0.960
OECD membership	–0.385	0.045
Air partners	–0.063	0.736
ICAO treaties ratified	0.183	0.133
Constant		0.000
N=134		

The addition of these rule-specific variables increases the overall strength of the model, as reflected in a higher R^2, but does not otherwise change the relative strength of the independent variables themselves.

Finally, we apply the same variables to compliance with the Montreal Protocol. Table 5.18 reports the results, which show that government effectiveness is the only variable that is highly correlated. Credit-worthiness is also more weakly correlated. Taken as a whole, however, much of the variance remains unexplained, as reflected in the low R^2 statistic (0.112).

More specific measures include the number of ozone-related treaties and protocols sponsored by the UN Environmental Programme, the number of years that have passed since ratification of the Montreal Protocol (relative to years of independence), and two measures of economic development – energy usage and CFC production. The first variables are intended to measure the degree of legal commitment to protecting the ozone layer and the latter are designed to gauge the level of industrialization and (indirectly) technological sophistication in a country on the one hand, and its degree of dependence on CFCs on the other. At the bivariate level, compliance correlates with the number of various Montreal-sponsored treaties a country has ratified (0.168**) but not with the number of years since it ratified the initial Protocol, or the level of energy usage and CFC consumption. We therefore incorporate the first variable into the model, as reported in Table 5.19.

The addition of treaty-signing behavior did not improve the model to a significant degree, nor did it alter the relative weight of the existing variables. Governing effectiveness still emerges as the most significant factor.

Regressions using the general indicators and topic-specific indicators are very weak with respect to ship safety norms, anti-piracy law, or anti-slavery rules. We therefore do not include them in the analysis.

At this point, and as mentioned in Chapter 1, the clear story is that reliance on a single theory to explain or predict international law compliance is unreasonable. Even though the theories explain much in isolation, it is clear that when they are pitted against each other as controls, none is able to explain compliance across a range of issues. Further, it is not easy to predict, based on the theory's causal logic, which issues it will better predict. As we see in Table 5.20, it is unclear why

Table 5.18 Regression on the Montreal Protocol

Independent variables	*Standardized coefficients*	*Significance*
Polity	–0.016	0.895
Credit-worthiness	–0.351	0.066
GNP per capita	–0.001	0.995
Government effectiveness	0.599	0.012
COW weighted s-score	0.075	0.531
Multilateral treaty signing	0.072	0.685
OECD membership	–0.100	0.685
Constant		0.433
R^2	0.112	
N	134	

Table 5.19 Second regression on the Montreal Protocol

Independent variables	*Standardized coefficients*	*Significance*
Polity	–0.032	0.792
GNP per capita	0.011	0.954
Credit-worthiness	–0.360	0.059
Governing effectiveness	0.555	0.021
COW weighted s-score	0.076	0.524
Multilateral treaty signing	0.058	0.741
OECD membership	–0.084	0.628
COW	0.076	0.524
Ozone-related treaty ratifications	0.108	0.277
Constant		0.987

Table 5.20 Summary of findings

Theory	*Rule for which compliance is explained*
Rationalism – Capacity	Anti-Trafficking, Montreal Protocol
Rationalism – Realism	none
Rationalism – Reputation	Anti-Terror, Airline Safety
Sociological – Socialization	none
Sociological – Domestic Culture	CEDAW (Model 2)
Sociological – Legitimacy	Anti-Terror (Model 2)
Liberalism	CEDAW (Model 1)

democratic regimes would be particularly eager to prevent harm to women, but not to slaves or trafficked persons. Likewise, it is not apparent why states with greater administrative capacity would be eager to prevent trafficking but not terrorism. Realism fared poorly, but even more surprising, it is odd that international and regional socialization does not appear to play much of a role – in fact it had a depressing effect on airline safety compliance.

Also as discussed in Chapter 1, the findings suggest that contextual and interactive factors play a key role – something that most statistical tests fail to adequately measure. Furthermore, historical patterns and institutional procedures likely influence policy outcomes to a greater degree than expected. Ultimately, what is needed is far more detail on precisely how governments arrive at particular decisions regarding compliance with international rules. It is therefore necessary that we undertake systematic country studies, to which we now turn.

Note

1 Note that we have adjusted the signs of the variables so that increased compliance is reflected in a higher score.

Appendix: variable sources

Air partners and air liberalization scores from Piermartini Roberta and Linda Rousova (2008) "Liberalization of Air Transport Services and Passenger Traffic," Staff Working Paper ERSD-2008–06, World Bank. Available at www.wto.org/english/res_e/reser_e/ersd200806_e.pdf.

Arab League, GCC, OECD, OIC memberships derived from organization websites.

CFC Output from UNEP (2002) at http://ozone.unep.org/Data_Reporting/Data_Access/.

Countries with permanent US military installations as of 1998, as reported in Jerel Rosati (2004) *The Politics of United States Foreign Policy*, 3rd edn. Wadsworth: Belmont, California, pp. 194–195.

CO_2 per capita figures (2004) and energy use (2004) from the World Bank at http://ddp-ext.worldbank.org/ext/DDPQQ/showReport.do?method=showReport.

Credit Risk for 2007 from *Institutional Investor* at www.iimagazinerankings.com/CountryCredit/GlobalRanking.asp.

Debt Service (PPG and IMF only, % of exports of goods and services) for 2005 as found at http://devdata.worldbank.org/dataonline/htm.

Economic Freedom Rankings 2005 from the Heritage Foundation. Available at www.heritage.org/index/ranking.

Europe, Sub-Saharan Africa categories derived from COW Project.

Foreign Debt Risk for 2005 as reported by *International Country Risk Guide* by The PRS Group, Inc. 2009.

Foreign Embassies tabulated from the *Europa Yearbook* (2008) at www.europaworld.com/welcome?authstatuscode=200.

Freedom House civil liberties scores for 2005, 2010 available at www.freedomhouse.org/template.cfm?page=15&year=2010.

Freedom House civil liberties scores (2007) available at www.freedomhouse.org/template.cfm?page=15&year=2007.

Globalization index for 2005 from http://globalization.kof.ethz.ch/.

GNP per capita calculated as GNI per capita, Atlas method (2006) from World Bank through its interactive data search at http://web.worldbank.org/WBSITE/EXTERNAL/DATASTATISTICS/0,,contentMDK:20394802~menuPK:1192714~pagePK:64133150~piPK:64133175~theSitePK:239419,00.html.

Gross Domestic Product in current US$ for 2005 as found at http://devdata.worldbank.org/dataonline/htm.

IGO memberships tabulated from the *CIA Factbook* (2008) at www.cia.gov/library/publications/the-world-factbook/fields/2107.html.

Land boundary in km. www.nationmaster.com/graph/geo_lan_bou_tot-geography-land-boundaries-total.

Member of the "coalition of the willing" as listed by the White House at www.whitehouse.gov/news/releases/2003/03/20030327–10.html.

Member-state of the Organization of the Islamic Conference as listed at www.oic-oci.org/.

Military expenditures (% of GDP) for 2005 as found at http://devdata.worldbank.org/dataonline/htm.

Military spending from SIPRI (2006) *Military Spending Trends 2006*, available at http://first.sipri.org/non_first/milex.php.

Moody's Monthly Bond-rating Index. Available at http://v3.moodys.com/productandsolutions.

Multilateral treaties endorsed as compiled by the author. See Robert Denemark, Matthew Hoffman, Lauren Twist, and Hasan Yonten (2007) "Dominance and Diplomacy: Trends in the Utilization of Multilateral Agreements by Global Powers," presented at the annual meetings of the International Studies Association, Chicago.

Muslim population derived from the Pew Research Center. http://pewforum.org/Mapping-the-Global-Muslim-Population.aspx.

Number of UN-designated international conventions against terrorism signed or ratified as of July 2001, as listed in UNGA doc A/56/160 and found at http://ods-dds-ny.un.org/doc/UNDOC/GEN/N01/447/63/PDF/N0144763.pdf?OpenElement.

Official development assistance and official aid (current US$) for 2005, divided by gross domestic product as found at http://devdata.worldbank.org/dataonline/htm.

Origin, Destination, Transit – from UNODC *2006 Trafficking in Persons* report at www.unodc.org/pdf/traffickinginpersons_report_2006ver2.pdf.

Ozone-related convention status available from UNEP (2007) at http://ozone.unep.org/Ratification_status/.

Percentage of teen girls who are married – UN Statistical Division at www.unstats.un.org/unsd/cdb/cdb_advanced_data_extract.asp.

Piermartini, Roberta and Linda Rousova (2009) "Free Sky and Clouds of Restrictions," Discussion Paper 2009–11, Volkswirtschaftliche Fakultät, Ludwig-Maximilians-Universität München.

Polity IVd 2004 score of government's overall democratization, –10 to +10, as found at www.cidcm.umd.edu/inscr/polity/index.htm#polity4d.

Public opinion survey results from the Pew Global Attitudes Project at http://pewglobal.org/.

Rule of Law scores from 2005 are reported in *International Country Risk Guide* by The PRS Group, Inc. 2009.

Slavery figures and in-trafficking and out-trafficking scores available at Kevin Bales (2005) *Understanding Slavery: A Reader*, Berkeley: University of California Press.

Sponsor of terrorism, as designated by the US Department of State in April 2003 and disseminated to US Embassies worldwide. An example is at http://usembassy.state.gov/posts/pk1/wwwh03050104.html.

TERATIT – Average number of terrorist acts, scaled from 1 to 5 (high) as compiled in the ITERATE data set for terrorist events and reported in S. Brock Blomberg, Gregory Hess, and Athanasios Orphanides (2003) "The Macroeconomic Consequences of Terrorism," manuscript, Claremont, California.

Trafficking in Persons scores from United States Department of State (2006) *Trafficking in Persons Report, June 2006* Publication 11335, Washington D.C.

Transparency International scores (2005) from www.transparency.org/.

US Aid for 2005 as measured by total of economic and military grants from the US (current US$) as listed in the USAID Green Book found at http://esdb.cdie.org/cgi-bin/broker.exe?_program=gbkprogs.ctypage_1.sas&_service=default.

Weighted s-scores generated from Correlates of War data by D. Scott Bennett and Allan C. Stam III. See D. Scott Bennett and Allan C. Stam III (2002) "Expected Utility Generation and Data Management," available at www.eugenesoftware.org and www.correlatesofwar.org/datasets.htm.

WomanStats index available at www.WomanStats.org/.

Women in parliament, women's vote come from data set used in Mark M. Gray, Miki Caul Kittilson, and Wayne Sandholtz (2006) "Women and Globalization: A Study of 180 Countries, 1975–2000," *International Organization* 60 (Spring): 293–333.

World Bank government effectiveness for 2005 of "government effectiveness" by firms, NGOs, and other observers as measured by various surveys and scaled on a 100-point scale, as listed in www.worldbank.org/wbi/governance/govdata/.

World Bank voice and anti-corruption scores available at http://web.worldbank.org/WBSITE/EXTERNAL/WBI/EXTWBIGOVANTCOR/0,,menuPK:1740542~pagePK:64168427~piPK:64168435~theSitePK:1740530,00.html.

World Trade Center casualties of a national of country, as listed in www.september11victims.com/september11Victims/COUNTRY_CITIZENSHIP.htm.

Part II

Case studies

6 Globalized democracies

Peru and Bolivia

Where democracy and globalization are combined, we might expect to also see other factors emerge – most of which can be expected to increase compliance. For one, such states may strive to be better partners to other democracies in the region. Where the number of democracies has reached a critical mass – as in Europe – this aim might lead to the formation of security communities and integrated markets, both of which will tend to increase incentives to comply with past agreements. Globalization and democracy will also likely have a transformative effect on domestic society, increasing the likelihood that international norms will penetrate more deeply than would be the case where each factor exists separately but not in tandem. In-bound and out-bound travel will tend to increase, interactions between legislators and jurists will expand, non-government organizations and other civil society actors will multiply and collaborate, and scholars and students will communicate and learn more from each other. Although not inevitable, there is also a correlation between democracy and globalization on the one hand and economic and technological advancement on the other. Where this occurs, governments will ultimately have access to more resources at their disposal, increasing the likelihood they will have the capacity to implement international norms.

We saw in Chapter 5 that democracy and globalization correlate with compliance on a number of rules, including CEDAW, anti-terror, anti-trafficking, airliner safety, and ozone depletion, although caveats should be mentioned. For one, only established democracies are more likely to comply and states with mid-range democracy scores were the least likely to comply. With respect to the regressions, democracy levels were helpful only with respect to explaining compliance with CEDAW, although even that fell away when domestic religious affiliation was included. Because democracy and globalization are closely correlated, globalization was not included in the regressions. But since some of the theories that explain the link between globalization and compliance hypothesize that this stems from a desire for a reputation for reliability, we can point out that measures of credit-worthiness also correlate with compliance on the five rules mentioned above. Further, credit-worthiness stands up to regression with respect to compliance with anti-terror law and airline safety regulations.

Clearly, although the logic is impressive, the empirical evidence is still mixed with respect to whether globalized democracies are more likely to comply with international law. For this reason we undertake the study of Peru and Bolivia in this chapter.

Peru

Overview

Peru is a diverse country with respect to its climate and topography, society, and political heritage. Located on the Pacific coast of Latin America and covering an area comparable to that of South Africa, its topography and climate include arid deserts, tropical plains, and mountainous jungles. It has known periods of considerable influence and power as well as dependency and foreign domination. Its politics are infused with large measures of radical nationalism, cosmopolitan internationalism, and ambiguous identity. For most of its history since Spanish forces were defeated in 1824, Peru has been governed by military regimes, interrupted by various democratic regimes. The current period of democratic government began in 1980 and its new constitution has been in place since 1993. It has adopted a pro-Western foreign policy orientation and in recent years has endeavored to be a strong regional partner to the US. Peru has adopted a pro-trade, pro-foreign direct investment economic strategy, particularly since the early 1990s, that has earned it the approval and support of the West. It has made efforts to reconcile with regional rivals, signing a number of agreements to resolve long-standing disputes with neighbors. It has also joined free-trade bodies in the region.

Peru's politics have been generally moderate of late, particularly in the wake of the "*autogolpe*" by President Alberto Fujimori in the early 1990s and his failed attempt at a third term in 2000. The resulting reaction has led to the creation of new oversight institutions, including the office of the Ombudsman to provide ordinary citizens with a point of access for expressing grievances, a Truth and Reconciliation Commission to investigate injustices of the past (Caistor and Villarán 2006, 91), and a Constitutional Court separate from the Supreme Court. While a large majority of Peruvians support democracy and voter turnout is very high (90 percent plus), there is still considerable disappointment with the level of corruption in all institutions of government, including political parties (Boidi 2008).

Peru's economy and society have struggled to modernize but it is currently enjoying a very strong growth rate and substantial technological improvement. Its GDP per capita of just over $8,000 places Peru in the World Bank's "upper middle income" category, along with Argentina and Brazil. While still heavily dependent on mineral and cash crop exports, the economy has become increasingly diversified in recent years, although the benefits have not spread evenly across the country. Literacy rates are strong at 92.9 percent, poverty is falling, and public services are available in much of the country. But the poverty rate is still over one-third (World Bank 2010), and is much higher in rural areas – particularly the Amazonian Basin where indigenous peoples make up the majority of the population. Illiteracy rates in rural areas are roughly five times those in cities. Rural populations complain of a lack of access to health care facilities (Andina 2008).

Political cleavages in the country line up along class, ethnic, region, and rural-urban lines, and generally reinforce a wealthy white, urban, coastal, and liberal society against a poor, *indio*, rural, highland, and somewhat radical society. The election of Alejandro Toledo Manrique represents an important watershed in that he was the first candidate with Indian ancestry to become the head of state (Freedom House 2010). Peru has struggled over recent decades with widespread political violence, primarily involving the Shining Path (*Sendero Luminso*) rebel group that began operations in the early 1980s as a Maoist-inspired defender of rural land workers and grew to pose a serious challenge to the government during the 1980s. President Alberto Fujimori (1990–2000) adopted draconian tactics that ultimately proved largely successful as the government captured the movement's leader in 1992 and his successor in 1999. Fujimori himself is presently incarcerated, having been convicted on various charges of corruption and abuse of power in connection with the deaths of two dozen people by the military in the early 1990s (*New York Times* 2009).

Liberalism

With this broad overview complete, we will now consider characteristics of Peru that relate specifically to the various theories of international law compliance. We will begin with a focus on liberal theories of institutions, values, and processes. The most dramatic shift came at the end of the Fujimori era in 2000. Despite intimidation of opposition parties and bribery of the press by his security advisor, Vladimiro Montesinos, Fujimori missed winning in the first round by 0.1 percent of the vote. An Organization of American States (OAS) monitoring team agreed with opponents that the election was flawed. The second-place vote getter (Toledo) boycotted the run-off and Fujimori won with 74 percent of the vote. Protests continued after the vote with denunciations of wrong-doing and large-scale street demonstrations. At this point videos of Montesinos bribing TV station owners came to light. Fujimori accepted responsibility and promised to hold new presidential elections in April 2001 for which he would not run. He ultimately flew to Asia and announced he would not be returning and resigned in Japan in November 2000. The interim president brought back celebrated diplomat Javier Perez de Cuellar to serve as interim prime minister and both set to work to organize a new election. The OAS and EU were invited to monitor the elections – and gave them their approval. Toledo won with 53 percent of the vote (Caistor and Villarán 2006, 68–78). Although his administration was heavily criticized, he completed his term and peacefully handed over power to Alan Garcia Perez in 2006.

A closer look also shows that even democratic institutions in Peru often lack the independence and responsiveness observers might expect. Corruption is pervasive in the country's paramount institutions, including especially the judiciary. As mentioned in the Freedom House survey, "According to an October 2008 survey, 92 percent of Peruvians characterized corruption as 'generalized' in politics. A National Anticorruption Office established in October 2007 was disbanded in August 2008..." (Freedom House 2010). Thirty percent of Peruvians reported having been victimized by a corrupt public official in 2006 (Zéphyr 2008, 256). One out of ten had paid a bribe to a judge to expedite a case. The judiciary investigated a few of the cases, but no arrests were made.

The police are distrusted. In 2009, following a declaration by the Minister of Justice that indigenous demonstrators in Bagua province were "encouraging rebellion, sedition and conspiracy," police began removing protesters from their blockades. Violence erupted and dozens were killed, including both police and protesters. But, as deplored by a United Nations special rapporteur, the government denies that the police abused their authority and did not undertake any investigation on the matter (Human Rights Council 2009a).

Although the Constitutional organs are not functioning, many proper procedures are followed and rights are protected. The press is fairly vocal, although corruptible. Non-government organizations and other civil society organizations thrive, although Garcia adopted new legislation requiring they register and publicize their sources of income (which the Constitutional Court mostly overturned – Freedom House 2010). To sum up, then, Peruvian institutions and practices present a mixed bag, and depending on one's coding methods, it might appear either very democratic or quite undemocratic.

To what extent is Peru open to the outside world? The answer is considerably, with some exceptions. In the area of trade and investment, Peru, like most of Latin America, has historically been ambivalent about the virtues of laissez-faire economics, but since the early 1990s has committed itself to a program of almost entirely free trade and free investment. This is true with respect not only to the United States but also to its Latin neighbors. The twenty-year commitment to free trade is all the more remarkable since it has been carried out by political figures who disagreed on nearly everything else (Dept. of State 2010a). Specifically, Fujimori lowered tariffs toward all trading partners, dropping them to almost nothing with respect to Latin American states. This coincided with the regional commitment to an Andean free trade area and restructuring of the Andean Community in the mid-1990s. The government announced plans to abolish tariffs on roughly 6,000 types of goods it was importing from members of the Community during the period 1997–2005. Peru became an associate member of the Southern Common Market (MERCOSUR) in 2003, then signed a free trade agreement with the United States in 2005 (Europa 2010a). It has also concluded free trade agreements with Canada, the EU, and China (CIA 2009). The Heritage Foundation gave Peru a score of 61.3 (out of a range of 8.0–89.5) in 2005 and 67.6 (on 1.0–89.7) in 2010, earning it a "moderately free" ranking (Heritage Foundation 2010).

Import levels nearly doubled in just three years in the mid-2000s and exports saw an increase from $17 billion to nearly $28 billion. Throughout the 1990s and 2000s, Peru's economy grew at significant rates, sometimes nearing 10 percent per year. Poverty has dropped considerably, although, as mentioned earlier, the benefits are not being shared proportionately across the population. Exports are weighted heavily toward petroleum, natural gas, and minerals (copper alone accounted for one-sixth of Peru's exports in 2007), all of which are notorious for their demand and price volatility.

Peru has also opened itself to increasing levels of foreign direct investment by privatizing state-owned firms in the 1990s and liberalizing profit repatriation laws. Inflows have averaged roughly one billion US$ since 1991 and total stock of FDI financing projects stood at roughly $18 billion in 2008 – a dramatic increase for Peru but still a relatively low figure by Latin American standards (Markwick 2009). Investments would likely be higher except for obstacles of bureaucratic red-tape and corruption. Bribes and kickbacks are rather routine, and one case involving a Norwegian investor and others involved in oil drilling led to the conviction of Prime Minister Jorge del Castillo in 2008 (Freedom House 2010).

Also significant was the increase in foreign borrowing during this period – especially from international financial institutions such as the IMF. Loans were forthcoming during the 1990s largely in response to Fujimori's efforts to impose fiscal discipline and monetary constraint – policies that cut Peru's inflation rate from over 1,000 percent to under 100 percent in a few years. These were met by loans of two billion dollars from the US and EU.

Anticipating the "reputational" school's material, it is worth noting that in 2008 the government's many efforts at financial discipline were rewarded with an increase in its credit rating from Standard and Poor's, which enabled the Garcia regime to issue bonds in 2009, thereby raising one billion dollars (Markwick 2009). It is clear from the above that, despite ambivalence with respect to domestic political liberalism, the Peruvian government since 1990 has been committed to a course of international economic liberalism. What is also interesting is that its economic liberalism has in fact fed back its political liberalism through the operations of politically motivated creditors and donors.

Taken together, Peru certainly qualifies as a state that is liberalizing along most dimensions, although the process has been incomplete and inconsistent over time. Peru is clearly as liberal as it has ever been and seems intent on persisting along this path.

Managerial school

The managerial school, as we have seen, argues that all states want to comply with international law, and their failure to do so stems primarily from a lack of administrative and enforcement capacity. It is a lack of customs agents and border patrols, not political will, that explains non-compliance, to put it simply. Peru sits squarely in the middle on most measures. We've already discussed the problem of corruption and the challenge of providing services to a large and sometimes impenetrable territory. Tax collection has historically been a serious weakness of the Peruvian government, amounting to only 6 percent of GDP in 1990. That figure has increased to 12 percent in recent years thanks to simplified tax rates, improved technology and training (IADB 2010). Concerns have also been raised about the impartiality of judges who have been accused of extorting funds from un-charged prisoners (Senior Peruvian Official 2010). Both with respect to supply and demand, then, Peru is suffering from important capacity deficiencies.

Unlike many countries with inaccessible areas, Peru makes considerable effort to provide services around the country. But such efforts are not generally successful, differential regional poverty rates mentioned earlier can attest. There are simply limits to what can be done in sparsely populated jungle regions such as Loreto to the north. Regulating many industries, such as logging, is impeded not only by distance and cost but also by the difficulty of identifying inspectors willing to live in inhospitable jungles far from amenities (McClintock 2010).

Penetration of Colombia *narcotrafficantes* into this region is matched only by the lawlessness of the Ayacucho region in the southern highlands where rebel groups have formed unholy alliances with drug traffickers (Europa 2010b).

Reputational theory

We have already broached this subject in our discussion of Peru's credit-rating and overall quest for approval from international creditors. Relatively speaking, Peru finds itself in a fairly strong position, particularly given its history. It is clear from the indicators and from the previous discussion that Peruvian governments of various political leanings have placed credit-worthiness near the top of the agenda – even at the peril of political unpopularity.

Aside from purely financial considerations, it is also clear that Peruvian governments for the past twenty years have worked assiduously to curry the favor of Western powers and international institutions. Rare have been the instances when Peru openly defied international opinion (one involved a repudiation of the Inter-American Court of Human Rights [IACHR] by Fujimori which was later reversed). As was mentioned, embrace of Western business and trade standards has been used to justify anti-*indios* actions, again showing that international approval may take precedence over domestic popularity for some Peruvian leaders. Particularly in the wake of Fujimori's ouster, the Peruvian government sought the international community's approval (Youngers 2010). This is less the case with the Garcia administration, which has defied international demands for prosecution of those suspected of graft in earlier administrations.

At the regional level, Peru strives for a moderate tone – distancing itself from Hugo Chavez and his populist rhetoric and anti-American positions – and embracing regional solutions to questions of trade, drug and human trafficking, environmental protection, and so forth. Peru strives to be a "good citizen" of such bodies as the IACHR and the OAS, respecting their judgments – even when these repudiate Peruvian actions (IACHR 2010). Peru is active in the United

Nations and saw one of its citizens – Javier Peres de Cuellar – preside as Secretary-General, and roughly 250 of its troops serve in peacekeeping operations (40th rank).

Cultural theory

Peruvians, as mentioned earlier, are generally liberal in their orientation to key political and cultural issues, although there are strong disagreements about specifics. Roughly 85 percent of Peruvians are Roman Catholic, and 43 percent attend church every week (U. Michigan 1997). While there are considerable differences between rural and urban areas, Peruvians are generally family-oriented and morally conservative. Two-fifths of Peruvians, for example, report that single motherhood and divorce are never acceptable, indicating a strong degree of support for traditional family structures and roles.

Peruvians have also been exposed to the full array of Western media and educational curricula, with the result that they are familiar with Western cultural values, science, philosophy, and so forth. These are available through relatively plentiful televisions, radios, and internet access points as well as numerous schools and universities. Close to one million Peruvians are enrolled in college and university graduates permeate society – particularly in government administration. Sixty-one percent of Peruvians have a favorable attitude toward the United States, according to a 2007 survey (down from 67 percent in 2002, but higher than for the EU, Russia, China, and Iran – Pew 2010a). Furthermore, four-fifths agree that trade with the outside world is good for Peru, although only half as many believe the free market itself is good for Peruvians generally (Pew 2010b). In general, then, Peruvians have embraced the Western world and its values – but with some reservations regarding new forms of family life.

Legitimacy theory

Finally, legitimacy theory asks whether Peru has internalized the view that international law is legitimate and serves the best interests of most countries. Although we will consider more systematically whether Peru has ratified international legal instruments that are central to the various issues below, it is enough to point out that Peru has signed over 340 multilateral treaties since 1960, is host to nearly fifty foreign embassies, and is a founding member of the United Nations, the OAS, and many other key international bodies (MATRS 2010). Peru accepted the compulsory jurisdiction of the International Court of Justice in 2003 and ratified the Rome Statute of the International Criminal Court in 2001 (following Fujimori's fall). As mentioned earlier, it is active in multilateral institutions at both the regional and international levels, and has submitted to international dispute settlement and human rights proceedings from time to time. In general, Peru inherits the legal legacy of all Latin American states borne of years of anti-American resistance and proclamation of national sovereignty and the right of non-interference (Smith 2007, 95–99).

Ratification and implementation of international treaties requires a lengthy process that includes internal debate and public discussion and consultation first at the level of the presidency, then the legislature, and finally the regulatory bodies tasked with implementing the agreement. At each stage, revision is possible and likely. Attempts to circumvent this process – as in the case when presidential decrees were issued to implement the Peru–US Free Trade Agreement in 2008 – will likely lead to reversals by the judiciary (Senior Peruvian Official 2010). This said, the Constitution states that once ratified, international treaties take precedence over domestic law.

Rationalism

As mentioned in Chapter 1, testing rationalism requires considerable information regarding stakeholders, their interests, the opportunities they face, and the strategies they select. Although we will consider these in greater detail under the issue-area headings, it is worth noting that Peruvian politics and society is a kaleidoscope of actors competing in a plethora of contests. Although the constitutional national governing institutions have fewer confrontations than might be expected on the basis of their nominal powers, there are alternative bodies that challenge the rights of these constitutional organs, as mentioned above. Likewise, although Peru is not a federal system, local sources of power and bureaucratic discretion – not to mention outright venality – contribute to important vertical contests. Outside of the institutions of governance, political parties are numerous and important players – especially during elections – as are civil society organizations and business groups. Indigenous groups and their defenders are a force to be reckoned with, as we have seen. Finally, extra-legal bodies from organized criminal organizations to rebel movements have in some instances defined Peruvian politics of late.

Although it is premature to predict which of these many groups will prevail and shape national policy with respect to implementation of international law, it is important to keep them in mind as we turn to the specific legal issue areas that are addressed in the next section. It is also worth noting that Peruvian leaders are capable of undertaking calculations of pure interest, as in the case of the Garcia administration that weighed the benefits of limiting the exposure of his cohorts who may have committed serious crimes during the 1980s versus the inevitable outcry from human rights defenders at home and abroad (Youngers 2010).

Performance across issue-areas

Rules governing territorial defense: anti-terrorism, anti-piracy, and anti-trafficking

Peru has struggled against significant terrorist and piracy threats as well as human trafficking. Its long borders across open jungle and its inaccessible mountainous terrain have created important opportunities for illicit movement of people, goods, weapons, and money. Peru has made considerable efforts to publicly commit itself to halting these threats and has been partially successful, although not always without corruption and abuse of powers.

Table 6.1 provides a snapshot of Peru's efforts to protect its territory and people from trans-border threats. The Counter-Terrorism Committee of the United Nations Security Council has endorsed many of the measures the government has taken to strengthen domestic terrorism laws. Its only shortcomings were a failure to submit the first status report before the deadline and a failure to adopt (as of 2004) a law on the financing of terrorism – although Peru has ratified the convention on this topic. As we have already seen, Peru's efforts to end terrorism have had mixed results.

With respect to combating maritime piracy, Peru responded in some tangible and official way to seven out of twenty-three pirate attacks between 2001 and 2007, which is a low rate in relative terms. This, despite the fact that it has endorsed the principal international instruments addressing the need to protect seafarers from piracy.

Peru's anti-trafficking scores are all in the middle range, whether measuring primarily the government's efforts (TIP) or the policy outcomes (UN and Bales). This is so despite the fact that Peru has signed and ratified the key legal instrument on the subject – the 2000 Anti-Trafficking Protocol.

With respect to international norms on terrorism, Peru has shown increasing concern. In 1992, the Fujimori government issued a series of strong decrees against terrorism without much regard for international norms. In particular, terrorism was defined very broadly – too broadly from the point of view of the Constitutional Court which overturned the decree in 2003. Terrorists were also denied the protections of due process since they could be tried in military courts without the opportunity to defend themselves. Other decrees outlawed any advocacy for terrorism anywhere in the world, potentially punishable by withdrawal of Peruvian citizenship. And convicted terrorists were to receive life in prison without the possibility of parole (UNCTC 2004).

Table 6.1 Indicators of compliance with rules governing territorial defense

UN CTC total score	5 (7 possible)
UN CTC score, minus treaty ratifications	3 (5 possible)
Pirate attack response rate	30%
Total pirate attacks	23
SUA endorsement	Yes
SUA Protocol endorsement	Yes
US State Dept. TIP score	2 (out of 3, with 1 the lowest rate)
UN origin score	3 (out of 5, with 1 the lowest rate)
Bales trafficking score	2 (out of 4, with 1 the lowest rate)
WomanStats trafficking score	3 (out of 4, with 1 the lowest rate)
2000 Trafficking Protocol signature	Yes
2000 Trafficking Protocol ratification	Yes

These laws were used to considerable effect during the 1990s. Hundreds of individuals were brought before secret military tribunals on the basis of little more than hearsay. Ninety-seven percent were convicted. The rebellion was essentially crushed in a war that cost nearly 70,000 lives (most of them civilian). The international community was generally tolerant of much of this activity until the late 1990s. In 1999 the Inter-American Court of Human Rights demanded a re-trial for four Chileans who had been convicted without due process (Caistor and Villarán 2006, 51).

In 2003 the new Constitutional Court overturned a variety of anti-terror decrees on due process grounds. As explained by Peru in its report to the UN's Counter-Terrorism Committee, "By rectifying this situation, national legislation to combat terrorism has been brought into line with international standards" (UNCTC 2004).

During 2007 the Garcia government imposed states of emergency in parts of the country where *Sendero Luminoso* have become active again, suspending certain civil liberties and expanding the military's authority over civilians (Dept. of State 2010b). The key problem seems to lie in a growing link between terror groups and narcotics traffickers.

Maritime piracy continues to represent a low-level problem in Peru. Between 2001 and 2009 there were forty-one attacks against shipping in and near Peru's territorial waters. These attacks were largely successful, although they involved low levels of violence. The overwhelming majority of these attacks occurred when ships were at anchor or at dock. The port of Callao was listed as a "piracy prone area" by the International Maritime Bureau (IMB 2010). Crews under attack could not count on the Peruvian port authorities or coast guard to perform either a deterrent or enforcement function consistently.

Peru's navy is mid-sized at just under thirty ships, and the coastline is very long at more than 2,400 kilometers. So it is understandable that Peru struggles to protect its entire maritime border. On the other hand, since almost all of the attacks occur in one port, the real question is why the government cannot secure such a small area. Ultimately, it appears to stem from lack of political will rather than lack of capacity.

Human trafficking is a concern in Peru, although figures are very difficult to verify. The official government statistic in 2009 was 185 trafficked persons, although it is generally thought the figure is far higher (Dept. of State 2010c).

> Peru is a source, transit, and destination country for men, women, and children subjected to trafficking in persons, specifically forced labor and forced prostitution. Several thousand persons are estimated to be subjected to conditions of forced labor within Peru, mainly in mining, logging, agriculture, brick making, and domestic servitude. Many trafficking victims are women and girls from impoverished rural regions of the Amazon, recruited and coerced into prostitution in urban nightclubs, bars, and brothels, often through false employment offers or promises of education. Indigenous persons are particularly vulnerable to debt bondage … Peru also is a

> destination country for some Ecuadorian and Bolivian females in forced prostitution, and some Bolivian citizens in conditions of forced labor. Child sex tourism is present in Iquitos, Madre de Dios, and Cuzco. Traffickers reportedly operate with impunity in certain regions where there is little or no government presence.
>
> (Dept. of State 2010d)

This is the case despite the fact that these actions are illegal under Peruvian law. Trafficking is punishable by 8–25 years in prison. Trafficking for purposes of sexual exploitation is punishable by 8–15 years – 12–25 years in prison if the victim is under eighteen. Child sex tourism is punishable by 2–8 years, and such related crimes as kidnapping, rape, child pornography are all punishable by lengthy prison sentences (Dept. of State 2010d). Private citizens can initiate an investigation into trafficking (Xinhua 2010).

The fact that violations are fairly widespread stems largely from an unwillingness to devote the necessary resources to enforcement. Only thirty officers were tasked with trafficking enforcement, and the budget for enforcement of forced labor laws allowed the hiring of only five inspectors. The net effect of this was a mere nine convictions for sex trafficking in 2008 and five in 2007 (Dept. of State 2010c). And if the lack of resources were not enough, there is evidence, according to the US State Department, of complicity in trafficking and protection of traffickers by judicial and law enforcement officers (Dept. of State 2010c).

It seems clear that with respect to anti-piracy and anti-trafficking policy, the Peruvian government does not take international norms seriously. There are indications that much of what is done amounts to lip service, aimed – it would seem – at deflecting criticism from abroad. On the other hand, the government's commitment to combating terrorism appears far more earnest – to the point that efforts have sometimes exceeded expectations in that they have violated the due process rights of suspects as defined under international law.

Returning to the theories, it seems clear that democracy matters, although not to the extent hypothesized. The Peruvian government is constrained by a Constitutional Court that limits executive power and by a judiciary that, although independent, does not consistently enforce the law. Liberal trade policies may to some degree undermine compliance with rules designed to promote territorial integrity by reducing border controls and promoting the free movement of goods and people. This appears to be particularly the case with activities like sex tourism. There is no good reason why maritime trade should not be safe in Callao. This brings us to the managerial school, the predictions of which are consistent with the outcomes, although it fails to explain the antecedents. In the case of Peru, the lack of resources to enforce certain laws appears more a matter of priority than possibility, which implies that a focus on resources alone is misplaced. That said – the country's problems with corruption and human rights abuse make it clear that good laws and good constitutions are not enough to create good government.

To what extent are Peruvian policies motivated by a desire to burnish its reputation overseas? As mentioned earlier, it appears that much of what Peru is doing involves lip service to international norms. It is clearly sensitive to international criticism, and was quick to raise anti-terror laws up to international standards in 2003 – although it seems the primary force in that change was internal, that is to say an effort to reverse the human rights abuses of the Fujimori regime by its successors. Overall, reputational theory explains our outcomes poorly. Related to this, Peru's willingness to ratify international instruments seems unrelated to its actual policies, implying that legitimacy theory is equally unable to explain outcomes.

Cultural theory – as defined broadly – seems somewhat promising. Peruvians have mixed views about a range of issues that are critical to these rules. Although corruption is lamented, it is tolerated. Although terrorism is deplored, many sympathize with particular groups and are complicit in the production of cocaine that provides them with resources. Although many wish the borders were more tightly controlled, trafficking in contraband, drugs, and people is a way of life for many in the far reaches of the country. These conflicting attitudes and lifestyles seem to better explain why the national government displays a split personality when it comes to controlling its borders and suppressing threats such as piracy and terrorism.

Finally we consider rationalism. We have seen that different actors in Peru have very different interests with respect to these issue-areas. Most obviously the drug lords and rebel movements have begun to combine their forces in an effort to carve out control over lawless territory. Viewing these actions as a direct threat to Peru's territorial integrity, the Fujimori government opted to ignore international norms regarding due process in a calculated fashion. The project was largely successful in stemming the rebel tide, although it did little to stem narcotics trafficking. But the cost in human lives and human dignity (not to mention the rule of law) was too great, and under pressure from without and from within, Fujimori was replaced by others with different priorities – priorities that were more consistent with international norms. It is apparent that although "norms matter" in this case, the key issue was "whose norms" and how much power the various norm-carriers had at their disposal.

With respect to trafficking and piracy, the picture is still more complex, since it seems clear that different government officials are working at cross-purposes. The conflict in this case is primarily vertical in that national administrators are unable or unwilling to bring to heel the lower-level functionaries and law enforcement officers who are themselves challenging the norms. At this point, the situation appears to be at a stalemate, as local authorities are able to wield considerable powers of discretion and the central government has few resources to deploy to the frontiers – particular where interdicting trafficking is concerned.

Rules designed to regulate the market: shipping and airline regulation and CFC control

Rules that regulate market transactions are different in important ways from those that protect national territory. In particular, they necessarily involve foreign governments and firms and can therefore be expected to touch on questions on liberal trade regimes and reputational issues. Table 6.2 shows indicators of compliance. The record, as we can see, is very strong in these areas.

Peru's merchant marine fleet is small. In 2005 it numbered only four vessels. The figure rose to eight in 2008 and thirteen in 2010 (Indexmundi 2010). This includes one Bahamian-owned ship, proving that Peru has made its registration available to foreign corporations as a flag of convenience. The regional Viña del Mar Accord of which Peru is a member received Peruvian flagged ships and has inspected some of them out of concern that they might be in violation of safety standards. Two Peruvian ships were detained for having been found unseaworthy – one in 2000 and one in 2002 (Viña del Mar 2010). The fact that none has been inspected or detained since then points to Peru's likely compliance with international norms in this area.

Peru's maritime authority is sophisticated. It includes numerous directorates covered by numerous up-to-date regulations that are widely disseminated (APN 2010). Inspectors are empowered to enter any facility or ship in Peru's ports (Peru 2007). We can conclude that Peru is compliant with international norms.

With respect to airline safety, Peru's performance is comparable to most advanced industrialized countries, particularly following its initial series of ICAO-sponsored inspections. The United States Federal Aviation Administration has determined that Peru's pilot and crew training and fleet inspection programs for its international flights meet international standards and are not a cause of concern. There is evidence that the government steps in preemptively when it deems aircraft are unsafe (Dept. of State 2010e). Peru has adopted thirty out of forty-five multilateral aviation-related treaties for which it is eligible, according to ICAO records. By comparison, Brazil has adopted forty out of forty-seven and the US has adopted thirty-six out of fifty-one (ICAO 2010a).

As mentioned earlier, Peru receives a large number of visitors each year – on the order of two million. Peru has regular direct flights to nearly all Latin American capitals, several cities in North America, and Paris, Madrid, and Amsterdam.

It is interesting to note that although Peru's international airlines have strong safety records, the same cannot be said of its domestic side. Four accidents

Table 6.2 Indicators of compliance with market regulating laws

Cumulative Montreal Protocol compliance score	3 (0–24; low=compliance)
Reported data to Ozone Commission 2002–2007	Yes
Found non-compliant 2002–2007	No
Broke existing program 2002–2007	Yes
1999–2001 ICAO non-compliance score	19.46 (on a scale of 0–100; 0=no defects)
ICAO follow-up 2004	2.4
ali_standard air liberalization score	124 (0–183; high=liberal)

involving civilian domestic flights occurred between 2003 and 2010 (ASN 2010a). The situation was serious enough that the IATA instructed Peru to hire an outside consultant to train pilots and others in flight safety in the mid-2000s (QSL 2010). The World Economic Forum ranked Peru's air transport infrastructure as 86th out of 121 (IATA 2009).

Peru's public commitment to minimizing ozone depletion is high, as measured by its ratification of relevant treaties, public statements of support for the norm, and engagement in international organizations such as the UN Environmental Programme's Ozone Secretariat and its various committees. At the same time, however, Peru has been a consumer of chlorofluorocarbons and other ozone depleting substances. By 2001, it was ranked as the 41st CFC consumer in the world (Globalis 2001). In 2000, Peru's failure to submit timely reports and bring CFC consumption to zero during a UNEP-imposed freeze resulted in its being labeled non-compliant with the Montreal Protocol (UNEP 2006a).

Following a concerted effort to remedy the situation, Peru was praised by a joint UNEP and World Meteorological Organization oversight committee: "We consider that it is a great advance implementing these in Peru which is a country subject to paragraph 1 of article 5 referring to countries in a special situation" (WMO n.d.).

As of 2007, Peru had officially ended consumption of all nine types of ozone-depleting chemicals except for HCFCs – a safer alternative to CFCs (consumption in 2008 was at twenty-eight ODP tons [ozone-depleting potential tons]).

Taken together, Peru's approach to international norms on market-regulating issues appears to be the reverse of its performance with respect to the first set of issues. Compliance, while not always perfect historically, met international standards during much of the 2000s and sometimes exceeded them. What explains this pattern?

To what extent do the various theories of international law compliance explain Peru's compliance with market regulating norms? In these three areas, it is clear that compliance does not require going against public opinion. In fact, with respect to ozone depletion in particular, Peruvians generally accept the need to make sacrifices for the sake of the health of the atmosphere and climate (Senior Peruvian Official 2010). Maritime and airline safety are also consistent with the desires and needs of many Peruvians who make use of these modes of transportation and depend on the tourists and goods that arrive thereby. Political liberalism therefore accurately predicts these outcomes.

Airline and ship safety seem to be intimately tied with Peru's commitment to free market liberalism, something which can be explained by the fact that failure to maintain acceptable safety standards naturally leads to drops in earnings. Remaining competitive requires that your customers feel safe, and so trade liberalization – combined with the profit motive – naturally results in compliance. There is no indication that Peru's culture helps to explain the outcomes.

Peru's capacity to govern, as emphasized by the managerial school, is put to the test in these issue-areas. But in these cases the government has risen to the occasion. Administration of the airports and airlines has either been handled by what appear to be competent and well-trained government officials or by private corporations – also well-managed. The government has invested considerable resources into policing not only its own merchant marine but foreign ships as well. Likewise, government efforts to control ozone consumption have been effective, perhaps in part because only a dozen firms are involved and can therefore be more easily monitored with a small staff.

The reputational theory offers perhaps the strongest explanation thus far, namely that Peru was well aware that it was being watched by competent outsiders. Although in the case of CFC consumption the financial stakes were relatively low, Peru's image would be tarnished by non-compliance. Likewise, earning a reputation for safety would significantly improve Peru's competitive edge in the area of air travel where the economic stakes are quite substantial. With respect to maritime safety, it seems reasonable to surmise that Peru has embraced the norm in part because it was found deficient in the early part of the decade.

Peru was openly committed to the international instruments governing ship and air safety and ozone protection, which made it vulnerable to international oversight. But it is not clear that the commitment alone made a difference. Perhaps this was more the case with respect to ozone depletion where Peru was not only committed to the norm but actively involved in international bodies that enforced it. But it is clear that Peru is making a considerable effort to internalize the international norms in the form of actively enforced domestic regulations and standards.

Finally, and perhaps most importantly, the theory of rationalism goes far in explaining the outcomes. As was mentioned, Peru has much to gain from establishing a reputation for air safety and trading freely in air transport services. The financial trade-off is clear: money and manpower devoted to air safety will translate into higher earnings in tourism (as well as cargo transport and exports of lightweight, high-end goods). The government is also investing a great deal in the area of ship and port safety – perhaps more than is required by international standards. With respect to CFCs, while a few firms benefited from its usage, they have been able to retrofit and re-engineer their plants to accommodate other inputs while maintaining profitable production for the most part.

Laws on human rights promotion: anti-slavery law and anti-discrimination against women

Table 6.3 presents some indicators of Peru's compliance levels with respect to anti-slavery norms and the protection of the physical security of women. The record is poor. Conditions are far better for those urban women who have enough training and skills to be able to defend themselves, while abuse is common for women and children in poor, rural areas. In other words, men in Peru have not generally internalized principles of self-control, but can be deterred by the law.

Table 6.3 Indicators of Peru's compliance with anti-slavery and women's security norms

Bales' slavery percentage (est.)	0.02%
WomanStat physical security of women 2007	4 (worst on a 4-point scale)
Share of women in parliament	10.8%
Average age for women at first marriage	23 years
Proportion of teenaged girls who are married	13%

Slavery and slave-like practices are relatively common in Peru, although they are all illegal. Slavery involves women and children from across the country as well as large numbers of indigenous peoples. The International Labour Organization estimates that between 20,000 and 40,000 individuals in Peru are forced to work. Indigenous workers in Amazonian logging and mining enterprises – including major foreign firms – make up the largest group of forced laborers, many of whom are in debt peonage (Dean 2009; Dept. of State 2010f). Many domestic workers are also required to work far more than the maximum forty-eight hour work week and paid less than the minimum monthly wage of $192. There are an estimated two million child laborers in Peru, almost all of them in the informal sector (Dept. of State 2010f).

Workers have little recourse. Although unions are legal, strikes must be permitted by the state and are rarely approved. The number of labor inspectors is small. Labor inspectors have been forced to pay their own way to job sites and are often greeted with hostility (Dept. of State 2010f). Even when companies are found to be negligent, fines are often not collected. When workers are permitted to strike by the government, they face retribution by the company – including foreign corporations.

Moving on to the status of women, Peru scores alarmingly low in the WomanStats scale and is generally seen as a place where poor, illiterate, and indigenous women cannot expect to be protected from abuse by men. All such women are at times subjected to abuse by those men with whom they are intimate.

Abuse against women has been described as "epidemic." Two-thirds of Peruvian women report having been physically or emotionally abused at some point, typically by a spouse or relative (Freedom House 2010). Men's attitudes are mired in a misogynistic tradition of domination and control in which women are expected to play a subservient role. Even though many laws have been adopted to outlaw abuse, including spousal rape, few women seek protection under them.

> NGOs stated that the majority of reported cases did not result in formal charges because of fear of retaliation or the expense of filing a complaint. The protections offered were limited because of legal delays, ambiguities in the law, and the shortage of shelters for victims.
>
> (Dept. of State 2009f)

This situation is not just the result of a failure to prevent private actors from abusing their peers, but also from active government involvement. The Truth and

Reconciliation Commission reported that more than 500 rapes were committed during the civil war, and that "sexual violence was used by the state armed forces as part of an anti-subversive strategy" (Paez 2009). Three-fourths of the women who were assaulted by both *Sendero Luminoso* guerrillas and Peruvian soldiers were indigenous rural dwellers, and most were under the age of eighteen. The military has refused to cooperate with the Commission's request for names of soldiers who served in the areas where most attacks occurred and the government has closed down the Reparations Council for the Victims of Violence.

On the economic side, women are paid far less than men for comparable work and enjoy far fewer protections. UNIFEM scores Peru's protection of equal pay norms in the middle range of all countries (JICA 2007). Women on average earn roughly one-quarter of what men earn. For similar occupations, age, and education attainment, women earn 19.4 percent less than men (Asensios 2009). Three-fifths of women work in the informal sector where only 15 percent have health coverage and 4 percent have a retirement plan (Asensios 2009).

Since the early 2000s, Peruvian governments have drafted and promulgated a number of new laws and initiatives aimed at improving the safety of women. Laws regarding family violence were strengthened in 2003 and in 2004 a law was passed to create a network of safe houses for victims of family violence (JICA 2007). This is in addition to laws providing for gender equality under family law and in employment. Increases in the number of women in elective office have been remarkable, aided by laws which require 30 percent of all candidates be women. The creation of the Ministry of Women and Social Development has provided a focal point for reform initiatives that promise at the very least to ensure that data on women's conditions are collected and attention to the issue increases (Paez 2009).

But, as described by the State Department, these laws fail to alter outcomes for most women. "The law criminalizes rape, including spousal rape, but enforcement was not effective. There were no reports on the numbers of abusers prosecuted, convicted, or punished" (Dept. of State 2010f). In its assessment of conditions for women in Peru, the CEDAW Committee was equally blunt:

> While the Committee takes note of various initiatives at the legislative and policy levels to reduce violence against women, including the National Plan against Violence towards Women, it remains gravely concerned about the extent, intensity and prevalence of such violence. In particular, the Committee remains concerned that women experience significant obstacles in accessing justice, particularly indigenous women who also face language barriers, the lack of enforcement measures which contribute to impunity for perpetrators, and the persistence of permissive attitudes in society towards violence against women.
>
> (CEDAW 2007)

These are not the only important international actors to have condemned Peruvian treatment of women. In *K.L.* v. *Peru*, the UN Human Rights Committee ruled in 2003 on a case involving Peru's then-restrictive abortion law that allowed the procedure only in the case of a threat to the mother's life or health. It decided that Peru had violated several provisions of the Convention, including the prohibition against torture and cruelty (Article 7), by requiring a teenaged mother to carry her pregnancy to term even though the fetus was diagnosed as anencephalic and expected to die shortly after birth (it died four days later) (Rudolf and Eriksson 2007, 518).

Which theories of international law compliance best explain these processes and outcomes? To begin, liberalism clearly opposes the violation of basic rights of workers and women, and so the failure of Peru to live up to these expectations indicates that for all of the country's democratization, it has yet to internalize the full array of liberal values. On the other hand, the exploitation of workers and women has been an integral, if regrettable, part of capitalism's history. As with trafficking, the unleashing of free market forces enables and even encourages the unscrupulous profit maximizer to minimize wages.

The government lacks the political will to address this issue. Resources are not being mobilized even though they are available. Furthermore, the fact that the state has had a direct hand in perpetrating abuse or preventing the prosecution of suspects indicates that the problem does not stem primarily from lack of resources as hypothesized by the managerial school.

Peru seems ambivalent about its international reputation with respect to anti-slavery and women's protection norms. On the one hand it seems eager to promulgate new laws that meet international standards and does not dispute criticism from abroad when it fails to implement them, but nonetheless it fails to do what is required to secure international approval in this area.

Cultural factors seem paramount in these cases, where a history of slavery, exploitation, racism, and misogyny combine to provide cover for those who commit abuses. While this does not explain the fact that foreign firms have also participated in the abuse, it goes far to explain its persistence – particularly where women are concerned. The inability or unwillingness of women to upend the status quo is a rational response to a situation in which doing so will expose them to still more violence.

The willingness of Peru to endorse human rights agreements seems disconnected from its performance. It may explain some of the more superficial reforms that have been undertaken, but we would argue that domestic performance and outcomes reflect the lack of internalization of international norms.

Is human exploitation and abuse a rational exercise in utility-maximization? Certainly maintaining low wages and few worker protections redounds to the benefit of the owners of factories, mines, and forests. The fact that there appear to be few negative repercussions from these activities no doubt galvanizes the perpetrators. It may be fairly rational for the state to calculate that enforcement of laws governing the protection of workers and women would be politically risky since so many employers and men would consider it an intrusion into their private sphere.

Concluding remarks on Peru and theories of international law compliance

As we now consider the performance of our various theories of compliance against the case of Peru, several conclusions can be drawn (see Table 6.4). To begin, all of the theories provide interesting insights, and none of the theories explain everything that we observed. This outcome was to be expected given our previous findings from our quantitative analysis. The case study, however, provides new information regarding the rationalist approach. It clearly performs best among the various theories, explaining a great deal of behavior, and one could argue it explain some of the policies on the protection of women.

We undertook the case study work primarily to see more clearly the dynamics of compliance. Several observations can be made. To begin, it is important to note that compliance involves a number of discrete elements. To begin, there is the public face of compliance which typically involves commitment to international instruments and reports to international monitoring agencies. Next there is the formal internalization of these commitments – which may occur without any instruments having been ratified. Finally, there is the implementation of these new domestic rules in the form of altered behavior and outcomes. When this is taken into account, we can see that the liberal theory, combined with the reputational theory, the theory of legitimacy, and even rationalism, can explain rather neatly Peru's conduct. As we have seen repeatedly, Peru considers its international reputation separately from other concerns and makes rational calculations on the basis of what it thinks the international community expects. In particular, it cares about whether its conduct will be judged as constitutional as well as whether it will comply with international norms. Because the international community itself is often content to validate a regime's efforts based purely on legalistic gestures, it is easy to understand why Peru approaches this task as a separate enterprise and is usually eager to please.

Internalizing international norms in the form of domestic law also seems at times to be an exercise in sophisticated rhetoric. Domestic actors play a much larger role, however, as well as the political preferences of elite decision-makers. Calculations of what will tolerable to these various players enter into the final decision, but outcomes are not easily predictable and depend on the nature of the issue. When regime survival is at stake, all other considerations are dismissed, as we saw in the case of the civil war of the 1990s. On the other hand, where compliance is relatively costless – as in the case of ozone depletion – compliance will generally be full (although sometimes delayed).

Finally, when it comes to implementation, the story changes rather dramatically. It is one thing to sign a treaty and even adopt a new statute. It is quite another to devote resources and personnel, not to mention political capital, to actually bringing about change. And outcomes seem largely unrelated to questions of capacity, since capacity itself is largely a political outcome itself. Again, much depends on the mix of players and their interests. Where foreign actors are dominant and in a strong position to impose sanctions, as in the case of airline

Table 6.4 Competing theories of international law compliance and the case of Peru

"To what degree does the theory explain outcomes?"

		Sovereignty defense			*Market control*			*Human rights*	
		Anti-terror	*Anti-piracy*	*Anti-trafficking*	*Air transport*	*Ship safety*	*Ozone depletion*	*Slavery*	*Protection of women*
Liberalism	Political	some	some	some	much	much	much	little	little
	Economic	little	some	much	much	much	some	much	some
	Managerial	much	much	much	much	much	much	little	little
	Reputational	some	little	little	much	some	much	some	some
	Cultural	some	some	some	little	little	little	much	much
	Legitimacy	little	little	little	much	much	some	some	some
	Rationalism	much	much	much	much	some	much	much	little

safety, we should expect to see full compliance with international standards. But this is not always the case. We would expect, for example, to see strong compliance with anti-piracy measures but we do not – presumably because of corruption. In general corruption throws many theories into a tailspin since it exposes the fact that resources are fungible and sometimes privately controlled, with the result that national interests and plans are often poor predictors of actual policy. Even where Peru cares deeply about its credit-worthiness, national authorities are willing to permit high levels of piracy, trafficking, slavery, and abuse of women in violation of international standards and domestic law. One can surmise that the local trumps the national, domestic culture trumps international norms, and powerful criminal operations can hold their own in most situations.

Bolivia

Overview

Bolivia shares much with Peru, including a border, climate, topography, and ethnic diversity. It also enjoys considerable mineral and petroleum resources, as well as problems with physical access to all parts of the country and preventing corruption in government. It also expelled Spaniards in the 1820s and has also integrated economically with the rest of Latin America.

One might argue that Bolivia is like Peru, only more so. Where Peru has a sizable minority of indigenous people, they make up a solid majority in Bolivia. While poverty is ubiquitous in Peru it is endemic in Bolivia where roughly two-thirds live on less than two dollars a day (Gigler 2009). While Peru is a major supplier of natural gas and petrochemicals, Bolivia has the second largest natural gas reserves in Latin America, second only to Venezuela. While Peru has a functioning democracy in which an autocrat was identified and removed by political moderates, Bolivia has a raucous and rambunctious political system in which a moderate was removed and replaced (along with the Constitution) by a leftist, propelled by widespread unrest and supported by unruly social movements. It is worth noting that, while Peru has powerful cocaine traffickers that ally with rebel groups, in Bolivia the popular President is the leader of the coca producers' alliance and is working to make it legal (while still banning cocaine trafficking).

It would be a mistake, however, to draw too many similarities between the countries. Both politically and economically, the two governments have charted largely independent paths. Bolivia has seen peaceful transitions in power through free and fair elections for nearly three decades. Although for the most part the elections have brought to power minority governments that were forced to rule in coalitions, there was remarkable policy agreement across administrations. Beginning in the late 1980s the Bolivian government initiated economic liberalization, privatizing state-owned mines and other operations and welcoming foreign direct investment as well as foreign goods. Unlike Peru, however, the current administration has reversed some of these policies and adopted a more confrontational posture toward foreign investors and Western governments while at the same time establishing closer ties to Venezuela, Cuba, Iran, and Russia. Likewise, where Bolivia's political elite tended to represent the *mestizo* and white communities of the eastern lowlands where plantation agriculture dominates, the current government represents – and has tried to empower – the indigenous peoples of the central and western highlands. It has also provoked a conservative backlash in those areas where the governing party is still in the minority. Despite this, Bolivia's economy is growing rapidly and state coffers are flush with revenue, much of which comes from the foreign investors who are being forced to pay higher royalties for hydrocarbons.

Liberalism

Bolivia has enjoyed uninterrupted democratic rule for nearly thirty years – longer than most of its neighbors in the region. The military has remained in its barracks and plays a smaller role than in Peru, although it has been involved with suppressing rebellions and unrest from time to time – especially in the late 1990s (Europa 2010c). A US-funded anti-coca military task force was criticized as unconstitutional in 2003 (Freedom House 2005). Freedom House downgraded Bolivia from "free" to "partly free" in 2003 due to the growing disturbances connected to the resignation of Sanchez de Lozada in October. The transition was a messy one and has its roots in the unequal distribution of wealth in Bolivia and a perception on the part of many – particularly the poor – that nearly twenty years of economic liberalization had left the country poorer and more dependent on the West. Coca growers resented the efforts of the central government – funded and encouraged (demanded?) by the United States – to eradicate coca farms in the highland regions and saw this, as well as the generous contracts offered to foreign oil and gas companies, as evidence of the country having sold out (Morales 2008, 219).

Indigenous groups are difficult to count in Bolivia, although the general consensus is that they make up nearly two-thirds of the population. The 2001 census lists 62 percent as indigenous and a survey conducted by a research team from Oxford found 57 percent to be indigenous. But other surveys, including one led by a team from Vanderbilt University, found the figure closer to 20 percent, with two-thirds *mestizo* (Reyles 2008, 52). Most Bolivians prefer not to self-categorize along ethnic lines.

At any rate, it is clear that large numbers of Bolivians have felt excluded and exploited by the pre-2003 political system. Most prosperous departments, such as Santa Cruz, have seen their circumstances improve with liberalization while many highland departments such as Oruro that were already poor have seen conditions deteriorate. This was occurring despite the fact that the economy grew at an average rate of nearly 4 percent each year. The distribution of wealth was the worst in Latin America and becoming more pronounced. Efforts to redistribute land moved too slowly through the Sanchez de Lozada administration in 2002 to stem the frustration (Europa 2010d).

The situation came to a head in early 2003 after the government of Sanchez de Lozada proposed construction of a pipeline through Chile to ship newly discovered natural gas to the US. The proposal provoked a firestorm as critics accused the government of selling out to the US and cozying up to Bolivia's traditional rival Chile (Crabtree 2010). What happened next is described below.

> A hunger strike by Aymara leader and congressional deputy Felipe "Mallku" Quispe led his followers to begin blocking roads near Lake Titicaca. About 800 tourists, including some foreigners, were trapped in the town of Sorata. After days of unsuccessful negotiations, Bolivian security forces launched a rescue operation, but on the way out, were ambushed by armed peasants and a number of people were killed on both sides. The incident ignited passions throughout the highlands and united a loose coalition of protestors to pressure the government.... Tensions grew and La Paz was subjected to protesters' blockades. Violent confrontations ensued, and approximately 60 people died when security forces tried to bring supplies into the besieged city.
>
> (Dept. of State 2010g)

In El Alto, anti-government clashes led to seventy-four deaths (Europa 2010c). Evo Morales, the second-highest vote-getter in the 2002 presidential campaign, organized massive demonstrations against the government in mid-October and Sanchez de Lozada resigned. His vice president and successor, Carlos Mesa Gisbert, tried to contain the unrest, but protests continued and in June 2005 Mesa resigned.

Evo Morales won the presidency on the first round in 2005 and immediately set to the task of "refounding" Bolivia. His style is confrontational, and while he was wildly popular with the indigenous peoples he represented, his actions provoked a backlash among white and *mestizo* elites. He had difficulty securing the supermajorities in the legislature and the cooperation from provincial leaders he needed to re-write the Bolivian constitution. His plan involved first the creation of a Constituent Assembly that would take responsibility for drafting the document. The 255-seat body was elected in July 2006 and the President's party (Movimiento al Socialismo or MAS) gained 137 seats – thirty-three short of the two-thirds majority needed. He secured the support of independent members – enough for the document to become a referendum in January 2009. It was approved by 61 percent of the electorate and became effective in February 2009 (Europa 2010e). Morales was reelected with 64 percent of the vote on the first ballot to begin the first of two five-year terms. The new institutions share a great deal with the US system, including an independently elected president, a bicameral legislature, and an independent judiciary with power to rule on an act's constitutionality (Dept. of State 2010g).

Throughout the first Morales term, questions of regional distribution of power polarized the country. Although the new constitution provided for the devolution of powers to departments and indigenous areas, Morales opponents sought to acquire increased autonomy directly through mass mobilization and local referenda. Several provinces in the eastern half of the country approved referenda providing for greater autonomy, which were declared illegal by the Morales government. Violence erupted in 2008 as anti-government organizers in the departments of Santa Cruz, Tarija, Beni, Pando, and Chuquisaca "raided government buildings, sabotaged gas pipelines and fought with government supporters" (Europa 2010e). The government imposed martial law in Pando and arrested its prefect (Dept. of State 2008a).

Opponents of the regime also deplored what they considered "unbounded democracy" – the inclusion of social movements directly into policy-making and an increased use of mass mobilization, protests, and even violence to achieve political aims.

Along with political change, Evo Morales undertook a number of economic measures that upended the economy. Specifically, he increased government control of the hydrocarbon sector, which allowed him to cancel the contracts then in place with foreign oil and gas companies. They were given six months to conclude new deals and pay up to 81 percent of the value of production in royalties. He also called on Argentina and Brazil to renegotiate the terms of their own contracts with Bolivia (Crabtree 2010). As a result, Bolivia's tax revenues and budget surplus increased dramatically. However, relations with Western states and foreign investors generally cooled. As put by Morales:

> Bolivia is currently [2008] experiencing a difficult relation with transnational investors. Although the data are not very robust, it seems to be the case that investment has fallen even lower. Rates of private investment, in particular, appear to have continued their downward trend. There is no doubt that the hydrocarbons nationalization harmed the investment climate, even though its negative effects were reduced by the signing of new contracts.
>
> (Morales 2008, 235)

Despite the lack of new foreign direct investment, Bolivia's economic situation has been solid. The value of trade increased across the board, with the exception of exports to Japan, which were more than offset by a dramatic increase in sales to the South Korean market. Even trade with the US has expanded, despite trade sanctions stemming from Morales' tolerance of coca production.

Morales also undertook a massive redistribution of land in order to provide indigenous people with small farms. The new constitution also limited the maximum size of a plantation.

Managerial school

While Bolivia's governance appears fairly liberal and the rule of law seem solid on paper, the government struggles with implementation and enforcement, much like Peru. As we have already seen, local governments can and have challenged the authority of the central government. As put by Molina, the Bolivian state displays a combination of strength and weakness. State institutions beyond the capital are sometimes so weak that they are ineffective, and local power centers have emerged to fill some of the tasks. The result is heterogeneity in governance (Molina 2008, 109–112). For example, "only 180 of the 327 municipalities had a judge, only 76 had a prosecutor, and only 11 had a public defender" (Dept. of State 2008a) Some local councils have taken it upon themselves to carry out court proceedings and even execute those convicted, separate from ordinary judicial channels. Aggressive eradication of coca fields in the Yungas valley and Chapare district succeeded in reducing production only by half. Morales – himself the leader of the coca producers' association – has opted to focus instead on interdicting cocaine trafficking rather than production. The new strategy appears to be a concession to the politics and realities of the situation (Crabtree 2010).

Even where the law is enforced by formal authorities, there is generally little confidence that justice will be served. Only 21 percent of Bolivians in 2007 believed that judges "mostly" or "always" enforce the rule of law (Molina 2008, 113). According to a 2006 survey, many Bolivians have seen official corruption first-hand. More than a third report having been a victim of government corruption, with a quarter having been asked for a bribe by a local official. Oddly enough, well over half of Bolivians reported satisfaction with the operation of democratic institutions in 2008 (Zéphyr 2008). In 2006, Bolivia's Transparency International corruption perceptions index ranking placed it 105th most corrupt out of 163 – better only than Ecuador, Guyana, Paraguay, and Venezuela. Its ranking in 2009 had slid to 120th out of 180 (TI 2010).

Reputational theory

During the 1990s, much like Peru, Bolivia worked considerably to improve its standing in the West, particularly in the financial markets. The IMF increased funding and forgave loans, and the EU and US provided support to reward various governments for reducing inflation from four figures to single digits and for increasing foreign direct investment and exports (Morales 2008, 231–232). Under Evo Morales, however, the tone of Bolivian policy has been more confrontational and dismissive.

The country is considered a poor risk by credit-rating agencies, especially with respect to the ability of the state's banks to cover their obligations and international indebtedness relative to the size of the national economy. But Bolivia is rated high with respect to fiscal and monetary policy.

The picture, then, is decidedly mixed. It appears that the rhetoric of the Morales government is not always matched by its behavior – particularly with respect to fiscal and monetary policy – and foreign economic observers have taken note.

Culture

Many facets of Bolivian culture affect implementation of international norms. In general, Bolivians have tended to be more skeptical of the benefits of globalization than their peers in Latin America. A survey conducted in 2007 shows that more Bolivians have a negative view of the US than those from any other Latin American country except for Argentina. Even for those who knew someone who had emigrated to the US, only 41 percent reported that the lives of those emigrants had improved after arriving.

Many in Bolivia have seen how dependence on mineral exports has served the country poorly in the past. The nation was once a leader in silver production, but the mines gave out in the late 1800s. Then tin production became the economy's foundation until the 1980s when tens of thousands were put out of work when government-owned mines were closed. And so to many the discovery of large natural gas reserves seemed to be yet another chapter in the country's commitment to a natural resources that was bound to leave only foreign investors better off (Crabtree 2010).

It is worth noting that Bolivians' direct contact with foreign ideas is limited. Tourism has been growing in the 2010s, although tourist mostly stay in La Paz and Sucre. Only 3 percent of the population is enrolled in college, and there are only around 250,000 computers in the country. Cellular phone coverage has expanded rapidly, and is projected to grow from less than three million in 2006 to around five million in 2010 – roughly half the population (ITU 2008).

Bolivian families tend to be larger, more traditional, and less educated than in Peru, although literacy rates are relatively high and school enrollment levels are generally strong (although roughly one-quarter of school-aged children work). The status of women, as we will see below, is relatively low, but they are becoming increasingly mobilized to press their rights. More than 150,000 are attending university in Bolivia. The form of Catholicism practiced by over 80 percent of the country has elements of traditional worship intermixed with orthodox ritual and belief.

The country tolerates a high degree of racism against indigenous peoples, even though they constitute a majority in the aggregate. There are nearly forty official ethnic groups in Bolivia, of which the Quechua and Aymara make up 31 and 25 percent, respectively. Indigenous peoples are a much smaller minority in the eastern regions, making up less than 20 percent (Human Rights Council 2009b). For many Bolivians ethnicity and race have little to do with genealogy and much more to do with class.

Legitimacy

Bolivia is an active participant in a wide range of international and regional multilateral treaties and organizations. A founder of the United Nations and the Organization of American States, it has signed 334 multilateral treaties since 1945 and belongs to more than fifty distinct international organizations. It hosts twenty-six foreign embassies and has its embassies in thirty-four countries. It has been involved in a few cases at the Inter-American Court of Human Rights, including one it lost in 2009 relating to damages to victims of government abuses in the 1970s (IACHR 2010, 78).

In recent years Bolivia has become part of a small voting bloc in the OAS known as ALBA with Venezuela, Ecuador, and Nicaragua – all of which are led by left-of-center regimes that propose to serve as a political counterweight to the United States in the Western hemisphere (Shifter and Jawahar 2006). Morales has negotiated agreements on technical assistance and peaceful nuclear activity that could bring $1 billion to Bolivia and signed a deal with Russia that could result in a $4.5 billion investment in Bolivia's oil and gas industries (Europa 2010f). Bolivia's more tolerant policies on coca production, as mentioned, have resulted in the withdrawal of trade benefits from the US.

Rationalism

As discussed thus far, Bolivia is politically heterodox, with active and highly motivated interest groups and social movements, regional political players, and foreign interests that clash in dramatic and often violent ways. As already implied, it is not enough to know what the President and Congress think to know what will be the policy implemented on the ground. Particularly where a rule requires local enforcement, we should expect to see considerable slack with respect to carrying out the national government's wishes.

We have also seen that class plays a key role in Bolivian politics and administration, and we should expect that this will influence not only policy formulation but also implementation. Where rules relate to the interaction between classes and in particular improving the status of low-class citizens (women, children, and the poor), we can expect considerable resistance. On the other hand, the recent upending of Bolivian politics means that new deals will perhaps be struck.

Performance across issue-areas

Rules governing territorial defense: anti-terrorism, anti-piracy, and anti-trafficking

Bolivia is surrounded on all sides by five relatively peaceful neighbors. Its military expenditures are modest, however, at less than 2 percent of GDP, particularly in relation to the extensive border it is expected to defend (nearly 7,000 km). The northern half of the country is covered by almost impassable rainforest and jungle while the border to the southwest is mountainous.

Table 6.5 provides some of the indicators of Bolivia's compliance laws governing terrorism and trafficking. We should note that because Bolivia is landlocked, we will not consider Bolivia's response to maritime piracy, although because it has a sizable merchant marine fleet under its flag, we will consider its actions with respect to maritime safety.

Table 6.5 Indicators of Bolivian compliance with territorial defense norms

UN CTC total score	4 (7 possible)
UN CTC score, minus treaty ratifications	2 (5 possible)
US State Dept. TIP score	3 (out of 3, with 1 the lowest rate)
WomanStats trafficking score	3 (out of 4, with 1 the lowest rate)
2000 Trafficking Protocol signature	Yes
2000 Trafficking Protocol ratification	No

With respect to anti-terrorism measures, the figures provided in Table 6.5 are depressed because the government recently signed the last of the twelve anti-terror instruments but had not yet ratified them when the score was tallied. In addition, Bolivia signed the regional anti-terror instrument, known as the Inter-American Convention Against Terrorism (Privacy International 2004). Between the attacks on September 11, 2001 and the inauguration of Evo Morales in January 2006, Bolivian governments were in lock-step with the United States' war against global terror. The government provided intelligence, logistical, and diplomatic support and was one of the darlings of the region from the American point of view. Eighty percent of the public supported the war on terror (Pew 2007).

At home, the US provided training and support for Bolivia's somewhat limited anti-terror efforts. The threat has come from two home-grown indigenous groups, including the Tupac Katari Guerrilla Army and the Nestor Paz Zamora Committee. The government established a centralized anti-terrorism unit in 2004 to bring under one roof a variety of anti-terror centers. The unit directs the operations of the military, the police, and intelligence organizations, primarily to pursue narcotics traffickers and their paramilitary wings (Terrorism Research 2010). As mentioned earlier, the effort has been partly successful, with the amount of acreage devoted to coca production dropping by half from 1998 to 2005.

With the election of Morales, the tone of Bolivia's anti-terrorism policy changed markedly. The country's improved relations with Iran – a state sponsor of terrorism according to the United States – is perhaps the most dramatic evidence of this shift. The government is cooperating less with the US in areas such as intelligence sharing and investigation of terror financing. It dragged its feet on creating an effective "financial intelligence unit" (FIU), which led to Bolivia's being dropped from the Egmont Group of national FIUs in 2007 (Dept. of State 2008b). Subsequently, the government introduced new legislation to tighter laws against money-laundering and was readmitted to the Group. Overall, commitment to and compliance with global anti-terror norms appear high, although it will be interesting to see whether the Morales government will maintain that commitment.

With respect to human trafficking, the picture is far more disturbing. The fact that Bolivia was given a score of 3 by the Trafficking in Persons unit of the US State Department is indicative of a serious problem and carries automatic sanctions. The WomanStats figure is 3 out of 4 – with 4 representing the worst situation with respect to controlling trafficking.

Bolivia is primarily a source country for trafficking. Because of this, the government of Bolivia has fewer incentives to address the problem. The victims of the crime are outside the country, after all.

With respect to the scale of the problem, only anecdotal evidence is available. It is estimated that a half million Bolivians are in Argentina illegally. As explained by the UN official responsible for trafficking in Bolivia:

> Between July 2006 and August 2007, 10 children disappeared monthly on the border between Bolivia and Argentina.... One major problem is that in Bolivia, it is common that parents in rural areas give their children to so-called godfathers or godmothers who pledge to provide the children with food and education in the city. This practice of entrusting children to friends or family is often a covered form of domestic trafficking in persons. Another issue is that many children are taken across the border by persons who are not their parents. In such cases, according to Bolivian law, two witnesses can simply sign the required authorization. Last year, it was found that a Judge for Minors had falsified these authorizations and ... signatures had been bought.
>
> (Albertin 2008)

The US State Department indicates that "hundreds" of children leave the country under "suspicious circumstances" each month. This implies that the number of Bolivian children being trafficked each year is likely in the thousands (Dept. of State 2010h).

In addition to children, vulnerable men and women are also leaving the country for uncertain futures. Bolivian women are routinely found in brothels and sweatshops in Buenos Aires, Rio de Janeiro, Santiago, Lima, Madrid, and the United States. This stems in large part from the lack of resources for border police as well as corruption. The government is taking steps to create new anti-trafficking police units. They have already been deployed in the four largest cities and plans are in place to establish them along the southern and western borders with Peru, Argentina, and Brazil (Dept. of State 2010h).

The government has also adopted new laws (2006) to outlaw and punish trafficking. But most of its efforts are focused on foreigners or *indios* who have been brought to La Paz and other cities. Although the efforts are timid, they have identified hundreds such individuals. Where Bolivia falls down is in the area of prosecution and conviction. As reported by the State Department, out of 288 open cases in 2009,

> [t]he Bolivian government reported 21 prosecutions initiated and seven trafficking offenders convicted in 2009; three of the seven convicted offenders were given suspended sentences and released, while the other sentences ranged from three to 12 years. These actions compare with 64 prosecutions initiated and seven convictions obtained in 2008.
>
> (Dept. of State 2010h)

This implies that a human trafficker has less than a 3 percent chance of being convicted and a less than 2 percent chance of serving a prison sentence (ten out of 517). Little of Bolivia's effort is funded by regular budget expenditures, but rather is paid for by international governmental and non-governmental efforts, and carries all the unpredictability inherent in project financing (Dept. of State 2010h).

To what extent do our theories of international compliance explain these outcomes? To begin, it appears that democratic institutions in Bolivia have restrained some excesses with respect to fighting terrorism. The state has generally operated within the confines of the laws – laws which embody international norms of due process and proper rules of engagement. With respect to fighting trafficking, it appears that the domestic political institutions are capable of drafting a reasonable strategy but not of implementing it. This may stem in part from the fact that Bolivia has largely embraced principles of free trade and the free movement of people. As a result, it is easy for individuals and groups to migrate from Bolivia to other countries.

It is fairly clear that the managerial school offers an explanation for both the strength of anti-terror measures and the weakness of anti-trafficking policies. Simply put, trafficked persons and their exploiters far outnumber terrorists in Bolivia. Furthermore, terrorists must make themselves known to be effective while traffickers generally prefer to hide. Applying the "squeaky wheel" model, it is understandable that the government would pursue terrorists more vigorously than traffickers. Add to that the likelihood that some officials benefit personally from human trafficking and it is easy to see why enforcement differs so much.

With respect to questions of reputation, Bolivia's recent history presents a puzzle. On the one hand, the government has consistently embraced anti-trafficking norms without putting them into practice, while on the other hand successive Bolivian governments have adopted very different rhetorical postures regarding terrorism even though the actual policies have changed very little. Bolivia has actually increased its commitment to halting money-laundering while publicly rejecting the US approach.

Cultural factors seem unrelated to Bolivia's current anti-terror regime, although they may help explain the ambivalence with respect to trafficking. Bolivians clearly have a tradition of emigration – some estimate that a quarter of all persons born in Bolivia are now living outside the country. Likewise, the status of indigenous people, women, children, and the poor is low, not only socially but also psychologically. Since many trafficked persons fall into more than one of these categories, it is certainly conceivable that their plight may be easy for most Bolivians to ignore. Finally, the participation of some officials in trafficking fits the culture of corruption we've discussed.

It is worth noting that although Bolivia pledges to comply with international trafficking norms, the fact remains that it did not ratify the 2000 Protocol until 2006 and that it has placed a reservation with respect to a dispute over the Protocol between two parties being referred to the ICJ (UN 2010a). With respect to anti-terror law, however, the formal commitment has been more impressive, implying that there is at least a correlation between Bolivia's choices to be bound by legal instruments on the one hand and its policy behavior at home.

Finally, rationalism seems to provide some conflicting explanations, particularly when we ask ourselves if the outcomes were predictable. It would be fairly easy to predict, for example, that right-leaning governments in Bolivia, a country which is dependent on foreign corporations for its key exports, might be willing to kowtow a bit to the US and make every effort to please. This explains Bolivian anti-terror policy rather neatly, although it leaves anti-trafficking policy a mystery. Likewise we might have predicted that a left-leaning populist government might take relish in turning its back on international rules dear to the US. But in fact there was no fundamental reversal, even in the controversial area of anti-terror law. Looking inside Bolivia, it seems clear that various elements within the governments and within society are competing to influence policy in these two areas. Terrorism appears to be the weapon of the politically weak while counter-terrorism is the concern of the politically powerful. Finally, the lack of enthusiasm for anti-trafficking measures seems consistent with rationalism, but only because of the pervasive cultural norm that discriminates against its victims.

Rules designed to regulate the market: shipping and airline regulation and CFC control

Given Bolivia's poverty and deficiencies with respect to governing capacity, we would expect that regulating private actors in the market would pose a substantial challenge. We will see below whether this is borne out. Table 6.6 provides some data on Bolivia's degree of compliance with these rules.

With respect to maritime safety, although Bolivia is landlocked, the government's tiny commercial fleet has become notorious. Bolivia is one of those "flags of convenience" that sells its official sponsorship for a fee (DeSombre 2008, 164). In 2010, seven ships out of a fleet of twenty-nine are foreign-owned (CIA 2010). It is alleged that another forty ships fly Bolivia's flag without its permission (IMO 2008, 2). Of course, for a land-locked state to become a flag of convenience presents one glaring problem: where would Bolivian officials go to inspect the ships that fly the Bolivian flag in the first place? It is a recipe for chaos.

And chaos is the result. Bolivian ships are routinely stopped and detained around the world. Based on the record, between 5 and 10 percent of the entire

Table 6.6 Indicators of Bolivian compliance with market regulating rules

ali_standard air liberalization score	83 (0–183; high=liberal)
Number of air partners	16
Cumulative Montreal Protocol compliance score	14 (0–24; low=compliance)
Reported data to Ozone Commission 2002–2007	No
Found non-compliant 2002–2007	Yes – four times
Broke existing program 2002–2007	Yes – twice

fleet is detained each year in Latin American ports alone (Viña del Mar 2010). Europeans have placed Bolivia's fleet on the Paris MOU's "black list." The fleet was ranked next to the bottom, besting only North Korea's derelict operation (EMSA 2010). Several specific vessels have been detained so many times that they have been given a warning that should they fail inspection one more time, they will be permanently banned from European ports (EU 2003). The IMO ranked Bolivia's fleet among the thirteen worst in the world (IMO 2009).

Bolivia naturally pleads poverty in its defense and also blames international authorities for failing to help. The Bolivian Maritime Administration (AMB) complained to the IMO in 2008: "As a developing country, Bolivia is in great need of technical cooperation. Since 2000 the AMB has benefited from only one IMO technical cooperation." It has also complained that port states do not always cooperate: "Late receipt of information from certain port State control regimes is making it impossible to take immediate action in cases of detention" (IMO 2008, 4, 5).

Bolivia asserts its commitment to maritime safety, and as of 2009 has ratified many of the relevant treaties (some are still under review by the legislature) in this regard (IMO 2009). It has taken steps to improve the situation by reorganizing the AMB and hiring more qualified staff. It has also revoked the registration of some of the worst offending shipping companies, dropping the total fleet by roughly a quarter as a result (IMO 2008, 4). It will also participate in the IMO's voluntary audit scheme, modeled on the ICAO's (see Chapter 3) (IMO 2008, 4).

Turning to aviation, the picture is far more impressive. Bolivia's airline industry is small, but important. Roughly half of the 500,000 foreign visitors who arrive in Bolivia each year come by air. The total economic effect of these visitors accounts for roughly 2 percent of the country's GDP (IATA 2007, 2). Bolivia is listed as "air partner" to sixteen countries, although a recent search of active destinations from La Paz indicates only Argentina, Bolivia, Chile, the US (Miami), and Peru. The La Paz airport is small and at 4,000 meters is one of the highest in the world. Most Bolivian cities have a small airport, and the safety record of local flights is good. Only six accidents have occurred since 2000 – no fatalities (ASN 2010b).

Bolivia has committed to the relevant international instruments related to air safety, and its domestic legislation and regulations are rated a nine on a ten-point scale developed by the FAA. Bolivia is at or above international averages with respect to safety oversight mechanisms, with its lowest score (5/10) coming in the area of personnel qualifications (ICAO 2010b). Overall, Bolivia's compliance with international civil aviation safety norms is very high.

Bolivia's compliance with the Montreal Protocol is relatively strong in substance, although ironically less so in form. Bolivia has committed itself to the battery of ozone-related international instruments and is active on the Ozone Secretariat of UNEP, including the powerful Implementation Committee (with which it has periodically run afoul). But Bolivia has routinely failed to submit the proper reports at the proper time, and has struggled to comply with all the demands placed upon it. It has been informed by the enforcement panel on a number of occasions that its use of certain ozone-depleting substances was unwarranted (UNEP 2006b, 283). Perhaps most significant, however, is that its annual CFC consumption fell from a high of 87.1 ODP tons in 1996 to 2.4 ODP (ozone-depleting potential) tons in 2007. It has suspended use of other ozone-depleting substances since 2001 (UNEP 2010).

In 2006 Bolivia was criticized by the Committee for its use of carbon tetrachloride – a banned substance. The Committee pointed out substitutes existed and that Bolivia was therefore not entitled to a laboratory usage exemption from the ban (UNEP 2006b). Consumption was suspended after 2007. Although Bolivia has been called to account for marginally inappropriate behavior, then, its overall record of compliance with the substance of the Montreal Protocol is strong.

Liberalism – or any theory that focuses on inputs that are relatively constant – can hardly explain the outcomes in this section of the study. Bolivia is extremely derelict – although improving – with respect to maritime safety, but it is fundamentally compliant where air safety and ozone depletion is concerned. There is no reason why Bolivia as a stable, albeit boisterous, democracy should have produced such radically different records. In all three cases the norms are crystal clear and the state should be capable of developing laws and regulations. Furthermore, considering the managerial school's predictions, it's worth noting that the sectors are all very small – involving just a handful of firms in each case. Although the expertise required to fully understand them may be demanding, it is not beyond the capacity of a government such as Bolivia's. Witness the fact that air safety – perhaps the most complex of any of the areas – has been the country's strong suit. What is particularly puzzling is that a democratic regime would authorize itself to essentially go rogue – to create a merchant fleet of virtual renegades and then leave them to themselves while collecting fees and royalties. This clearly violates any notion of rule of law embodied in liberal democratic principles. Nor does it reflect the capacity of the Bolivian government which simply chose not to deploy its resources. Perhaps it was an expression of extreme libertarianism – it is worth noting that things began to turn around roughly when the Morales government took office, both with respect to ratifying conventions and cleaning up the fleet.

The reputational school seems to help explain why Bolivia repeatedly promised to comply when given the opportunity, and it may also explain why it has generally responded to public reprimand. With respect to the legitimacy school, it is clear that – on paper at least – Bolivia was making every effort to internalize rules governing air safety and ozone depletion. But with respect to maritime safety, even though it subscribed to international maritime safety law, it defied it. Its first response to criticism was to turn on its critics by blaming the IMO for not providing enough assistance and the EU for not providing enough information. Surely government officials in Bolivia would have known that this is no way to prove one's bona fides.

There also does not seem to be a cultural component to this behavior. Culture also appears not to have a played a part with respect to air safety or ozone issues since these would have been handled by a small cadre of experts – most of them probably educated in the West.

The rational choice approach might have predicted that, despite all the international attention and disapproval, Bolivia would find the chance to earn a bit of hard currency through flags of convenience an irresistible temptation. It was not until international monitoring increased that it decided to discipline its fleet. With respect to air safety, international monitoring was always very high – as we saw in the Peru case. It would not be possible for weak safety standards to go unnoticed. The same is true for CFC consumption. So it would seem that where the market is concerned, Bolivia decided to see what it could get away with. It only complied after it got caught.

But this doesn't explain why Bolivia persists with the flag of convenience arrangement when the costs have risen so high. And it doesn't explain why Bolivia actually exceeds the international average for air safety. And it doesn't explain why Bolivia requested permission to violate a rule (with respect to carbon tetrachloride) then complied immediately when it was denied. But despite these reservations, the rationalist approach seems promising.

Laws on human rights promotion: anti-slavery law and anti-discrimination against women

A quick glance at Table 6.7 tells us that conditions in Bolivia are virtually identical to conditions in Peru. Roughly the same number of women serve in government (although the figure is rising for Bolivia), women marry at roughly the same age, and roughly the same number of teenaged girls are married. Female literacy, as we saw earlier, is lower in Bolivia, but women are generally safer.

With respect to slavery, Bolivia has outlawed chattel slavery and other forms of unpaid work. It has decreed a minimum wage of $55 per month and has enshrined a right to unionize, collectively bargain, and strike. The maximum work week is forty-eight hours and children under fourteen may not be hired (although they may be apprenticed). The police are charged with enforcing these laws and the Ombudsman may hear complaints of violations (Dept. of State 2008c). It has also ratified all the pertinent major international instruments on the subject, although it waited until 2005 to ratify the ILO's flagship convention on forced labor.

While no one knows the exact number, there are thousands of slaves in Bolivia despite these laws. Bolivia has a long tradition of servitude in haciendas, typically involving indigenous peoples and women who are compelled to herd

Table 6.7 Indicators of Bolivia's compliance with human rights norms

WomanStat physical security of women 2007	3 (1–4; 4 = worst treatment)
Share of women in parliament 2006	11.5%
Average age for women at first marriage	23 years
Proportion of teenaged girls who are married	12%

cattle, farm, and provide domestic service. The land reforms of the Morales administration were aimed at giving some of these people an escape route. But, as explained by the UN's Human Rights Council representative:

> The agrarian reform did not affect the system of relations that prevailed in the east, in the Chaco and in the north, thus perpetuating relations of servitude through a variety of formulas: *pongueaje* (compulsory unpaid domestic service), *enganche* (improper hiring practices) and debt bondage.
>
> Such relations continue to this day in certain medium and large-sized properties that are characterized by low levels of technology and productivity, and entire communities remain subjected to a system of servitude that prevails in agricultural and/or stockbreeding haciendas in exchange for paltry wages. According to International Labour Office estimates, between 5,100 and 7,200 Guaraní are subjected to such servile arrangements.
>
> (HRC 2009b, 13–14)

In an account passed along by the US State Department, we find more evidence of the problem:

> In 2005 the ILO reported that between 26,000 and 30,000 persons, mostly of indigenous origin, were victims of forced labor, harvesting Brazil nuts in Beni Department. The work was seasonal, lasting approximately three months per year. During that time landlords sold basic foodstuffs to workers at inflated prices; workers subsequently incurred large debts and were not permitted to leave the property until the debts were satisfied. Similar conditions existed in the sugar industry in Santa Cruz Department.
>
> (Dept. of State 2008c)

There are still other reports that to 100,000 children are working eight to twelve hours a day. Others estimate that roughly 22 percent of children (as many as 32 percent of those aged 12–14) are economically active (Dept. of State 2008c). The government acknowledges that more than 3,000 children are engaged in mining, trapped in a Dickensian hell. In general, child labor is considered normal. Half the parents in Santa Cruz felt their children should participate in the sugar harvest (ILO/UNICEF 2004, 16 in Sharma 2006, 14). Parents are also involved and often perpetuate it by sending children (10–12 years old) out to illegally work for middle-class families in exchange for room and board and schooling. Still others sell their children – sometimes to families out of the country.

The government devotes relatively few resources to enforcing anti-slavery law. There are merely thirty inspectors tasked with monitoring and enforcing worker safety laws throughout the entire country (Dept. of State 2008c). Child labor laws are therefore generally not enforced, although the government welcomes efforts by NGOs to monitor and publicize violations.

The government is committed to a plan to eradicate child labor and has created a national task force toward that end. But the body is under-funded (it has only one full-time employee) and lacks the capacity and authority to implement government plans (Sharma 2006, 18).

When addressing the status of women in Bolivia, much depends on whether one is speaking of plans and reforms on the one hand or outcomes and behavior on the other. For twenty years, successive governments in Bolivia have established and re-established many high-level bodies to address women's issues. In 1991 a National Policy Council launched a ten-year plan for women and children, which spawned the National Agency for Minors, Women, and the Family. In 1993 the Ministry of Human Development was created, housing the National Secretariat of Ethical, Gender, and Generational Affairs. In 1997 a vice-ministry of Gender, Generational and Family Affairs was created and in 2002 the Vice-Ministry of Women was created under the Ministry of Sustainable Development (UN 2010b). The frequency of change prompted the CEDAW Committee to warn against a "lack of institutional stability" in 2008 (CEDAW 2008).

The Morales government has dramatically expanded opportunities for women in government as well. The 2009 elections brought far more women into the legislature (28 percent of lower house seats and 47 percent of Senate seats) and the Cabinet (50 percent women), prompting a senior woman's rights activist to exclaim "Not long ago, 10 years ago, nobody talked about women in power in this country, that was unimaginable" (Menkendick 2010). This change has also been reflected at departmental and local levels, although much less so.

Finally, the government has passed pro-woman laws with remarkable speed. A short list over the past ten years includes the Family and Domestic Violence Act, the Law on Protection for Victims of Crimes against Sexual Freedom, Act #3325 on Trafficking in Persons and Related Offenses, the National Reproductive Health Act, and the National Public Policy Plan for the Full Exercise of Women's Rights (CEDAW 2008). Added to this are the large numbers of land transfers being done for women around the country – 10,300 in 2006, 2007, and 2008 (Menkendick 2010). Without question, successive Bolivian governments – and particularly the Morales administration – have devoted attention to the status of women. The CEDAW Committee was unimpressed:

> While the Committee takes note of various legislative and political initiatives to reduce violence against women, including domestic and sexual violence, it remains gravely concerned about the extent, intensity and prevalence of such violence in the State party, which borders on feminicide, and about the lack of statistical data thereon.
>
> (CEDAW 2008)

Violence against women is endemic, to be sure. One NGO reports that 70 percent of women have been abused at some point, 40 percent have been sexually assaulted, although others believe the figures to be even higher (Dept. of State 2010g). There is no law against marital rape, and assaults against women are under-reported out of a fear of social stigma or retaliation. Of those few women who report assault (less than 20,000 in 2009), only two in 100 actually see their cases go to trial (Ireland 2010).

Economic discrimination against women is also severe, although diminishing. Overall, women with equal training earn less than men despite laws prohibiting wage discrimination. Nationwide, women earn 54 percent what men earn, although in rural areas the figure is 27 percent. To make matters worse, indigenous women in rural areas generally earn half of what other women earn (UN 2010b). Overall, women own one-fifth of the land and in some areas tribal laws prohibits a remarried widow from remaining on the land of her deceased husband (UN 2010b). Roughly one-quarter of all households are headed by a woman, and of those, 23.3 percent suffer from extreme poverty.

To what extent do our various theories explain Bolivia's performance in these human rights areas? Democracy has had a profound effect on the empowerment of women in recent years, to be sure, and the increased presence of women in decision-making capacities promises that current reforms will be sustained – at least on paper. On the other hand, the decentralized nature of Bolivian governance is inhibiting nation-wide rapid reform, especially with respect to slavery. Economic liberalism also does not predict outcomes consistently since, as we have seen in other areas, it provides incentives to both empower and enslave. The search for reduced production costs can lead to enslavement and marginalization just as opportunities for entrepreneurship may empower and enrich. We see evidence of both in Bolivia.

Bolivia's poverty looms large as both cause and effect of its struggles in implementing human rights law and improving the status of women and the poor. Combined with a traditional – virtually feudal – culture and social structure that discriminates against women and the poor, the resources available to the state are small in relation to the task at hand. Although oil revenue has been increasing, it is not enough to carry out land reform on the scale that is needed, provide services and training to all who need them, and enforce the laws that have been passed. Add to this the problems of decentralized administration and official corruption and the situation appears virtually hopeless. But the fact is corruption could be addressed with administrative discipline, administration could be more centralized, and efforts could be more targeted to address most urgent problems first.

The Bolivian government is concerned about its international reputation with respect to human rights. Its commitments to international legal instruments are fairly clear, if somewhat slow. It has endeavored to internalize these rules to a high degree through a variety of institutional and legal reforms. In some cases the national policy-makers have even made common cause with international monitoring bodies and foreign governments to accelerate reforms.

Finally, Bolivian policy can be explained in part by actors pursuing their interests. But it is important to note that in at least one important respect, the interests of the elites coincide with those of the poor and women in the country. In a country where the powerful have rarely used their positions to bring benefits to the weakest members of the society, it is hard to say that this behavior is strictly speaking rational – or predictable. Clearly an ideological component drives the formulation of national policy today, just as opposition to the policy stems in part from traditional values and social structures. Of course, opposition to changes in labor practices is consistent with the short-term economic interests of many plantation and mine owners – not to mention some parents.

Concluding remarks on Bolivia and theories of international law compliance

Bolivia has made a good faith effort to acknowledge and adopt most of the international rules we've discussed – with the possible exception of ship safety norms. But the reasons for this are not easily explained by our theories. In fact, their records are even less impressive than was true for Peru (Table 6.8).

Using the same informal scoring system, we can see that none of the theories explains much of what happened in more than three issue areas, while once again political liberalism fares poorly, as does cultural theory. If points were awarded on the basis of one for "little," two for "some," and three for "much," then economic liberalism and the managerial school would score one more point than the reputational, legitimacy, and rationalism schools.

More substantively, this points once again to the fact that many factors are at work here, and some factors interact with each other in interesting ways. In the case of Bolivia, the market and state capacity to control it reinforce each other by limiting what the state is able and willing to do to alter domestic social structures and practices. On the other hand, democratic institutions are inherently constrained by what citizens – especially powerful ones – are willing to tolerate. Where the problem is smaller in size and more technical in nature, and especially where international monitoring is easy, these forces come together to increase the odds of compliance. Otherwise, the obstacles are considerable.

Overall conclusions on globalized democracy and theories of international law compliance

As stated previously, developments in Bolivia bear some superficial resemblance to those in Peru, as should be expected given that they are both globalized democracies. But when examined more closely we see that in fact the governments have responded quite differently to international norms. Most importantly, Peru's government took an autocratic turn in the face of a serious guerrilla threat while on the other hand Bolivia's government took a leftist turn to address endemic social problems. In both cases, the change of government was ultimately settled at the ballot box.

With respect to compliance, we have seen that except where air safety and ozone-depleting substances are concerned both countries have mixed records. For the most part they made what appears to have been a sincere effort to understand, accept, and internalize international norms and responded to international concerns when raised. Both Peru and Bolivia have at least one clear exception,

Table 6.8 Competing theories of international law compliance and the case of Bolivia

"To what degree does the theory explain outcomes?"

		Sovereignty defense		*Market control*			*Human rights*	
		Anti-terror	*Anti-trafficking*	*Air transport*	*Ship safety*	*Ozone depletion*	*Slavery*	*Protection of women*
Liberalism	Political	much	some	little	little	little	some	some
	Economic	little	much	much	some	some	much	some
	Managerial	much	much	some	some	some	some	some
	Reputational	some	some	much	little	much	some	some
	Cultural	little	some	little	little	little	much	some
	Legitimacy	some	some	much	little	much	some	some
	Rationalism	some	some	much	some	much	some	little

however, when they openly defied the international community – Peru with respect to prosecuting terrorists and Bolivia with respect to maritime safety.

In a side-by-side comparison, it is interesting to note that out of the six issue-areas common to both cases, our seven theories explained the outcomes to the same degree in twenty-six out of forty-two cases, and in no case was the difference greater than one degree. Put that way, then, the pattern of explanation is relatively consistent across cases. Specifically, we find that political liberalism and cultural theory struggle to explain most of what takes place in our cases. The managerial and legitimacy schools, along with the reputational approach explain the most with economic liberalism and rationalism in the middle.

What accounts for these results? Central to this work is the argument that compliance with international law is a multi-faceted phenomenon in which important factors interact with each other. This means that single-factor or unidirectional theory is unlikely to explain a wide range of phenomena. With respect to our two globalized democracies, several interactive and trigger mechanisms become apparent.

Rhetoric vs. reality. These two democratic regimes appear to seek membership in and approval from the broader international community for the most part. As a result, governments routinely seek opportunities to show their acceptance of international norms. This begins with signing international instruments and ratifying them (although sometimes after several years have passed). This also means adopting legislation to internalize these norms. And finally, governments are often willing to submit to adverse opinions of international tribunals.

On the other hand, actual implementation runs aground under certain circumstances. Certainly much depends on the interests and capabilities of key stakeholders; it isn't always easy to predict how these will matter. Nor is it easy to even predict what the interests themselves will be.

Democracy is inherently a struggle between groups, both vertically and horizontally. Actors gain and lose power, shift priorities, and form coalitions depending on the issue. The larger the number of actors and the deeper and more complex the policy shift proposed, the less predictable the outcomes. The more determined and entrenched the opposition, and the more institutionally powerful the opponents, the less likely democratic governments will be to actually implement their policies unless they can secure the support of still more powerful elements. Lack of resources or expertise in the government, official corruption or decentralized governing institutions can weaken a state's ability to overcome this opposition. Sometimes external actors can tip the balance, but at other times foreign intervention can backfire, which brings us to our next point.

Nationalism vs. community. Democratic regimes that are intertwined in the world economy always run the risk that the engagement will backfire. The globalized market can distort local wealth and power distribution, reinforcing stratification in some cases and disrupting them in others. Foreign ideas may lead some to challenge existing roles and prompt opposition from traditionalists.

How governments and international bodies deal with this tension is difficult to predict but vitally important. Consider how the Morales government dealt with terrorism. It knew that this would require it to take action against certain indigenous people who advocated some of the same social changes Morales himself sought. Doing so might have undermined his status as leader of the indigenous community, especially if it were known that he had done so with American insistence. On the other hand refusing to comply with Western demands on a key issue could provoke unpleasant outcomes. And so, as we saw, he apparently calculated that it was best to comply with American demands in private while criticizing them in public.

Capacity is a choice. Although Peru and Bolivia clearly lack the resources to do everything governments can take specific actions that will enhance or waste resources. And, of course, they can make choices about where to deploy them. In both cases we found specific instances where each government clearly chose to limit its own capacity to implement international law and other cases where considerable resources were mobilized and concentrated on efforts they considered important. Contrast Peru's efforts to combat terrorism in which no expense was spared with its meager efforts to combat maritime piracy taking place in the port adjacent to the capital. Conversely, there is considerable irony in the fact that Bolivia was able to dramatically increase its national income from oil and gas royalties almost overnight, but did not deploy resources to inspect the seventy ships that sailed under its flag. This is not to say that enforcement is possible – only that it often reflects the culmination of a series of choices by governments.

References

Albertin, Christina (2008) "Encountering Human Trafficking in Bolivia," UN Gift. June 9. Available at www.ungift.org/ungift/en/stories/encountering-human-trafficking-in-bolivia.html. Accessed October 21, 2010.

Andina: Agencia Peruana de Noticias (2008) "Analfabetismo en el Perú se redujo a 7.1%, revela último censo nacional," July 22. Available at: www.andina.com.pe/Espanol/Noticia.aspx?id=NiBnWpBzahw=. Accessed October 11, 2010.

Asencios, Martiza (2009) "Women Workers Forced into Informal Economy," *IPS* 2 December. Available at http://ipsnews.net/news.asp?idnews=49511. Accessed August 6, 2010.

Autoridad Portuaria Nacional (2010) Available at www.apn.gob.pe/c/document_liberary/get_file?p_l_id=32081&folderId=78135&name=DLFE-3480.pdf. Accessed December 4, 2010.

Aviation Safety Network (2010a) "Peru Air Safety Profile," *Flight Safety Foundation.* Available at http://aviation-safety.net/database/country/country.php?id=OB. Accessed August 27, 2010.

Aviation Safety Network (2010b) "Operator Index for Bolivia," *Flight Safety Foundation.* Available at http://aviation-safety.net/database/operator/airline-country.php?id=CP. Accessed August 27, 2010.

Boidi, María Fernanda (2008) "'Throw Them All Out?' Attitudes Towards Political Parties in the Americas," in Mitchell A. Seligson, ed., *Challenges to Democracy in Latin America and the Caribbean: Evidence from the AmericasBarometer 2006–2007.* Nashville, TN: Vanderbilt University, pp. 53–72.

Caistor, Nick and Susana Villarán (2006) *Picking Up the Pieces: Corruption and Democracy in Peru.* London: Latin American Bureau.

Central Intelligence Agency (2009) *World Fact Book – Peru.* Available at www.cia.gov/library/publications/the-world-factbook/geos/pe.html. Accessed June 5, 2010.

Central Intelligence Agency (2010) *World Fact Book – Bolivia.* Available at https://www.cia.gov/library/publications/the-world-factbook/geos/bl.html. Accessed November 30, 2010.

Convention on the Elimination of Discrimination against Women (2007) Concluding Comments of the Committee on the Elimination of Discrimination against Women: Peru. Thirty-seventh session, January 15–February 2. CEDAW/C/PER/CO/6.

Convention on the Elimination of Discrimination against Women (2008) Concluding Comments of the Committee on the Elimination of Discrimination against Women: Bolivia. Fortieth Session, April 8. CEDAW/C/BOL/CO/4.

Crabtree, John (2010) "Economy (Bolivia)," in Europa World online. London: Routledge. Available at www.europaworld.com.erl.lib.byu.edu/entry/bo.ec. Accessed August 26, 2010.

Dean, Bartholomew (2009) "Machetes in Our Hands, Blood on Our Faces: Reflections on Violence and Advocacy in the Peruvian Amazon," *Anthropological Quarterly* 82(4) (Fall): 1069–1072.

Department of State, United States, Bureau of Democracy, Human Rights, and Labor (2008a) "Bolivia." Available at www.state.gov/g/drl/rls/hrrpt/2007/100629.htm. Accessed August 20, 2010.

Department of State, United States, Office of the Coordinator for Counterterrorism (2008b) "Country Reports on Terrorism 2008. Chapter 2. Country Reports: Western Hemisphere Overview." Available at www.state.gov/s/ct/rls/crt/2008/122435.htm. Accessed August 26, 2010.

Department of State, United States, Bureau of Democracy, Human Rights, and Labor (2008c) "Bolivia." Available at www.state.gov/g/drl/rls/hrrpt/2007/100629.htm. Accessed August 24, 2010.

Department of State, United States (2010a) "Background Note: Peru." Available at www.state.gov/r/pa/ei/bgn/35762.htm. Accessed July 7, 2010.

Department of State, United States (2010b) Office of the Coordinator for Counterterrorism. "Country Reports on Terrorism 2008. Chapter 2. Country Reports: Western Hemisphere Overview." Available at www.state.gov/s/ct/rls/crt/2008/122435.htm. Accessed August 23, 2010.

Department of State, United States (2010c) "Trafficking in Persons – Peru," June 14. Available at: www.unhcr.org/refworld/docid/4c1883ce31.html. Accessed August 23. 2010.

Department of State, United States (2010d) "Trafficking in Persons – Peru," May 28. Available at: www.unhcr.org/refworld/docid/4c1883ce31.html. Accessed August 23. 2010.

Department of State, United States (2010e) Bureau of Consular Affairs. "Peru Country Specific Information," August 24. Available at http://travel.state.gov/travel/cis_pa_tw/cis/cis_998.html#aviation_safety. Accessed August 26, 2010.

Department of State, United States (2010f) "2009 Country Reports on Human Rights Practices – Peru," March 11. Available at: www.unhcr.org/refworld/docid/4b9e52cb8c.html. Accessed July 27, 2010.

Department of State, United States (2010g) "Background Note: Bolivia." Available at www.state.gov/r/pa/ei/bgn/35751.htm. Accessed August 25, 2010.

Department of State, United States (2010h) "Trafficking in Persons Report 2010 – Bolivia," June 14. Available at: www.unhcr.org/refworld/docid/4c188407c.html. Accessed August 24, 2010.

DeSombre, Elizabeth (2008) *Flagging Standards: Globalization and Environmental, Safety, and Labor Regulations at Sea*. Cambridge: MIT Press.

European Maritime Safety Agency (2010) "Quality Performance List of Flags (Black-Grey-White)." Paris MOU. Available at https://extranet.emsa.europa.eu/index.php?option=com…task… Accessed August 26, 2010.

European Union (2003) "IP/03/1116." Europe Press Releases. July 25. Available at http://europa.eu/rapid/pressReleasesAction.do?reference=IP/03/1116&format=HTML&aged=0&language=EN&guiLanguage=en. Accessed August 26, 2010.

Europa World (2010a) *Foreign Affairs (Peru)*. London: Routledge. Available at www.europaworld.com.erl.lib.byu.edu/entry/EE001628. Accessed August 26, 2010.

Europa World (2010b) *The Resurgence of Sendero Luminoso (Peru)*. London: Routledge. Available at www.europaworld.com.erl.lib.byu.edu/entry/EE001626. Accessed August 26, 2010.

Europa World (2010c) *A Return to Democratic Rule (Bolivia)*. London: Routledge. Available at www.europaworld.com.erl.lib.byu.edu/entry/EE000350. Accessed August 25, 2010.

Europa World (2010d) *Indigenous Peoples' Rights (Bolivia)*. London: Routledge. Available at www.europaworld.com.erl.lib.byu.edu/entry/EE000354. Accessed August 26, 2010.

Europa World (2010e) *The Government of Evo Morales (Bolivia)*. London: Routledge. Available at www.europaworld.com.erl.lib.byu.edu/entry/EE000351. Accessed August 26, 2010.

Europa World (2010f) *Other External Relations (Bolivia)*. London: Routledge. Available at www.europaworld.com.erl.lib/entry/EE000357. Accessed on August 26, 2010.

Freedom House (2005) "Bolivia." Available at www.freedomhouse.org/template.cfm?page=363&year=2005. Accessed October 19, 2010.

Freedom House (2010) "Freedom in the World – Peru," February 15. Available at: www.freedomhouse.org/template.cfm?page=22&year=2009&country=7683. Accessed August 23, 2010.

Gigler, Björn-Sören (2009) "Poverty, Inequality and Human Development of Indigenous Peoples in Bolivia," March. Center for Latin American Studies. Working Paper. Georgetown University.

Globalis (2001) "Indicator: Consumption of Ozone-depleting Chlorofluorocarbons – 2001." Available at http://globalis.gvu.unu.edu/indicator.cfm?IndicatorID=82&country=BY#rowBY. Accessed August 2, 2010.

Heritage Foundation (2010) Economic Freedom Rankings. Available at www.heritage.org/index/ranking. Accessed December 15, 2010.

Human Rights Council (2009a) "Report of the Special Rapporteur on the situation of human rights and fundamental freedoms of indigenous people, S. James Anaya* Addendum Observations on the situation of the indigenous peoples of the Amazon region and the events of 5 June and the following days in Bagua and Utcubamba provinces, Peru." A/HRC/12/34/Add. 8, August 18.

Human Rights Council (2009b) "Report of the Special Rapporteur on the situation of human rights and fundamental freedoms of indigenous people, Rodolfo Stavenhagen – Mission to Bolivia." A/HRC/11/11, February 18.

IATA Economics (2007) IATA Economics. *Economic Benefits From Air Transport in Bolivia.* Available at http://clacsec.lima.icao.int/IATA-Estudio/Bolivia_eng.pdf. Accessed August 26, 2010.

IATA Economics (2009) IATA Economics. *Economic Benefits From Air Transport in Peru.* Available at http://clacsec.lima.icao.int/IATA-Estudio/Peru_eng.pdf. Accessed August 26, 2010.

Indexmundi (2010) Peru Merchant marine. Available at www.indexmundi.com/peru/merchant_marine.html. Accessed December 3, 2010.

Inter-American Court of Human Rights (2010) *2009 Annual Report*. Washington D.C.: OAS.

Inter-American Development Bank (2010) "The Simpler, the Better: Peru's Tax Reform Program Succeeds by Making it Easier for Companies and Individuals to Pay," IDBAmérica, October 13.

International Civil Aviation Organization (2010a) "Status of Individual States with Regard to International Air Law Multilateral Treaties." Available at www.icao.int/icao/en/leb/StatusForms/. Accessed October 16, 2010.

International Civil Aviation Organization – Flight Safety Information Exchange (2010b) "USAOP Status for States which have Authorized the Release of Information Including Progress Validated by ICAO." Available at www.icao.int/fsix/AuditRep1_icvm.cfm. Accessed August 26, 2010.

International Labour Organization and UNICEF (2004) "Caña dulce, vida amarga: el trabajo de los niños, niñas y adolescentes en la zafra de cañ de azúcar," ILO/UNICEF, La Paz, Bolivia.

International Maritime Bureau (2010) "Piracy Prone Areas and Warnings." International Chamber of Commerce. Available at www.icc-ccs.org/index.php?option=com_content&view=article&id=70:piracy-prone-areas-and-warnings&catid=56:quarterly-piracy-update&Itemid=167. Accessed October 15, 2010.

International Maritime Organization (2008) Bolivia. "Responsibilities of Governments and Measures to Encourage Flag State Compliance." IMO Sub-Committee on Flag State Implementation 16th Session Agenda Item 3. FSI 16/3/12. March 28.

International Maritime Organization Secretariat (2009) "Shipping Industry Flag State Performance Table: 2009 Update." London: Maritime International Secretariat Services Limited. Available at www.marisec.org/FlagStatePerformanceTable09.pdf. Accessed August 26, 2010.

International Telecommunications Union Newslog (2008) "3G Network Launched in Bolivia." September 1. Available at www.itu.int/ITU-D/ict/newslog/3G+Network+Launched+In+Bolivia.aspx. Accessed October 21, 2010.

Ireland Refugee Documentation Centre (2010) "Bolivia: Information about Violence against Women and State Protection in Bolivia," May 25, Q12171. Available at www.unhcr.org/refworld/docid/4c07780e2.html. Accessed July 26, 2010.

JICA (2007) "Peru: Country Gender Profile." Available at www.jica.go.jp/activities/issues/gender/pdf/e06per.pdf. Accessed August 4, 2010.

Markwick, Sandy (2009) "Economy (Peru)," in Europa World online. London: Routledge. Available at www.europaworld.com.erl.lib.byu.edu/entry/pe.ec. Accessed August 26, 2010.

MATRS (2010) Multilateral Agreement and Treaty Record Set. Author's personal data set.

McClintock, Cynthia (2010) Professor of Political Science, George Washington University. Interview with the author, September 2, Washington D.C.

Menkendick, Sarah (2010) "Bolivian Women Making Big Strides in Evo Morales' Government." *Change*, February 17. Available at http://womensrights.change.org/blog/view/bolivian_women_making_big_strides_in_evo_morales_government. Accessed August 15, 2010.

Molina, Gray (2008) "State-society Relations in Bolivia: The Strength of Weakness," in John Crabtree and Laurence Whitehead, eds., *Unresolved Tensions: Bolivia Past & Present.* Pittsburgh: University of Pittsburgh Press, pp. 109–124.

Morales, Juan Antonio (2008) "Bolivia in a Global Setting: Economic Ties," in John Crabtree and Laurence Whitehead, eds., *Unresolved Tensions: Bolivia Past & Present.* Pittsburgh: University of Pittsburgh Press, pp. 217–237.

New York Times (2009) "Peru's Ex-President Convicted of Rights Abuses," April 7. Available at www.nytimes.com/2009/04/08/world/americas/08fujimori.html?ref=alberto_k_fujimori. Accessed October 10, 2010.

Paez, Angel (2009) "IACHR Calls for Justice for Victims of Forced Sterilisation." *IPS*, November 26. Available at http://ipsnews.net/news.asp?idnews=49430. Accessed August 5, 2010.

Peru, Government of (2007) Resolucíon de Acuerdo de Directorio #010–2007-APN/DIR, Callao, March 16.

Pew Research Center (2007) Latin America and the Pew Global Attitudes Survey. Available at www.cipcol.org/?p=450. Accessed October 20, 2010.

Pew Research Center (2010a) Global Attitudes Project: Peru. Available at http://pewglobal.org/database/?indicator=1&country=172. Accessed October 14, 2010.

Pew Research Center (2010b) Global Attitudes Project: Peru. Available at http://pewglobal.org/database/?indicator=16&country=172. Accessed October 14, 2010.

Privacy International (2004) "Terrorism Profile – Bolivia." Available at www.privacyinternational.org/article.shtml?cmd%5B347%5D=x-347–359608. Accessed August 23, 2010.

Reyles, Diego Zavaleta Reyles (2008) "Oversimplifying Identities: The Debate over What Is *indigena* and What Is Mestizo," in John Crabtree and Laurence Whitehead, eds., *Unresolved Tensions: Bolivia Past & Present.* Pittsburgh: University of Pittsburgh Press, pp. 51–60.

Rudolf, Beate and Andrea Eriksson (2007) "Women's Rights under International Human Rights Treaties: Issues of Rape, Domestic Slavery, Abortion, and Domestic Violence." *International Journal of Constitutional Law* 5(3): 1474–2640.

QSL Consultants (2010) "Aviation Courses Developed and Delivered by QSL Consultants in the Field of Quality, Safety, Security, and Human Factors." Available at www.qsl.cl/english/toc.html. Accessed August 26, 2010.

Senior Peruvian Official (2010) Interview with the author, November 3. Provo, Utah.

Sharma, Bhavna (2006) *Contemporary Forms of Slavery in Bolivia.* London: Anti-Slavery International.

Shifter, Michael and Vinay Jawahar (2006) "The Divided States of the Americas," *Current History* 105(688) (February): 51–57.

Smith, Peter H. (2007) *Talons of the Eagle: Latin America, the United States, and the World.* New York: Oxford University Press.

Terrorism Research (2010) "Bolivia." Available at www.terrorismresearch.biz/bolivia.php. Accessed August 25, 2010.

Transparency International (2010) Corruption Perceptions Index. Available at www.transparency.org/policy_research/surveys_indices/cpi/2009. Accessed October 20, 2010.

United Nations (2010a) Treaty Series: Status as at 22–10–2010 01:48:00 EDT, 12 a Protocol to Prevent, Suppress and Punish Trafficking in Persons, Especially Women and Children, supplementing the United Nations Convention against Transnational Organized Crime, New York, November 15, 2000. Available at http://treaties.un.org/Pages/ViewDetails.aspx?src=TREATY&mtdsg_no=XVIII-12-a&chapter=18&lang=en. Accessed October 22, 2010.

United Nations (2010b) "Bolivia: Beijing Report Questionnaire." Available at www.un.org/womenwatch/daw/Review/responses/BOLIVIA-English.pdf. Accessed August 26, 2010.

United Nations Counter-Terrorism Committee (2004) "Letter dated 19 July 2004 from the Chairman of the Security Council Committee established pursuant to resolution 1373 (2001) concerning counter-terrorism addressed to the President of the Security Council." July 22, New York S/2004/589.

United Nations Environment Programme (2006a) "Decision XIII/25: Compliance with the Montreal Protocol by Peru." In *Handbook for the Montreal Protocol on Substances that Deplete the Ozone Layer.* 7th edn. Available at www.unep.ch/Ozone/Publications/MP_Handbook/Section_2_Decisions/Article_8/decs-non-compliance/Decision_VII-17.shtml. Accessed August 3, 2010.

United Nations Environment Programme (2006b) "Decision XV/29: Non-compliance with the Montreal Protocol by Bolivia." In *Handbook for the Montreal Protocol on Substances that Deplete the Ozone Layer.* 7th edn. Available at http://ozone.unep.org/Publications/MP_Handbook/Section_2_Decisions/Article_8/decs-non-compliance/Decision_XV-29.shtml. Accessed August 3, 2010.

United Nations Environment Programme (2010) Data Access Centre. "ODS Consumption" and "Imports of Recovered/Recycled/Reclaimed." Ozone Secretariat. Available at http://ozone.unep.org/Data_Reporting/Data_Access/. Accessed July 28, 2010.

University of Michigan (1997) Study identifies worldwide rates of religiosity, church attendance. Available at http://ns.umich.edu/htdocs/releases/story.php?id=1835. Accessed October 14, 2010.

Viña del Mar (2010) Statistics from various Annual Reports. Available at www.acuerdolatino.int.ar/. Accessed December 3, 2010.

World Bank (2001) "Peruvian Education at a Crossroads: Challenges and Opportunities for the 21st Century." World Bank Country Study. May. Washington D.C.

World Bank (2010) Bolivia Brief. Accessed October 11, 2010 at http://web.worldbank.org/WBSITE/EXTERNAL/COUNTRIES/LACEXT/PERUEXTN/0,,contentMDK:22252133~pagePK:1497618~piPK:217854~theSitePK:343623,00.html.

World Meteorological Organization (no date – *c.*2002) "Stratospheric Ozone and Human Health Project: Report of the Third Meeting of the Ozone Research Managers." Available at http://sedac.ciesin.org/ozone/WMO/peru.html. Accessed July 28, 2010.

Xinhua (2010) "Bolivia Mulls Military Buildup on Borders with Peru, Brazil." Available at http://english.peopledaily.com.cn/90001/90777/90852/7098521.html. Accessed August 25, 2010.

Youngers, Coletta (2010) Senior Fellow, Washington Office on Latin America, telephone interview with the author, October 12.

Zéphyr, Dominique (2008) "Corruption and its Impact on Latin American Democratic Stability," in Mitchell A. Seligson, ed., *Challenges to Democracy in Latin America and the Caribbean: Evidence from the AmericasBarometer 2006–2007*. Nashville, TN: Vanderbilt University, pp. 251–276.

7 Globalized autocracies

Tunisia and Pakistan

In this chapter, we focus on pre-Arab Spring Tunisia and Pakistan. The two nations are clearly not mature democracies but they are tightly intertwined with the rest of the world – particularly the West.

Liberal theory is of two minds on these cases. On the one hand, since democracy and rule of law are important predictors of compliance, we should see weak internalization and implementation of international norms. On the other hand, since economic liberalism correlates with the type of societal penetration by foreign influences – especially Western – we should expect to see relatively high degrees of compliance. Other theories offer varied predictions. For example, the managerial school would expect autocracies will be able to mobilize resources while cultural theory predicts low compliance where international norms conflict with local traditions. Taken together, the cases are likely to present paradoxes for our theories.

Tunisia

Overview

Tunisia has been independent from France since the 1950s and saw two leaders prior to 2011: Habib Bourguiba and Zine el Abidine Ben Ali, who replaced Bourguiba in a bloodless coup in 1987. Ben Ali was reelected every five years and his party, the Constitutional Democratic Rally, dominated the bicameral legislature until his precipitous departure on January 14, 2011 following large-scale nation-wide demonstrations. The population of roughly ten million is almost entirely Muslim and Arabic-speaking.

The country is known for its attempt to achieve a precarious balance in policies on a wide variety of issues. For example, the Ben Ali government encouraged Islam, but worked to prevent fundamentalism by placing all imams on the state payroll (Freedom House 2010a). It encouraged Western tourism and investment, but placed severe restrictions on internet access and website creation. It worked with the US and European governments to combat terrorism, but opposed US intervention in the Middle East.

The country is situated in the Maghreb in North Africa, which places it at a crossroads in the Eastern hemisphere. It neighbors Libya and Algeria and sits

140 kilometers from Sicily. On the other hand, Tunisia is more isolated than most states due to topographical obstacles. It enjoys peaceful borders with its neighbors. The bulk of Tunisia's vegetation – and population and economic activity – are in the north. Most of the tourism and trade occur on the coastline while most of its mineral and petrochemical wealth is in the south. This lends itself to an economically diversified country.

Not only was Tunisia's political leadership remarkably stable over the years, its economic growth has been virtually constant since the 1980s, averaging roughly 4 percent per year. This stemmed largely from a strategic alliance between governing elites, urban business leaders, large rural landholders, and foreign capital (King 1998). The country trades most heavily with its European neighbors, exporting foodstuffs, textiles, petrochemicals, and an increasing variety of manufactured goods. Its imports consist primarily of finished goods of high quality, allowing Tunisian producers which have been increasingly exposed to foreign competition as a result of gradually declining tariffs to find a niche in the low end of the product spectrum (World Bank 2009, 28). Job creation could not keep up with population growth, however, and the unemployment rate remained at between 10 and 15 percent during this period (Europa 2010a). Poverty (those living on less than $2 a day) stood at roughly 8 percent in 2010.

The government used violence to suppress labor unrest and demonstrations demanding greater political openness (Freedom House 2010a). Widespread protests involving primarily unemployed college graduates and other professionals forced President Ben Ali to flee the country in early 2011 (The Guardian 2011). In particular, the nation's principal trade union, the police, and the army all joined the demand for political renewal, which led to a dismantling of Ben Ali's party apparatus and seizure of his family's considerable wealth (*The Economist* 2011; *LA Times* 2011).

Liberalism

We will now turn to a consideration of the factors that are of greatest interest to the various theories of international law compliance we've been examining in this work. Although opposition parties were repressed, they were not entirely outlawed. Opposition candidates routinely ran quixotic campaigns against the dominant party (Dept. of State 2010a). In 2009, a quarter of parliamentary seats were set aside for opposition candidates – up from 20 percent (Europa 2010b).

In 1988 the Constitution was amended with the creation of a Constitutional Council which took over the monitoring of presidential and legislative elections from the legislature itself. In 1999, a National Elections Observatory was created to monitor all elections and submit a report on their fairness (World Bank 2008, 42–46). The Constitutional Council could rule on the constitutionality of laws passed by the legislature. And freedom of association, press, and expression were enshrined in constitutional law, along with gender equality. In fact, as we will see later, the status of women under the law was among the highest in the Arab world.

Many of these laws were ignored in practice, however.

> Ben Ali carefully crafted these reforms in ways that set very real limits on the amount of actual power that the opposition can win at the ballot box and the amount of criticism they can level through the media or human rights organizations
>
> (Alexander 2010, 115)

The Constitutional Council members acted as if they served at the pleasure of the President (Dept. of State 2010a).

In the society at large, bodies that might articulate alternative perspectives were either repressed or self-censored. The NGO community was filled with groups that were led by friends or cronies of the government (Henry 2007, 308). Academia was self-censored, although criticism of the government is permissible in private. It is noteworthy, however, that prior to his ultimate departure from Tunisia on January 14, President Ben Ali gave orders to security forces to cease using violence.

The press experienced repression under Ben Ali. Journalists were harassed, roughed up, fired from their positions, and imprisoned, with their presses starved for paper, ransacked, and destroyed.

Finally, treatment of prisoners – especially Islamic fundamentalists – fell far short of international standards for due process. Political prisoners numbered as many as 1,000, although the government released a few from time to time, presumably for cosmetic reasons.

Corruption on the part of the ruling family itself was carefully concealed, and most Tunisians appeared to be content with the level of police and army protection and performance. For those who opposed the regime, risks were great. A judge in 2001 wrote an editorial deploring the fact that his judgments were required to "reflect nothing by the interpretations of law that political authority wishes to impart." He was sacked for his comments (Yahtaoui 2001).

With respect to economic liberalism, Tunisia is among the more progressive in Africa and the Arab world. Since the early 1990s, the Ben Ali government moved away from state controls of the market and key industries in favor of gradual but deliberate reduction of tariffs and quotas on the one hand and of controls on private investment on the other. Combined with some steps in the direction of privatization of state-owned assets, the Tunisian economy is currently quite open. The value of Tunisia's exports in 2006 and 2007 was roughly equal to half the GDP and imports outpaced exports by a small margin.

France and Tunisia have enjoyed a relatively warm relationship which culminated in a $100 million aid package and an agreement to support Tunisia's nuclear power program in mid-2009 (Human Rights Watch 2010). Even as Ben Ali faced off against demonstrators in 2011, France stood by him (*New York Times* 2011b). The EU and Tunisia entered into negotiations to lower the latter's tariff and quota structure over a period of time, beginning in 1995, by granting Tunisia associate status. The government lowered what was an average 100 percent tariff rate in 1996 to 4 percent in 2007, taking care to provide support for firms that were especially vulnerable to foreign competition (World Bank 2009, 3). Tunisia's membership in the World Trade Organization also pushed it to lower trade barriers and by the mid-2000s its textile industry was unprotected. Some European and American firms have moved production into Tunisia to take advantage of free access to the EU market, although the level of FDI has not grown as quickly as expected (Alexander 2010, 83–84). Cronyism and favoritism in business transactions among the major political players and their families may account for some reticence on the part of investors (Freedom House 2010a).

Tunisia's foreign debt is sizable but manageable, running at roughly 60 percent of GDP in recent years – down from 70 percent in the 1980s. And Tunisia's foreign reserves have increased dramatically of late, reaching $8 billion in 2008. Tourism from Europe remains high, with close to four million arriving annually and another 2.5 million coming from neighboring Libya and Algeria. Taken together, tourism brings in roughly $3 billion to the Tunisian economy each year, or nearly 10 percent of GDP – although this sometimes drops during periods of recession in the West (Europa 2010c).

Managerial school

Tunisia's police force stood at 100,000 members in 2005 – or roughly one policeman for every one hundred Tunisians (in Britain the figure is around one for every 380 citizens). Some estimate that figure was matched by the number of plainclothes officers (Henry 2007, 301; The Guardian 2011). In addition, one in five Tunisian workers had a government job (Lust 2011, 711). Tunisia spent more than 7 percent of its GDP on education in recent years. Total government spending was 30 percent of GDP indicating a high capacity to mobilize tax revenues. What the state could not do, however, was give its young population hope.

Tunisia's governance capacity is above the average for the world and well above the average for developing countries. For example, Tunisia's World Bank anti-corruption score placed it in the top third of all countries rated (50/152). Likewise for governing effectiveness. It ranked 65th out of 180 in the Transparency International rankings – just below Italy but well above Greece. Of course, it is likely that this rank would have been much lower had the full extent of Ben Ali's financial abuses been fully understood (*The Economist* 2011).

The military is professionalized and has avoided a political role, especially where repressing Islamic groups was concerned (Lawson 2007, 125). Corruption was a serious issue as the ruling family secured control over large swaths of the nation's economy. The President's second wife, Leila Trabelsi, and her relatives rose from very humble positions to great wealth as a result of privileges and favors stemming from her marriage (Nawaat 2010). Note, for example, this analysis from the World Bank in 2007:

> Weaknesses in economic governance, particularly regarding the predictability and transparency of the regulatory framework and limited market contestability constitute an important constraint for private investment.... Discretionary intervention by the government, low levels of public

> accountability, voice and participation contribute to weakening the investment climate and strengthening the hand of "insiders," mostly in the absence of strong competitive forces. This contributes to reducing market contestability and discouraging risk taking by less well-connected entrepreneurs.
>
> (World Bank 2008, 4)

Reputational theory

Tunisia's concern about its reputation varies from topic to topic, however. While under Ben Ali it was eager to attract Western aid, investment, and travelers, it did not necessarily seek Western approval for its domestic policies. Tunisian authorities bristled when French or American diplomats suggest the need to open up the political system, even as they strongly defended the course of democratization (or lack thereof) in Tunisia (see especially Tunisia's rebuttal to the World Bank's criticism of the government's lack of accountability in World Bank 2008, 42–47).

Tunisia qualified to receive a rating by Moody's and that rating was in middle range – strong relative to what we find in Africa and the Arab world and enabled Tunisia to be fully engaged with the global market.

Tunisia has been eager to be seen as a trusted ally in the war against terror. Even before 9/11, Tunisia worked closely with Western countries to monitor and curtail the activities of Islamic fundamentalists, and since 9/11 it continued to provide intelligence and participate in American-led operations to root out Al Qaeda and its cohorts. Ben Ali was rewarded with a steady stream of senior Western diplomats coming to Tunis to pay their respects and offer moral and material support (Lawless *et al.* 2010).

The strategy paid off, in that Western governments generally turned a blind eye to Tunisia's more egregious human rights violations. As explained by Alexander:

> French officials occasionally have issued carefully worded statements about the importance of human rights and the rule of law. But they have never taken stronger measures because, in the final analysis, Ben Ali's value as a leader who maintains stability and encourages economic development trumps concerns about his authoritarianism.
>
> (Alexander 2010, 93)

Culture

Tunisians are almost all Muslim, albeit moderates for the most part. Imams were on the government payroll and mosques were closed except during prayer time. There were no anti-Western diatribes during long Friday services, and active Islamic fundamentalists, as we have seen, risked imprisonment, torture, or death. Individual practice of Islam is disrupted by the state, which discouraged the wearing of head scarves (*hijab*) by women. And publications by mosques were reviewed by government officials prior to dissemination.

Family courts sometimes applied Shari'a law in particular cases, although in general the equal status of women is protected. Inter-faith marriages are even tolerated so long as any Tunisian Muslim who was married to a non-Muslim had the ceremony performed outside of the country (Dept. of State 2009a).

At a social level, Tunisian family life varies in its degree of tradition. Tunis and other cosmopolitan coastal cities are more Westernized than their counterparts to the south, something that becomes apparent to casual visitors. But throughout the country there is a general acceptance of women having a prominent role in society. Women's numbers in school at all levels – including tertiary – is nearly equal to men's, although female literacy is substantially lower (70 percent vs. 86 percent in 2007). Women have been voting since independence and nearly a quarter of legislators are female.

Perhaps most significant, large numbers of both men and women in Tunisia agree that women deserve a status in society roughly equal to that of men. In a survey conducted by Gallup in 2007, 73 percent of men and 83 percent of women agreed that women should have rights equal to men. Seventy-nine percent of men and 84 percent of women agreed that women should be able to choose candidates freely when it came time to vote. Eighty percent of women and 72 percent of men believed women should be able to work outside the home. And 76 percent and 65 percent of women and men, respectively, agreed that women should be able to hold the most senior posts in government (Rheault 2007).

Legitimacy

Tunisia has been an active member of the United Nations and a wide range of other universal and regional international organizations. It has signed 361 multilateral treaties since 1945 and has a reputation as a conciliator and solid negotiator. It was elected for a two-year term on the UN Security Council, serving from 2000 to 2002, and on ECOSOC in 1996–1998. More than 6,000 Tunisians have been deployed in more than a dozen UN peacekeeping missions over the years (Tunisia Ministry of Defense 2010).

Tunisia is engaged in the Arab League, albeit not a leader, and recently hosted a League conference on women's issues. It has also worked to revitalize the Arab Maghreb Union.

It is not clear that Tunisia is in the habit of internalizing international norms. Domestic statutes generally derive from the priorities of the executive, passed by a compliant legislature and unchallenged by the judiciary. When these coincide with international norms, internalization occurs – but the direction of causality appears to begin with the President's priorities.

Rationalism

Other than a small Jewish and Christian community (around 1 percent of the population each), Tunisian society could be described as "homogenous." A recent quantitative study ranked Tunisia as the 17th least ethnically divided or contentious country (out of 138) – similar to Greece or Malta (Montalvo and Reynal-Querol 2005).

Class conflict has historically been muted in Tunisia, although strikes have occurred from time to time – often over fairly straightforward complaints about failure by management to fulfill contracts (ICFTU 2005). Likewise, as illustrated by the self-immolation of Mohamed Bouazizi on December 17, 2010 and the response it generated, the principal cleavage was between frustrated, unemployed young adults and a state that seemed indifferent to their plight.

One way class conflict was expressed was through fundamentalist Islam. While most opposition parties drew from the middle and upper classes of Tunisian society, the Islamic fundamentalist parties drew from lower class Tunisians, polling better than 15 percent in 1989 (Gasiorowski 1992, 90).

Within the Tunisian governing circles there was little evidence of dissent or systematic conflict, although one would expect a certain degree of rivalry between members of the ruling elite with respect to business ventures and so forth.

Any discontent that existed in Tunisian society was assumed to be either low or contained. As explained by Entelis:

> For all intents and purposes, Tunisia is a one-party state governed by an unaccountable autocrat. Yet for many if not most ordinary Tunisians, the absence of genuine democracy seems acceptable as long as political stability is maintained and socioeconomic development sustained. The absence of significant challenge to the Ben Ali regime can be attributed in great measure to its pursuit of progressive social policies, including the priority given to education and health, to measures to alleviate unemployment, poverty and regional inequalities, and to legislation that has successfully promoted women's rights.
>
> (Entelis 2007, 32)

Performance across issue-areas

Rules governing territorial defense: anti-terrorism, anti-piracy, and anti-trafficking

Tunisia is a relatively open country with moderate border controls. The closer to Tunis, the stronger are the controls. It is known as a relatively easy transit point for migrants from Sub-Saharan Africa seeking access to Spain, Italy, and the rest of Europe (Cook 2008). Islamic terrorists are able to cross the southern border undetected (Bitzan 2009). The maritime border is also not secured tightly enough to prevent illegal migrants from entering or leaving the country, although considerable efforts have been expended to remedy this.

With respect to specific questions of implementing laws on territorial defense we can see from Table 7.1 that Tunisia's record is mixed. It is firmly committed to international norms on terrorism and has become a trusted ally in the West's

Table 7.1 Indicators of compliance with rules governing territorial defense

UN CTC total score	6 (7 possible)
UN CTC score, minus treaty ratifications	4 (5 possible)
Total pirate attacks	0
SUA endorsement	Yes
SUA Protocol endorsement	Yes
US State Dept. TIP score (2006)	2 (1–3, with 1 the lowest rate)
UN origin score	2 (1–5, with 1 the lowest rate)
WomanStats trafficking score	3 (1–4, with 1 the lowest rate)
2000 Trafficking Protocol signature	Yes
2000 Trafficking Protocol ratification	Yes

fight against Islamic extremism. With respect to anti-piracy measures, it appears Tunisia's efforts to defend its maritime borders have had a deterrent effect – but it is probably also benefiting from regional efforts to suppress piracy that have been on-going for more than a century. Finally, although the levels of human trafficking into the country are low, outbound trafficking occurs and there are indications that the government does not take this problem seriously.

Islamic fundamentalism presented a serious threat to the Ben Ali regime and to international trade and tourism. In 2003, at the encouragement of the West, Tunisia tightened its already strict laws against Islamic militancy. The new law banned not only the commission of violence against civilians for political purposes, but also planning attacks, financing them, joining an organization involved in attacks, and – in practice – even the intention of becoming a member of such an organization. International observers, including a UN envoy, have criticized the law for being too broad (Human Rights Watch 2010; UNOHCHR 2010). Hundreds were arrested under the law – 300 by the government's estimate, 2,000 by the reckoning of some human rights organizations (Dept. of State 2010a).

A UN envoy expressed concern that allegations of torture by prison guards, among other abuses, were rarely investigated (UNOHCHR 2010). He said "The most disturbing experience during my mission was the existence of serious discrepancies between the law and what was reported to me as happening in reality" (UNOHCHR 2010).

Western countries were reticent to focus attention on the deficiencies. As explained by Lawless *et al.* (2010),

> Following the September 2001 suicide attacks on New York and Washington DC, President Ben Ali vehemently denounced those who had carried out the attacks and reiterated Tunisia's "principled and deeply anchored stand against terrorism in all its forms and manifestations"

With respect to anti-piracy norm compliance, Tunisia – and the entire Maghreb – has the enviable distinction of having had no pirate attacks in recent years (IMB 2010). This likely stems from deterrent actions taken over the years by all port and national authorities in the region.

Tunisia's naval forces consist of nine small fast attack ships (less than 500 tons) with one more under construction that primarily serve as border patrol rather than as a force projection fleet (World Warships 2006; Tunisia Online News 2010). The three port authorities in Tunis have solid reputations as secure facilities for cargo and cruise ships.

The principal mission of the naval forces is to interdict trafficking and illegal emigration. In 2007 thirty-five African migrants who were trying to reach Italy from Libya were picked up at sea when their motor failed and they drifted into Tunisian waters (Magharebia 2010). In 2008, a private environmental monitoring ship was stopped and boarded by the Tunisian Navy beyond the twelve-mile limit (Ellenbogen 2008). These and other cases indicate that Tunisia is capable of interdicting pirates as well, which is likely known to would-be attackers.

Tunisia is committed to roughly half of the available conventions sponsored by the International Maritime Organization (a typical number for IMO members), including each of the three Safety of Life at Sea (SOLAS) agreements and the 1988 Convention for the Suppression of Unlawful Acts against the Safety of Maritime Navigation (SUA), although not the 2005 protocol that prohibits the use of a ship as a weapon of mass destruction by terrorists (IMO 2010). Taken together, Tunisia's commitment to anti-piracy norms is roughly above average.

Tunisian authorities do not consider human trafficking to be a cause of concern, despite the fact that trafficking does occur (Dept. of State 2010b). But these efforts are deemed inadequate:

> The Penal Code prescribes punishments of 10 years' imprisonment for capturing, detaining, or sequestering a person for forced labor, and up to five years' imprisonment for forced prostitution of women and children.... [However t]here were no investigations or prosecutions of trafficking offenses, or convictions of trafficking offenders, during the year [2009]...
>
> ...[T]he government did not show evidence of progress in prosecuting and convicting trafficking offenders, proactively identifying or protecting trafficking victims, or raising public awareness of human trafficking over the last year...
>
> The government did not offer trafficking victims access to shelters or other services during the reporting period. The government lacked formal procedures to identify trafficking victims among vulnerable groups, such as undocumented migrants and those persons detained for prostitution offenses. As a result, persons whose trafficking victim status was not recognized by Tunisian authorities were vulnerable to imprisonment and deportation if caught engaging in illegal activities under Tunisian law. The government neither undertook efforts to identify trafficking victims among the undocumented migrants in its detention centers, nor did it allow outside parties to screen these detained migrants to determine if any were victims of abuse.
>
> (Dept. of State 2010b)

The more significant Tunisian effort is aimed at apprehending and detaining migrants on their way to Italy and other European destinations. The distance between Tunisia's coast and Sicily is a mere 150 km. In 2008 roughly 1,000 Tunisians sailed to Italy illegally and were held in a facility on the island of Lampedusa until the Tunisian and Italian interior ministers agreed to measures to facilitate their deportation in 2009 (ADN Kronos 2009).

Taken together, then, Tunisia's records on anti-terror and anti-piracy measures are very strong, while its efforts with respect to trafficking are mixed. To what extent do our theories of international law compliance explain this outcome? It is not surprising that an autocratic regime would take forceful action against threats to the state – especially a terrorist threat from groups with which large segments of the society sympathizes. Furthermore, we should not be surprised to see it apply draconian measures to achieve this end. We should also expect to see such a regime take serious measures against maritime piracy – particularly where it threatens key state interests. Even its actions with respect to trafficking are reasonable. After all, it would be surprising to see such a regime expend a great deal of effort to prevent private individuals from abusing women and children.

Liberalism in trade and migration may help explain some of the difficulties Tunisia faces with respect to human trafficking and the inflow of terrorists across the border. The borders are relatively open. Smuggling cheap fuel, cars, marijuana, and other goods from Libya has been common (Magharebia 2010). Corruption within the ranks of border police has undermined law enforcement as well. This dovetails with the managerial school, of course, and we have noted that corruption is a concern throughout the country. But our evidence shows that the very large Tunisian police pursued priority targets, such as human rights activists and Islamic fundamentalists. This means that failure to apprehend traffickers reflects not a lack of capacity but a lack of will.

It is clear that Tunisia dearly values its standing in the international community, especially with respect to its business ties to the West. Fighting terrorism both stabilized the regime and made Tunisia a much safer and more stable place to invest, trade, and travel. Ben Ali learned that becoming a staunch Arab ally in the fight against Al Qaeda created considerable room for diplomatic maneuver. From the perspective of legitimacy theory, it is difficult to say that international norms were internalized into Tunisian law and policy. Rather, the government seemed willing to ratify some rules without regard to their enforcement, as in the case of the UN Protocol on Trafficking. In other cases, it appears that the government endorsed instruments which it was already willing to implement for its own reasons.

Cultural theory does not seem to go very far in explaining Tunisian policy in these areas. If anything, Tunisian attitudes, beliefs, and behavior were ignored, altered, and suppressed in the interest of political stability.

The interests of the state – especially short-term concerns for Ben Ali to maintain power – seem to explain most of what we observe in this section. Ben Ali was willing to ignore international norms that were inconvenient or unimportant for the sake of ensuring his regime's prosperity. Even some of his economic and foreign policies seem to have been primarily aimed at his own long-term survival in that he can count on both Western powers and the majority of his citizens (especially the business and political classes) to approve of his regime.

Rules designed to regulate the market: shipping and airline regulation and CFC control

Table 7.2 shows that Tunisia is doing a reasonable job of complying with international rules governing the market. The ship detention rate for the Paris and Tokyo MOUs is well below the average, although more will be said about this below. Its airline safety rate is solid and improving, and its compliance with the Montreal Protocol is one of the best in the developing world.

Tunisia has a merchant fleet of roughly seventy-five vessels, although only twenty are over 1,000 gross tons. The fleet consists of a wide variety of ships, including tankers, passenger ships, cargo vessels, and a myriad other fishing and transport ships (Europa 2010d; Med. MOU 2010). It also has eight ports, including a significant complex of three ports near Tunis, and has a solid reputation for safety.

The best measure of Tunisia's fleet safety is the frequency of inspection and detention in European ports as measured by the Paris Memorandum of Understanding. The record is rather spotty. Relatively speaking, 2002 was the worst year of the group in that more than a third of the Tunisian ships that were inspected were prevented from leaving port until repairs were made. In contrast, only one of twenty inspected ships were detained in 2000. In 2008, Tunisia was fifty-fifth out of eighty-three flag states with respect to ship safety (EMSA 2009).

Tunisia is participating in the "5+5" maritime cooperation program involving countries around the Mediterranean (it has hosted a number of regional meetings on maritime safety), as well as the Mediterranean MOU which aims at increasing port safety (Med. MOU 2010; Tunisia 2010).

Tunisia's commitment to international air safety norms appears to be equally solid. Roughly 4,500,000 tourists arrive in Tunisia by air each year, most from

Table 7.2 Indicators of compliance with market regulating laws

Ship detention rates from Paris, Tokyo MOU	3.17 (0–581; 13.89 average)
1999–2001 ICAO non-compliance score	13.38 (on a scale of 0–100; 0=no defects)
ICAO follow-up 2004	3.53
ali_standard air liberalization score	87 (0–183; high=liberal)
Cumulative Montreal Protocol compliance score	0 (0–24; low=compliance)
Reported data to Ozone Commission 2002–2007	Yes
Found non-compliant 2002–2007	No
Broke existing program 2002–2007	No

Europe. Flights arrive from eighteen different countries on thirty different airlines, not including four domestic carriers (OACA 2010). Tunisair is the principal domestic carrier, and is 75 percent government-owned. Tunisair also owns 83 percent of Sevenair, but two smaller carriers are entirely private (Endres 2009).

The country had very few infractions upon the first ICAO inspections in 1999 and almost none by the time of its 2004 follow-up. The ICAO gave Tunisia's air safety structures and practices a clean bill of health in 2008 (ICAO 2008).

A serious blemish to its record occurred in 2005 when a Tunisair (now Sevenair) flight carrying thirty-five passengers ditched off the northern coast of Sicily due to lack of fuel. Fifteen passengers and one crew member were killed. Investigations found that the wrong type of fuel gauge had been installed and provided inaccurate readings. Rather than landing at a nearby airfield, the pilot panicked, prompting Italian authorities to convict him of manslaughter and also banned all Tunisair flights for a time (Flight Safety Foundation 2008; BBC 2009).

Finally, in the area of protecting the ozone layer from damaging chemicals, Tunisia has performed what can only be called an about-face that has brought universal accolades. Tunisia's consumption of ozone-depleting substances in 2001 was twenty-fourth out of ninety-five countries ranked. By 2008 the country had eliminated almost all CFC and other ODS consumption (Globalis 2001). It also had the lowest carbon dioxide emissions in all of Africa (tied with Mauritius) and earned a seat on the Implementation Committee of the Montreal Protocol and the Executive Committee of UNEP (UNEP 2007, 2009, 2010).

The World Bank provided assistance from the beginning of the Montreal Protocol process. The following provides its favorable assessment at the conclusion of the project:

> From the beginning of the project, Tunisia has shown a strong sense of ownership of the project, and benefitted from the leadership of the Government of Tunisia to make ozone depleting substance phase-out a national priority. This strong national ownership has been an asset to the Tunisian … program at the level of the Montreal Protocol, where the country was among the early movers on this issue. The strong political commitment from the Government of Tunisia has also been instrumental, as has the existing institutional foundation upon which the project has built and strengthened the capacity of the National Ozone Bureau.… This project achieved its Global Environmental Objectives; namely, Tunisia was able to achieve the complete phase-out of CFC and halons by January 1, 2010.… This was a reduction 14% greater than the reduction target … set for Tunisia by the Montreal Protocol.
>
> (World Bank 2012, 13–17)

Taken together, Tunisian compliance with laws governing the regulation of the market is generally strong, although weakest with respect to maritime safety.

The heavy involvement of the government in key sectors – including transportation and industry – and the autocratic nature of decision-making mean that once the regime made up its mind to implement a particular economic program, it was able to do so. So it comes as no surprise that an autocratic, *dirigiste* regime as we've seen in Tunisia was able to cause private (and not-so-private) business entities to comply with international standards. Ben Ali staked his fortunes on delivering economic growth to ordinary Tunisians (taking care to favor family members and wealthy urban and rural businesses). Ensuring that shipping – whether in-bound or out-bound – and air transportation meet international standards was naturally a key component to this effort. Tunisia's efforts to force local companies to comply with international CFC standards may also stem from this effort to make Tunisian exports competitive in Europe. But this does not entirely explain the adoption of these standards for goods that are produced and consumed locally.

As has been mentioned, the Tunisian government has the capacity to ensure that its regulations are implemented. We see this clearly with respect to ozone-depleting substances. Even where it lacks resources at home, it is capable of mobilizing support from abroad. It stands to reason, though, that it would struggle to identify sufficient numbers of well-trained aircraft inspectors – its most glaring weakness according to the ICAO – and that it might not be able to carry out adequate inspections of the merchant marine fleet, given its extraordinary mobility.

The reputational, legitimacy, and rationalist approaches work together in these cases to show that where establishing a reputation for compliance can help enhance economic benefits for key stakeholders, the rules will be internalized and implemented. This is clearly the case where transportation regulation is concerned. We see evidence that Tunisia paid close attention to the norms and to the criticisms it received from the international community – particularly with respect to air safety and ozone-depleting substances. It is entirely possible that the government made a judgment that since its failings would be obvious, it may as well embrace the norms and receive some kudos in the process (Entelis 2007).

Finally, the cultural approach does little to explain these outcomes, since compliance with international norms does not seem to dovetail with any particular Tunisian value system or social customs.

Laws on human rights promotion: anti-slavery law and anti-discrimination against women

In many respects, Tunisian policies on slavery and women's rights anticipated international norms. Slavery was outlawed in 1846 under orders from the British. Women's equality was enshrined in the Constitution, more specifically in the Personal Status Code in 1957. In most respects, these principles have been codified in specific statutes and implemented as official policy. Enforcement, however, and internalization at the level of private individuals and local courts are less certain.

Table 7.3 Indicators of Tunisia's compliance with anti-slavery and women's security norms

WomanStat physical security of women 2007	3 (1–4; 1 is most secure)
Share of women in parliament	22%
Average age for women at first marriage	27 years
Proportion of teenaged girls who are married	3%
Ratification of ILO Conventions #29, 105, 182 on slavery	All 3

Table 7.3 shows a bit of a contradiction. Women clearly are in a strong position with respect to charting their own futures, as evidenced by a high average age of first marriage and low numbers of teenagers marrying. The government committed itself to all the relevant international instruments on forced labor and the rights of women (it has ratified CEDAW). Nearly a third of all lawyers are women and women and children routinely appear in court to defend their rights (over 9,000 rape cases were brought to trial in 1989–1990) (Labidi 2007, 289; Freedom House 2010b).

On the other hand, the WomanStats figure of 3 – far from the best level of treatment for women – warns of troubles that are not captured by the other data. This may reflect the fact that the state has not considered trafficking or violence against women a high priority.

We will begin with a consideration of slavery and forced labor in Tunisia. Workers are entitled to a contract and may collectively bargain for one "without discrimination" (Dept. of State 2010a). All industrial workers are guaranteed a minimum wage of roughly $200 a month. Nearly 400 labor inspectors fan out across the country to verify compliance with these rules in each firm at least every two years (Dept. of State 2010a). Child labor under age thirteen is outlawed, and specific restrictions apply to youth between the ages of thirteen and eighteen, with gradually easing restrictions. The penalty for forcing a child to work is up to ten years' imprisonment.

While these laws appear appropriate and even impressive, the reality is quite different. To begin, only one labor union was permitted to operate under Ben Ali. Roughly one-sixth of Tunisian workers belonged to it. The union bargained collectively once every three years to develop a contract covering much of the economy (Dept. of State 2010a). Naturally, this did not affect farm workers or the half-million workers in the informal sector. Even members of the national union face difficulties if they choose to mount an unauthorized strike, as occurred at the Zarrouk brickyard in 2004 when workers were attacked as they gathered to discuss what to do about fifty former co-workers who had been fired unfairly (ICFTU 2005). The penalty for engaging in an illegal strike was up to eight months in prison – a sentence considered disproportionately harsh by the International Confederation of Free Trade Unions and the International Labour Organization (ICFTU 2005).

With respect to children and those working in the informal economy, it appears that abuse of children in the workplace occurred on a regular basis. In a survey conducted in 2008, 130 domestic workers were asked to assess their working conditions. As detailed by the US State Department:

> It was found that 52 percent were younger than 16; 23 percent claimed to be victims of physical violence, and 11 percent claimed to be victims of sexual violence. The majority received salaries below the minimum wage, and 99 percent indicated they had not work contracts. These conditions are indicators of possible forced labor.
>
> (Dept. of State 2010a)

The ICFTU concluded that

> [w]hile child labor is not widespread, unacceptable exploitation of children is occurring to some degree, mainly in the informal economy, in domestic services and in agriculture. Although efforts of the Tunisian government to tackle this problem have to be recognized, there is still a compelling need for further research in this area.
>
> (ICFTU 2005)

Women have been formally free to engage in a wide range of activities that are normally restricted in conservative countries, regardless of the dominant faith. They secured the right to vote at independence and have been allowed to run for office since 1959. They can initiate divorce proceedings, make a claim on their ex-husbands for alimony and other assets, testify in court, own property, start a business, and so forth. Polygamy was outlawed and women were given essentially equal rights in the home (Labidi 2007, 281).

Tunisia has adopted laws against marital rape unlike many of its counterparts in the developing world. In fact, penalties for rape and sexual abuse increase dramatically if the suspect is a relative of the victim (Canada 2009). The maximum penalty for domestic violence is life in prison (equivalent to the penalty for manslaughter – Freedom House 2010b). Girls are also protected with graduated penalties that increase as the age of a victim goes down (Labidi 2007, 289). The state also provides shelters and emergency services to women who have been victimized, as well as sensitivity and awareness training and campaigns (Canada 2009).

Attitudes in Tunisia are remarkably supportive of women's rights, as mentioned earlier, with three-fourths of men supporting the principle of gender equality with respect to civil law (Ray and Younis 2009). Particularly in urban areas, women are increasingly self-reliant and men accept the notion that housework and child-rearing duties should be shared (Labidi 2006).

While the formal status of women under the law and even in the minds of more cosmopolitan men is among the best in the developing world, in practice many of the laws are enforced tentatively or not at all, and women continue to experience low status and abuse at home. To begin, the laws regarding rape and sexual abuse are conditional on the victim pressing charges. Perhaps as a result, spousal rape is very rarely prosecuted. Women are constrained by social norms not to press charges against a husband who sexually assaults a child and judges often set aside cases involving family members (Labidi 2007, 289). In general, violence within the home is considered a personal matter and the police often hesitate to interfere (Canada 2009).

Attitudes towards women are still quite conservative. According to a 2007 survey:

> Two thirds of women believed that women who had no children had a lower social status, reflecting a continuing strong belief in the proper role of women as mothers. These women still believed in social restrictions on single women and unmarried girls: only 16% unconditionally agreed that single women could live alone; 10% unconditionally approved of girls being allowed to travel alone; and 7.5% unconditionally approved of girls going out with boys, compared to 42% who "don't mind." Among unmarried youth (both male and female) aged between 18 and 19 years, 93% declared that they chose/would choose their future spouse; and 70% declared it was unacceptable to use contraception before marriage.
>
> (Tunisian NOFP 2001 cited in Watts 2007, 4)

Some of this is reflected in the attitudes of lower court judges who apply Shari'a principles to divorce cases, inheritance cases, and other cases involving family law. Despite a generally favorable review, the CEDAW Committee in 2002 raised concerns about "the lack of legal remedies to ensure that the Constitutional provision on equality is enforced or court decisions in which women have obtained redress for acts of discrimination" (UN CEDAW 2002).

Liberal theory is presented here with a genuine puzzle: can we explain progressive, secular policies towards women and workers in an autocracy? On the one hand, Tunisia's founders had internalized the progressive civil rights views of their European teachers and created a national coalition that included women's rights activists. That the first and particularly the second regimes discarded meaningful electoral procedures does not diminish the significance of this initial infusion of liberal principles. On the other hand, as we have seen elsewhere, participation in the world economy – economic liberalism – does not seem to play much of a part. Certainly, the expansion of urban businesses in which women have a prominent role is facilitated by trade liberalization. But it seems that this is not a proximate cause.

The state developed the capacity to regulate firms suspected of discrimination, but it isn't always clear that it used this capacity to ensure implementation. International observers, in particular, are frustrated with the lack of data on key issues such as child labor, prostitution, and domestic service, which they seem to believe reflects a lack of will rather than a lack of capacity.

Tunisia has made it clear that it is formally committed to the norms we've discussed in this section, and has generally internalized these norms in the form of statutory law. It seems to have done so in part to please the international community. But it also does not seem that this is the most pressing concern. The lack of data, the lack of enthusiasm for questions relating to slavery, and the incorporation of women's rights principles long before they were on the international agenda all point to this conclusion.

What prevented Tunisia from fully implementing all international norms as presently constituted appears to be local culture. The state tolerated deviations from the secular civil law code in favor of Shari'a law principles regarding family law cases. The commitment to conservative Islamic traditions persisted under Ben Ali. This was reflected in the traditions that discourage women from pressing charges against abusive husbands and so forth – something which the state has explicitly tolerated.

Finally, to what extent do Tunisian policies reflect a rational calculation of basic interests – especially economic ones? While there does appear to have been a calculation on the part of state elites that promoting the rights of women would strengthen their hold on office, it is also clear that doing so came at considerable risk. The state seems to have had an incentive to make important compromises with traditionalists and perhaps even fundamentalists given the level of repression. Likewise, Tunisia derived some benefit with respect to international status as it protects women's rights, and even seemed to calculate just how far it could deviate from international norms before sanctions would be imposed.

Concluding remarks on Tunisia and theories of international law compliance

The case of Tunisia shows that a globalized but autocratic regime is capable of complying with a wide range of international norms. In some respects, because it had the capacity to function without requiring the consent of the governed, the Tunisian regime was better able to implement norms that would face domestic opposition. This is particularly apparent with respect to fighting terrorism, protecting the ozone layer, promoting women's rights, and suppressing piracy. Under Ben Ali, it was more difficult for Tunisia to plead poverty, public unrest, or lack of capacity.

Table 7.4 offers a summary of the relative strength of each theory's explanation of the outcomes we've seen. In this head-to-head comparison, we see that rationalism does the best job of explaining the most outcomes. It does in fact appear that the Tunisian government tended to be fairly pragmatic – even opportunistic – linking issue-areas such as human rights and anti-terrorism to insulate itself from the type of sanctions other regimes have faced. It could provide information where it was flattering and conceal it where it presumably was not. It was able to calculate the pay-off structures of different policies, in other words.

Given the ability and willingness of the regime to suppress traditional and extremist traditions in Tunisian culture, these factors did little to shape national policy under Ben Ali. On the other hand, the government elites' commitment to

Table 7.4 Competing theories of international law compliance and the case of Tunisia

"To what degree does the theory explain outcomes?"

		Sovereignty defense			*Market control*			*Human rights*	
		Anti-terror	*Anti-piracy*	*Anti-trafficking*	*Air transport*	*Ship safety*	*Ozone depletion*	*Slavery*	*Protection of women*
Liberalism	Political	much	much	much	some	some	some	some	some
	Economic	some	some	some	much	some	some	much	some
	Managerial	much	much	little	some	much	some	some	some
	Reputational	some	some	little	much	some	much	some	some
	Cultural	little	little	some	little	little	little	some	some
	Legitimacy	some	some	little	much	some	much	some	much
	Rationalism	much	much	much	much	some	much	much	much

certain liberal norms – particularly economic competitiveness and women's rights – explains many of policies and their degree of implementation. There is an interaction between the liberal school with respect to state interests and the managerial school with respect to implementation. The reputational and legitimacy schools also overlap in their explanation of how these developments relate to international norms.

Pakistan

Overview

Pakistan is a house divided surrounded by enemies – or at least this is the perception of most Pakistani elites. The country was largely a fabrication of Muslim intellectuals in the 1940s who feared being overwhelmed by Hindus in a unified post-independence state. Even though both India and Pakistan were governed by secular leaders at independence Pakistan's leaders have identified the state as a haven for Muslims. Pakistan, by definition, is not India.

This "negative" definition of Pakistan has proven to be too little to unify the country (Shaikh 2009, 180). Few groups see beyond their own narrow religious or ethnic identity. These ethnic identities shape Pakistani politics and society generally. Each of the four major groups can claim a large segment of the population – or at least a large swath of territory. Most also have their preferred political party as well. Nawaz Sharif finds almost all of his support in Punjab, while President Asif Ali Zardari's power base is in Sind. The Awami National Party wins seats in the Pashtun and Taliban-dominated North-west Frontier Province (now Khyber-Pakhtunkhwa) while the Balochistan National Party is supported only by the Balochs (Dept. of State 2010c). Add to this the *Muhagirs* – Muslims who were living in India at Independence and who now live mostly in Karachi – who dominate the business world in Sind province (Malik *et al.* 2009, 195–201).

Ethnicity also shapes the country's foreign policy to a considerable extent. Most Pakistani ethnic groups are closely tied to co-ethnics in neighboring countries. Pashtuns sometimes express stronger ties to their counterparts to the west than with fellow Pakistanis, which shaped Pakistani sympathies toward the Taliban regime in Afghanistan. Kashmiris to the north are the least interested in being part of the Pakistan state (Minority Rights 2010). But acceding to their wish for independence or surrendering them to India would profoundly undermine Pakistan's raison d'être as a Muslim sanctuary.

The differences between the various regions and ethnic groups in Pakistan are stark. Large urban areas, such as Islamabad and Karachi, enjoy relative prosperity compared to the rural areas of the country which are endemically poor (Pakistan 2003, 17–18). This is reflected in a variety of measures of well-being, including especially female literacy. West of the Indus River along the Afghan border as many as 85 percent of women cannot read or write, while female literacy rates exceed 70 percent in Islamabad and Karachi.

The average age in Pakistan is barely 21, with 37 percent of the country's 180 million inhabitants under fifteen. Although economic growth has been fairly robust in recent years, it has not kept pace with population growth and as a result there are large numbers of unemployed young men (World Bank 2010). Add to this the frustration that comes with pervasive corruption, poor infrastructure, and lack of access to decision-making, and violence is to be expected. As put by Faisal Edhi, "The jobless youth fall into the hands of criminals who use them for their purposes. Some elements in political parties are also involved in such activities" (IRIN 2010).

In addition, many armed groups have engaged in human rights abuses against not only the civilian population generally but more specifically women and children (Dept. of State 2010d). The central government, although secular, has tolerated considerable discretion for the application of Shari'a law to not just family but also criminal law. As explained by Freedom House:

> The FATA [Federally Administered Tribal Areas] are governed under a separate legal system, the Frontier Crimes Regulation, which allows collective punishment for individual crimes and preventative detention of up to three years and authorizes tribal leaders to administer justice according to Shari'a and tribal custom. Feudal landlords and tribal elders throughout Pakistan adjudicate some disputes and impose punishments – including the death penalty or the forced exchange of brides between tribes – in unsanctioned parallel courts called jirgas. In 2004, responding to growing concern over the potential for abuse in this practice, the Sindh High Court banned all trials conducted under the jirga system in the province. However, such proceedings continue to take place. Tensions between national laws and the efforts of provincial assemblies to pass restrictive Islamist legislation remain a problem.
>
> (Freedom House 2010c)

Add to these troubles the continued presence of nearly two million Afghan refugees and various internally displaced persons, along with a resurgent Taliban and we can begin to understand the severe constraints within which Pakistan strives to eke out an existence.

Liberalism

We now turn to the various features of interest to our different theories of international law compliance. To begin, we ask whether Pakistan is liberal politically. Pakistan's politics have been volatile over the last fifteen years. The government has suspended and amended the Constitution several times, elected several new Presidents and Prime Ministers, none of which served a full term, and seen two coups – one of which technically involved the president-as-general removing his civilian self (Malik *et al.* 2009, 171)!

Through it all, Pakistan's government retained its basic institutions: a President elected for a five-year term, a bicameral parliament with seats reserved for women and religious minorities, a Supreme Court with powers of judicial review, and a preeminent role for Islam – including a supreme court for Shari'a law.

Pakistan holds regular elections, but governments routinely replace each other under "extraordinary" circumstances. As put by Cohen: "By the 1990s the idea of Pakistan no longer included genuine democracy. More Pakistanis would have settled for the appearance of democracy with a modicum of good government – they got neither" (Cohen 2004, 87). Pakistanis generally support the effort to create democracy, as reflected in surveys that show three-fourths prefer an unstable democracy to a stable dictatorship. But two-thirds of Pakistanis believe that the military has a right to intervene in an emergency (IRI Index 2009).

Civil society is relatively active in Pakistan, with thousands of NGOs, several independent television stations and newspapers, and the academy functioning under the protection of formal freedom of expression and assembly. Journalists find working in Pakistan among the riskiest assignments in the world, mostly due to threats from armed rebels and militants. In 2007, it was President Pervez Musharraf's decision to remove the sitting Supreme Court chief justice that precipitated widespread protests from lawyers, which in turn forced him to permit the return of exiled opposition leaders Benazir Bhutto and Nawaz Sharif and the holding of elections in 2008 (Europa 2010e).

Under Musharraf, elections were generally tainted, although they were not meaningless. As explained by Freedom House:

> The Musharraf government continued to constrain opposition party activity through mass arrests and preventative detention in 2007 and early 2008, and although the 2008 elections marked a distinct improvement over those held in 2002, they were not completely free and fair. State resources and media were used to support pro-government parties and candidates, and inaccuracies in the voter rolls that were noted in 2002 were not corrected. The voting results were generally not displayed at each polling station, allowing for rigging in some areas as the overall constituency results were tallied; the European Union observer mission noted suspicious results in a number of constituencies.
>
> (Freedom House 2010c)

Opposition parties swamped the ruling government in the legislature, leaving Musharraf politically isolated. He resigned under threat of impeachment a few months later. The ruling coalition of Zardari and Sharif proved fragile. The military continues to reserve the implicit right to interfere in civilian governments. In March 2009 during a series of large-scale protests by Nawaz Sharif, the Army Chief of Staff Ashfaq Parvez Kayani confided in the US Ambassador in Islamabad that he might need to ask Zardari to step down – with the proviso that he would be replaced by a member of the ruling party, so this would not be a "formal coup" (Wikileaks 2010a). When the government failed to provide relief to flood victims in September 2010, he met with Zardari. He expected heads to roll in the Cabinet (*New York Times* 2010). Zardari adamantly refused in private but took no steps to discipline the general for intruding on politics.

Taken together, Pakistan is a mixed system, including some democratic and liberal elements while at the same time abusing these norms during crises and tolerating judicial and customary practices that are clearly undemocratic.

With respect to economic policy, Pakistan has followed the path of other South Asian governments privatizing numerous state-owned firms, lowering tariffs and generally working to deregulate the economy, thereby making the country more accommodating to foreign investors. As explained by the Ministry of Finance:

> [T]he Government of Pakistan has implemented a comprehensive program of trade reforms gradually moving their economies away from protectionism towards greater trade openness and global economic integration. Currently, the maximum tariff is 25 percent, down from 125 percent in 1990–91. The effective tariff, defined as collection net of custom duties relative to dutiable imports, declined from 73 percent in 1990–91 to 16 percent in 2002–03. The total number of tariff lines with specific tariffs has also declined from 103 in 1995 schedule to 43 lines.
>
> (Pakistan 2003, 38)

Trade rose dramatically in the years before the financial crisis in the 2000s. Total exports rose from $8.4 billion in 1998 to $20.4 billion in 2008 while imports also rose from $10.3 billion to $35.5 billion during the same period, leading to a dramatic increase in the trade deficit (World Bank 2010). Trade with Middle Eastern countries and China rose significantly, while exports to the US remained flat. This increasing variety of trade partners will help protect Pakistan in the future.

Trade with Western countries has been affected by sanctions that were imposed over Pakistan's support of the Taliban and its failure to pursue Osama Bin Laden, as well as its detonation of a nuclear device in 1998. Most sanctions were lifted after 9/11 when Pakistan became a key player in the war against terror. During the 2000s, the US provided roughly ten billion dollars in various forms of aid (Malik *et al.* 2009, 230).

On balance, the efforts to liberalize are paying off:

> Despite fears that the political strife, domestic and regional security concerns, bureaucratic obstacles, corruption and inadequate infrastructure would continue to deter potential investors, foreign direct investment (FDI) increased substantially in the latter half of the first decade of the 2000s; in 2005/06 FDI more than doubled, compared with the previous year, to reach $3,450 million and rose by a further 45.7% to a total of $5,026 million in 2006/07.
>
> (Dept. of State 2010c)

Managerial school

It was recently reported that only two million Pakistanis pay income taxes (*New York Times* 2010). Government revenue amounts to only 13 percent of GDP as a result. The country has unsurprisingly struggled to maintain a balance in its fiscal accounts.

Not only are tax collections and national expenditures difficult for Pakistani governments to control, but administration in general suffers from a lack of professionalism. Corruption is rampant. Transparency International listed Pakistan among the fifty most corrupt countries in the world in 2009. It charged the government with mismanagement of tax revenues and donor funds. As put by TI's Pakistan office:

> Pakistan needs to seriously tackle this cancer on a war footing, in the same manner that it is engaged in the war against terrorism. The rise in extremism is linked to corruption, because massive pilferages to the tune of over Rs500 billion to Rs700 billion has denied investment by the state in welfare, education, health, provision of security and basic needs to the people.
>
> (Shamsuddin 2009)

Zardari himself (nicknamed "Mr. Ten Percent" for the cut he routinely took on government contracts while his wife served as Prime Minister) served eight years for corruption (Freedom House 2010c). He was convicted in 2003 by a Swiss court of money-laundering (BBC 2010). Even the military is knee-deep in questionable financial transactions involving its many business ventures (Anderson 2010).

Beyond issues of mis-use of funds, Pakistan's central government has had great difficulty establishing a presence throughout the territory. The problem has risen to a first-order international issue since Taliban fighters, not to mention dozens of local rebel groups, have been able to control large segments of Pakistan. The Pakistani government controls only about two-thirds of the northern areas. The situation was perhaps most serious in the narrow Swat valley where Taliban forces established such firm control that in May 2008 the government negotiated a deal (later reversed) to allow them to govern the area under Shari'a law (Europa 2010f). Balochistan is another region where the reach of the government is tentative. In both areas, various Afghan groups routinely seek refuge as American forces pursue them – typically with attacks from unmanned drones. The result is considerable diplomatic and political tension over questions of Pakistani sovereignty (Mayar 2009). Eighty percent of Pakistanis oppose the Taliban's use of Pakistani territory as a base for launching attacks into Afghanistan, but three-fourths also oppose drone attacks on bases in Pakistan (IRI Index 2009).

As can be imagined, the inability to control its territory and its borders means that the smuggling of contraband, drugs, weapons, people, and almost anything one can imagine are very high. As put succinctly by the CIA:

> [Pakistan is a] significant transit area for Afghan drugs, including heroin, opium, morphine, and hashish, bound for Iran, Western markets, the Gulf States, Africa, and Asia; financial crimes related to drug trafficking, terrorism, corruption, and smuggling remain problems.
>
> (CIA 2010)

Reputational theory

As was mentioned, successive Pakistani governments have been working to improve the country's reputation on a number of fronts. Perhaps the most dramatic is in the area of economic relations where its efforts to open its markets and bring its financial house in order seem to be making some progress.

On most measures of financial responsibility Pakistan sits squarely in middle range – which is something to be commended given the profound difficulties it faces with respect to security and governance. Of note is the fact that it has earned a rating from Moody's above junk-bond status (B1). Likewise its currency stability was very high. This effort has borne fruit in the form of IMF support and other forms of official development assistance. Pakistan has also been able to borrow on the open market.

At the political level, as alluded to earlier, Pakistan decided after September 11th that it would join the West in its war on terror (Lavoy 2005, 55). In the short term, this meant abandoning the Taliban which it had supported directly and indirectly for several years. The choice was a dangerous one because elements of the military – especially in the Inter-Service Intelligence (ISI) – were among the Taliban's strongest supporters. Relations with the new Afghan government of Hamid Karzai have been tense as Pakistan has seen him as pro-India while Karzai has accused the ISI of providing sanctuary and support to Taliban leaders (Europa 2010g).

Culture

Like Tunisians, almost all Pakistanis are Muslim. Unlike Tunisians, many Pakistanis are openly militant. The sub-standard state-run educational system is supplemented with a large number of *madrasas* that focus on religious and non-technical education.

> The system has had an impact – less than 25 percent of Pakistan's workforce is literate, which makes it difficult to train workers for any but the most menial tasks and discourages industry and foreign companies from investing in Pakistan. Pakistan's public education system has failed because it is not valued enough by the politically important components of the state's leadership.... Pakistan's business community saw no need for an educated workforce that could adapt to changing production requirements since the companies had no such vision for themselves.
>
> (Cohen 2004, 241–242)

We already took note of the low level of women's education, particularly in rural areas. This generally correlates with high levels of traditionalism with its emphasis on a male-dominated, conservative family life and disdain for the development of women's skills beyond child rearing. It is worth noting that nine out of ten Pakistanis believe that Islamic fundamentalism is a threat to the country (IRI Index 2009).

Legitimacy

Pakistan is an active participant in the United Nations and other multilateral organizations. It served as president of the Economic and Social Council in 2005 and sits on the Human Rights Council among other bodies. It has been the number one provider of peacekeeping troops during the 2000s. Pakistanis currently participate in eleven different UN peacekeeping operations.

In the early 1990s, Pakistan helped revitalize the Economic Cooperation Organization which includes Iran and Turkey as well as a number of Central Asian states. Their hope is to lower trade barriers with each other (Europa 2010g). More significantly, Pakistan has been a key party to the South Asian Association for Regional Cooperation with India.

On the other hand, Pakistan has refused to ratify the Non-Proliferation Treaty and its position on nuclear weapons runs counter to international norms – especially with respect to its refusal to punish A.Q. Khan who was caught selling nuclear secrets to the North Koreans (Lavoy 2005, 58).

Generally, then, Pakistan gives the impression of a country that is eager to play by international rules, even when those rules produce unwelcome results. But when matters of national survival are at stake, it is clearly willing to ignore international norms.

Rationalism

Finally, we should consider some of the key stake-holders and power-wielders in Pakistani politics in anticipation of explaining outcomes with reference to calculations of interest. Central to the governance of Pakistan is something called "the Establishment." It is a fairly small circle of strategically placed groups and individuals who, regardless of constitutional provisions or the ebb and flow of electoral politics, keep a hand on the tiller of Pakistani policy (Cohen 2004, 94). First among them is the military, to which various governments have yielded control of national security (Anderson 2010). Next are senior bureaucrats who have the uncanny ability to survive coups and elections. There are the business elites – although the large number of business ventures by military officers and senior bureaucrats makes this category somewhat fuzzy. Finally we find the large landowners. These groups – almost entirely made up of Punjabis – generally agree on the basics of Pakistani policy (Shaikh 2009, 184).

This circle ensures the character of Pakistan remains relatively stable and that members of the Establishment will always come out ahead. Close to this circle, but not entirely on the inside, is a ring of civil society actors such as journalists, NGO activists, and lawyers. We've already seen that they can play critical roles when the policies of the government in power exceed certain parameters – especially with respect to flouting the law.

Outsiders include the Islamic fundamentalists, who are both appeased and repressed and who seek nothing less than control of the state and its nuclear weapons. These groups sometimes find common cause in the short run with secessionists who, by definition, seek autonomy and ultimately independence from the central government. Likewise, traditional power centers such as tribal councils and courts agree that the state should withdraw and give them free rein, although the scope of their vision is usually far smaller than the secessionists. Women, children, and the poor – particularly the rural poor – are the furthest removed from power. Their focus generally is on survival rather than influence.

Performance across issue-areas

Rules governing territorial defense: anti-terrorism, anti-piracy, and anti-trafficking

As already indicated, Pakistan's ability to defend its territory is limited and the threats are considerable. We will review its anti-terror policies first, followed by its efforts against maritime piracy and human trafficking. Table 7.5 provides some indicators in these areas.

Pakistan's efforts to combat terrorism after September 11, 2001 have come at considerable cost. At the time the decision was made to sever formal ties to the Taliban, the internal debate was intense. The military cabinet meeting is said to have lasted six hours and more than one senior officer was very reluctant to support the decision (Hoyt 2005, 285–286).

At the international level, Pakistan has endorsed almost all of the key international anti-terror conventions, although it has applied reservations to some. In

Table 7.5 Indicators of compliance with rules governing territorial defense

UN CTC total score	4 (7 possible)
UN CTC score, minus treaty ratifications	3 (5 possible)
Total pirate attacks	0
SUA endorsement	Yes
SUA Protocol endorsement	Yes
US State Dept. TIP score (2006)	2 (1–3, with 1 the lowest rate)
UN origin score	4 (1–5, with 1 the lowest rate)
UN transit score	1 (1–5, with 1 the lowest rate)
UN destination score	4 (1–5, with 1 the lowest rate)
WomanStats trafficking score	3 (1–4, with 1 the lowest rate)
Trafficking score (Bales)	3 (1–4, with 1 the lowest rate)
2000 Trafficking Protocol signature	No
2000 Trafficking Protocol ratification	No

particular, it has chosen not to extradite suspects of terror financing under the 1999 convention. It also has yet to ratify the 1991 convention on plastic explosives.

At home, Pakistan has adopted a wide range of statutes against terrorism, beginning with the 1997 Anti-Terrorism Act that defined the crime broadly and established fast-acting anti-terror courts. The Act was mostly struck down by the Supreme Court, however, for violating defendants' due process rights (Kennedy 2004, 391–392). The military was granted the authority to establish its own tribunals for terror suspects (Kennedy 2004, 395). Musharraf added crimes to those covered under the now-amended Anti-Terrorism Act. In August 2001 he further expanded the Act to include membership in terrorist organizations. Hundreds were rounded up in August 2001, and since the Supreme Court had been reconstituted with Musharraf sympathizers, there were no appeals (Kennedy 2004, 404).

The military and regional paramilitary forces have taken the lead in the fight against terror suspects under both Musharraf and Zardari. Thousands of terror suspects have been apprehended and hundreds killed in operations since 2001. As many as 100,000 troops have been deployed in the Federally Administered Tribal Areas alone (Dept. of State 2009b).

Government efforts to curb terrorist activities are ineffective in other respects as well. During the floods in the summer of 2010, it was Jamaat-ud-Dawa, widely considered a charitable front for Lashkar-e-Taiba (responsible for the November 2008 Mumbai attacks), that provided vast amounts of relief to the victims (*Seattle Times* 2010).

There are indications that the government's heart is not entirely in the fight. In 2006, for example, the American Ambassador confronted the foreign secretary to ask why two banned NGOs were still operating. His reply was that steps were being taken to rein them in, but there were no plans to go further. This prompted the Ambassador to wonder aloud to his Washington superiors whether Pakistan "is committed to implementing the sanctions..." (Wikileaks 2010b).

With respect to piracy, Pakistan shares Tunisia's status as a country that has had no pirate attacks in or near its waters since 2000 (IMB 2010). This distinction is all the more remarkable since all of its neighbors have seen many pirate attacks. It is not for lack of opportunity, as thirty million tons of cargo passes through the port of Karachi alone each year (Europa 2010h). The port is very busy – even chaotic – and has seen problem with collisions. The Pakistani Navy and Coast Guard have their headquarters in the area (Hassan 2009). Pakistan has acceded to all the relevant regulations regarding port security and mitigating violence on ships.

The Karachi Port Trust (KPT) administers the port and is composed of both civilian and military officials appointed by the state as well as elected representatives of various private stake-holders. In 2008, Zardiri appointed Nasrin Haq as the KPT's first civilian head since 1990 (and first female leader ever). She replaced Vice Admiral (ret.) Ahmed Hayat, who came under investigation of

KPT embezzlement involving $10 million (Frontier Star 2009). The port nonetheless has a good reputation and seems to comply with most international standards of security and safety.

It is difficult to overstate the seriousness of the problem of trafficking in Pakistan. The State Department estimates there are more than one million trafficked persons in the country. Hundreds of thousands more have been trafficked out of the country – especially to the Gulf states and Southeast Asia (Baloch 2009; Dept. of State 2010f). Tens of thousands of children were shipped off to the Gulf states to become camel jockeys. Hundreds of thousands of Bangladeshi women have been trafficked into the country to work as prostitutes or sold as wives. In parts of Pakistan, women and girls are bought and sold at illicit slave auctions according to NGO and police reports (Dept. of State 2010f). Thousands of women and children have also been forced into bonded labor at a variety of export-oriented companies, including sporting goods manufacturing, clothing and textile industries, rug making, and mining (Dept. of State 2010f).

The UN Fund for Population Activities, the UN Office on Drugs and Crime, and the International Organization for Migration routinely cite Pakistan for its high levels of trafficking (Masud 2005; UNFPA 2006; UNODC 2010). It is rated poorly with respect to reports of inbound and outbound trafficking, and the State Department has listed it as a major source, transit, and destination country (see Table 7.5). Pakistani officials have criticized the UN's continuing harsh judgment, accusing European countries and NGOs of "trying to defame Pakistan" (PakTribune 2006).

Many government officials have been complicit in the trade. Some receive bribes from traffickers in exchange for turning a blind eye to the practice (Dept. of State 2010f). The highway between Karachi and the Iranian border has become a key conduit for traffic of persons by land (Baloch 2008). In the villages and towns of the Western provinces, local landlords and village chiefs use bonded laborers with little regard for national regulations; they are protected from national and provincial police forces by their sizable private militias (Dept. of State 2010f).

Despite all this the government's efforts have been considerable. To begin, it has passed a law (PACHTO) imposing a sentence of 7–14 years for anyone who "knowingly plans or executes any … plan for human trafficking into or out of Pakistan" (PACHTO 2002, 3[i]) It has also outlawed kidnapping, bonded labor, and prostitution. Some police (250 in 2009) are being trained to deal specifically with trafficking cases (Dept. of State 2010f). The number of prosecutions of various aspects of trafficking has been rising in recent years. For example, in 2009, roughly 3,000 were prosecuted for various offenses under PACHTO and related offenses, of which several hundred were convicted.

Still, one gets the sense that Pakistani officials are insincere in their efforts to turn the tide against trafficking. Consider, for example, the case described by the UN Human Rights Commission involving Pakistani children who were deported home after working as camel jockeys in the UAE. The government promised the UN it would create a fund to assist them. After three years their cases were not yet resolved (UN Human Rights Council 2010).

To begin, the theory of political liberalism seems to do a relatively good job explaining anti-terror policies, in that it shows how during democratic periods the courts have reined in some policies because they were deemed to violate constitutional provisions. On the other hand, under military rule policies were generally unconstrained. The theory, however, does not explain the outcomes for anti-trafficking or anti-piracy measures. In both cases the policies changed little even as democratic and autocratic regimes traded places. Economic liberalism seems to have little to offer to explain anti-terror policy, except perhaps that free trade also makes borders somewhat more porous. But it goes far to explain anti-piracy measures since port security is vital to maritime trade. It helps explain some of the incentives that lead to trafficking, as we have seen in other cases.

The managerial school offers some useful insights. Pakistan lacks the wherewithal to address the overwhelming problems it faces. The problem of piracy appears to be far more manageable than terrorism and the response is naturally more effective. With respect to trafficking, however, the problem stems not only from lack of resources but also a lack of will.

Pakistani leaders seem to care deeply about maintaining at least the appearance of compliance with international norms. With respect to anti-terror policies, the effort seems to be genuine. It is hard to imagine the sort of pressure any government must endure when satisfying the international community requires destroying large swaths of its own territory and killing thousands of its citizens. Recent revelations show that Pakistani governments have often had more than one policy toward terrorists at the same time – one that was secret and involved far more complicity than eradication (Crilly and Spillius 2010). We see evidence of the same duplicity with respect to anti-trafficking policy.

Pakistani culture goes far to explain the origins of terrorism and trafficking as well as government responses. The failure to consolidate a multi-ethnic nation leaves millions without a sense of belonging to Pakistan. The long history of slavery and exploitation of women and children helps explain trafficking.

Pakistan has internalized some international norms, although not fully. Terrorism itself has not been entirely repudiated, as is revealed by the government's willingness to supply and train the Taliban in Afghanistan. Following international norms with respect to the means of fighting terrorism have not been embraced. But Pakistan has been a useful ally to the US in the war on terror – certainly better than might have been the case with a less committed government. With respect to anti-trafficking law, however, even were existing laws to be perfectly enforced, it would come up short of international standards. On the other hand, Pakistan appears to have embraced and acted upon international norms with respect to maritime safety.

Finally, to what extent are Pakistani policies on our three issues the product of cold calculation on the part of elites? The answer could well yes be for all of them. After all, successive governments have had strong incentives to battle anti-regime terrorists with or without international norms to guide them. After 9/11 the choice was to appease certain groups and risk losing the billions in aid from the world's only superpower, or to press the fight and stay in America's good graces. Officials may have concluded that trafficking allows local industry to benefit from lower labor costs, sex tourism to flourish, and some "surplus" children to leave the country. This probably overstates the case, however, since there seem to be at least some efforts against trafficking that are more than cosmetic. Likewise the defense against piracy – it may be good for business but it may also simply be the right thing to do.

Rules designed to regulate the market: shipping and airline regulation and CFC control

Table 7.6 shows that with respect to regulating market actors Pakistan's performance is lackluster. It fares slightly better than the average with respect to transport regulation and worse than the average with respect to preventing ozone depletion.

Pakistan has a relatively small fleet, with roughly fifty ships. It is interesting to note that many if not most ships owned by Pakistanis are registered under another country's flag (CIA 2010; Europa 2010h). One might conclude this is due to Pakistan's rigorous inspection regime, but that would be incorrect. Nearly all of Pakistan's fleet is viewed with suspicion in foreign ports, and with good reason. The Tokyo Memorandum of Understanding member-states have repeatedly found Pakistani flagged vessels to be deficient. Asian port authorities routinely inspect Pakistani ships and find deficiencies in nearly all of them. Almost every year they detain at least one Pakistani vessel that is not seaworthy. Four Pakistani ships accounted for roughly one-quarter of all the detentions (Tokyo MOU 2010b).

Despite this unimpressive record, Pakistan has managed to remain off the black lists for both the Paris and Tokyo MOUs (Tokyo MOU 2010a, p. 31). Although it has ratified the key maritime safety instruments, Pakistan is not especially active at the International Maritime Organization (MARISEC 2009).

The small size of Pakistan's merchant marine and its poor performance upon inspection in Asian ports tells a fairly clear story – namely that the Pakistani

Table 7.6 Indicators of compliance with market regulating laws

Ship detention rates from Paris, Tokyo MOU	6.52 (0–581; 13.89 average)
1999–2001 ICAO non-compliance score	16.97 (on a scale of 0–100; 0 = no defects)
ICAO follow-up 2004	7.98
ali_standard air liberalization score	60 (0–183; high = liberal)
Number of air partners	53
Respondents who believe global warming is a serious problem	41%
Cumulative Montreal Protocol compliance score	7 (0–24; low = compliance)
Reported data to Ozone Commission 2002–2007	No
Found non-compliant 2002–2007	Twice
Broke existing program 2002–2007	Yes

government is not devoting adequate resources to the task. Some efforts may be taking place as the record since 2006 shows clear improvement.

Pakistan's airlines and airports have reached the minimum standard for safety according to the ICAO and the US government (see Table 7.6; ICAO 2008; IRIN 2010). Pakistan does not yet have the confidence of the international community. In 2007, the European Union banned most of the aircraft belonging to Pakistan International Airlines (PIA) – the flagship carrier owned mostly by the government and led by the Minister of Defense. PIA's fleet of forty-two aircraft at the end of 2007 included fifteen that were more than twenty years old and another twelve that were fifteen years old (BBC 2007; PIA 2008). Pakistan experienced ten aircraft accidents during the decade beginning in 2000, including one on July 28, 2010 that resulted in the loss of all 152 passengers and crew members (Hasan 2010). Some blamed the congestion at the airport while other blamed pilot error (Aviation Safety Network 2010).

The Civil Aviation Authority (CAA) is currently at odds with the pilot's association, which claims that pilots and their crews are being forced to work longer hours than is safe. The pilots have also criticized the CAA for pushing the industry to keep up with growing demand and cutting corners on safety in the process. The CAA denies these charges (Hasan 2010). In an otherwise favorable assessment the ICAO expressed concerns about a number of issues, including resolving safety issues and carrying out continued surveillance (ICAO 2008).

Pakistan certainly has a strong incentive to maintain a high quality airline industry. More than eight million foreigners arrive by air each year and tourism accounts for roughly 5 percent of GDP (CAA 2010; World Travel 2010). Air Blue, a new private airline, is expanding rapidly and PIA is working hard to get out of debt by expanding flights (PIA 2008). Pakistan has ratified all the key airline safety instruments and regulations and is nominally committed to (and claims to have succeeded in) bringing Pakistan's airlines and airports up to international standards.

Finally, with respect to ozone-depleting substances, until recently Pakistan's consumption levels were clearly out of compliance with international expectations and commitments. As part of its becoming subject to the Montreal Protocol, Pakistan and the Implementation Committee arrived at a "baseline" against which performance would be judged. The level was set quite high at 1,679.4 tons of ozone depletion potential, putting it at #14 worst offender (Globalis 2001). This relatively generous starting point took into account the large population and GDP of the country along with the rather low level of technology in its industry. What is impressive is the fact that Pakistan's CFC consumption not only rose during the early 1990s, owing to fairly rapid industrial expansion and weak efforts to find CFC substitutes, but that it continued to rise in the late 1990s.

At the same time Pakistan's CFC consumption was surpassing its baseline, it was failing to keep its other obligations regarding the Montreal Protocol. It failed to submit reports and to implement programs design to remedy the problem with over-consumption. It was also over-consuming carbon tetrachloride, methyl bromide, and Halon gas (ECO Environment 2010).

This is not to say that Pakistan was ambivalent about the Protocol. It was active at the agency headquarters, serving on the Implementation Committee and as co-chair of the Open-ended Working Group of states parties (UNEP 2009, 418). Beginning in the mid-2000s, the government began reporting on a regular basis. Pakistan requested aid from the World Bank and other international agencies, as well as technical assistance (Ozone Depletion Today 2004). As explained in *ECO Environment*, a newsletter of the Economic Cooperation Organization, Pakistan:

> [c]onverted [21] CFC-based projects into Ozone friendly technology in foam and refrigeration sector through the World Bank.... [C]onverted [33] CTC-based projects into Ozone friendly technology in the metal cleaning and solvent sector through UNIDO.... Trained [350] Customs officials ... to enhance their capacity to curb illegal trade of ODS [and 3000] refrigeration servicing technicians.... [The] Ozone Cell, Ministry of Environment, imposed ban on imports of CFC-based compressors in July, 2008 under the new Trade Policy 2008–09 although it was not obligatory under the provisions of the Montreal Protocol.... Pakistan is the only country in the region which has taken this initiative voluntarily...
>
> (ECO Environment 2010, 1–2)

The net effect of these and other recent efforts is that since 2002 Pakistan's consumption of CFCs dropped to nearly nothing. The same is true for other ozone-depleting substances. It is worth noting that this outcome was achieved by 2009 – ahead of the December 31, 2009 deadline fixed by the Implementation Committee (Alam 2010).

Reviewing these three topics, then, which of our theories does a better job explaining what we've seen? To begin, the only topic regarding which the Pakistani electorate is likely to have become involved is air safety, and the government seems to be digging in its heels. It has resisted criticism from the pilots, engineers, and technicians and instead has persisted in what appears to be a fairly weak and opaque regulatory regime. Maritime safety does not affect most Pakistanis, and the imposition of strict new guidelines regarding ozone-depleting substances encountered some domestic resistance. Political liberalism does not seem to explain the outcome, then. Economic liberalism, on the other, may explain why the government seems to be cutting corners with respect to airline safety. Likewise, encouraging the shipment of cargo by ignoring safety concerns is a short-term response to competitive pressures. Substituting non-ozone-depleting chemicals across various sectors of the economy, on the other hand, runs counter to short-term profit motives.

To what extent does the lack of capacity explain compliance patterns? With respect to maritime safety since the fleet is small and could be dramatically improved by focusing on just a handful of vessels, lack of capacity seems a thin reed on which to rest the failure to comply fully with international maritime safety standards. Likewise, the inability to bring aircraft safety standards up to international levels does not seem to stem from lack of capacity itself – particularly since the CAA actually cut some inspectors. The fact that the pilots and other professionals have diagnosed the systems problems also implies that the country does lack for technical expertise. And finally, the fact that Pakistan was able to quickly deploy large numbers of regulators and re-train thousands of technicians to bring down CFC consumption in the late 2000s implies that this could have been done sooner.

It is fairly clear that Pakistan knows exactly what is expected of it with respect to these three areas and does only what is required. The case of ozone depletion is instructive, in that the country was able to mobilize once the 2009 deadline loomed. Likewise, the various regulatory agencies seem capable of keeping the ports and ships just safe enough to avoid sanctions. It misjudged, though, where airline safety was concerned. It is interesting to note that it still maintained the approval of the US and ICAO throughout the period and has taken steps to return to favor in Europe. Only in one area – banning the importation of CFC-based compressors – did Pakistan go beyond the minimum.

It is difficult to see where Pakistani culture explains our outcomes. There is no evidence that minimal-compliance has anything to do with ethnic tensions or even a culture of corruption. Rather, it appears as though Pakistani leaders make fairly cold calculations of interest, as predicted by the rationalist approach, and expend the fewest resources in order to avoid international sanction.

Laws on human rights promotion: anti-slavery law and anti-discrimination against women

While Pakistani officials seem genuinely concerned about keeping up appearances with respect to ozone depletion, aircraft safety, and even anti-terror measures, this does not seem to apply with respect to important areas of human rights. To be certain, laws have been passed and sentences have even been handed down regarding certain abuses, but they are having very little effect.

Beginning with slavery and slave-like practices, we should note that although Pakistan has not ratified the anti-trafficking instruments, it has committed to a wide range of international instruments related to forced and bonded labor, as we can see in Table 7.7. Pakistan has outlawed slavery and bonded labor, most recently with a fairly strong law entitled the Bonded Labor System (Abolition)

Table 7.7 Indicators of Pakistan's compliance with anti-slavery and women's security norms

Population in slavery	2.3%
Ratification of ILO Conventions #29, 105, 182 on slavery	All 3
WomanStat physical security of women 2007	4 (1–4; 1 is most secure)
Share of women in parliament	20.5%
Average age for women at first marriage	21 years
Proportion of teenaged girls who are married	21%

Act of 1992. The law requires all workers who owe their employers more than one week's wages to be freed of the debt. It establishes fines and penalties for employers who do not comply and establishes a "District Vigilance Committee system" to promote enforcement nation-wide (Dept. of State 2010e). Some provinces have made considerable efforts to implement the law. In 2001, the government launched a nation-wide program "for the Abolition of Bonded Labor and the Rehabilitation of Freed Bonded Laborers to promote law (AntiSlavery 2010).

For all of the violence and abuses that occur there, the North-west Frontier Province has few cases of bonded labor. As explained in a 2004 International Labor Organization study:

> the prevalence of debt bondage is quite insignificant in NWFP (Swabi). The principal reason for lack of bonded labor is the pattern of social organization in Swabi district whereby landowners and tenants belong to same tribe. In the tribal system, each household is socially important, irrespective of its economic status. Migration, both internal and external, is common in NWFP. The tribal system and reliance on non-agriculture sources certainly prevents bondedness in NWFP.
>
> (Arif 2004, 19)

In addition, the government has spent roughly $1.4 million to register brick kiln workers and provide them with microcredit to help them pay off their debts (Dept. of State 2010e). Conditions are nonetheless deplorable.

As mentioned earlier, the US estimates that roughly one million people have been trafficked into Pakistan for the purpose of sex work, domestic service, or other forms of bonded work or slavery. The ILO estimated that the province of Sindh had up to a million indentured farm workers in 2004 (Skinner 2009). The Pakistani government estimated in 2000 that the number of indentured farm workers nation-wide was over 1.8 million and another million may be in bonded labor in the country's brick kilns (AntiSlavery 2010). The BBC quotes a figure of five million total slaves or bonded workers in Pakistan, which corresponds roughly to Bale's estimate in Table 7.7 (BBC 2010). No one has been convicted under the Bonded Labor Act, and no funds have been spent to help rehabilitate former bonded workers.

The authorities are sometimes part of the problem. We already mentioned that soldiers in remote areas routinely abuse local citizens. In 2009, the Asian Human Rights Commission reported on the existence of fifty-two "torture cells" in which young women are used as sex slaves (AHRC 2009). The police demand bribes from the poor:

> Because beggars live in illegal settlements in urban centers, the security of their homes is dependent on patronage from people in authority. In some cases, *madrasa* owners encourage them to live under their protection in return for a cut of their earnings, but in other cases they find themselves without effective protection. In Singpura, Lahore, residents complain of police harassment. They also say that Railway authorities regularly come to

> destroy their shanties. They will take Rs.20–30 for each [one] so as not to destroy it. In Shaukat Park, Sargodha, some members of a family were arrested during recent police action against beggars and they had to pay Rs.3,000 per person to the police for their release.
>
> (CSSR/ILO 2004a, 39)

Provincial governments are charged with implementing the law, and most lack the funding, political will, and integrity to do it effectively. Even the law itself has many loopholes. For example, firms with fewer than ten employees are exempt from inspection (Dept. of State 2010e).

Two key factors seem to explain why enforcement is so lax and workers have so few rights. To begin, there are cultural elements that justify bonded labor. For example, the system known as *peshgi* has a long tradition in Pakistan.

> [A] worker-borrower contracts a cash or kind advance … from the employer-creditor. The worker-borrower then works on a piece-rate or wage-rate basis, and a part (in some cases all) of earnings goes to repay the advance. The worker-borrower cannot change employers or locations as long as the loan remains unpaid unless the new employer takes over the loan, thereby becoming the creditor.
>
> (CSSR/ILO 2004b, 56)

It is difficult to overstate the precariousness of these workers' situations. Bonded labor is carried out with violence and other forms of physical coercion at times. Large semi-feudal landowners are known as *zamindars*. *Hari* is a name for bonded agricultural labor, the conditions of which are described below:

> Several *zamindars* and *haris* informed the team that bonded *haris* are settled on the landowner's land away from the village. In some cases, the settlement is open and appears to be unguarded, but checks are made on them. In other cases, a small fortress, *kot*, is constructed, which consists of a large wall surrounding the houses of the *haris*. All bonded *haris* reside inside the *kot*, guarded by the *zamindar's* watchmen. In extreme but rare cases, the *haris* are even chained inside their houses. *Haris* are closely watched while they work in the field, sometimes by guards employed for that purpose. In exceptional situations, the *haris* are even chained while working in the field.
>
> (Hussein *et al.* 2004, 29)

The Committee on the Rights of the Child in 2009 told the Pakistani representative that the country had to account for its failure to comply with the most basic international standard with respect to slavery. It listed five key deficiencies:

> (a) No comprehensive survey on the extent of child labour in Pakistan has been conducted since 1996, making it difficult to assess the severity of the issue and address the problem appropriately;

(b) The prevalence of child labour is extremely high and has increased in recent years due to growing poverty;
(c) Despite legislation prohibiting slavery and all forms of forced labour, including bonded labour, and the 2001 National Policy and Plan of Action, bonded and forced labour continue to occur in many industries and the informal sector, affecting the poorest and most vulnerable children;
(d) The ineffectiveness of labour inspection machinery reduces the likelihood of investigations of reports of child labour, making unlikely prosecution, conviction, or punishment for the exploitation of children in bonded labour; and
(e) There are insufficient programmes to identify and protect victims of forced labour, particularly bonded labour, and child labour in the informal sector including domestic work.

(UN CRC 2009)

Turning to the status of women, Pakistan is deficient. We have already seen its performance with respect to the trafficking of women, the education of girls, and sexual exploitation and violence against women and girls in the work environment and in their encounters with the police and army. Table 7.7 shows other statistics relating to public policy toward women, in particular its having earned the lowest possible rating on the WomanStats measure of security.

According to the Aurat Foundation, a major local women's NGO, during 2009 there were 2,655 crimes of violence against women formally reported to the authorities in Pakistan, including 485 murders, 126 honor killings, and 374 instances of gang rape, some of which were ordered by local village councils as punishment for infractions by the woman's family (ADB 2010; Ireland 2010). The actual number of attacks was likely several times greater because of the social constraints on women against reporting crimes of violence – especially those perpetrated by relatives. According to the Asian Development Bank,

> [p]atriarchal values embedded in local traditions and culture predetermine the social value of gender. An artificial divide between production and reproduction, created by the ideology of sexual division of labor, has placed women in reproductive roles as mothers and wives in the private arena of home and men in a productive role as breadwinners in the public arena. This has led to a low level of resource investment in women by the family and the State. Thus, low investment in women's human capital, compounded by the ideology of *purdah* (literally "veiled"), negative social biases, and cultural practices; the concept of honor linked with women's sexuality; restrictions on women's mobility; and the internalization of patriarchy by women themselves, become the basis for gender discrimination and disparities in all spheres of life.
>
> (ADB 2010, 1)

This is reflected in female literacy rates which are half those of men, the low earning power in the marketplace where women are generally relegated to agricultural and informal sector work, the fact that only 1 percent of rural women own land (ADB 2010, 9), and pervasive violence and fear (eight out of ten Pakistani women experience a physical attack during their lifetimes – Freedom House 2010c). Although the Constitution guarantees the legal equality of men and women, it also accepts Shari'a law on family questions, with the result that women lack rights with respect to divorce, custody, inheritance, and so forth. Polygamy is legal, as is marital rape (ADB 2010, 10).

This is not to say that the government is not making efforts. Not only has it endorsed all of the pertinent international instruments, but it has attempted to codify some of them, although not all. Honor killings, rape as a criminal penalty (used by tribal courts), and domestic violence have all been outlawed. In some cases special enforcement panels and inspectors have been hired and Pakistan developed a National Plan of Action in 1998 and established a new National Commission on the Status of Women in 2002 to gather better data and advise the government on new programs. In 2010, Zardari signed into law a new bill on preventing sexual harassment (New Pakistan 2010).

Perhaps more fundamental is the government policy since 2002 to reserve a large proportion of seats in national, provincial, and local legislatures for women – a total of one-third of all seats. Women are still free to compete for the other open seats. The hope is, naturally, that these women will advocate for progressive reforms (Khan 2009, 23–24).

To what extent do our theories fit the facts? Liberal principles are frequently invoked and applied both in the area of bonded labor and women's rights. The effort to include more women in the policy-making process may lead to more progressive reforms in the future. But even military regimes have enacted progressive policies toward women, so it is difficult to say that liberalism is the best explanation. Economically, it appears that many industrialists and land-owners have a strong vested interest in frustrating efforts to free Pakistan's slaves.

While the task of pursuing exploiters and discriminators is perhaps overwhelming, the conclusion of key actors in the international community seems to be that Pakistan is not doing what it could with what it has. At least part of the failure to internalize international norms seems to stem from a pack of political will at many levels of government. Likewise, the legitimacy school does not seem to explain why a government so eager to endorse international human rights instruments would be so reticent about implementing them.

The cultural theory seems to explain women's issues and some of what occurs in the area of forced labor. Certainly the low status of women and children as well as certain religions and castes, combine to justify an exploitative and oppressive system. Even senators and cabinet officials seems to be of two minds with respect to the treatment of women, and many of the worst exploiters of workers are prominent law-makers in their own rights.

Finally, politicians no doubt make calculations about the advantages of confronting these institutions. They seem to weigh the risks of international sanctions – which appear to be low – against the likelihood of suffering possibly fatal political consequences at home. But there is more to it than an objective weighing of costs and benefits, because many prominent leaders have already committed to a particular world view that makes dramatic policy reform seem inappropriate as well as imprudent.

Concluding remarks on Pakistan and theories of international law compliance

We will now summarize the findings of our country study. Naturally, as before, some judgment is required to categorize the explanatory power of our theories with respect to the different issues, and reasonable observers may disagree. But we feel the evidence, on balance, points in the direction of these conclusions.

Table 7.8 provides the overall findings. As we can see, once again, no single theory explains all of the outcomes and processes we've observed. Rationalism fares better than the rest, but it leaves something to be desired in some respects, particularly with respect to issues that seem to be driven by cultural factors.

The political liberal school explains the least, followed closely by the managerial school. All of the other schools explain at least two issue-areas fairly well. Unlike other cases we've considered, the theories do not seem to explain our issue clusters. In almost every case, the fact that an issue involves sovereignty defense, market regulation, or human rights does not seem to matter – there are few patterns there. What is perhaps most intriguing is the fact that one issue-area – anti-piracy measures – seems to be over-determined.

General conclusions

Even though both of our cases involve states with high engagement with the outside world and little genuine democracy, there are relatively few other parallels. This allows us to isolate more clearly the variables that count most in explaining international law compliance.

Tunisia looks much more like a genuine autocracy in which the executive attempted to re-make the state and the nation according to his model. For twenty-three years, Ben Ali appeared to have succeeded. His fall came as a surprise to nearly all observers.

Pakistan, on the other hand, is teetering on failed statehood. Neither autocratic nor democratic governments can control policy – including policies related to national identity and survival. Pakistani governments are weak when it comes to mobilizing the resources required for governance and enforcing the law. At the same time, opposition groups are far more able to threaten the state.

Various regimes in Tunisia and Pakistan demonstrate that decisions about implementing international norms require trade-offs and calculations of likely costs and potential benefits. More so than was the case with Peru and Bolivia, autocratic governments seem more shrewd and calculating, setting aside with little afterthought whatever moral or ideological principles are in play.

Table 7.8 Competing theories of international law compliance and the case of Pakistan

"To what degree does the theory explain outcomes?"

		Sovereignty defense			*Market control*			*Human rights*	
		Anti-terror	*Anti-piracy*	*Anti-trafficking*	*Air transport*	*Ship safety*	*Ozone depletion*	*Slavery*	*Protection of women*
Liberalism	Political	some	little	little	little	little	some	some	some
	Economic	little	much	much	some	some	some	much	some
	Managerial	some	much	some	little	some	little	little	little
	Reputational	much	much	some	much	much	much	little	little
	Cultural	much	little	much	little	little	little	some	much
	Legitimacy	some	much	little	some	some	much	little	little
	Rationalism	much	much	some	much	much	much	much	some

This section, then, points to a few more general propositions regarding the interaction between the variables identified by the different theories.

Capacity is not just a choice – it is based on a contextual frame that itself can be manipulated. These two cases demonstrate that while governments face certain relatively fixed cultural, political, and economic domestic and international environments, it is possible to re-invent and re-design these environments to a certain extent. Tunisia has demonstrated that it is possible to substantially alter a nation's political, economic, and social structure as well as its fundamental culture. Pakistan has shown that there are always choices to be made, even when circumstances are desperate and seem to point to no good solution. In fact, Pakistan has perhaps limited its own options by not considering seriously other more fundamental changes to the environment, from withdrawing from Kashmir by supporting a referendum to dismemberment (namely granting independence to Balochistan or FATA). Alternatively, the judiciary could be strengthened to root out corruption and the tax regulators could be provided the resources needed to increase government revenue. Granted, all of these steps would produce dramatic upheaval and pose tremendous risks, but the same is true of past decisions to test nuclear weapons, impose and then abandon military rule, to accommodate and then oppose the Taliban. Each path creates new contingencies that affect which rules will be easy or difficult to follow.

The "executive tenacity" and "constitutional succession" factors. The cases of Tunisia and Pakistan also point to an element that appears to be missing from most of the theories – what we call "executive tenacity." This refers to the commitment on the part of the executive to remain in power. It is a difficult thing to measure since it involves the thought processes of an individual, some of which he may not even understand consciously. It is only when faced with the possibility of a term coming to an end that the executive knows how he will respond. Ben Ali thought he would institute democracy in the late 1980s, but decided remaining in power and ensuring political stability was more important once he saw the electoral strength of Islamic fundamentalists (although one wonders whether his calculations were really correct). Calculating his will to remain in power was not possible, however, until the demonstrators attacked his nephew's villa (Brooks 2013). On the other hand, Pervez Musharraf so feared the Supreme Court and the legal community – as well as other groups – that he conceded the demand for elections and ultimately resigned his post. All of this directly affects implementation of international law, in that governments that are tenacious – and successful in maintaining power – see international commitments differently. Namely, the "shadow of the future" (Keohane 1984) weighs more heavily on the executive's mind and makes the act of committing to a norm a more serious decision. Reputation matters more to those who intend to be in office indefinitely. Likewise, when commitments are made, because they are weighed more carefully, it is more likely that the appropriate legislation and resources will be devoted to implementation in the hope that this in turn will buttress the state's international credibility. Such a state may also find that success in implementing one norm gives the government some breathing room in other areas.

Pakistan, on the other hand, shows that where tenure is unpredictable and governments are unwilling to resist efforts to unseat them, international commitments mean less. We see in the case of Pakistan a certain degree of cynicism with respect to international commitments. Rather than trying to build a national reputation by measuring carefully international commitments and earnestly working to implement international norms, the act of committing seems disconnected from the act of codification, which in turn seems unrelated to the act of implementation – if it happens. Rather, the country seems to stumble from one near-failure to another, like a poor money manager who pays off one credit card with another. This is all the more true because each new government feels no need to honor the agreements made or statutes enacted by the prior regime, unlike what we see in a stable constitutional democracy.

References

ADN Kronos International (2009) "Italy: Agreement Reached with Tunisia over Illegal Immigration," January 28. Available at www.adnkronos.com/AKI/English/Security/?id=3.0.2959735796. Accessed October 27, 2010.

Alam, Mikhtar (2010) "Sale of CFC-based Inhalers Allowed for Two More Years," Dawn.com. January 3. Available at http://news.dawn.com/wps/wcm/connect/dawn-content-library/dawn/the-newspaper/local/karachi-sale-of-cfcbased-inhalers-allowed-for-two-more-years-310. Accessed November 4, 2010.

Alexander, Christopher (2010) *Tunisia: Stability and Reform in the Modern Maghreb*. London: Routledge.

Anderson, Walter (2010) Director, South Asia Program, Nitze School of Advanced International Studies, Johns Hopkins University, Washington D.C., Interview with the Author, September 2.

AntiSlavery (2010) "Background: Bonded Labour in Pakistan." Available at www.anti-slavery.org/english/campaigns/take_action/background_bonded_labour_in_pakistan.aspx. Accessed November 5, 2010.

Arif, G.M. (2004) "Bonded Labour in Agriculture: A Rapid Assessment in Punjab and North West Frontier Province, Pakistan," March. Geneva: ILO. Available at www.ilo.org/wcmsp5/groups/public/--ed_norm/--declaration/documents/publication/wcms_082027.pdf. Accessed November 5, 2010.

Asian Development Bank (2010) "Situational Analysis of Women in Pakistan – An Overview." Available at www.adb.org/Documents/Books/Country_Briefing_Papers/Women_in_Pakistan/chap01.pdf. Accessed August 26, 2010.

Asian Human Rights Commission (2009) "Pakistan: Young Women Held in Military Torture Cells and Forced into Sexual Slavery." Available at www.ahrchk.net/ahrc-in-news/mainfile.php/2009ahrcinnews/2434/. Accessed November 5, 2010.

Aviation Safety Network (2010) "Operator Index for Pakistan." *Flight Safety Foundation*. Available at http://aviation-safety.net/database/operator/airline-country.php?id=AP. Accessed August 30, 2010.

Baloch, Shafi (2008) "Human Trafficking on the Rise in Pakistan," *The Nation*. June 13. Available at www.nation.com.pk/pakistan-news-newspaper-daily-english-online/Regional/Karachi/13-Jun-2008/Human-trafficking-on-the-rise-in-Pakistan. Accessed November 3, 2010.

BBC News Online (2007) "EU Bans Pakistan Airline Flights," March 5. Available at http://news.bbc.co.uk/2/hi/6418891.stm. Accessed August 30, 2010.
BBC News Online (2009) "Pilot Jailed for Sicily Air Crash," March 24. Available at http://news.bbc.co.uk/2/hi/europe/7962082.stm. Accessed October 29, 2010.
BBC News Online (2010) "Pakistan to Ask Switzerland to Reopen Zardari Cases," March 31. Available at http://news.bbc.co.uk/2/hi/8596708.stm. Accessed November 2, 2010.
Bitzan, John (2009) "Tunisia: General Political Environment." *EDC.* Available at www.edc.ca/english/docs/gtunisia_e.pdf. Accessed August 26, 2010.
Brooks, Risa (2013) "Abandoned at the Palace: Why the Tunisian Military Defected from the Ben Ali Regime in January 2011," *Journal of Strategic Studies* 36(2): 205–220.
Canada (2009) Immigration and Refugee Board of Canada. "Tunisia: Domestic Violence, Legislation and Protection Available to Victims (2007–2009)," November 24, TUN103273.FE. Available at www.unhcr.org/refworld/docid/4b20f04a3c.html. Accessed August 29, 2010.
Central Intelligence Agency (2010) *CIA Factbook – Pakistan.* Available at www.cia.gov/library/publications/the-world-factbook/geos/pk.html. Accessed November 2, 2010.
Civil Aviation Authority (2010) Statistical information. Available at www.caapakistan.com.pk/AviationStatistics/MTF%20by%20Airports%202008_09.pdf. Accessed November 4, 2010.
Cohen, Stephen Philip (2004) *The Idea of Pakistan.* Washington D.C.: Brookings Institution.
Collective for Social Science Research, Karachi and International Labour Organization (2004a) "A Rapid Assessment of Bonded Labour in Domestic Work and Begging in Pakistan," March. Geneva: ILO. Available at www.ilo.org/wcmsp5/groups/public/--ed_norm/--declaration/documents/publication/wcms_082030.pdf. Accessed November 5, 2010.
Collective for Social Science Research, Karachi and International Labour Organization (2004b) "A Rapid Assessment of Bonded Labour in Hazardous Industries in Pakistan: Glass Bangle-making, Tanneries and Construction." March. Geneva: ILO. Available at www.ilo.org/wcmsp5/groups/public/--ed_norm/–declaration/documents/publication/wcms_082031.pdf. Accessed November 5, 2010.
Cook, Maria Lorena (2008) "Unauthorized Migration and Border 'Control': Three Regional Views." *Cornell University ILR School.* Available at http://digitalcommons.ilr.cornell.edu/cgi/viewcontent.cgi?article=1005&context=conference. Accessed August 26, 2010.
Crilly, Rob and Alex Spillius (2010) "Wikileaks: Pakistan Accused of Helping Taliban in Afghanistan Attacks." *Daily Telegraph,* July 26. Available at www.telegraph.co.uk/news/worldnews/asia/afghanistan/7910687/Wikileaks-Pakistan-accused-of-helping-Taliban-in-Afghanistan-attacks.html. Accessed November 3, 2010.
Department of State, United States (2009a) *International Religious Freedom Report 2009 – Tunisia.* October 26. Available at www.state.gov/g/drl/rls/irf/2009/127359.htm. Accessed October 26, 2010.
Department of State, United States (2009b) Office of the Coordinator for Counterterrorism, *Country Reports on Terrorism 2008.* Chapter 2: South and Central Asia Overview. Available at www.state.gov/s/ct/rls/crt/2008/122434.htm. Accessed August 26, 2010.
Department of State, United States (2010a) *2009 Country Reports on Human Rights Practices – Tunisia.* March 11. Available at www.unhcr.org/refworld/docid/4b9e52b17c.html. Accessed August 23, 2010.
Department of State, United States (2010b) *Trafficking in Persons Report 2010 – Tunisia.* June 14. Available at www.unhcr.org/refworld/docid/4c1883bc2d.html. Accessed August 26, 2010.

Department of State, United States (2010c) *Background Report: Pakistan*. July 21. Available at www.state.gov/r/pa/ei/bgn/3453.htm. Accessed August 26, 2010.

Department of State, United States (2010d) *Trafficking in Persons Report 2010 – Pakistan*. June 14. Available at www.unhcr.org/refworld/docid/4c1883d1c.html. Accessed August 23, 2010.

Department of State, United States (2010e) Bureau of Democracy, Human Rights, and Labor, *2009 Human Rights Report: Pakistan*. Available at www.state.gov/g/drl/rls/hrrpt/2009/sca/136092.htm. Accessed August 26, 2010.

Department of State, United States (2010f) *Trafficking in Persons Report 2010 – Pakistan*. June 14. Available at www.unhcr.org/refworld/docid/4c1883d1c.html. Accessed August 25, 2010.

ECO Environment (2010) "Pakistan's Achievements in Environment Sector." *Economic Cooperation Organization Bulletin on Environment* no. 8. Available at www.ecosecretariat.org/ftproot/Publications/Bul_Env/8th%20Issue%20of%20ENV%20Bulletin-Final%20113.pdf. Accessed August 27, 2010.

Economist, The (2011) "Ali Baba Gone, But What About the 40 Thieves?" Available at www.economist.com/node/17959620/print. Accessed January 25, 2011.

Ellenbogen, Keith (2008) "Tunisia Navy Boards the Oceana Marviva Med." *Oceana* (June). Available at http://rallen.oceana.org/en/our-work/oceana-on-the-water/the-marviva/expedition-diaries/mediterranean-expedition-2008/tunisia-navy-boards-the-oceana-marviva. Accessed October 27, 2010.

Endres, Gunter (2009) World Airline Directory 2009. *Flight International* 175(5184). April 14–20.

Entelis, John (2007) "The Unchanging Politics of North Africa," *Middle East Policy* 14(4) (Winter): 23–41.

Europa World (2010a) "Economic Affairs (Tunisia)." London: Routledge. Available at www.europaworld.com.erl.lib.byu.edu/entry/tn.is.49. Accessed August 26, 2010.

Europa World (2010b) "President Ben Ali Re-elected (Tunisia)." London: Routledge. Available at www.europaworld.com.erl.lib.byu.edu/entry/EE001962. Accessed August 26, 2010.

Europa World (2010c) "Tourism (Tunisia)." London: Routledge. Available at www.europaworld.com.erl.lib.byu.edu/entry/tn.ss.72. Accessed August 26, 2010.

Europa World (2010d) "Transport (Tunisia)." London: Routledge. Available at www.europaworld.com.erl.lib.byu.edu/entry/tn.ss.64. Accessed August 26, 2010.

Europa World (2010e) "Recent Developments: The Abolition of the Seventeenth Amendment; Increasing Violence (Pakistan)." London: Routledge. Available at www.europaworld.com.erl.lib.byu.edu/entry/EE001566. Accessed August 26, 2010.

Europa World (2010fh) "Regional Relations (Pakistan)." London: Routledge. Available at www.europaworld.com.erl.lib.byu.edu/entry/EE001568. Accessed August 26, 2010.

Europa World (2010g) "Other External Relations (Pakistan)." London: Routledge. Available at www.europaworld.com.erl.lib.byu.edu/entry/EE001569. Accessed August 26, 2010.

Europa World (2010h) "Transport (Pakistan)." London: Routledge. Available at www.europaworld.com.erl.lib.byu.edu/entry/pk.ss.68. Accessed August 26, 2010.

European Maritime Safety Agency (2009) "Quality Performance List of Flags (Black-Grey-White)." Paris MOU. Available at https://extranet.emsa.europa.eu/index.php?option=com…task… Accessed August 26, 2010.

Flight Safety Foundation (2008) "News." Flight Safety Foundation: Aviation Safety Network. Available at http://aviation-safety.net/news/news.php?var=200509%#1508. Accessed August 15, 2010.

Freedom House (2010a) "Freedom in the World 2009 – Tunisia," February 15. Available at www.freedomhouse.org/template.cfm?page=22&year=2009&country=7721. Accessed July 3, 2010.

Freedom House (2010b) "Women's Rights in the Middle East and North Africa 2010 – Tunisia," March 3. Available at www.unhcr.org/refworld/docid/4b99011cc.html. Accessed August 26, 2010.

Freedom House (2010c) "Freedom in the World 2010 – Pakistan." Available at www.freedomhouse.org/template.cfm?page=363&year=2010. Accessed November 1, 2010.

Frontier Star (2009) "PAC for Putting Name of Former Chairman KPT on ECL," April 6. Available at www.thefreelibrary.com/PAC+for+putting+name+of+former+Chairman+KPT+on+ECL-a0197380068. Accessed November 3, 2010.

Gasiorowski, Mark J. (1992) "The Failure of Reform in Tunisia," *Journal of Democracy* 3 (4) (October): 85–97.

Globalis (2001) "Indicator: Consumption of Ozone-depleting Chlorofluorocarbons – 2001." Available at http://globalis.gvu.unu.edu/indicator.cfm?IndicatorID=82&country=BY#rowBY. Accessed August 30, 2010.

Guardian, The (2011) "Tunisia Protests: 'The Fear Has Gone ... I've Been Waiting 20 Years for Today'," January 14, by Angelique Chrisafis. Available at www.guardian.co.uk/world/2011/jan/14/tunisia-protests-tunis-ben-ali. Accessed January 14, 2011.

Hasan, Syed Shoaib (2010) "Pakistan Crash Raises Questions About Air Safety." *BBC News*, July 28. Available at www.bbc.co.uk/news/world-south-asia-10792774. Accessed August 26, 2010.

Hassan, Raza (2009) "Karachi: Port Vulnerable to Looming Terror Threat," December 7. Available at http://news.dawn.com/wps/wcm/connect/dawn-content-library/dawn/the-newspaper/local/karachi-port-vulnerable-to-looming-terror-threat-729. Accessed November 3, 2010.

Henry, Clement (2007) "Tunisia's 'Sweet Little' Regime." in Robert I. Rotberg, ed., *Worst of the Worst: Dealing with Repressive and Rogue Nations*. Cambridge, MA: World Peace Foundation; Washington D.C.: Brookings Institution Press, pp. 300–324.

Hoyt, Timothy D. (2005) "The War on Terrorism: Implications for South Asia," in Devin T. Hagerty, ed., *South Asia in World Politics*. Lanham, MD: Rowman & Littlefield, pp. 281–300.

Human Rights Watch (2010) *World Report 2010 – Tunisia*, January 20. Available at www.unhcr.org/refworld/docid/4b586cdd7b.html. Accessed August 31, 2010.

Hussein, Maliha H., Abdul Razzaq Saleemi, Saira Malik, and Shazreh Hussain (2004) "Bonded Labour in Agriculture: A Rapid Assessment in Sindh and Balochistan, Pakistan," March. Geneva: ILO. Available at www.ilo.org/wcmsp5/groups/public/—ed_norm/—declaration/documents/publication/wcms_082026.pdf. Accessed November 5, 2010.

International Civil Aviation Organization (2008) "List of States that have Authorized ICAO to Release Information on their Safety Oversight Audit Conducted Between 1999 and 2004." *ICAO-Flight Safety Information Exchange*. November 7. Available at www.icao.int/fsix/auditRep1.cfm. Accessed August 26, 2010.

International Confederation of Free Trade Unions (2005) "Internationally-Recognised Core Labour Standards in Tunisia: Report for the WTO General Council Review of the Trade Policies of Tunisia." Geneva. September 28–30. Available at www.icftu.org/www/pdf/clstunisia2005.pdf. Accessed August 28, 2010.

International Maritime Bureau (2010) IMB Live Piracy Map. Available at www.icc-ccs.org/index.php?option=com_fabrik&view=visualization&controller=visualization.googlemap&Itemid=219. Accessed October 27, 2010.

International Maritime Organization (2010) "Convention for the Suppression of Unlawful Acts Against the Safety of Maritime Navigation, Protocol for the Suppression of Unlawful Acts Against the Safety of Fixed Platforms Located on the Continental Shelf." Available at www.imo.org/About/Conventions/ListOfConventions/Pages/SUA-Treaties.aspx. Accessed February 23, 2010.

Integrated Regional Information Networks (IRIN) (2010) *Pakistan: IDPs Reluctant to Return*. July 11. Available at www.unhcr.org/refworld/docid/4c3adfca1a.html. Accessed August 30, 2010.

Ireland: Refugee Documentation Centre (2010) *Pakistan: Information About Honour Killings in Pakistan. Information About Women's Groups that Support Potential Victims*. May 26. Q12187. Available at www.unhcr.org/refworld/docid/4c0779cf2.html. Accessed August 26, 2010.

IRI Index (2009) Pakistan Public Opinion Survey (July 15–August 7). Available at www.iri.org/sites/default/files/2009%20October%201%20Survey%20of%20Pakistan%20Public%20Opinion,%20July%2015-August%207,%202009.pdf. Accessed September 24, 2010.

Kennedy, Charles H. (2004) "The Creation and Development of Pakistan's Anti-terrorism Regime, 1997–2002," in Satu P. Limaye, Robert G. Wirsing, and Mohan Malik, eds., *Religious Radicalism and Security in South Asia*. Honolulu: Asia Pacific Security Center, pp. 387–413.

Keohane, Robert (1984) *After Hegemony: Cooperation and Discord in the World Political Economy*. Princeton: Princeton University Press.

Khan, Rabia (2009) "Situational Analysis and Mapping of Women's Human Rights in Pakistan." *CIDA Pakistan Progam*. Available at www.mowdalumni.com.pk/pdf/GenderGovernanceCitizenshipRights/Final-Report-on-Women-Human-Rights-in-Pakistan-PublicVersion.pdf. Accessed August 26, 2010.

King, Stephen J. (1998) "Economic Reform and Tunisia's Hegemonic Party: The End of the Administrative Elite – Beyond Colonialism and Nationalism in North Africa," *Arab Studies Quarterly* (Spring): 59–86.

Labidi, Lilia (2006) "The New Psychology of Tunisian Women and the Personal Status Code." Paper presented at Women and Change in the Middle East. Woodrow Wilson School Middle East Program, May 21. Available at www.wilsoncenter.org/index.cfm?topic_id=1426&fuseaction=topics.event_summary&event_id=181101. Accessed October 28, 2010.

Labidi, Lilia (2007) "Islamic Law, Feminism, and Family." In Valentine M. Moghadam, ed., *From Patriarchy to Empowerment: Women's Participation, Movements, and Rights in the Middle East, North Africa, and South Asia*. Syracuse, NY: Syracuse University Press, pp. 278–292.

Lavoy, Peter (2005) "Pakistan's Foreign Relations," in Devin T. Hagerty, ed., *South Asia in World Politics*. Lanham, MD: Rowman & Littlefield, pp. 49–70.

Lawless, Richard I., Francesco Cavatorta, and Philip McCrum (2010) "History (Tunisia)," in Europa World online. London: Routledge. Available at www.europaworld.com.erl.lib.byu.edu/entry/tn.hi. Accessed August 26, 2010.

Lawson, Fred (2007) "Intraregime Dynamics, Uncertainty, and the Persistence of Authoritarianism in the Contemporary Arab World," in Oliver Schlumberger, ed., *Debating Arab Authoritarianism: Dynamics and Durability in Nondemocratic Regimes*. Stanford: Stanford University Press, pp. 109–127.

Los Angeles Times (2011) "Tunisia's Uprising was Three Years in the Making," January 27. Available at www.latimes.com/news/nationworld/world/la-fg-tunisia-uprising-20110127,0,7541408.story. Accessed January 27, 2011.

Lust, Ellen, ed. (2011) *The Middle East.* 12th edn. Washington D.C.: Congressional Quarterly Press.

Magharebia (2010) "Police in Medenine (480 km South of Tunis) Intercepted a Human Trafficker…" October 22. Available at http://magharebia.com/en_GB/articles/awi/newsbriefs/general/2010/10/22/newsbrief-04?change_locale=true. Accessed October 27, 2010.

Malik, Yogendra, Ashok Kapur, Charles Kennedy, Mahendra Lawoti, Robert Oberst, and Syedur Rahman (2009) *Government and Politics in South Asia.* Boulder, CO: Westview Press.

Maritime International Secretariat (MARISEC) (2009) "Shipping Industry Flag State Performance Table: 2009 Update." London: Maritime International Secretariat Services Limited. Available at www.marisec.org/FlagStatePerformanceTable09.pdf. Accessed August 30, 2010.

Masud A., A.K.M. (2005) "Treading Along a Treacherous Trail: Research on Trafficking in Persons in South Asia," in Frank Laczko, ed., *Data and Research on Human Trafficking: A Global Survey*. Geneva: IOM, pp. 141–164.

Mayar, Abdul Hadi (2009) "Pakistan Urges Tightened Border Control to Prevent Amrs, Militants Movement." *China View*, October 22. Available at http://news.xinhuanet.com/english/2009–10/22/content_12298359.htm. Accessed August 30, 2010.

Mediterranean MOU on PSC (2010) Tunisia. Available at www.medmou.org/. Accessed October 27, 2010.

Minority Rights Group International (2010) *State of the World's Minorities and Indigenous Peoples 2010 – Pakistan.* July 1. Available at www.unhcr.org/refworld/docid/4c33310cc.html. Accessed August 24, 2010.

Montalvo, Jose G. and Marta Reynal-Querol (2005) "Ethnic Polarization, Potential Conflict, and Civil Wars." Working paper, Universidad Pompeu Fabra Department of Economics and Business, March. Available at www.econ.upf.edu/docs/papers/downloads/770.pdf. Accessed October 26, 2010.

Nawaat (2010) "The Tunisian Intifada…" January 3, by Rob Prince. Available at http://nawaat.org/portail/2011/01/03/the-tunisian-intifadah%e2%80%a6/. Accessed January 14, 2011.

New Pakistan (2010) "President Signs Historic Women's Right Bill," March 10. Available at http://new-pakistan.com/2010/3/10/president-signs-historic-women-s-rights-bill. Accessed November 5, 2010.

New York Times (2010) "Generals in Pakistan Push for Shakeup of Government," September 28.

New York Times (2011a) "Power Again Changes Hands in Tunisia as Chaos Remains," January 15. Available at www.nytimes.com/2011/01/16/world/africa/16tunis.html. Accessed January 16, 2011.

New York Times (2011b) "France Seen Wary of Interfering in Tunisia Crisis," January 16. Available at www.nytimes.com/2011/01/17/world/africa/17france.html. Accessed February 7, 2011.

Office de l'Aviation Civile et des Aéroports (2010) Service d'Information Aéronautique. Available at www.oaca.nat.tn/index.php?id=673. Accessed February 23, 2010.

Ozone Depletion Today (2004) "Pakistan Calls on Nations to Share Ozone Policy Expertise," February 20. *Ozone Depletion Today*. Available at www.allbusiness.com/public-administration/administration-environmental/751418–1.html. Accessed July 30, 2010.

Pakistan International Airways (2008) *2007 Annual Report.* Available at www.piac.com.pk/PIA_About/profiles/2007/annualreportfull_05052008.pdf. Accessed November 4, 2010.

Pakistan, Government of, Ministry of Finance, Poverty Reduction Strategy Paper Secretariat (2003) "Accelerating Economic Growth and Reducing Poverty: The Road Ahead," December 31. Available at http://siteresources.worldbank.org/PAKISTANEXTN/Resources/PRSP.pdf. Accessed November 1, 2010.

PakTribune (2006) "The Senate Was Told on Wednesday that Government of Pakistan Has Rejected the Report of United Nation Regarding Pakistan Not Doing Enough to Stop Human Smuggling," September 14. Available at www.paktribune.com/news/index.shtml?154101. Accessed November 3, 2010.

Prevention and Control of Human Trafficking Ordinance (2002) Government of Pakistan: An Ordinance to Prevent and Control Human Trafficking. Available at www.hsph.harvard.edu/population/trafficking/pakistan.traf.02.doc. Accessed January 18, 2011.

Ray, Julie and Mohamed Younis (2009) "Approval of US Leadership Up in Some Arab Countries," Gallup, June 1. Available at www.gallup.com/poll/118940/approval-leadership-arab-countries.aspx. Accessed February 24, 2010.

Rheault, Magali (2007) "Majorities Support Women's Rights in North Africa: Most Men Agree with Principles of Gender Equality." Gallup On-line, November 6. Available at www.gallup.com/poll/102595/Majorities-Support-Womens-Rights-North-Africa.aspx. Accessed October 25, 2010.

Seattle Times (2010) "U.N.-listed Terrorist Front Group Aids Pakistan Flood Victims," August 3. Available at http://seattletimes.nwsource.com/html/nationworld/2012525118_pakflood04.html. Accessed November 3, 2010.

Shaikh, Farzana (2009) *Making Sense of Pakistan*. New York: Columbia University Press.

Shamsuddin, Mian (2009) "Corruption and Governance." *Dawn*, November 23. Letter to the Editor. Available at www.transparency.org.pk/news/newsnov09.htm. Accessed November 2, 2010.

Skinner, E. Benjamin (2009) "Pakistan's Forgotten Plight: Modern-Day Slavery," *Time*, October 27.

Tokyo MOU (2010a) *2009 Annual Report*. Available at www.tokyo-mou.org/ANN09.pdf. Accessed November 4, 2010.

Tokyo MOU (2010b) Memorandum of Understanding on Port State Control in the Asia-Pacific Region. Asia-Pacific Computerized Information System. Available at http://212.45.16.136/isss/public_apcis.php?Action=getSearchForm. Accessed November 4, 2010.

Tunisia (2010) 5+5 Summit. Available at www.tunisie.gov.tn/index.php?option=com_content&task=view&id=571&lang=english&Itemid=236. Accessed October 29, 2010.

Tunisia Ministry of Defense (2010) "Tunisian Participation in the Operations of Preservation of Peace in the World." Available at www.defense.tn/en/index.php?option=com_content&task=view&id=43. Accessed October 27, 2010.

Tunisian National Office of Family and Population (2001) "Tunisian Health Survey" – performed in conjunction with the Pan Arab Project for Family Health, Tunis. Available at www.papfam.org/index.php?option=com_content&view=article&id=48. Accessed February 20, 2014.

Tunisia Online News (2010a) "Tunisian Navy to Build New Patrol Boat." Available at www.tunisiaonlinenews.com/tunisian-navy-gives-launch-to-the-building-of-a-patrol-boat/. Accessed October 27, 2010.

UN Committee on the Elimination of Discrimination against Women (2002) "Concluding Comments of the Committee on the Elimination of Discrimination against Women: Tunisia." June 21. A/57/38, paras.171–210.

UN Committee on the Rights of the Child (2009) "Consideration of Reports Submitted by States Parties under Article 44 of the Convention – Concluding Observations: Pakistan." Fifty-second session – October 15.
UN Environmental Programme (2007) Decisions of the Parties Related to the Con-Compliance Procedure of the Montreal Protocol on Substances that Deplete the Ozone Layer. Available at www.unep.ch/ozone/Meeting_Documents/impcom/MOP_decisions_on_NCP.pdf. Accessed August 29, 2010.
UN Environmental Programme (2009) Ozone Secretariat. 2009 *Handbook for the Montreal Protocol on Substances that Deplete the Ozone Layer.* 8th edn. Available at www.unep.ch/ozone/Publications/MP_Handbook/MP-Handbook-2009.pdf. Accessed July 31, 2010.
UN Environmental Programme (2010) Executive Committee of the Multilateral Fund for the Implementation of the Montreal Protocol. 61st Meeting, July 5–9, Montreal. UNEP/OzL.Pro/ExCom61/48. Available at www.multilateralfund.org/files/61/6148.pdf. Accessed October 29, 2010.
UN Fund for Population Activities (2006) *State of World Population 2006: A Passage to Hope – Women and International Migration.* New York: UN. Available at www.unfpa.org/swp/2006/english/notes/indicators.html. Accessed November 3, 2010.
UN Human Rights Council (2010) *Report Submitted by the Special Rapporteur on Trafficking in Persons, Especially Women and Children, Addendum: Communications to and from Governments*. May 31. A/HRC/14/32/Add.1. Available at www.unhcr.org/refworld/docid/4c29bd512.html. Accessed August 30, 2010.
UN Office on Drugs and Crime (2010) Pakistan Profile. Available at www.unodc.org/pakistan/en/country-profile.html. Accessed November 3, 2010.
UN Office of the High Commission for Human Rights (2010) "UN Expert on Human Rights and Counter Terrorism Concludes Visit to Tunisia." UNOHCHR Press Release, January 26. www.ohchr.org/EN/NewsEvents/Pages/DisplayNews.aspx?NewsID=9772&LangID=E. Accessed October 27, 2010.
Watts, Susan (2007) "The Impact of Women of Changes in Personal Status Law in Tunisia." *WHO*: *Women and Gender Equity Knowledge Network.* Available at www.who.int/social_determinants/resources/changes_personal_status_tunisia_wgkn_2007.pdf. Accessed August 29, 2010.
Wikileaks (2010a) "Secret US Embassy Cables," Message from the US Embassy in Islamabad to the State Department, February 21, 2009. Available at http://cablegate.wikileaks.org/index.html. Accessed December 1, 2010.
Wikileaks (2010b) "Secret US Embassy Cables," Message from the US Embassy in Islamabad to the State Department, November 27, 2006. Available at http://cablegate.wikileaks.org/index.html. Accessed December 1, 2010.
World Bank (2008) *Country Assistance Strategy Progress Report for the Republic of Tunisia for the Period FY05–08*. Washington D.C.: The World Bank.
World Bank (2009) *Tunisia's Global Integration: Second Generation of Reforms to Boost Growth and Employment*. Washington D.C.: The World Bank.
World Bank (2010) Pakistan data. Available at http://data.worldbank.org/country/pakistan. Accessed November 1, 2010.
World Bank (2012) *Implementation Completion and Results Report on a Grant in the Amount of US$5.12 Million to the Republic of Tunisia for a Demonstration Project for the Phaseout of Ozone Depleting Substances*. Report No: ICR2530, Washington D.C., December 21.

World Travel & Tourism Council (2010) "Key Facts at a Glance." Available at www.wttc.org/eng/Tourism_Research/Economic_Research/Country_Reports/Pakistan/. Accessed August 30, 2010.

World Warships (2006) Tunisia. Available at www.worldwarships.com/warships_tunisia.htm. Accessed October 27, 2010.

Yahtaoui, Mukhtar (2001) "Open Letter to President Ben Ali," July 6. Available at www.humanrightsfirst.org/middle_east/tunisia/open_letter.pdf. Accessed October 29, 2010.

8 Isolationist autocracies

Belarus and Equatorial Guinea

Theoretical predictions regarding isolationist autocracies

The isolated dictatorship is widely seen as the most recalcitrant character in international law. Liberal thinking, joined by reputational and legitimacy theory, predict that such a regime will be an obdurate opponent of most efforts at creating an international society governed by law. It will likely pride itself on its non-compliance.

Rationalist and managerial theories hold out more hope. Rationalists may argue that such a regime has the virtue of being easy to understand. If only the international community can learn what makes the dictator tick, it may be possible to cajole, bribe, or even coerce him into compliance. There may be some weakness or dependency that can be exploited. The managerial school would argue that if you ever manage to change the state's priorities, there is a good chance the policy will be implemented.

Cultural theory has no clear predictions, however, in that much depends on whether the leadership is in tune with and a product of the prevailing culture. In some cases, dictatorship may simply be in the bones – in others it may be an alien imposition.

Belarus

Overview

Belarus has been described as a "time capsule" (Henko 2010) and the "worst of the worst" (Freedom House 2010a). It is the only former Soviet republic that has adopted neither economic nor political liberalization but rather has chosen to remain a Cold War relic. The political system is dominated by President Aleksandr Lukashenko who since 1994 has governed by increasingly autocratic means over a society where four out of five people depend on the state for their livelihood (State Dept. 2010a). Overall, the leader appears to be popular and benefits from the country's political lethargy (Zadora 2009, 141).

The country is land-locked, bordering Russia, with which it has experienced an on-again-off-again relationship. Russia is its most important supplier of energy and foreign aid, as well as a primary export market. This dependency, however, makes Belarus anything but pliant, and from time to time Russia has moved to punish its obstreperous neighbor (Suzdaltsev 2009). The European Union, for its part, imagines that one day Belarus will become an active associate, but in the meantime puts pressure on the regime to release political prisoners and hold fair elections (Rossmann 2009). These efforts generally coincide with American pressure as well (Kramer 2010). The government generally protests such intrusions into domestic affairs and adopts a generally antagonistic posture toward the West.

Liberalism

Belarus democracy scores are very low. Certainly, Lukashenko has governed through a combination of illiberal strategies, including wide-spread election manipulation, intimidation, violence, censorship, and cooptation. Belarus briefly experimented with Western-style reforms (Dept. of State 2010a). Lukashenko came to power in 1994 in the country's last free and fair elections, inheriting already vast presidential powers (Rossmann 2009, 237). He then set about expanding those powers to entrench himself. In 1996, he engineered a constitutional amendment via referendum that granted the president a five-year renewable term. He also declared that his first "term" began that year, rather than 1994, and therefore kept himself in office at least until 2001 by the stroke of a pen (Freedom House 2010a). In 2004 he removed term limits (Dept. of State 2010a). Lukashenko relies heavily on his special security forces and the bureaucracy. The legislature provides validation for his policies – not debate. The judiciary is not independent.

Lukashenko was reelected at the end of each term. Each time the elections were rejected by international observers (Rossmann 2009, 243; *New York Times* 2010). The infractions involved both preelection campaigning and the conduct of the election itself. The government controls access to the media, with the exception of some foreign broadcasts, and does not hesitate to arrest independent-minded journalists (Dept. of State 2010a; Freedom House 2010a). Opposition candidates have been harassed and sometimes imprisoned (Europa 2010b).

> In June 2001 two former investigators at the Office of the Prosecutor-General, who had been granted asylum in the USA, claimed that senior government officials had organized the assassinations of political opponents to Lukashenko's regime, and alleged them to be responsible for the deaths of the missing opposition figures [Viktar] Hanchar and [Yuri] Zakharenka [kidnapped in 1999], as well as Dmitrii Zavadski, a cameraman for a Russian television channel, whose location had been unknown since July 2000. The allegations were supported by the Chairman of the Federation of Trade Unions of Belarus, Uladzimir Hancharyk, who in July 2001 revealed documents that apparently linked the Prosecutor-General, Viktar Sheyman,

> and the former Minister of Internal Affairs, Yuriy Sivakow, with the disappearance and presumed murder of Hanchar and Zakharenka.
>
> (Europa 2010b)

Opposition figures have sometimes been released from prison and a few civil society organizations have been given a freer rein, under pressure from American and European governments (Kramer 2010). But the gains are often short-lived. Following relatively small peaceful protests following the December 2010 elections, NGO websites were frozen, seven presidential candidates were arrested and face up to fifteen years in prison, and more than 600 protesters were arrested for several days (RFE/RL 2010).

The government in Belarus has also taken an unusual approach to economic development. The government owns or controls roughly three-fourths of the national economy, according to most counts (figures are unreliable because of currency manipulation). As put by Ryder:

> Since 1994 the Government has aimed to implement a socially orientated market economy. This means that the state controls over three-quarters of the economy through centrally mandated wage targets; directing bank loans to key sectors and firms regardless of their solvency; administering controls on prices and profit margins; and through legislation that allows the Government to overturn management decisions in any firm that is partially state-owned or was formerly state-owned. Privatization has been slow.
>
> (Ryder 2010)

For many years, the government reserved the right to control any firm in which it had a single share (the "golden share"), even if the firm was private (Ryder 2010). Agriculture has remained largely collectivized (Europa 2010a). Foreign investors and entrepreneurs find conditions daunting, however. These include "complex bureaucratic procedures and the red tape of complicated legal provisions regulating credit and investment operations" (Katibnikov 2009, 55). There are indications this may be gradually changing, however, as hundreds of firms have been privatized in recent years, including Priorbank – acquired by an Austrian bank in 2003 (Ryder 2010).

Belarus engages in a considerable degree of international trade, although Russia is the single biggest customer and supplier, providing 60 percent of imports and purchasing 37 percent of exports. Belarus has signed a variety of trade agreements with Russia and a number of former Soviet republics, culminating in a customs union with Russia and Kazakhstan which came into effect in 2010 (Europa 2010c). This isn't to say that economic relations with Russia have been smooth, however. Belarus routinely re-sells its discounted Russian gas and oil for considerable profit in Europe. Russia, in return, has taken half ownership of the principal oil company in Belarus and negotiated higher prices for gas exports (Europa 2010c).

While it is doubtful that tensions with Russia will necessarily push Belarus to the West, it is worth noting that exports to EU countries have increased in recent years. The Netherlands nearly doubled its purchases of Belarusian goods (mostly oil) from 2005 to 2006 and is now importing roughly half as much as Russia.

Taken together, Belarus scores poorly with respect to both political and economic liberalism, and we should expect to see poor performance with respect to international law if liberal theory holds true.

Managerial school

Autocratic regimes are often capable of strict implementation of international norms through their ability to mobilize resources and ensure enforcement of regulations. In the case of Belarus, the state is obviously capable of mobilizing considerable resources. Belarusians are taxed heavily – government revenues amount to half of the GDP (Ryder 2010). Corporate taxes are especially high, amounting to 144 percent of profits according to a 2007 World Bank study (Ryder 2010). Governing elites have devised extralegal means of increasing revenue, as explained by the Human Rights Council:

> On the basis of the available data, the Special Rapporteur concludes that the budgetary expenditures of Belarus (especially those related to the internal security forces and to the social safety net policies) cannot possibly be supported by the performance of the country's highly centralized and relatively closed economy. A thorough international investigation into the origin of the financial resources funding these expenditures is therefore necessary. That origin may very well be of an illicit nature.
>
> (HRC 2007, 12)

Later in the report, reference is made to alleged illegal arms trafficking through government agents – most likely under the direction of Lukashenko himself – as has been mentioned in other research (Kramer and Wilson 2010). Generally speaking, low- and mid-ranking government officials, including the police, are careful to comply with instructions – mostly out of fear of serious repercussions (Kramer 2010). The police and regulators are capable of deploying across large areas of Belarus, to the point that they are often guilty of harassment and abuse.

Local governments also generate considerable revenue through taxation and service fees, although this does not translate into local control.

> Local authorities play an important role in the provision of various services, including primary health care. However, the regional and district levels of government lack legally defined limits of authority and guaranteed financing amounts. Consequently, although responsibility for health care services is devolved to the local government level, this mandate is frequently not matched by appropriate resources and a legal entitlement to generate revenue for the local budget. A strong executive power structure organized in a top-down

> manner and reporting directly to the President undermines the accountability of the executive branch to locally elected people's representatives.
>
> (Richardson and Anker 2008, 5)

The result is often discriminatory. While the country enjoys a surfeit of medical professionals, they are not distributed evenly across the country. There is an urban bias, with 8.24 doctors for every 1,000 residents of the city of Minsk and only 4.36 doctors per 1,000 residents of the Minsk district (Richardson and Anker 2008, 62).

Belarus has reasonably strong border controls in part to protect against nuclear materials trafficking (Belarus 2010a; BelTA 2010). Travel across the western and northern borders is a concern, however, and the government has adopted plans to develop biometric passports to better track the movement of people (Belarus 2010a).

Reputational theory

Belarus struggled during the 1990s to establish international credibility. Although it has viewed relations with the West with disdain, government leaders sought to maintain strong enough fiscal and monetary policies to entitle them to international credit should the need arise.

Belarus receives close to perfect marks from creditors. The overall risk rating for foreign direct investment is among the lowest in the world. Even Moody's and Standard & Poor's bond ratings for Belarus are quite strong (B+), particularly for a country that has not embraced economic liberalism. The government was even able to successfully float a bond (Kramer 2010).

Belarus' financial reputation does not carry over to other areas. Lukashenko has a reputation for blunt confrontations with foreign leaders (Ioffe 2004, 106). He has been strongly criticized and put under sanctions by both Western European states and the Russia government. Sometimes he speaks in chauvinistic anti-Western terms that embarrass Moscow (Balmaceda 2007, 203). He has blocked EU and OSCE election monitors, acquiescing to their presence only under duress. As put by Balmaceda:

> The centerpiece of Belarussian ideology is the elevation of Belarussian sovereignty. The importance of sovereignty is used to justify ignoring calls for change in the regime's domestic policies. With a periodic deterioration of Lukashenko's relations with Russia, this anti-Western rhetoric sometimes turns into something resembling North Korea's *juche* (self-reliance), but in a mild and rather pathetic form since Belarus cannot in practice isolate itself from the rest of the world.
>
> (Balmaceda 2007, 208)

It is difficult to say whether Belarusian leaders really want a reputation for compliance. It would seem that they hope to be taken seriously – and also left alone – two positions that in most cases are mutually contradictory.

Culture

Belarusian nationalism is something of an oxymoron as there is little evidence that Belarusians feel attached to any particular identity. Even before World War II, many Belarusian lands were collectivized and absorbed into Soviet structures while many elite were admitted into leadership positions in the Party (Ioffe 2004, 102). During World War II, Belarus was divided between Nazi Germany and Soviet Russia. Both occupiers committed atrocities and slaughtered vast numbers of local inhabitants. Figures vary widely, but most agree that at least one out of every four Belarusians died during the war (Henko 2010). These factors may help to explain why Belarus is the only former Soviet republic that has seriously entertained the possibility of reunification with Russia (Europa 2010c).

Belarusians are modernized with respect to their beliefs about the role of the state and the nature of the family and society. While the Belarusian Orthodox Church plays an important part in society (it is heavily supported by the state), most Belarusians have adopted a secular approach to life and politics.

Family life in Belarus echoes that of many Central European states. While women have enjoyed legal equality since the Soviet occupation, they do not enjoy social equality in every respect. Spousal abuse is widespread, as are cases of women leaving their husbands and filing for divorce as a result (Human Rights Council 2007, 12). Alcohol is a factor in many incidents (Radio Free Europe 2006).

Economic conditions are worrisome for many in the country – particularly those living in rural areas where poverty has been a serious concern for government officials. Partly as a result of increases in wages in state-run firms, incomes increased dramatically during the 2000s and the poverty rate fell from 27 percent to 11 percent.

> At the end of 2005 only 70% of dwellings in rural areas had running water, only 65% had sewerage, only 54% had central heating, only 41% had hot water, and only 56% had indoor bathrooms or showers (versus 90%–95% for dwellings in urban areas).
>
> (Ryder 2010)

Rather than causing anger and resentment, however, these conditions tend to increase resignation. Although some have joined in protests against the government over the past ten years, the numbers are decreasing (Freedom House 2010a). Even the elites – both in the government and in business – are generally passive, and civil society has yet to emerge as autonomous from the state.

Legitimacy

In general, it does not appear that Lukashenko considers the norms established by the international community to be entirely legitimate in the first place, nor does he consider himself bound even after committing to them. Emphasis on the norm of sovereignty generally indicates skepticism and even hostility toward all other norms (Shen 2000).

The rhetoric, however, conceals a more cooperative approach. Belarus hosts several important international organizations, including the EU, the OSCE, and the UNDP. The UNDP 2010 Human Development Report praised the progress Belarus has made in the area of poverty alleviation and reducing unemployment (Broek 2010). The government has also received considerable financial support from the International Monetary Fund including a $2.45 billion stand-by arrangement in 2009 to support government efforts. As put by the IMF:

> Macroeconomic policies have been generally appropriate. Fiscal policy has served as an important anchor to the economic program, with the deficit in 2009 being less than 1 percent of GDP. The decision to cut lending under government programs and reaffirmation of the binding nature of the lending limit will make more financial resources available to private business, creating conditions for gradually reducing market interest rates. The re-centering of the exchange rate band at end-2009 and the depreciation of the ruble against the currency basket have supported external adjustment.
>
> (IMF 2010)

Belarus is quite active in the United Nations. It was a member of ECOSOC and the UN Environmental Programme's Governing Council in the late 2000s and has sat on UNICEF's Executive Board as well as commissions dealing with women's rights (CEDAW), sustainable development, narcotic drugs, and economic, social, and cultural rights (Belarus 2010b).

Rationalism

Looking back at the material presented thus far, there are clearly cases where the government of Lukashenko calculates benefits and weighs risks before decided whether to comply with a particular international norm. The scope of actors that are included in these decisions is remarkably narrow. The legislature and judiciary, as mentioned, do not initiate policy and generally endorse what is proposed by the executive. The public – and even the business elites – are generally submissive (even passive). As put by Zadora: "The mentality of the Belarusian elite as well as the Belarusian people as a whole are passivity, lack of ambition and a minimalist attitude: little is better than nothing" (Zadora 2009, 141–142). On the men and women in power, she says:

> The political elite in Belarus is an amorphous group, which is preoccupied with its own security and well-being. The fear factor and the weak consolidation of this group are responsible for the fragility of the political elite. The Soviet heritage with its closed, corporatist and undemocratic rules has shaped the present elites. The total absence of controls from the society, the absence

> of a checks and balance system, the nonexistence of political opposition and alternatives is responsible for the weakness of the political elite.
>
> (Zadora 2009, 148)

With little to fear at home, Lukashenko worries mostly about balancing Russia with the EU. His principal priorities appear to be maximizing policy flexibility and political autonomy, combined with ensuring access to cheap energy and foreign markets and capital. Only when sanctions seriously threaten the country's economy is he willing to grant additional prerogatives to opposition figures (Kramer and Wilson 2010).

Performance across issue-areas

We now turn to Belarus' performance across our issue-areas. We will begin with norms related to defending territorial integrity.

Rules governing territorial defense: anti-terrorism and anti-trafficking norms

As a land-locked country without a merchant marine, we will naturally set aside the issue of piracy in Belarus. Instead, we will consider the government's efforts to comply with international norms against terrorism and against trafficking. Table 8.1 presents a snapshot of its performance.

Generally speaking, the level of compliance across these issue-areas is middling. Belarus has endorsed a number of key international conventions. In 2002, for example, Permanent Representative Sergey Ling declared to the UN General Assembly: "Belarus is going to continue cooperation with the Anti-terrorist committee of the UN Security Council and is working for complete implementation of all UN decisions concerning the fight against international terrorism" (Belarus 2002). He also emphasized that

> [T]he president and the government of Belarus consider the fight against terrorism to be of the highest priority. The republic has a reliable border and

Table 8.1 Indicators of compliance with rules governing territorial defense

UN CTC total score	5 (7 possible)
UN CTC score, minus treaty ratifications	3 (5 possible)
US State Dept. TIP score	2 (out of 3, with 1 the lowest rate)
UN origin score	5 (out of 5, with 1 the lowest rate)
UN transit score	3 (out of 5, with 1 the lowest rate)
Bales trafficking score	1 (out of 4, with 1 the lowest rate)
WomanStats trafficking score	2 (out of 4, with 1 the lowest rate)
2000 Trafficking Protocol signature	Yes
2000 Trafficking Protocol ratification	Yes

> customs control for prevention of the illegal transportation of weapons and ammunition through the Belarusian border, suppression of illegal migration; trade in drugs and other activity connected with terrorism.
>
> (Belarus 2002)

As a victim of Chernobyl's fallout, Belarus has worked with the international community to minimize the risk of nuclear terrorism and the trafficking of nuclear materials. This includes a joint project with Japan to install radiation monitors along the border and a "network of mobile laboratories" (BelTA 2010).

The country does not have any known indigenous terrorist groups, nor is there any evidence of foreign activity. However, in 2008, the country was rocked by an explosion that injured fifty people and "cast doubt on the government's ability to prevent any such events" in the future (OSAC 2009).

These indicators of Belarusian support for the war on terror are profoundly contradicted by its practice of selling weapons to states that are listed as sponsors of terrorism. At one point in the early 2000s, Belarus was reportedly selling military equipment to six of the seven countries listed as state sponsors of terrorism in open defiance of international norms and sanctions. Lukashenko is reported to have responded to Western criticism of arms sales to Syria by saying "No matter how severely we are admonished for it, we'll continue to help Syria militarily, because they have promised to help us in the same way" (Sannikov and Lenzi 2004).

Belarus has very high levels of human trafficking – particularly as a source country for Western Europe. There are relatively few obstacles to the many under-employed young women to travel west, and many are trapped in trafficking rings and forced sex work (Sims 2009, 628–629; UNDP 2010. This likely explains Belarus receiving the worst possible score as an origin country from the UN Office on Drugs and Crime (see Table 8.1).

Belarus has ratified the Trafficking Protocol and has adopted a wide range of statutes, decrees, and policies – both unilaterally and multilaterally – to address the problem. Even the US State Department, which has no reason to flatter the regime, has acknowledged that it is making "significant efforts" to comply (Dept. of State 2010b). For example, the penalty for trading in people is up to ten years in prison, kidnapping for sexual exploitation can bring fifteen years, and recruiting someone for sexual exploitation can result in a ten-year sentence, according to Belarusian government sources (Belarus 2004). Efforts are expanding to regulate modeling agencies and other trafficking fronts, with the help of NGOs (Dept. of State 2010b).

Belarus has engaged the help of numerous international organizations and foreign governments in these efforts. The International Organization for Migration, UNDP, and EU each has supported projects to improve border controls (Belarus 2004; UNDP 2010). The government has worked with the police forces of Poland, Germany, the Czech Republic, Israel, and Turkey to identify and disrupt international trafficking rings (Dept. of State 2010b). The results have been impressive. In the first three years of the past decade, the government claims to have identified 2,500 victims of trafficking and arrested 1,000 traffickers (Naumov 2007). Since then, hundreds more victims have been identified each year, along with their traffickers.

As put by the UN's trafficking rapporteur following a 2009 official inspection:

> Of note is the high number of cases prosecuted resulting equally in high number of convictions. The evidence of this huge success in prosecution indicates that the trafficking problem is not only real and serious in Belarus but also that measures are being undertaken to deal with the menace. Some of the good and perhaps unique practices found include compensation to victims of trafficking; international training center on migration and human trafficking;... extensive media campaigns directed at prevention of human trafficking and cooperation with international and regional organizations.... All of these are commendable developments...
>
> (Ezeilo 2009)

There is concern that the current initiatives will expire once the problem begins to subside (Ezeilo 2009).

To what extent are our various theories of international law compliance consistent with the outcomes in these areas? To begin, the fact that Belarus is an autocratic regime does not seem to help us understand why it complies fairly well with certain norms and not others. It is unclear, for example, why the government should devote so much energy to rescuing trafficked persons and apprehending their captors. But the regime is apparently eager to protect its citizens as they travel abroad, consistent with what one might expect from a democracy. Likewise, the concern on the part of the government to prevent nuclear trafficking and terrorism seem consistent with what any democratic government would do. On the other hand, its willingness to support regimes that have ties to terrorists seems more typical of a rogue state.

On the economic side, the illiberality of the regime contributes to compliance in these areas since it has no compunction about regulating private firms, restricting international travel and commerce, and limiting transnational communication. With respect to capacity, Belarus is redirecting resources toward border control, as predicted by the managerial school.

Belarus has a curious view of its reputation. On the one hand, it is happy to announce that it has received international approval for conforming to international norms. On the other hand, it seems to take just as much pride in getting caught when violating international norms. This is not entirely the attitude one might expect from a country that trumpets its sovereignty above all else. Ultimately, then, since it is very difficult to pin down how much Belarus cares about international approval.

It is difficult to say to what extent national culture informs national policy. Since the culture is characterized by a high degree of passivity and government paternalism, one would expect the regime to operate autonomously, albeit somewhat protectively. In some respects, this is what we observe.

As we discussed earlier, it is clear that Belarus does not believe international rules are intrinsically legitimate. But neither does it reject all international norms out of hand. It is fairly selective, but persuadable. Particularly with respect to human trafficking and border control policy, the government is eager to conform to international standards and has exposed itself to considerable international scrutiny and interference. Where the government considers the norm inappropriate to Belarus, the regime seems compelled to declare its intent to break the rule, lest there be any confusion about its intentions.

We have already noted that Belarus seems to calculate the costs and benefits and risks of different strategies with respect to international law compliance. With respect to the decision to provide military hardware and training to rogue states, Belarus may have calculated that there was little to lose and something to gain from working with these regimes. In the process, Lukashenko could demonstrate to his people that he was nobody's patsy. Likewise, taking a hard line on nuclear terrorism was a low-cost/high-payoff policy. Not only would it demonstrate to Belarusians that he cared about their safety, but by tightening controls on nuclear materials, Lukashenko could stop other sorts of threats.

It isn't entirely clear why the regime calculated that limiting human trafficking was worth the effort, however. Some regimes ignore outgoing trafficking and focus instead on those being trafficked into the country.

Rules designed to regulate the market: shipping and airline regulation and CFC control

Table 8.2 shows that, overall, Belarus has made a considerable effort to endorse and apply international norms in the areas of maritime and airline safety and preventing ozone depletion. To begin, although Belarus does not have an ocean-going merchant fleet, it has considerable experience with ship and port safety since the country is ringed and criss-crossed by navigable rivers and the town of

Table 8.2 Indicators of compliance with market regulating laws

Ratified SUA	Yes
Ratified SUA Protocol	Yes
1999–2001 ICAO non-compliance score	26.95 (on a scale of 0–100; 0=no deficiencies)
ICAO follow-up 2004	16.08
ICAO treaties ratified	24 (out of 43)
ali_standard air liberalization score	73 (0–183; high=liberal)
Cumulative Montreal Protocol compliance score	3 (0–24; low=compliance)
Reported data to Ozone Commission 2002–2007	Yes
Found non-compliant 2002–2007	No
Broke existing program 2002–2007	Yes

Mayzr serves as a port. Shipbuilding is an important industry and both it and local shipping are heavily regulated (Belarus 2010d). The government is inviting shipping companies to help the country create a merchant fleet worthy of the name (Naviny.by 2010).

Although Belarus has not joined the International Maritime Organization, it has endorsed a number of conventions, including SUA, SOLAS, and MARPOL (on pollution prevention). On the other hand, it has chosen not to ratify a number of important and widely accepted treaties, including two SOLAS and one MARPOL protocol (IMO 2010).

Airline regulation has a much clearer history. The country is an active hub in European and Central Asian travel. Belavia, the flagship airline – government owned, of course – is a member of the International Air Transport Association, which required it to comply with basic rules on safety of operations and aircraft (Belavia 2010). The average age of the carrier's thirteen aircraft is low at thirteen years (Airfleets.net 2010). Service has been expanding rapidly as the airline added six new destinations in 2010 alone bringing the total to thirty-two (Airline Analysis 2010). Two other airlines transport cargo overseas and passengers locally (Endres 2009a, 2009b). Belarus-flagged aircraft have a relatively strong safety record. Four accidents occurred during the 2000s. But overall flying in Belarus appears to be safe (Airport.by 2010).

The ICAO's opinion of the Belarusian airline safety record is generally positive, although it has noted that statutory provisions are inadequate and inadequately enforced. After the 2004 follow-audit of its safety oversight systems, Belarus was found to have more problems with respect to operating regulations than the world average, but otherwise has improved across the board (ICAO 2008). Of particular concern was a failure to give inspectors unlimited access to all aviation facilities. There are some indications that the state is currently taking steps to tighten laws and regulations to bring them up to ICAO standards (Belarus 2010c).

Belarus ratified the Montreal Protocol in 1993 as a developed country. Its chlorofluorocarbon consumption of 1986 was established as the baseline and it was given roughly a decade to find substitutes (UNEP 2010b). Belarus, with most other members of the Commonwealth of Independent States asked for assistance and for extensions to the deadlines, both of which were granted (UNEP 2009, 342–343). In particular, Belarus benefited from a generous exception made to Russia that allowed it to continuing exporting CFCs to CIS members until 2000.

Belarus failed to submit annual plans and reports until in 1996 it was declared non-compliant by the Ozone Secretariat (UNEP 2006). It still declined to submit a remediation plan and announced that it would likely continue to be out of compliance until 2000. In 1997, however, Belarus received a generous grant of nearly $7 million from the World Bank's Global Environmental Fund. The funds would be provided to help Atlant, the country's only refrigerator manufacturer, to replace CFCs in its products, substituting non-ozone-depleting chemicals for cleaning electronic components (World Bank 1997).

Belarus met the 2000 deadline for eliminating CFC consumption, according to data received by the Ozone Secretariat. This earned the country close to the best world ranking for low CFC usage at the time (Globalis 2001). The government has taken pride in its performance since then and has even chastised other developed countries for failing to meet their own environmental targets (Belarus 2009).

There are still concerns within the Ozone Secretariat. The ozone layer has thinned directly above Belarus. By 2005, it was 7 percent thinner than should be expected, leading some to wonder whether CFC consumption is still taking place and whether despite the government's assurances (UNEP 2005).

Turning to our theories of international law compliance, Belarus earns relatively high marks in all three areas, despite the fact that it is an isolated autocracy. In general, then, liberal theory fails. But in its defense, it is worth noting that in the cases of air traffic and ozone consumption, Belarus is far less isolated than in most other areas. Belarus wants to attract more tourists (Belarus 2011) and carry more cargo, and so keeping its airlines and airports above the minimum international safety standards makes good sense. Likewise, because it does not produce CFC at home, all CFC consumption is a matter of international trade. The implication is that what may matter more than a country's overall international economic policy is its degree of international engagement from issue to issue.

Belarus, as we have seen, has considerable capacity to govern, and so it comes as no surprise that it is able to regulate airlines, airports, ships, and trade in ozone-depleting substances. What is perhaps surprising is that it has taken so long to develop appropriate laws on airline safety and CFC usage. Within Belarus, then, it may matter more whether Lukashenko wishes a policy to change rather than whether specific legislation has been adopted by the Assembly.

With respect to questions of reputation, we see again a pattern – at least with respect to CFC usage. When the government knows that its performance will fall short of international standards, it freely admits as much. For the first four years after ratifying the Montreal Protocol, Belarus was rather obstinate. There is no evidence of this attitude with respect to ICAO demands, but neither is there evidence of serious failures after the 2001 audit. On the other hand, once the performance of the country began to improve, we see evidence of greater levels of enthusiasm for the norm – to the point of self-righteousness.

There is no evidence that cultural factors entered into government decisions regarding compliance in these issue-areas, other than the possibility that ruling elites took for granted that their preferences would be implemented.

As in the case of reputational theory, legitimacy theory offers a mixed bag. While the rhetoric seems rather self-serving, the efforts at policy implementation indicate a fairly high degree of commitment and, by implication, an acceptance of the norms.

Much of what we observe can be explained by Lukashenko's cost-benefit analysis. He showed a willingness to comply with international standards when doing so helped the country's bottom line and the costs are not exorbitant. In the case of ozone-depleting substances, it is worth noting that the regime did not move aggressively toward eliminating consumption until it had secured funding. Likewise, it did not bother to adopt the types of laws and regulations expected by the ICAO once it had achieved a moderate level of safety first. It seems that the performance in these areas would likely be lower without international standards and monitoring.

Laws on human rights promotion: anti-slavery law and anti-discrimination against women

Moving into the realm of human rights, we would normally expect compliance with international norms to be far lower, given the government's practice of minimizing dissent. Table 8.3 presents a mixed picture.

The Bales estimate suggests that there may be as many as 20,000 individuals living under slave-like conditions. We have already said that persons are being trafficked in and through Belarus, although the numbers are difficult to ascertain. "There were [also] reports that women from low-income families in Belarus' regions were subjected to forced prostitution in Minsk. Belarusian men, women, and children continued to be subjected to forced begging" (Dept. of State 2010b) The state has outlawed these practices and engages in periodic enforcement. In 2005–2006, it identified and freed 350 slaves and quasi-slaves (Naumov 2007, 2).

On the surface, statutes in Belarus internalize – and even cite – international instruments relating to slavery and work conditions. The 1992 Trade Union Act, for example, specifically refers to the Universal Declaration of Human Rights, the International Covenant on Economic, Social and Cultural Rights, and International Labour Organization conventions as the basis for Belarusian labor law (Belarus 2007, article 1).

In fact, the government consistently violates basic workers' rights. To begin, it sometimes requires workers in state-owned firms to work on the week-end and "donate" their wages to social causes (Dept. of State 2009). More important, it repeatedly interferes with the activities of labor unions and takes measures to prevent the emergence of independent worker associations. To begin, registration of a trade union – as is the case with any NGO – requires a legal address. But obtaining an office space is difficult because the government must approve the lease (Balmaceda 2007, 200). Unions must also meet a 10 percent threshold

Table 8.3 Indicators of Belarus' compliance with anti-slavery and women's security norms

Bales' slavery percentage (est.)	0.02% (0–10.79)
WomanStat physical security of women 2007	3 (4-point scale – 1 is best)
Share of women in parliament	32%
Average age for women at first marriage	23 years
Proportion of teenaged girls who are married	6%

to be approved, meaning that at least 10 percent of the workers at a particular factory must sign up in advance, thereby drawing attention to themselves (ILO 2004, 165). Since 1999, no independent union has been approved (Dept. of State 2009).

Workers are routinely put on short contracts of one to five years to reduce their job security and make them more malleable. Those involved in independent union activity are often fired and worse (Dept. of State 2009). Government officials since 2000 have intervened to manipulate union leadership elections, control access to union accounts, and otherwise control union practices. Workers who complain of mistreatment by employers are targeted for penalties and even dismissal (Dept. of State 2009).

The situation has not escaped international attention. In a bold move, Belarusian union activists have filed grievances against their government at the International Labour Organization and the International Confederation of Free Trade Unions. Both have issued damning reports following extensive hearings. In 2004, the ILO grievance commission sided with the independent trade unions and called upon Belarus to remove obstacles to union registration and permit the free operation of all trade unions (ILO 2004, 175–177).

> While the Commission acknowledges the special circumstances of Belarus, the application of these fundamental ILO Conventions cannot be made contingent upon its level of economic development or its policy priorities. Indeed, the Commission considers that free and independent workers' and employers' organizations are indispensable partners in economic development and the advancement of social justice.
>
> (ILO 2004, 178)

There is a profound irony in the fact that this statement was made to a regime that claims to represent workers. They are even given the right to contribute to the shaping of national policy and monitoring its implementation under the law (Belarus 2007, Article 19). But the fact is that the regime gives only lip service to many international labor norms.

Women in Belarus are probably better off than many of the women we have considered in this study. They are well educated, have longer life-spans than men, are well represented in the legislature, and have many protections in the workplace, including a generous maternity leave policy (van Klaveren and Martin 2010, 23). Spousal abuse and rape are outlawed and men can receive prison sentences of up to fifteen years for spousal abuse (Fair Fund 2010). Women are guaranteed legal equality with men and enjoy the type of protections one would expect to find in Western Europe with respect to matters of parental rights, inheritance, divorce, and so forth (van Klaveren and Martin 2010, 23). They make up over two-fifths of all the town councils in the country (Petina and Burova 2003, 4).

While these rights indicate that women in Belarus have the possibility of achieving substantive equality with men, the reality is quite different. To begin,

Belarusians view the woman's place as squarely in the home, or else in "women's professions" such as teaching, nursing, and social work. Not only do they tend to get jobs in certain sectors, but they tend to enter and stay at relatively low ranks, almost never rising to the most senior positions (Chutkova *et al.* 2005, 20; Freedom House 2010a). They make up two-thirds of the ranks of the unemployed (Chutkova *et al.* 2005, 20). In rural areas, they suffer poverty at far higher rates than men – research in the early 2000s indicated that more than 70 percent of women are poor (Petina and Burova 2003, 6).

While spousal abuse is illegal and the police generally handle situations well, it is under-reported. Surveys conducted by UN-affiliated agencies in the early 2000s indicate that between 20 percent and 30 percent of women had been abused by their spouses (Amnesty International 2006; Human Rights Council 2007, 12). As explained by the NGO Fair Fund:

> The major barriers to addressing domestic violence are societal traditions that tell a victim that it is shameful to make family business public. Many women also fear that their abusers will not be arrested, or that they will be blamed for "dishonoring" their families. Additionally, due to the economy, the majority of abused women (as opposed to abused men) are dependent on their husbands for income and support. Thus, reporting the abuse would most likely mean leaving the home, with potential homelessness or the shame of returning to the birth family. Outside the capital of Minsk, there are very few shelters offering support to women who want to leave their abusers.
>
> (Fair Fund 2010)

Given the wide range of statutes available to law enforcement officials it is possible for authorities to intervene at an early stage in marital conflict. As explained by an official in the Ministry of Internal Affairs:

> Here it is different. It is not like in your country where the police only get involved when there has been an act of violence. We have various articles such as hooliganism which mean that the police are involved when there are relationship problems.
>
> (Amnesty International 2006)

Much depends, however, on changing social attitudes. The government has yet to mount a significant campaign to raise awareness of domestic violence (unlike its considerable efforts on trafficking). A national council on women was established in 2000 and abandoned in 2002 (Petina and Burova 2003, 10). Another national plan unveiled in 2008 was unfunded (van Klaveren and Martin 2010).

Formal legal protections are considerable, but they are not given enough energy to overcome some entrenched cultural norms. The potential for progress exists, however. Women have kept their jobs at higher rates than men in recent years, with the result that female poverty is coming down (van Klaveren and Martin 2010, 20, 25).

To what extent do our theories of international law compliance explain these outcomes? Although Belarus is clearly authoritarian, because it was founded on socialist principles of worker supremacy and egalitarianism, the legal structure carries over some principles that were progressive in their early days and are still consistent with many contemporary international liberal norms. Slavery and gender discrimination are inconsistent with the governing principles of the country. This stems from the fact that some cultural norms have not been addressed directly and the fact that the state benefits from worker passivity. To the extent that rights are protected, it is because the regime is being true to its ideals.

Economic liberalism also explains much of the compliance we observe, although it does not explain non-compliance – particularly with respect to discrimination against women. In its efforts to compete in the international market, one would expect that Belarus officials would be more determined to ensure that all those who are qualified would rise to the highest level – something they could certainly bring about if they wanted. But instead chauvinism seems to influence the weight they place on ensuring that women rise to senior positions. The government seems more interested in protecting women than advancing them. As far as workers in general, the refusal to adopt international labor standards appears consistent with autocratic economic policies.

The government again demonstrates that it has the capacity to achieve its highest priorities. Despite the fact that harassing and abusing independent trade unionists requires considerable time and energy, the government has sadly made this a priority. Conversely, since those in power seem largely uncommitted to the advancement of women, the measures taken are half-hearted. The protection of women and the elimination of slavery seem to fall in the middle range.

Belarus again shows that it values its reputation only so far. Where its priorities coincide with international norms, it is happy to receive international support and encouragement. But where the norm conflicts with regime stability, it is capable of defiance, foot-dragging, and pleading poverty.

Culture – both social and political – seems to matter a great deal in this area. The government seems to accept a protective role with respect to women and those who are enslaved. On the other hand, because socialism is the state ideology, defiant workers threaten more than just productivity, and are treated as traitors to the regime. Angry, drunken men are still able to abuse women with little fear of retribution. Women who stand up for themselves are still viewed with suspicion (Amnesty International 2006).

Belarus has endorsed a number of international conventions on the topics at hand and has even incorporated them into specific domestic statutes. But where the international community provides an interpretation that conflicts with Belarusian policy, the state is willing to challenge the international community. But even when its conduct directly violates international norms, it does not generally repudiate the norm itself, nor does it deny international organizations the right to investigate compliance.

Not all of what we see in this section is consistent with a short-term materialistic rationalism. Certainly policies toward women do not fit neatly into this rubric since the state would benefit from elevating women to positions of leadership where their talents and training warrant, and encouraging them to defend themselves against abusers. But cultural factors seem to mitigate against this. Policies on labor are more consistent, however, for reasons we have seen. The state benefits both politically and economically when the workforce is pliable. Even its efforts to root out unregulated slavery make sense as symbolic of its role as defender of workers. Extracting resources from unwilling workers, on the other hand, seems risky since it is bound to cause resentment.

Concluding remarks on Belarus and theories of international law compliance

As in our other cases thus far, we have not found a theory that explains the majority of what we see. However, rationalism goes far. More so than with our other cases, taking into account the short-term material interests of the country's leadership – particularly those of Lukashenko – helps to explain a wide range of policy outcomes. This is so in large part because cultural factors are less pronounced but also because of the extraordinary concentration of power in the hands of a single-minded individual. Cultural factors sometimes inhibit or stimulate policy in particular directions, and the international community sometimes wins. But by and large the dictator prevails.

This is not to say that other factors do not matter, as we see in Table 8.4. It is surprising that a rule's legitimacy and the country's reputation seem to matter at some level, albeit sometimes in the negative and never predictably. The influence of these immaterial factors seems largely secondary, though, and often after-the-fact.

On the other hand, Belarus does not behave as predicted by liberalism. Rather than being consistently hostile or stand-offish to the rules, it is clear that they sometimes matter a great deal. And while much of the commitment to international norms seems self-serving and shallow, they sometimes provide an overarching rationale for policy. It is doubtful, for example, that Belarus would have cut its CFC consumption without the Ozone Secretariat or mounted an aggressive anti-trafficking campaign without the Trafficking Protocol and the US State Department looking over its shoulder. At the same time, even the strictest autocracies are capable of endorsing at least some liberal principles. One thing is clear, however. Just as we saw in the case of Tunisia, Belarus is capable of mobilizing whatever resources are needed to implement its top policy priorities.

Equatorial Guinea

Overview

"…[I]t is probably fair to say that Equatorial Guinea is less of a functioning country than it is a lucrative family business that happens to come with a flag, an

Table 8.4 Competing theories of international law compliance and the case of Belarus

"To what degree does the theory explain outcomes?"

		Sovereignty defense		*Market control*		*Human rights*	
		Anti-terror	*Anti-trafficking*	*Air transport*	*Ozone depletion*	*Slavery*	*Protection of women*
Liberalism	Political	little	little	little	little	some	some
	Economic	little	little	some	some	much	some
	Managerial	much	much	little	little	little	little
	Reputational	little	little	some	some	some	some
	Cultural	some	some	little	little	much	much
	Legitimacy	little	some	some	some	some	some
	Rationalism	much	some	much	much	much	some

anthem, and army, and a seat at the United Nations" (Ghazvinian 2007, 177). This statement sums up Equatorial Guinea, situated just north of the Equator on Africa's west coast. Its continental land mass is separated from its most prosperous territory – the island of Bioko. Its population is uncertain, but thought to be roughly 700,000. Its gross domestic product is considerable – roughly equal to Iceland's, and its GDP per capita is nearly equal to Saudi Arabia's. This prosperity is due almost entirely to its oil exports, which have been running at around half a million barrels a day.

This should have allowed the country to pull its citizens out of grinding poverty. But officials in Equatorial Guinea "have been ... using public funds for personal gain at the expense of providing key social services to the country's population, and squandering other potential revenues through mismanagement" (HRW 2009, 3). From 2004 to 2007, the country's Human Development Index ranking actually fell from 109th to 127th (Castro 2010a).

> Even in the major cities of Malabo and Bata, more than 60% of the population has no running water or access to electricity. The country lacks a functioning healthcare system, and the educational system is hobbling on a decrepit infrastructure left from the colonial era.
>
> (Fredriksson 2007, 29)

The government of President Teodoro Obiang Nguema Mbasogo is among the most despotic in the world, earning a solid 14 out of 14 on Freedom House's scale. It "engage[s] in significant human rights violations, acts with impunity, and is fundamentally corrupt, undemocratic and unaccountable to its citizens" (Fredriksson 2007, 29). The government routinely arrests and tortures leaders of opposition parties, even though they rarely win a seat in legislative elections. Obiang routinely polls over 95 percent of the vote, although in 2004 he won more than 100 percent in some precincts (Smoltczyk 2006)! The legislature is passive, as are the courts.

The country, despite its importance in the world economy, is still relatively isolated. To be certain, a few countries have fairly close ties with Equatorial Guinea. It has made efforts to build bridges with neighboring states. But it hosts a mere thirteen foreign embassies. The Lonely Planet guidebook warns visitors that they will not feel welcome, especially by the security forces (Lonely Planet 2009).

Equatorial Guinea provides a critical test for a number of our theories of international law compliance, in part because it embodies so many extremes. Most of our theories would predict very low levels of compliance, although some might predict selective compliance.

Liberalism

In 1993, Obiang announced to a crowd that his authority came from God (Liniger-Goumaz 1998, 81). From all the evidence, that statement appears to have been sincere. As mentioned earlier, the current Freedom House ranking places the regime at the bottom, and World Bank good governance scores also place it near the bottom with respect to public participation and rule of law.

For all its despotism, the Equatoguinean government has allowed opposition political parties, elements of a free press, and unrestricted internet access (HRW 2009, 64; Dept. of State 2010c). Looking for a silver lining, one observer notes "Obiang is actually a big improvement on his uncle [deposed in 1979], who managed to reduce the population by a third and run coffee production into the ground" (Soares de Oliveira 2007, 224). As we will see, the regime seems to understand that the international community expects at least lip service to international democratic norms, but generally does not go beyond that.

The president has virtually unlimited powers. He serves for renewable seven-year terms and can dissolve the legislature. He enjoys indefinite immunity from prosecution for any illegal acts done before or during his term of office (Europa 2010d). Obiang has surrounded himself with relatives, placing uncles, sons, and others in senior ministerial positions (see below). But this has not provided security or stability, as rivalry within the ruling family and threats from outsiders continually threaten the regime. As explained by Roberts:

> As oil wealth grew, loyalty became less predictable. Decisions were taken in the shadows. As more power and wealth were invested in one man, Obiang, it grew more tempting for others to kill him. And by 2003 Obiang grew frail. A deadly competition to succeed arose. Though simplified, one could see the domestic battle as one between two brothers, Obiang's two sons. On one side Teodorin, the playboy elder brother, an arrogant and power-hungry man.... The second son, Gabriel, represented another part of the ruling family, opposed to Teodorin, who feared that if he took power they would be pushed aside, possibly killed.
>
> (Roberts 2006, 95)

Almost every year, some threat appears on the horizon and prompts retribution. An attack on the presidential palace in 2008 prompted the imprisonment of ten major opposition figures, who were then beaten while in custody and charged with acts of terrorism (Freedom House 2010b). In 2004, a plot involving an exiled opposition figure and South African mercenaries was uncovered, leading to dozens of arrests and summary trials (Heilbrunn 2007, 231; Dept. of State 2010c). The UN Special Rapporteur on Torture has found

> torture by the police to be systematic in the initial period after arrest and during interrogation, including by suspension, severe beatings, electroshocks, etc.... [I]n many cases, victims of torture experience a total lack of justice, which, combined with the physical and psychological consequences of ill-treatment and the absence of any rehabilitation or compensation mechanism, may cause ongoing suffering that might amount to inhuman treatment.
>
> (Human Rights Council 2010)

The government in recent years has expressed concern over the methods of the police and has invited foreign specialists to help re-train some of them, and there are reports that conduct is improving (Dept. of State 2010c; Human Rights Council 2010). But there are no human rights organizations, and foreign NGOs are barred from addressing civil liberties (Human Rights Watch 2009, 15–16). In response to a question from a Human Rights Watch reporter, Obiang declared in 2003: "The international groups need to understand the real situation in the country because there is no abuse of human rights here. The press is free ... and we have the Commission for Human Rights" (Human Rights Watch 2009, 53).

Is Equatorial Guinea's economy more liberal than its political system? To be sure, it has opened up its oil fields to foreign exploitation. Since 1991, production has grown steadily from a mere 1,200 barrels a day to 580,000 in 2008 (Castro 2010a). Investors come from Spain, France, the US, China, and a number of other countries, attracted by the relatively low royalties (Roberts 2006, 227). The country's trade balance is naturally very positive, with exports roughly four times greater than imports. The country's Economic Freedom score was 48.6 (out of 89.7) in 2010 (Heritage Foundation 2010).

While inviting high levels of foreign investment – largely because it lacked the expertise to extract and refine the oil itself – the government has tended to adopt a mercantilist view of international political economy. It has routinely pitted Spaniards against French, Europeans against Americans, and, more recently, non-Westerners against Westerners. China's presence has increased substantially. As explained by Esteban, "the Chinese government offers Obiang more extensive and stable support than Western governments to the extent that most of the undeniable developmental potential of Chinese co-operation is wasted through clientelist networks" (Esteban 2009, 667).

Multinational corporations are caught in an awkward dilemma. They are well aware that complicity with a regime that so brazenly abuses its citizens will likely come back to haunt them, but they cannot pass up on the opportunity to earn billions. Because the oil fields are off-shore, they have created an enclave on the island of Bioko within which they can operate in peace (Smoltczyk 2006). They have been willing to collaborate with the regime, providing senior government officials with numerous supplemental revenue streams (Senate 2004). For its part, the government has tried to accommodate its guests, by, for example, removing families from land where corporate offices are to be erected (Freedom House 2010b). As put by Amnesty International: "Multinational corporations conducting business with President Obiang willfully ignore the impact of their economic engagement in Equatorial Guinea and their role in enabling the worst offenses of its regime" (Fredriksson 2007).

A silver lining to the presence of foreign investors in Equatorial Guinea may be that this will force the regime to improve its accounting practices in particular and its overall standards of economic conduct (Soares de Oliveira 2007, 225). The signs are not promising, however, as it has managed to alienate almost all international financial institutions – primarily among them the International Monetary Fund which has refused to extend funding since 1996 over issues of governance (Castro 2010a). It has generally refused to divulge its oil income, claiming the figures are a state secret.

Managerial school

The World Bank scores Equatorial Guinea in its lowest tier with respect to controlling corruption. It scores very poorly with respect to other governance indicators as well. The principal reason for this poor showing is rampant corruption. In 1998, for example, Obiang appears to have stolen nearly $100 million of the country's $130 million oil earnings (Simser 2010, 322). Several cabinet ministers own corporations in sectors their ministries regulate (Dept. of State 2010c). As put by Human Rights Watch:

> Perhaps the most brazen and troubling examples of corruption are repeated instances involving the president's eldest son, Teodorin Nguema Obiang, whose globetrotting and extravagant lifestyle is filled with purchases of multimillion-dollar houses and exotic sports cars throughout the world. Teodorin Obiang's official title is minister of forestry, and from that position he earns a salary equivalent to approximately $4,000 per month. Nonetheless, Teodorin Obiang has been able to buy mansions in Los Angeles and Cape Town, and there have been press reports that he has purchased homes in Buenos Aires and Paris as well.
>
> (HRW 2009, 34)

The government gave contracts to foreign logging firms without providing for domestic firms in what appears to have been an effort to impoverish individuals whose wealth was gained independently of the regime (Heilbrunn 2007, 228). The government has passed anti-corruption laws, but fails to enforce them (Dept. of State 2010c).

The government has at times been held to account, not only by the IMF and World Bank but also by foreign governments and courts. In 2004, hundreds of millions of dollars were found to have been laundered through Riggs Bank in Washington D.C., prompting lengthy and embarrassing Senate hearings. It was revealed that the bank opened numerous accounts for members of the Obiang clan worth millions. In one case the deposit was made with "a suitcase of plastic-wrapped dollar bills weighing 60 pounds" (Senate 2004).

The net effect of this rampant corruption is the constriction of spending on public welfare. Total spending on health and education has stayed below 5 percent of the national budget since the 1990s (Heilbrunn 2007; Human Rights Watch 2009, 46). The results are palpable. The country suffers from weakness ranging from poor infrastructure to inadequate schools to poorly trained civil servants and teachers. "[C]hildren living outside of the capital have very limited access to health and social services and constitute some of the most disadvantaged groups in the country" (UNICEF 2010, 2). Although some oil revenue is beginning to be applied to improving the public sector, it is merely a trickle.

Private oil companies seem to be doing a better job helping the country through philanthropic activities (UNICEF 2010, 4). Overall, the oil sector accounts for 95 percent of the income earned by all workers; fewer than one in ten workers are employed there (UNICEF 2010, 2).

The government has repeatedly promised to set aside funds for development, as other oil-rich countries have done. Most plans have not come to fruition, however, or – even worse – have been co-opted by corrupt officials (Fredriksson 2007; Human Rights Watch 2009, 46). In 2007, in response to an IMF report, the government acknowledged that it had the resources then to eradicate poverty and could achieve developed country status by 2010 (Castro 2010a). On the other hand, some infrastructure projects have moved forward, including a hydroelectric power plant and an expanded international airport (Castro 2010a).

Reputational theory

Equatorial Guinea's reputation has generally been quite poor. As mentioned, the IMF stopped doing business with the government on governance grounds, and at one point the European Union suspended all aid on human rights grounds (Liniger-Goumaz 1998, 86).

Among Obiang's most enthusiastic supporters have been the oil companies that invested in the country. They helped finance a public relations initiative in 1998 and helped Obiang lobby the US government, even arranging a meeting with George W. Bush (Soares de Oliveira 2007, 229; Esteban 2009). In 2006, Condoleezza Rice met with Obiang, calling him a "good friend" to the US (Roberts 2006, 269).

In more recent years, the Obiang regime moved to join the Extractive Industries Transparency Initiative, a non-profit created by Western governments with the backing of the World Bank. Its purpose is to encourage oil exporters to play by the rules – particularly with respect to accounting practices. In 2008 it was accepted as a "candidate" with instructions to get its house in order by 2010 as a condition of full admission (Dept. of State 2010c). The government was quick to trumpet this tentative accomplishment as evidence of its intentions to play by the rules (ARB 2009). The impetus soon stalled, however, and it ultimately failed to meet the membership criteria (EITI 2010).

Obiang's sincerity can be doubted since his statements on fighting corruption and working with the West contradict his actions. Not only have few efforts been made to end corruption and increase the public's welfare, but it is apparent that Obiang has decided to hedge his bets by warming up to non-Western regimes (Frynas and Paulo 2006). As explained by Human Rights Watch, Obiang is well aware that his oil resources have increased his leverage on the world stage. He said as much in his autobiography, cynically titled *My Life for My People*. He writes:

> I have realized that the discovery of oil in Equatorial Guinea and especially the importance of these resources have completely changed the attitude of many of our partners, especially those who were more critical. Suddenly they have become more permissive. I know it is human nature, but not only

> men have changed in this fashion, institutions have done the same. And I specifically mean the International Monetary Fund, the World Bank, and the European Union.
>
> (151, cited in Human Rights Watch 2009, 87)

The strategy, combined with the public relations initiative, may be paying off as several Western actors have apparently begun muting their criticisms of the regime in recent years (Soares de Oliveira 2007). Closer to home, the African Union monitors pointed out that although security forces were a conspicuous presence during the 2009 presidential elections, the polling was "generally in line with electoral law" and took place in an atmosphere "of calm, order and discipline" (ARB 2010).

Culture

Central to Equatorial Guinea's politics and society are the ethnic tensions between the Fang and Bubi groups. The Fang, from which the Obiang family originates, are generally located on the mainland and constitute a large majority of the total population. The Bubi occupy much of Bioko island, numbering 40,000. They are repressed by the Obiang family. Leaders of the Bubi have sometimes resorted to violence to no avail (Dept. of State 2010c).

Traditional tribal law and custom are explicitly protected in Equatorial Guinea's constitution and are considered in legal cases (Dept. of State 2010c). Beyond these elements, the predominant trait of Equatoguinean culture is the requirement to submit to Obiang rule.

Legitimacy

Equatorial Guinea, as we have seen, has a tendency to keep international norms at arm's length without repudiating them outright. Formally, international law matters a great deal:

> Under Equatorial Guinea's legal system, international conventions prevail over any existing or future domestic law once they have been ratified by the President of the Republic following approval by the House of Representatives (article 64 (h) of the Constitution of Equatorial Guinea). The applicability of international conventions derives from the provisions of article 8 of the Constitution, which states: "The State of Equatorial Guinea shall abide by the principles of international law and hereby reaffirms its support for the rights and obligations deriving from the charters of the international organizations and agencies to which it belongs."
>
> (CEDAW 2004)

It is a member of numerous international organizations, although does not participate actively. As explained by Heilbrunn, "Equatorial Guinea['s] … resource base requires the dictatorship to establish and maintain relations with international oil firms. Although these relations may overwhelmingly favor the Nguemist regime, some concessions to international norms are necessary" (Heilbrunn 2007, 245).

It seems clear that Obiang and his government have not internalized many international norms. The warming of relations with China seems to be a calculated move to deflect international pressure. As explained by Estaben: "If the time comes, Obiang expects the Chinese delegation to shield him from United Nations sanctions just as it did with his good friend Robert Mugabe in July 2008" (Esteban 2009, 678).

Rationalism

All of the above makes clear that Obiang's policies are rarely driven by anything other than short-term material calculations. His cynicism is rather shocking. Even before oil was discovered, he played political games with Machiavellian single-mindedness. With the addition of oil in his arsenal, he has taken a more confident and even defiant tone. But throughout, he has made it clear that his aim is to remain in power in order to enrich himself and his relations. He does not hesitate to use brute force against his enemies, even when he knows he will be castigated by international watchdog groups.

The cynicism and strategizing may well be justified in today's post-9/11 world. Note the following anecdote about Bush administration policy-making in 2001:

> A few months after the terrorist attacks on New York and Washington, Walter Kansteiner, assistant secretary of state for African Affairs in the Bush administration, called together a meeting of oil barons [and said]: "Bring that oil home." He was talking about African oil, and "home," in his view, wasn't Malabo.
>
> (Smoltczyk 2006)

Performance across issue-areas

Rules governing territorial defense: anti-terrorism, anti-piracy, and anti-trafficking

With a small territory that includes several islands, one might think that Equatorial Guinea's government would have a relatively easy time controlling its borders. It has indeed proven itself capable of shutting down borders and deporting foreigners (IRIN 2008; Castro 2010b). Table 8.5 shows, however, that with respect to our three issue-areas, performance is relatively poor.

Transnational terrorism is not a serious issue for Equatorial Guinea. The closest things to it are transnational criminal organizations and isolated anti-regime militant groups (OSAC 2010). The government has dragged its feet on

Table 8.5 Indicators of compliance with rules governing territorial defense (2005)

UN CTC total score	3 (7 possible)
UN CTC score, minus treaty ratifications	3 (5 possible)
Total pirate attacks	1
SUA endorsement	Yes
SUA Protocol endorsement	Yes
US State Dept. TIP score	2 (out of 3, with 1 the lowest rate)
UN origin score	5 (out of 5, with 1 the lowest rate)
UN transit score	3 (out of 5, with 1 the lowest rate)
UN destination score	3 (out of 5, with 1 the lowest rate)
Bales trafficking score	3 (out of 4, with 1 the lowest rate)
WomanStats trafficking score	3 (out of 4, with 1 the lowest rate)
2000 Trafficking Protocol signature	Yes
2000 Trafficking Protocol ratification	Yes

implementing many of the UN's anti-terror norms. It was not until 2004 that it ratified most of the major anti-terror conventions, and it has yet to endorse the 1991 agreement on marking explosives and the 2005 agreement on nuclear terrorism. It waited until 2007 to establish a government body to address terrorism financing (Castro 2010b).

Equatorial Guinea has been fortunate to have been spared the types of pirate attacks that are common in the area. In the 2000s, only one attack occurred – fifteen nautical miles off the coast of Bioko island in 2008 – and involved ten individuals who identified themselves as rebels from Nigeria. They managed to board a ship that was underway and demanded food. No one was harmed and no damage was done (IMB 2008).

In another incident, a cargo ship carrying supplies for the UN Mission in the Democratic Republic of Congo was attacked in 2006. Fifteen armored personnel carriers from Belgium were stolen and are alleged to now be under the control of the Equatoguinean army (DID 2006). Finally, in 2009, seven Nigerians arrived by boat at the walls of the Presidential Palace in Malabo and carried out an armed attack against the facility. They were repelled by security guards and later apprehended (ARB 2010).

According to the International Maritime Organization, Equatorial Guinea is not compliant in the area of port security, having failed to provide a port security plan for Bata and an alternative plan for Malabo (IMO 2010). The coast guard and navy virtually ceased to exist in the late 1990s (it consisted of two leaky ships) and but was abruptly expanded to seven vessels in the 2000s (Jane's 2010). The United States has provided material support and training to Equatorial Guinea's coast guard in recent years to help protect oil tankers (Castro 2010a).

The picture is a mixed one. One the one hand, the government has not only done little to prevent piracy and may have even participated. On the other, it has spent considerable sums to beef up its capacity.

While numbers are difficult to come by, it is presumed that hundreds if not thousands of individuals – mostly women and children – are trafficked into

Equatorial Guinea each year. In 2009, for example, a single ship was detained in Gabon with hundreds of adults and dozens of children en route to Equatorial Guinea – obviously being trafficked (Dept. of State 2010d). They are drawn by the expanding economy and increasing wealth of the elite which creates demand for domestic servants and sex workers. The country currently rates a "tier two watch list" ranking from the US State Department and was given poor marks by the UN.

Some efforts are being made to address the problem. In 2004 an anti-trafficking law was passed which prohibits most of the acts related to trafficking and imposed stiff prison sentences for violators (CEDAW 2004). The law also protects minors who committed crimes while under the control of traffickers. The government also launched anti-trafficking advertising campaigns (Dept. of State 2010d). It has also collaborated with UNICEF and has become involved with the African Regional Conference "Fight against the Traffic of Human Beings" to improve border controls and coordinate anti-trafficking efforts in the region (Dept. of State 2010d).

These efforts largely fail, however. No one has been prosecuted under the new anti-trafficking law, even though there is evidence that the numbers of trafficked persons are still high (Dept. of State 2010d). Border controls are lacking, as evidenced by problems with arms trafficking (Keili 2008). The anti-piracy measures mentioned earlier may actually help to control illegal immigration and trafficking by sea. There is also evidence that many young Equatoguinean women have been trafficked to Spain (Muni *c.*2005). But the fact that the government deports hundreds of undocumented foreigners each year demonstrates it has the capacity to police trafficking.

How well do our theories of international law compliance explain Equatorial Guinea's performance with respect to terrorism, piracy, and trafficking? To begin, policy seems to take place within the inner sanctum of government and is not the product of any open discussion or debate, as predicted by political liberalism. The timing of the government's decision to ratify anti-terror treaties seems more than happenstance but rather a product of overall scrutiny of anti-terror law. One can surmise that its decision to create a unit on financing of terror was also a direct response to international pressure. The fact that Equatorial Guinea sometimes responds to this pressure has nothing to do with political liberalism, however.

Economic liberalism helps to explain anti-piracy measures in part. As international maritime traffic has become more dense and the cargos more valuable, foreign interests have pressed for improved security and even offered material assistance to bring this about. The market may also have had a perverse effect on Equatorial Guinea's trafficking problem since oil-driven economic growth has increased demand for workers. The theory seems unrelated to the country's anti-piracy measures. The theory offers a less persuasive explanation of policy in other two areas, except that Equatorial Guinea's overall economic isolation seems to correlate with a lack of concern about international norms.

Equatorial Guinea has underutilized capacity. Non-compliance is not a product of the nation's poverty. It is worth noting that once the regime decided to expand its naval forces, it went from two leaky ships to seven relatively new vessels in four years. On the other hand, little has been done, beyond an advertising campaign, to systematically address trafficking. The State Department offers this damning assessment: "Given the government's substantial financial resources, it could greatly increase its response to Equatorial Guinea's human trafficking problem" (Dept. of State 2010d). Overall, the managerial approach does not explain the country's track record.

It is possible that the government has responded to international pressure out of concern for its international reputation. This is not clear, however, since we cannot be certain of the type of reputation it seeks. Other than its willingness to ratify or accede to relevant international conventions, it is not clear that the government in Malabo wants to be known as compliant with respect to these issue-areas. One can surmise that this might be the case where anti-piracy norms are concerned, but since there is evidence the government has actually participated in piracy even this tentative conclusion is open to question. Where anti-terror norms are concerned, Equatorial Guinea has delayed implementation and enforcement.

Equatoguinean culture seems best correlated with trafficking policy, although it should be said that the government is trying to change that by training police forces and educating the public. But by and large the population – except for a few activists – seems disengaged from the problem. With respect to terrorism and piracy, local culture may contribute to a lack of serious problems in these areas. As far as government policy, there is little evidence that culture matters. The decision to give low priority to the security needs of women and children seems more to stem from the individual value systems of the President.

Equatorial Guinea has made commitments in each of the three issue-areas discussed above, and in some cases this is reflected in domestic law. However, contrary to the provisions of the Constitution, it is clear that there is nothing automatic or precedential about the implementation of international law. Adoption of policies is unrelated to the intrinsic merit of the rules and seem to stem more from international pressures and the President's priorities.

This brings us to the rationalist theory, which again seems to carry us a considerable distance. We have seen that the President and his cronies are interested in spending as little as possible on programs that benefit the poor and powerless, and so the decision to limit funding for trafficking victim assistance makes perfect sense. On the other hand, knowing the importance of oil to Obiang explains why he was willing to create a navy from scratch nearly overnight to protect foreign oil tankers. What is perhaps surprising is the degree to which the government tries to stay just barely within compliance with trafficking norms when it is essentially immune from sanctions at this point, especially given the importance of trade with China.

Rules designed to regulate the market: shipping and airline regulation and CFC control

Generally speaking, Equatorial Guinea does a poor job of controlling market related activities and complying with international norms in this area. Table 8.6 shows some of the indicators of compliance, although they do not necessarily reflect the contour or tone of government policy.

Equatorial Guinea has never been an important player in international maritime commerce. To its credit, it has endorsed the key international conventions related to ship safety. But its fleet is insignificant. All the oil tankers are foreign-flagged as are most of the ships that fish in its Exclusive Economic Zone (Castro 2010a). Currently, Equatorial Guinea's merchant fleet consists of only four ships, one of which is owned by a Norwegian firm.

It continues to make its flag available to foreign shipping companies despite a rather disastrous experience ten years ago. It was obvious that the country had no mechanism or standards for inspecting ship safety or conduct and was only interested in collecting fees, and it didn't take long before some marginal firms decided to shift their registration as a way of avoiding scrutiny. The country's merchant fleet swelled from three to nineteen in just one year. It appears that almost all of these newcomers were tuna fishing vessels, and their approach to their trade violated international norms. In retaliation, the governing body of the International Convention for the Conservation of Atlantic Tunas banned the importation of fish caught by ships under the flag of Equatorial Guinea in 1999 (DeSombre 2005, 81). In 2001, of the twelve ships flying under Equatorial Guinea's flag, six were inspected in European ports and three were detained due to lack of seaworthiness (Paris MOU 2002). This rate of detention to inspection was among the worst of any flag state in the world.

The country's merchant marine fleet dropped precipitously, most likely because the tuna fishers changed flags once they realized that sailing under Equatorial Guinea's flag was bad for business.

Equatorial Guinea has many tiny airlines – the largest of which has only six aircraft (Endres 2009a; Castro 2010a) primarily serving to link the island of Bioko to the mainland. The bulk of air traffic tying the country to the rest of the world is carried out by foreign airlines. The principal airport at Malabo has

Table 8.6 Indicators of compliance with market regulating laws

Number of IMO Conventions ratified	20 out of 61
Ratified SOLAS and two Protocols	Yes
Number of ICAO Conventions ratified	7 out of 45
Ratified Chicago '44, Tokyo '63	Yes
Cumulative Montreal Protocol compliance score	1 (0–24; low=compliance)
Reported data to Ozone Commission 2002–2007	No
Found non-compliant 2002–2007	No
Broke existing program 2002–2007	No
ali_standard air liberalization score	57 (0–183; high=liberal)

recently undergone expansion with the assistance of the French government (Castro 2010a).

The government has endorsed a few key international air safety conventions, but left the bulk of them unendorsed. It has also adopted the Civil Aviation Code of the Central African Economic and Monetary Community (CEMAC Code) (ICAO 2001). It has not fully codified these agreements in domestic law and regulation, however. Overall, its safety record is deplorable. Despite the small number of aircraft carrying its flag, there have been four serious accidents that have left sixty-six people dead since 1998. Largely as a result of this track record, the European Union banned all aircraft registered in Equatorial Guinea from European skies in 2006 (USA Today 2006; Castro 2010a). The International Air Transport Association in 2006 singled out Equatorial Guinea as one of the worst of the worst with respect to air safety (ASW 2006).

This outcome was foreseeable in light of the almost complete lack of aviation safety oversight in the country.

> Equatorial Guinea does not have an organization capable of meeting the requirements of safety oversight activities. The financial resources of the DGTAC [Civil Transportation and Aviation General Directorate] are insufficient to recruit qualified personnel, develop training programmes or purchase sufficient office equipment. The organization does not have specialized staff in the areas of licensing, aircraft operations or airworthiness. The DGTAC does not have a technical library nor can it provide its staff with the necessary reference documents. It has not developed guidance material (general policy, manuals, procedures, checklists, etc.) concerning licences, operations and airworthiness.... Due to a lack of qualified staff, the DGTAC has not implemented a system for performing the basic duties of an airworthiness inspection agency (issuance and renewal of certificates of airworthiness, certification and supervision of air operators, maintenance matters and maintenance facilities). The DGTAC cannot accurately determine the number of aircraft registered in Equatorial Guinea or the number of valid certificates of airworthiness issued. Lastly, Equatorial Guinea has not established an accident and incident investigation system involving civil aircraft.
>
> (ICAO 2001)

With respect to ozone-depleting substances, Equatorial Guinea has been a laggard, although it is gradually coming into compliance. It did not ratify the Montreal Protocol until 2006 (Latvian EGM Center 2010; UNEP 2010a, 2010c). Despite this lack of commitment, the government had reduced CFC imports from a high of 32.2 ozone-depleting potential tons in 1997 to 2.3 in 2008 (UNEP 2010b). The bulk of CFC usage in the country is devoted to servicing used refrigeration equipment, much of which is being replaced (UNEP 2009).

In 2007 the country organized a "terminal phase-out" program with the Ozone Secretariat that it estimated would cost a mere \$280,000. The goal was to eliminate CFC and halon imports by 2010, and it would appear to have been successful (UNEP 2009). The government instituted a new National Ozone Committee and adopted the CEMAC rules governing ozone-depleting substances.

To what extent do our theories of international law compliance help us understand what we have just described? To begin, the government's poor track record is consistent with what one might expect of an autocratic regime, according to political liberalism. Commitment to norms seems unrelated to the wishes of the people. Policies on transportation are particularly undemocratic, in that the government's actions have exposed the nation and its people to increased risk. Only in the area of ozone-depleting substances has the government behaved in a way that may improve the human condition – albeit very marginally.

Economic liberalism may explain more. Where breach of international rules is easily perceived and has economic consequences, the government usually alters its conduct. This is particularly true where international business is concerned. It is fairly easy to monitor much of the behavior of ships at sea since they must always return to port. It was therefore possible to establish that ships sailing under Equatorial Guinea's flag were violating basic safety standards and fishing illegally. Likewise, aircraft must land, and so monitoring their airworthiness was a matter that could be taken up by the receiving nations. The same principle applies to CFC consumption, since all of it was imported. Of course, local flights are another matter, which makes the government's decision to ground local airlines somewhat impressive.

While Equatorial Guinea clearly lacks the types of resources one might encounter in a developed country, it is interesting to recall the ease with which it increased the size of its navy. This type of energy does not seem to have been invested where air safety is concerned. It is difficult to tell whether the drop in extralegal maritime activity stems from a commitment of additional resources, but this is at least possible. If nothing else, we can see that the only foreign ship carrying the Equatorial Guinean flag is from Norway – a country famous for its strong record on ship safety. The government's performance in reducing the import of CFCs attests to a substantial technical and policing capacity. Where air safety is concerned, it would seem that an investment of one or two hundred million dollars might be enough to bring the country up to international standards. The challenge, of course, is to find – as expressed by the new manager of Ecuato Guineana de Aviacíon – "some committed men" (Equatorial Guinea 2010a). Overall, then, the managerial school may provide some explanation for the outcomes.

With respect to reputation, it appears that Equatorial Guinean authorities are at least somewhat sensitive to the expectations of others and seek to improve their reputation for rule compliance. This is clear where ozone-depleting substances are concerned. It may also be reflected in changes on maritime safety policy. They seem far less concerned about its international reputation where air safety is concerned, especially given the lack of effort invested in removing the EU ban.

It does not seem that culture is much of a factor. It is possible that the lack of a major maritime tradition helps to explain why the regulatory infrastructure is so weak. At any rate, most of the decisions regarding these technical problems are handled by a few people in the central government, some of whom are not native to the country.

As we saw with respect to reputation, it appears that Equatorial Guinea has mostly failed to internalize the norms in question. We say "mostly" because there is some evidence that internal regulations and policy priorities are in transition and may soon more closely reflect international standards. Evidence of this transition can be found particularly with respect to maritime safety and banning CFC imports.

Once again, much of what we see in these three areas reflects short-term materialist calculations on the part of the country's leadership. It seems reasonable to assume that a few senior administration officials chose to either increase revenue (in the form of ship registration fees, for example) while minimizing expenses (by not hiring more inspectors). This is clearly the case with respect to maritime policy from 1996 to 2003. It is also possible that the presence of so many foreign air carriers has taken the pressure off the government to tighten standards for its own airlines. Plenty of Equatoguineans can fly to Europe, after all, so long as they book their trips with Lufthansa or Air France. It is also plausible that the regime feared sanctions for failing to meet CFC consumption targets, perhaps calculating that they had little to lose from coming into compliance.

Laws on human rights promotion: anti-slavery law and anti-discrimination against women

Equatorial Guinea has made some efforts – mostly cosmetic – to improve conditions for women and children and to minimize forced labor. As we can see in Table 8.7, the government has ratified the major conventions related to both forced labor and the safety of women. It has also adopted a number of laws related to these topics, including outlawing compulsory labor and protecting the right to unionize and strike. Women are equal under the Constitution, and violence against women, including specifically rape as well as prostitution, is illegal and subject to serious penalties (Dept. of State 2010c; Equatorial Guinea 2010a). However, as we will see, these efforts collapse in the face of overwhelming economic, social, and cultural conditions due to a lack of enforcement and resources.

Table 8.7 Indicators of Equatorial Guinea's compliance with anti-slavery and women's security norms

Bales' slavery percentage (est.)	0.15 (0–10.79)
Status of ILO Conventions #29, #105, and #182	All ratified
WomanStat physical security of women 2007	3 (on a 4-point scale – 1 is best)
CEDAW status	2 (ratified)
Share of women in parliament	10%

While the figures are perhaps only estimates, it is interesting to note that over a thousand people in a country of 700,000 may be in bondage. Child labor laws – which prohibit work by anyone under fourteen – are largely unenforced. Vendors who hire children are subject to heavy fines and forced closing, but none were prosecuted in 2009 (Dept. of State 2010c). Half of children of school age are working as street vendors, car washers, field hands, and in domestic work – many of them against their will. "[T]here is an almost complete absence of social protection mechanisms" in the country (UNICEF 2010, 3).

In general, protecting the rights of workers appears to be a low priority for the government. It is worth noting that it was not until 2001 that it ratified the 1930 International Labour Organization Forced Labour Convention and the 1957 Abolition of Forced Labour Convention (ILO 2010). Voluntary unions are legal, but must register at least fifty workers in a factory and receive official approval. Thus far, only the Union Organization of Small Farmers has been legalized (Dept. of State 2010c).

Some reforms may be in process. The state has hired many more labor inspectors to ensure worker safety and the petroleum industry applies an international standard for its workers (Dept. of State 2010c). More likely a bifurcated labor market will emerge.

Women in Equatorial Guinea suffer under a tremendous burden of poverty and abuse. This, despite legal equality, bars on violence against them, a few government programs to promote their status, and the ability of a few to gain access to positions of prominence and power. Roughly 12 percent of teenaged girls become pregnant each year (CEDAW 2004).

Marriage presents its own set of dangers since it is generally governed by local custom. Dowry and arranged marriages are the norm, with the caveat that upon divorce the wife must reimburse the dowry (CEDAW 2004, 3). Polygamy is widespread, especially among the Fang (World Trade Press 2010). In general, social mores are discriminatory and involve

> deep-rooted adverse cultural norms, customs, and traditions, including forced and early marriage, and levirate marriage (the practice by which a man may be required to marry his brother's widow) [discriminate] against women. Lack of legislation regulating customary marriages and other aspects of family law also [discriminate] against women, particularly with respect to polygyny, inheritance, and child custody.
>
> (Dept. of State 2010c)

Rape and domestic violence are not generally prosecuted (Dept. of State 2010c). New family courts may offer some hope for victims of violence (Freedom House 2010b).

Most women work in the agricultural sector where they are subject to grinding poverty and limited opportunities for advancement. A few have managed to received advanced degrees and rise to positions of prominence, including ten who serve in the legislature. Overall, however, it is estimated that only 10 percent of the country's money is in women's hands (World Trade Press 2010).

As mentioned, the government has taken steps to enhance the status of women, including the passage of laws dealing with labor discrimination and a new draft Family Code (CEDAW 2004, 15; Equatorial Guinea 2010b). It has also established a network of adult education programs aimed at helping women who failed in school (CEDAW 2004, 7). It has trumpeted its acceptance of international conventions on women and claims to have played "a leading role in all international and regional meetings and has also taken the domestic measures necessary to give concrete form to its political will to promote women's advancement" (CEDAW 2004, 3).

These gestures and this rhetoric are greeted with skepticism abroad, however. The NGO Nord-Sud based in Switzerland argues that the government of Obiang tolerates violence against women and even perpetrates it. "Each time the authorities organize a wave of political repression, the mothers and the wives are the first victims" (Muni ca. 2005). We have already noted that the police abuse women in custody.

In light of its failure to mobilize its considerable resources to protect women, the CEDAW Committee concluded that the government had only a "limited understanding of its obligations under the Convention" (CEDAW 2004).

To what extent do our theories explain government actions in the area of human rights? The outcome – especially with respect to the status of women – seems consistent with political liberalism, which predicts the abuse. There appears to be little pressure from below on the government to make dramatic changes to the treatment of women and workers.

Economic liberalism does not seem to explain much of what we see. Except in the petroleum industry, the country's growing ties with the rest of the world do not seem to correlate with respect for human rights. What we seem to be witnessing in Equatorial Guinea is a classic bifurcated economy in which one small segment of the country is advancing with the aid of foreign capital while the other is left to remain in squalor and isolation.

As we have seen, Equatorial Guinea lacks the resources to manage a national government, both due to poor infrastructure and institutions and lack of capital and expertise. But much of what we see in the area of human rights could be addressed with the resources that are currently available. The state has demonstrated that it is perfectly capable of apprehending and incarcerating whomever it wishes. Add to this the complicity of the authorities in the abuse of women and we must conclude poverty and unenforced laws are therefore a result of Obiang's preferences, not a lack of capacity in itself.

The government appears particularly hypocritical with respect to human rights as it proclaims its commitment to international human rights norms on the one hand and abuses its citizens on the other. Its inability and/or unwillingness to address directly the concerns raised by prominent international observers is rather stunning in light of the unanimity and severity of the critique. From a theoretical point of view, we must conclude that the reputational theory is correct: those who don't care don't do.

Culture looms large in this issue-area, to be sure. As we have seen, there are deeply rooted traditions that militate against the progress of women and children. This situation seems to provide the government with an excuse to limit its efforts with respect to enhancing the status and improving the security of women. With respect to labor, there is little evidence that slavery is deeply rooted in the society.

While it is always difficult to discern the personal values of a dictator it seems clear that Obiang has not moved to fully internalize the international norms he has publicly endorsed. The CEDAW Committee said as much. The government has made few efforts to instill these norms in either government circles or society as a whole.

To what extent is all of this consistent with rationalism? Since promoting human rights will cost the governing elite money in the short run, there is little incentive to change course. In the long run educating and empowering the poor and disenfranchised could jeopardize the entire political system. On the benefit side, while it is conceivable that the regime's stability could be enhanced through the cooptation of women and workers, Obiang rarely shows this sort of forethought. Taking a page from Machiavelli, he seems to have calculated that generosity is dangerous.

Concluding remarks on Equatorial Guinea and theories of international law compliance

Because of the country's autocracy, isolation, and disdain for its international reputation, its compliance levels are generally low across our issue-areas. However, the fact that compliance is rather high in a few cases means that it is not enough to know the country's overall political and economic situation. One must also look closely at the bargain being struck in each particular area. Thus, despite his disdain for international norms on justice and human security, Obiang has calculated that oil tankers and their crews are worth protecting from pirates.

Ultimately, though, none of the theories does an adequate job explaining the hypocrisy the regime so often displays, as we see in Table 8.8. His public support for many international norms bears no relationship to his actual performance – for which he has no apologies. Equatorial Guinea's government seems to disassociate its foreign commitments from its domestic policy, leaving international observers bewildered.

More so than any case in this book, Equatorial Guinea provides almost no support for the managerial school. It is abundantly clear that Obiang has the means to do whatever he wants, and failure to mobilize resources is a choice.

General conclusions

The cases of Belarus and Equatorial Guinea allow us to once again observe how factors that are generally addressed in isolation interact with each other. Among

Table 8.8 Competing theories of international law compliance and the case of Equatorial Guinea

"To what degree does the theory explain outcomes?"

		Sovereignty defense			*Market control*			*Human rights*	
		Anti-terror	*Anti-piracy*	*Anti-trafficking*	*Air transport*	*Ship safety*	*Ozone depletion*	*Slavery*	*Protection of women*
Liberalism	Political	much	much	some	much	much	some	much	much
	Economic	some	much	some	some	much	much	some	some
	Managerial	little	some	little	little	some	some	little	little
	Reputational	some	some	much	some	some	some	much	much
	Cultural	little	little	much	little	some	little	some	some
	Legitimacy	little	little	little	some	some	much	much	much
	Rationalism	some	much	some	some	some	some	much	much

other things, we can see that local culture is far less fixed than is generally thought. Governments may dramatically alter a nation's fundamental social and economic structure in a fairly short period of time. In the case of Belarus, the passivity of the population and its ethnic homogeneity give tremendous license to the government. In Equatorial Guinea ethnic conflict creates yet another excuse to marginalize those who do not belong to the ruling family. That said, certain dimensions of local culture resist transformation and governments may elect to leave them be – as in the case of traditional family law in Equatorial Guinea.

The cases also illustrate the point that executive tenacity correlates negatively with international law compliance for the most part. When retaining power is the paramount priority, elections cannot be free and fair, opposition parties cannot be tolerated, even public service NGOs and poetry must be closely monitored and quickly controlled at the first sign of dissent. Such a regime will never be a full participant in the international society as presently constituted.

Two more insights can be gleaned from these cases.

Autocrats and resource mobilization: Autocratic governments are often more adept at mobilizing the resources required for law compliance than their democratic counterparts, although a caveat is in order. The government's position in the international economic system makes a great of difference in whether it can mobilize resources at will. In particular, energy dependency or independence is a key factor. Energy dependency opens a wedge into which the international community may be able to insert itself. On the other hand, resource independence may reverse the flow of power and allow a state to resist international pressure or to recruit allies.

The cynical core of rationalism: The advantage of studying isolated autocracies is that much of the diplomatic rhetoric is stripped away and outside observers are better able to identify genuine motivations. Further, we have the opportunity to see what governments do when they are largely unrestrained by ethics or public opinion or checks and balance. In fact, short-term calculations of narrow material self-interest seem to matter a great deal under these circumstances. Reference was already made to Machiavelli – the great philosopher of necessity and fate. His guidance seems to animate the policy decisions of Lukashenko and Obiang to a considerable degree – far more than other leaders we have observed (with the possible exception of Musharraf). Rationalist should feel vindicated.

But does this mean that these leaders are simply behaving openly in the way other leaders behave privately? Are concerns about reputation, legitimacy, and rule of law merely window-dressing for what is essentially a pragmatic, interest-driven enterprise? Perhaps. But it also seems clear that Lukashenko and Obiang are atypical.

References

Africa Research Bulletin (2009) "Lofty Aspirations," 46(3), May 1. Economic, Financial and Technical Series. Accessed December 1, 2010.

Africa Research Bulletin (2010) "Obiang Wins," 46(12), January 24. Political, Social and Cultural Series. Accessed December 1, 2010.

Airfleets.net (2010) Belavia. Available at http://airfleets.net/ageflotte/Belavia.htm. Accessed August 25, 2010.

Airline Analysis (2010) "Belavia Now Serving 32 Destinations from Minsk," August 11. Available at www.anna.aero/2010/08/11/belavia-now-serving-32-destinations-from-minsk/. Accessed November 24, 2010.

Airport.by (2010) Belarus. "Security of Flights." Available at www.airport.by/air_travellers.htm#2. Accessed August 24, 2010.

Amnesty International (2006) "Belarus – Domestic Violence: More than a Private Scandal," November 9. London, UK. Available at www.amnesty.org/en/library/asset/EUR49/014/2006/en/9c159a36-d401–11dd-8743-d305bea2b2c7/eur490142006en.pdf. Accessed November 24, 2010.

Aviation Safety World (2006) "We Need to Do Even Better," by Giovanni Bisignani. August. Available at http://flightsafety.org/asw/aug06/asw_aug06_p11–12.pdf. Accessed December 1, 2010.

Balmaceda, Margarita M. (2007) "Understanding Repression in Belarus," in Robert I. Rotberg, ed., *Worst of the Worst: Dealing with Repressive and Rogue Nations*. Cambridge, MA: World Peace Foundation; Washington D.C.: Brookings Institution Press, pp. 193–222.

Belarus, Republic of, Ministry of Foreign Affairs (2002) "Belarus Fulfills its International Obligations in Fight Against Terrorism," January 29. Available at www.mfa.gov.by/en/press/news/2002–01–29–1.html. Accessed August 25, 2010.

Belarus, Republic of, Embassy of Belarus to the United States of America (2004) "Efforts of the Government of Belarus in Fighting Trafficking in Persons (as of December 2004)." Washington D.C. www.belarusembassy.org/humanitarian/trafficking2.htm. Accessed August 25, 2010. Note: link is inoperative. Embassy location is estimated.

Belarus, Republic of (2007) Law of the Republic of Belarus. *Legal Acts on Trade Unions. No. 1605-XII of 22 April, 1992 In edition of the Law of the Republic of Belarus No. 371-Z of 14 January, 2000 [Amended as of May 10, 2007]*. Available at www.law.by/work/englportal.nsf/6e1a652fbefce34ac2256d910056d559/751672711037eef5c2256dee00500967?OpenDocument. Accessed August 25, 2010.

Belarus, Republic of, Ministry of Foreign Affairs (2009) Statement by His Excellency Sergei N. Martynov, Minister of Foreign Affairs of the Republic of Belarus. United Nations General Assembly Sixty-Fourth Session, General Debate. New York, September 26. Available at www.un.org/ga/64/generaldebate/pdf/BY_en.pdf. Accessed August 25, 2010.

Belarus, Republic of (2010a) National Legal Internet Portal of the Republic of Belarus. "Belarus President Approves State Border Security Policy for 2010," January 18. Available at http://law.by/work/EnglPortal.nsf/0/207DF24A4F0011E0C22576AF0054629D?OpenDocument. Accessed August 25, 2010.

Belarus, Republic of, Permanent Mission to the United Nations (2010b) Current Membership of the Republic of Belarus in the United Nations Bodies. Available at www.belembassy.org/un/Current%20membership.htm. Accessed November 23, 2010.

Belarus, Republic of, State Committee for Standardization (2010c) "Thematic Search." National Fund of Technical Normative Legal Acts. Available at www.tnpa.by/TematichPoiskGoEN.php. Accessed August 25, 2010.

Belarus, Republic of, State Committee for Standardization (2010d) "About the Fund." National Fund of Technical Normative Legal Acts. Available at www.tnpa.by/ZakonOsnovEN.php. Accessed August 27, 2010.

Belarus, Republic of (2011) National Tourism Agency portal. Available at http://eng.belarustourism.by/. Accessed on February 15, 2011.

Belavia (2010) "History of the Airline," July 20. Available at http://en.belavia.by/company/history/. Accessed August 24, 2010.

BelTA (2010) "Nuclear Terrorism Prevention Called Priority of Belarus' Border Guards," July 2. Available at http://news.belta.by/en/news/society?id=552886. Accessed August 28, 2010.

Broek, Antonius (2010) UNDP Resident Representative, at the launch of Human Development Report 2010, November 5. Available at http://undp.by/en/undp/zayavnews/belarus/08–11–2010-sp.html. Accessed November 23, 2010.

Castro, Marisé (2010a) "Economy (Equatorial Guinea)," in Europa World online. London: Routledge. Available at www.europaworld.com.erl.lib.byu.edu/entry/gq.ec. Accessed August 25, 2010.

Castro, Marisé (2010b) "Recent History (Equatorial Guinea)," in Europa World online. London, Routledge. Available at www.europaworld.com.erl.lib.byu.edu/entry/gq.hi. Accessed August 25, 2010.

Chutkova, Irina, Stephan Polonik, Anatoly Bogdanovich, Alexander Bondar, Valentina Dobritskaya, Galina Gasiuk, Taisa Kopusova, Galina Korzh, Victor Pinigin, Natalie Privalova, and Ivan Udovenko, eds. (2005) "National Report of the Republic of Belarus: Status of Achieving the Millennium Development Goals." Available at www.undg.org/docs/7740/MDG%20Report%202005.pdf. Accessed August 25, 2010.

Committee on the Elimination of Discrimination against Women (2004) "Responses to the List of Issues and Questions for Consideration of the Combined Third, Fourth and Fifth Periodic Reports: Equatorial Guinea," April 1. CEDAW/PSWG/2004/II/CRP.2/Add.2. Available at www.un.org/womenwatch/daw/cedaw/cedaw31/EqGuinea-crp2add2-e.pdf. Accessed November 29, 2010.

Defense Industry Daily (2006) "Dude, Where's my Pandur?" February 10. Available at www.defenseindustrydaily.com/dude-wheres-my-pandur-01873/. Accessed December 1, 2010.

Department of State, United States, Bureau of Democracy, Human Rights, and Labor (2009) *2009 Human Rights Report: Belarus*. March 11. Available at www.state.gov/g/drl/rls/hrrpt/2009/eur/136021.htm. Accessed November 24, 2010.

Department of State, United States (2010a) Background Note: Belarus, Bureau of European and Eurasian Affairs, August 27. Available at www.state.gov/r/pa/ei/bgn/5371.htm. Accessed August 25, 2010.

Department of State, United States (2010b) *Trafficking in Persons Report 2010 – Belarus*, June 14. Available at www.unhcr.org/refworld/docid/4c188409c.html. Accessed August 25, 2010.

Department of State, United States, Bureau of Democracy, Human Rights, and Labor (2010c) "2009 Human Rights Report: Equatorial Guinea." Available at www.state.gov/g/drl/rls/hrrpt/2009/af/135951.htm. Accessed August 25, 2010.

Department of State, United States (2010d) *Trafficking in Persons Report 2010 – Equatorial Guinea*, June 14. Available at www.unhcr.org/refworld/docid/4c1883f7c.html. Accessed August 26, 2010.

DeSombre, Elizabeth (2005) "Fishing under Flags of Convenience: Using Market Power to Increase Participation in International Regulation," *Global Environmental Politics* 5(4), November: 73–94.

Endres, Gunter (2009a) "World Airline Directory 2009." *Flight International* 175(5182), March 31–April 6.

Endres, Gunter (2009b) "World Airline Directory 2009," *Flight International* 175(5184). March 7–April 14.
Esteban, Mario (2009) "The Chinese Amigo: Implications for the Development of Equatorial Guinea," *The China Quarterly* 199, September: 667–685.
Europa Yearbook (2010a) "Recent History (Belarus)," in Europa World online. London: Routledge. Available at www.europaworld.com.erl.lib.byu.edu/entry/by.is.4. Accessed May 5, 2010.
Europa Yearbook (2010b) "Treaty of Union with Russia (Belarus)," in Europa World online. London: Routledge. Available at www.europaworld.com.erl.lib.byu.edu/entry/EE000317. Accessed August 26, 2010.
Europa Yearbook (2010c) "Regional Relations (Belarus)," in Europa World online. London: Routledge. Available at www.europaworld.com.erl.lib.byu.edu/entry/by.is.12713464221. Accessed August 26, 2010.
Europa Yearbook (2010d) "Constitution and Government (Equatorial Guinea)," in Europa World online. London: Routledge. Available at www.europaworld.com.erl.lib.byu.edu/entry/gq.is.31 Accessed on August 25, 2010.
Equatorial Guinea, Government of (2010a) Constitution of the Republic of Equatorial Guinea. Available at www.ceiba-guinea-ecuatorial.org/guineeangl/nvelle_const.htm. Accessed August 25, 2010.
Equatorial Guinea, Government of (2010b) Institutional Web Site of the Republic of Equatorial Guinea – Important Project for Government Reforms. Available at www.ceiba-guinea-ecuatorial.org/guineeangl/indexbienv1.htm. Accessed December 1, 2010.
Esteban, Mario (2009) "The Chinese 'Amigo': Implications for the Development of Equatorial Guinee," *The China Quarterly* 199 (September): 667–685.
Extractive Industries Transparency Initiative (2010) Letter to H.E. Teodoro Obiang from Peter Eigen, Chairman. April 29. Available at http://eiti.org/files/2010_04_29_letter_he_president_obiang_equatorial_guinea.pdf. Accessed November 29, 2010.
Ezeilo, Joy Ngozi (2009) "UN Expert on Trafficking in Persons Ends Visit to Belarus," May 26. HR09073E. Minsk, Belarus. Available at www2.ohchr.org/english/issues/trafficking/docs/PressReleaseVisitBelarus.doc. Accessed November 23, 2010.
Fair Fund (2010) "Belarus." Available at www.fairfund.org/subpage.asp?P=about&S=countries&T=belarus. Accessed November 23, 2010.
Fredriksson, Lynn (2007) "U.S. Foreign Policy Saps Human Rights Improvements in Ethiopia and Equatorial Guinea," Testimony, Committee on Foreign Affairs, Subcommittee on International Organizations, Human Rights, and Oversight, Subcommittee on Africa and Global Health, May 10.
Freedom House (2010a) *The Worst of the Worst 2010 – Belarus*, June 3. Available at www.unhcr.org/refworld/docid/4c0e0af91a.html. Accessed August 30, 2010.
Freedom House (2010b) *Freedom in the World 2010 – Equatorial Guinea*, May 3. Available at www.unhcr.org/refworld/docid/4c0ceaf428.html. Accessed August 25, 2010.
Frynas, Jedrzeg George and Manuel Paulo (2006) "A New Scramble for African Oil? Historical, Political, and Business Perspectives," *African Affairs* 106(423) (November): 229–251.
Ghazvinian, John (2007) *Untapped: The Scramble for Africa's Oil*. New York: Houghton Mifflin Harcourt.
Globalis (2001) Indicator. "Indicator: Consumption of Ozone-depleting Chlorofluorocarbons – 2001." Available at http://globalis.gvu.unu.edu/indicator.cfm?IndicatorID=82&country=BY#rowBY. Accessed August 25, 1020.

Heilbrunn, John R. (2007) "Equatorial Guinea and Togo: What Price Repression?" in Robert I. Rotberg, ed., *Worst of the Worst: Dealing with Repressive and Rogue Nations*. Cambridge, MA: World Peace Foundation; Washington D.C.: Brookings Institution Press, pp. 223–249.

Henko, John (2010) Georgetown Law, interview with the author, August 31, Washington D.C.

Heritage Foundation (2010) Economic Freedom Rankings. Available at www.heritage.org/index/ranking. Accessed December 15, 2010.

Human Rights Council (2007) Implementation of General Assembly Resolution 60/251 of 15 March 2006 entitled "Human Rights Council." Report of the Special Rapporteur on the situation of human rights in Belarus, Adrian Severin. A/HRC/4/16. January 15.

Human Rights Council (2010) "Report of the Special Rapporteur on Torture and Other Cruel, Inhuman or Degrading Treatment or Punishment," Thirteenth session Agenda item 3 Promotion and protection of all human rights, civil, political, economic, social and cultural rights, including the right to development. Mission to the Republic of Equatorial Guinea, Manfred Nowak, January 7.

Human Rights Watch (2009) "Well Oiled: Oil and Human Rights in Equatorial Guinea," July. Available at www.hrw.org/node/84253. Accessed December 1, 2010.

Integrated Regional Information Networks (IRIN) (2008) "Burkina Faso: Would-be Migrants Stuck on Border," February 4. Available at: www.unhcr.org/refworld/docid/498ab640c.html. Accessed August 25, 2010.

International Civil Aviation Organization (2001) ICAO Audit Report: Executive Summary – Initial 2001 audit: Equatorial Guinea. Available at www.icao.int/fsix/auditRep1.cfm. Accessed November 21, 2010.

International Civil Aviation Organization (2008) Flight Safety Information Exchange. "List of States That Have Authorized ICAO to Release information on Their Safety Oversight Audit Conducted Between 1999 and 2004." Available at www.icao.int/fsix/auditRep1.cfm. Accessed August 23, 2010.

International Labour Organization (2004) "Trade Union Rights in Belarus: Report of the Commission of Inquiry appointed under article 26 of the Constitution of the International Labour Organization to examine the Observance by the Government of the Republic of Belarus of the Freedom of Association and Protection of the Right to Organise Convention, 1948 (No. 87) and the Right to Organise and Collective Bargaining Convention, 1949 (No. 98)." International Labour Office, Geneva, July 23. Available at www.ilo.org/wcmsp5/groups/public/—dgreports/—dcomm/documents/meetingdocument/kd00067.pdf. Accessed November 24, 2010.

International Labour Organization (2010) ILOLEX Database of International Labour Standards. Available at www.ilo.org/ilolex/english/convdisp1.htm. Accessed December 1, 2010.

International Maritime Bureau, International Chamber of Commerce (2008) Piracy Map. Available at www.icc-ccs.org/home/piracy-reporting-centre/imb-live-piracy-map-2010/another-live-piracy-map/details/21/11. Accessed December 1, 2010.

International Maritime Organization (2010) Status of Conventions. Available at www.imo.org/About/Conventions/StatusOfConventions/Pages/Default.aspx. Accessed November 24, 2010.

International Monetary Fund – External Relations Department (2010) "IMF Completes Fourth Review Under Stand-By Arragnment with Belarus, approves US$662.9 Million Disbursement: Press Release No. 10/119." March 26. International Monetary Fund. Available at www.imf.org/external/np/sec/pr/2010/pr10119.htm. Accessed November 23, 2010.

Ioffe, Grigory (2004) "Understanding Belarus: Economy and Political Landscape," *Europe-Asia Studies* 56(1) (January): 84–118.
Jane's (2010) Navy (Equatorial Guinea) Navy. Available at www.janes.com/extracts/extract/cafrsu/eqgus130.html. Accessed December 1, 2010.
Katibnikov, Igor (2009) "Economic Reforms in Belarus," in Hans-Georg Heinrich and Ludmilla Lobova, eds., *Belarus: External Pressure, Internal Change*. Frankfurt am Main: Peter Lang, pp. 51–58.
Keili, Francis Langumba (2008) "Small Arms and Light Weapons Transfer in West Africa: A Stock-taking." *The Complex Dynamics of Small Arms in West Africa*. Available at www.unidir.org/pdf/articles/pdf-art2832.pdf. Accessed August 24, 2010.
Kramer, David (2010) Senior transatlantic fellow – German Marshall Fund of the United States, interview with the author, September 2, Washington D.C.
Kramer, David J. and Damon Wilson (2010) "When Sanctions Work: The Belarus Buckle," *The American Interest* (November–December).
Latvian Environment, Geology and Meteorology Centre (2010) "Ozone Layer Protection in the World." Available at www.meteo.lv/public/28976.html. Accessed August 24, 2010.
Liniger-Goumaz, Max (1998) *Guinée équatorial: 30 ans d'état délinguant nguemiste*. Paris: Harmattan.
Lonely Planet (2009) Equatorial Guinea. Available at www.lonelyplanet.com/equatorial-guinea. Accessed November 29, 2010.
Muni, El (*c.*2005) "Women are a Lucrative Commodity in Equatorial Guinea," *Afrol News*. April 13. Available at www.afrol.com/articles/16115. Accessed August 27, 2010.
Naumov, Vladimir (2007) Statement by H.E. Vladimir Naumov, Minister of Internal Affairs of the Republic of Belarus at the United Nations Headquarters International Conference, "Trafficking in Women and Girls: Meeting the Challenge Together." March 5. Available at www.un.int/belarus/conference/statement_naumov_en.pdf. Accessed August 25, 2010.
Naviny.by (2010) "Transport Ministry Considering Offers from Foreign Companies Willing to Invest in Creation of Belarus' Merchant Fleet," Belarus News. July 2. Available at http://naviny.by/rubrics/english/2010/07/02/ic_media_video_259_4406/. Accessed November 22, 2010.
New York Times (2010) "European Engagement with Belarus Takes a Blow," December 22. Available at www.nytimes.com/2010/12/23/world/europe/23iht-letter23.htlm. Accessed December 23, 2010.
Overseas Security Advisory Council (2009) *Belarus 2009 Crime & Safety Report*. August 17. Available at www.osac.gov/Reports/report.cfm?contentID=106505. Accessed August 25, 2010.
Overseas Security Advisory Council (2010) Equatorial Guinea 2010 Crime & Safety Report. May 10. Available at www.osac.gov/Reports/report.cfm?contentID=117150. Accessed August 23, 2010.
Paris Memorandum of Understanding on Port State Control (2002) Annual Report 2001. Available at www.parismou.org/upload/anrep/anrep2001.pdf. Accessed November 30, 2010.
Petina, Lyudmila and Svetlana Burova (2003) "Shadow Report on the Implementation of the Convention on the Elimination of all Forms of Discrimination Against Women in the Republic of Belarus." Available at http://un.by/pdf/2003%20Belarus%20CEDAW%20Shadow%20Report.pdf. Accessed November 30, 2010.

Radio Free Europe (2006) "Belarus: As Drinking Increases, Government Declares War," by Valentinas Mite. July 26. Available at www.rferl.org/content/article/1070115.html. Accessed November 22, 2010.

Radio Free Europe/Radio Liberty (2010) "Rights Group: Seven Belarusian Presidential Candidates Face 15 Years in Prison." December 22. Available at www.rferl.org/article-printview/2256148.html. Accessed December 23, 2010.

Richardson, Erica and Svetlana Anker, eds. (2008) "Belarus: Health System Review," *Health Systems in Transition* 10(6): 1–118.

Roberts, Adam (2006) *The Wonga Coup: The British Mercenary Plot to Seize Oil Billions in Africa*. London: Profile Books.

Rossmann, Martin (2009) "Elections and Political Pluralism in Belarus," in Hans-Georg Heinrich and Ludmilla Lobova, eds., *Belarus: External Pressure, Internal Change*. Frankfurt am Main: Peter Lang, pp. 237–247.

Ryder, Andrew (2010) "Economy (Belarus)," in Europa World online. London: Routledge. Available at www.europaworld.com.erl.lib.byu.edu/entry/by.econ. Accessed August 30, 2010.

Sannikov, Andrei and Mark Lenzi (2004) "Belarus's Terrorist Ties," June 12. *Washington Post*. Available at www.washingtonpost.com/wp-dyn/articles/A35748–2004Jun11.html. Accessed August 25, 2010.

Senate, United States (2004) "Money Laundering and Foreign Corruption: Enforcement and Effectiveness of the PATRIOT Act." Hearings before the Permanent Subcommittee on Investigations of the Committee on Governmental Affairs. One Hundred Eighth Congress, Second Session. July 15. S. Hrg. 108–633.

Shen, Jianming (2000) "National Sovereignty and Human Rights in a Positive Law Context," *Brooklyn Journal of International Law* 26: 417–446.

Sims, Roxanne (2009) "A Comparison of Laws in the Philippines, the USA, Taiwan, and Belarus to Regulate the Mail-Order Bride Industry," *Akron Law Review* 42: 607–637.

Simser, Jeffrey (2010) "Asset Recovery and Kleptocracy," *Journal of Financial Crime* 17(3): 321–332.

Smoltczyk, Alexander (2006) "Rich in Oil, Poor in Human Rights: Torture and Poverty in Equatorial Guinea," Spiegel Online. August 28. Available at www.spiegel.de/international/spiegel/0,1518,434691,00.html. Accessed December 1, 2010.

Soares de Oliveira, Ricardo M.S. (2007) *Oil and Politics in the Gulf of Guinea*. New York: Columbia University Press.

Suzdaltsev, Andrey I. (2009) "Relations between Moscow and Minsk (2005–2007)," in Hans-Georg Heinrich and Ludmilla Lobova, eds., *Belarus: External Pressure, Internal Change*. Frankfurt am Main: Peter Lang, pp. 349–364.

UNICEF (2010) *Annual Report for Equatorial Guinea*. New York: UNICEF. Available at www.youthpolicy.org/wp-content/uploads/library/2010_UNICEF_Equatorial_Guinea_Report_Eng.pdf. Accessed February 25, 2010.

United Nations Development Programme (2010) "New Centre to Help Belarus Youth Avoid 'Modern Slavery'." Available at http://europeandcis.undp.org/home/show/BB4BC545-F203–1EE9-B11C14D2C9954CE4. Accessed August 25, 2010.

United National Environment Programme (2005) "Belarus." Ozone Secretariat. Available at http://ozone.unep.org/Meeting_Documents/research-mgrs/6orm/resmgr6-rpt-part3-a.pdf. Accessed November 24, 2010.

United Nations Environment Programme, Ozone Secretariat (2006) "Decision VII/17: Compliance with the Montreal Protocol by Belarus." In *Handbook for the Montreal Protocol on Substances that Deplete the Ozone Layer*. 7th edn. Available at www.unep.ch/Ozone/Publications/MP_Handbook/Section_2_Decisions/Article_8/decs-non-compliance/Decision_VII-17.shtml. Accessed August 21, 2010.

United Nations Environment Programme, Ozone Secretariat (2009) *Handbook for the Montreal Protocol on Substances that Deplete the Ozone Layer*. 8th edn., pp. 286–287, 342–343. Available at www.unep.ch/ozone/Publications/MP_Handbook/MP-Handbook-2009.pdf. Accessed August 23, 2010.

United Nations Environment Programme (2010a) Division of Technology, Industry and Economics OzonAction Branch. "French-speaking Africa Regional Network of Ozone Officers." Available at www.unep.fr/ozonaction/networks/africa_f.asp. Accessed August 23, 2010.

United Nations Environment Programme (2010b) Data Access Centre. "ODS Consumption" and "Imports of Recovered/Recycled/Reclaimed." Ozone Secretariat. Available at http://ozone.unep.org/Data_Reporting/Data_Access/. Accessed August 26, 2010.

United Nations Environment Programme (2010c) Ozone Secretariat. "Status of Ratification." Available at http://ozone.unep.org/Ratification_status/ratif_by_country.shtml?cntryname=Equatorial+Guinea&submit_country=Submit+Query. Accessed August 21, 2010.

USAToday (2006) "EU bans 92 Mostly African Airlines from Landing at European Airports." *USAToday*, March 22. Available at www.usatoday.com/travel/flights/2006–03–22-eu-blacklist_x.htm. Accessed August 25, 2010.

van Klaveren, Maarten and Nuria Ramos Martin (2010) "An Overview of Women's Work and Employment in Belarus: Decisions for Life MDG3 Project Country Report No. 11." *Wage Indicator*. Available at http://dfl.wageindicator.org/uploadfolder/documents/Decisions_for_life-Country_Report-Belarus.pdf.

World Bank (1997) "GEF Grant Supports Environment in Belarus," Press release #97/1329 ECA. Available at http://web.worldbank.org/WBSITE/EXTERNAL/PROJECTS/0,,contentMDK:20016554~menuPK:64282138~pagePK:41367~piPK:279616~theSitePK:40941,00.html. Accessed November 24, 2010.

World Trade Press (2010) *Equatorial Guinea Society and Culture: Complete Report*. Petaluma, CA: World Trade Press.

Zadora, Anna (2009) "The Belarusian Elite: Formation, Conduct and Developmental Dynamics. A Socio-historical Perspective," in Hans-Georg Heinrich and Ludmilla Lobova, eds., *Belarus: External Pressure, Internal Change*. Frankfurt am Main: Peter Lang, pp. 139–152.

9 Isolationist democracies

Botswana and Papua New Guinea

Theoretical predictions regarding isolationist autocracies

Democratic regimes that have relatively few ties to the outside world may act unpredictably with respect to international law. On the one hand, they will internalize most rules respecting human rights and public participation, and will probably have relatively higher standards of governance due to their increased accountability. On the other hand, if they are relatively uninvolved with international society, they may not have been socialized to operate in the realm of law. There may be relatively few points of access whereby the international community can communicate with or influence the government. And it's possible that the society may not have been indoctrinated to broader principles of international law.

In the end, what we may encounter is a sort of legal tone-deafness in which the state may join in the chorus but not able to read the music. One might anticipate many miscues and offenses stemming primarily from ignorance and misunderstanding.

Botswana

Overview

Botswana has been widely praised as a model of good governance. It has enjoyed uninterrupted democracy since its founding in 1966, and has seen consistently strong growth. Although dependence on diamond exports has been a cause for concern, efforts are being made to expand manufacturing and increase agricultural productivity (World Bank 2009). The country's finances are well managed, inflation is low, debt is moderate, and the country's savings in hard currency are enough to cover many months' worth of imports.

Botswana is land-locked, bordering South Africa, Zambia, Zimbabwe, and Namibia. Its relations with its neighbors are somewhat tense, mostly due to their troubles that spill over (US Committee for Refugees 2009). It aspires to provide a leadership role in the southern African region. It has already sent peacekeepers to Lesotho (1998 – Europa 2010a). But it hosts only a dozen foreign embassies, making it a relatively marginal player in world affairs.

Around four out of five of Botswana's nearly two million inhabitants live near the South African border and belong to the Tswana ethnic group (IRIN 2010). There are forty-five other distinct ethnicities and two dozen languages spoken. Some groups, including the San, consider themselves the victims of discrimination (UN Human Rights Council 2009). Income inequality in Botswana is among the worst in the world, despite efforts to expand educational, health, and job opportunities by the government for decades. In particular, conditions in the cities are generally better than in rural areas (unemployment in most cities is below 10 percent), and some rural districts are in serious trouble. In Ngamiland North in the northernmost regions of the country, unemployment stood at 48.4 percent in 2008.

Although government officials have a presence throughout the country and many services are available even in remote corners, in some pockets the people feel cut off. In Ngwaketse West district, just two hundred miles from the capital, only 49.7 percent of households had a working radio, a quarter had a television set, and 8.3 percent had access to the Internet (Botswana 2009, 124).

By far the most serious and tragic problem facing Botswana at this point in its history is the HIV/AIDS epidemic. Estimates suggest that a quarter of the population is infected and as many as one in three children are born with AIDS. The country has nearly 150,000 "AIDS orphans" – children who have lost both parents to the illness. As explained by the World Bank:

> Life expectancy has quickly fallen from 60 to 56 years (2007). Infant mortality is up from 45 (per 1,000 births) in 1990 to 90 in 2007.... Botswana's Human Development Index (HDI) rankings have declined from number 72 (of 130 countries) in 1990 to 126 (of 179 countries) in 2008, largely explained by the decline in life expectancy due to the HIV/AIDS epidemic.
>
> (World Bank 2009)

Liberalism

Botswana is widely considered a stable democracy. The praise lavished on Botswana no doubt stems in part from how much it stands out from the neighborhood. We should therefore take care to compare the government to those around the world rather than just southern Africa.

Botswana's political liberalism is widely acknowledged. Polity and Freedom House scores consistently give Botswana high marks. Likewise, Botswana's "rule of law" scores are well above the mean.

Botswana's government is what might be called a "strong parliamentarian" system. Every five years the voters elect a legislature handing the Botswana Democratic Party (BDP) consistent majorities. In 2009, for example, although the BDP won only 53.5 percent of the vote, it gained forty-five of the fifty-seven contested seats (six other seats are filled by appointment by the majority party). The National Assembly selects the President, who in turn appoints the Cabinet from among the ranks of the legislature. He also has the power to dissolve the legislature and call fresh elections if needed before the five years are up (Good 2008, 33). The President routinely proposes legislation and has the power to veto acts of parliament, which enhances party discipline. The Vice-President succeeds the President upon the former's resignation – something that often happens just before he completes his second term. The result is that the BDP's candidate runs as an incumbent:

> This authoritarian state system was legitimized by the past, quickly established in the nation-state at independence and extended thereafter. Presidential successions have occurred smoothly on two occasions, over the heads of the people. Regular parliamentary elections have never produced a change of government and are equally notable for their low turnout of eligible voters. Since 1998 he is effectively chosen by only one person, his predecessor, by the act of his appointment as vice-president.
>
> (Good 2008, 25–26)

The government-owned radio and television stations are censored (and self-censored) to weed out stories that might be especially critical of the regime. In recent years, efforts have been made to limit the media even further:

> In July 2008, the government announced a new Media Practitioners Bill, which would set up a media regulatory body and mandate the registration of all media workers. The measure was withdrawn in August after the opposition and press freedom advocates objected, but the government reintroduced it in November and passed it the following month without holding promised consultations with the bill's detractors.
>
> (Freedom House 2010a)

The key reason for the BDP's longevity appears to be the inability of opposition parties to combine. Given the first-past-the-post system, the outcome is far from surprising. The Batswana are very supportive of democracy, favoring it over autocracy by 85 percent to 5 percent in a 2008 poll (Afrobarometer 2009, 3). Eighty-three percent agree that violence in politics is never justified – the highest level for any of the fifteen African societies surveyed (Afrobarometer 2004, 22).

National policy debates are common. The courts generally monitor and restrain the executive, and several acts and policies have been ruled unconstitutional. Many active NGOs and advocacy groups also strive to hold the government accountable. This was true in the case of the government's efforts to forcibly relocate the San people, for example (Good 2008, 140; Dept. of State 2010a).

Continued strong economic growth (averaging around 7 percent during the 2000s) has also played its part. In 2003 75 percent acknowledged that they are doing "better" or "much better" than their neighbors on the African continent (Afrobarometer 2004, 7).

Botswana is formally committed to economic liberalism. This is expressed in its commitment to free trade arrangements, including a customs union with

South Africa, and the South African Development Community (SADC). It has special access to the European Union and non-EU-member European countries (UNCTAD 2006, 8). It received the highest score in Africa for economic freedom from the Heritage Foundation at 70.3 out of 89.7 in 2010, besting Belgium by 0.2 points (Heritage Foundation 2010).

The total value of Botswana's imports and exports are greater than the country's GDP (Van Buren 2010). Its trade is not geographically diversified, however, in that the United Kingdom buys roughly two-thirds of the country's exports (mostly diamonds) and South Africa provides more than 80 percent of its imports – mostly food and other staples.

Foreign direct investment is strong, although much of this involves the mining sector – something the government is hoping to change by increasing incentives to expand manufacturing and diversify agriculture (Van Buren 2010). The government has begun weaning itself from foreign aid in recent years, receiving less and less from the major international financial institutions (World Bank 2009).

Taken together, then, it is fair to say that the Botswana economy is very open – perhaps dangerously so – and so predictions from theories related to economic liberalism should be borne out.

Managerial school

We have already mentioned that one of Botswana's claims to fame is its ability to govern. The 1999 World Bank Botswana country study was subtitled: "A Case Study of Economic Policy Prudence and Growth" (World Bank 1999). Botswana benefits from favorable comparisons to its neighbors. According to one senior government official, the government has taken care from the outset to ensure that revenue collection, expenditure decisions, and actual payments are each at arm's length from the other to minimize the opportunity for corruption. The country also benefits from a dedicated officer corps that has internalized a spirit of public service (Botswana official 2010).

The Batswana generally agree that the government's presence is strong. The following are the numbers who agreed they were either "likely" or "very likely" to get caught: 85 percent for committing a serious crime, and 78 percent for failing to pay taxes (Afrobarometer 2004, 39).

Concerns have been raised about government procurement methods since well-connected individuals seem to receive "sweetheart deals" (Good 2008, 74). The government did not sign or ratify the African Union's anti-corruption treaty. Some policemen have been convicted of various crimes (Dept. of State 2010a). The Directorate on Corruption and Economic Crime is relatively active in pursuing cases of official corruption (Dept. of State 2010a).

The government spends a great deal on education, health, and other services. Roughly 80 percent of Batswana agree that it does well providing education, health care, and other services, although only half feel they receive adequate policy protection (Afrobarometer 2004, 49). The military is small at roughly

15,000 – although defense expenditures are relatively high at nearly 4 percent of GDP (Henk 2010). The government has around thirty border stations. While impressive, this is not enough to prevent a steady flow of migrants from Zimbabwe (US Committee for Refugees 2009). The Botswana government fears the implications of an open door policy (Botswana official 2010).

> Illegal immigrants from Zimbabwe face increasing xenophobia and are accused, sometimes legitimately, of criminal activity. These immigrants are subject to exploitation in the labor market. Botswana is building an electric fence along its border with Zimbabwe, ostensibly to control foot-and-mouth disease among livestock, but the barrier is popularly supported as a means of halting illegal immigration; thousands of Zimbabweans have been deported in recent years.
>
> (Freedom House 2010a)

Otherwise, there are no apparent pockets of lawlessness as is typically the case in a country with this type of geography and environment. In general, the government is capable of generating revenue and ensuring that its policies are implemented with relatively few miscues.

Reputational theory

Establishing and maintaining a reputation for honoring debts and limiting financial risk has been a key priority for the government since independence. The international financial community has given Botswana high marks. Particularly noteworthy is the fact that both Moody's and Standard and Poor's have not only rated Botswana's bonds, but have given them a solid "A" grade since 2004 (Van Buren 2010). In other areas, Botswana seeks and receives international approval. This is especially so with respect to human rights, environmental policy, and health and education (Botswana official 2010).

Culture

While most of Botswana's inhabitants live in cities near the South African border, tribal life in the villages is still important. Tribal headmen are represented in a presidential advisory council (Freedom House 2010a). Certain local customs are allowed to supersede national law, especially with respect to the status of women (UN CEDAW 2008, 11). But the vast majority of the people are entirely Westernized and most have easy access to international media streams not only from the government-owned media but also from South African broadcasts.

Batswana attitudes about key social issues are mixed, but strongly tend toward modern Western values. Two-thirds believe people should be free to act for themselves rather than defer to their social groups. Seventy-eight percent believe women should have the same rights as men. Eighty-one percent believe everyone has the right to vote (Afrobarometer 2004, 19).

The collapse of rural agriculture prior to independence had the effect of leveling traditional society and forcing many former aristocrats into mining and business, with the long-term result that the country developed a bourgeoisie far sooner than many of its neighbors (Parsons 1999). The government does not emphasize the variety of ethnicities in Botswana, preferring to emphasize Tswana identity. Batswana, by a margin of 77 percent to 19 percent, do not believe politicians should look out for their own once they come to power, but rather look out for the country as a whole (Afrobarometer 2004, 19). Members of the second largest ethnicity – Kalanga – have dealt with the situation in one of two ways:

> while some opt for a militant assertion of Kalangahood in the face of the Tswana (particularly Ngwato) who have appropriated the post-Independence Botswana state, others (probably a majority, and including many members of the rising Botswana middle class) limit expressions of Kalangahood to private situations, and in the public sphere exchange submission to Tswana domination for personal political and economic success.
>
> (van Binsbergen 2002)

Kalanga leaders take their grievances to the press, community meetings, national conclaves, and even the corridors of power, and are able to be heard. They have secured additional services and benefits for their community (Werbner 2004). The San – a large hunter-gatherer society that has survived in the Kalahari for millennia – have not fared as well. The government decided in the late 1990s to begin assimilating them into mainstream society by relocating them from the Kalahari to areas where they would be provided with potable water, job training, and other services. Some groups resisted the move and remained behind. When a few hundred sought access to boreholes in the Kalahari in 2002, they were denied, but appealed and won (BBC 2002).

Legitimacy

Botswana sees itself as a peaceful and cooperative member of the international community. There are situations in which its standards are actually higher than what is expected, as in the case of protecting the fragile Okavango Delta (Botswana official 2010).

With respect to international law generally, we've seen that Botswana is happy to participate in international organizations, and international peacekeeping operations. It has accepted compulsory ICJ jurisdiction and even participated in a contentious case with Namibia (Saunders 2010). It serves as host to SADC Secretariat and participates actively in the African Union. It served on the UN Security Council during the 1990s.

Generally speaking, Botswana is able to codify and internalize international conventions. The legislature does not oppose international agreements that have been signed by the executive and the courts do not become involved in foreign policy as a rule. There are concerns about whether domestic courts pay adequate attention to international norms in their rulings, however (UN Human Rights Committee 2008).

Rationalism

Botswana's elites are agreed on a wide range of fundamental governing principles, including especially export-driven growth and public service provision. There is little elite conflict and virtually all seem committed to the general welfare. While there is evidence of favoritism for elites with respect to business transactions, there is also relatively little evidence of class conflict across the country. Serious cases of corruption are sometimes exposed and addressed. Thus far in Botswana's history, there has been enough money to go around to appease most disadvantaged groups, as we saw with respect to the Kalanga.

Botswana does not have a long history of interest group activism or even civil society engagement (Hope and Somolekae 1998). We've already seen that the state occupies a considerable public space and may be suffocating some would-be activity. Taken together, then, Botswana's civil society is smaller than might be expected given the considerable freedoms at hand. But this is not to say it is feeble. We have already noted cases when civil society organizations have protested or influenced government policy.

Even relations with DeBeers – potentially conflictual given the latter's monopoly of technical expertise – have improved in recent years. In 2006, the contract was renegotiated and the government's royalties were increased. The two also organized new arrangements that would bring more of the diamond processing, sorting, and marketing back to Botswana (Van Buren 2010).

Performance across issue-areas

Rules governing territorial defense: anti-terrorism, anti-piracy, and anti-trafficking

Botswana has no domestic terrorist groups, although it is concerned about infiltration from neighboring states. The lack of urgency to address the war on terror may explain some gaps in the law, and the relatively poor CTC scores (see Table 9.1). The country has nonetheless ratified all the pertinent anti-terror conventions and has passed a number of statutes outlawing terrorism (Botswana 2010).

Table 9.1 Indicators of compliance with rules governing territorial defense (2005)

Ratification of 2000 Trafficking Protocol	Yes
State Dept. Trafficking in Persons score (2009)	Tier 2
UN CTC total score	4 (7 possible)
UN CTC score, minus treaty ratifications	2 (5 possible)

Of greatest concern to Western interests is the lack of a law specific to financing of terrorism and the formation of a financial intelligence unit. But despite this the government's approach has provided fairly strong protections. The national anti-corruption agency has had the capacity to identify and track "suspicious transactions" (Dept. of State 2010b). The government has created a counter-terrorism national committee to coordinate anti-terrorist measures. It has designated a unit of its army to focus on counter-terror tactics and strategies, and it has collaborated with Interpol in information-sharing (Skelemani 2011).

Botswana is land-locked, has no navy, and currently registers no ships, according to the World Shipping Register. Despite this lack of involvement in matters relating to piracy, it is interesting to note that its penal code includes three specific references to piracy (Botswana 2010). This is consistent with Botswana's commitment to the SUA convention.

Human trafficking is a matter of some concern. It was not a priority for the government until very recently, perhaps because the country was not assessed by the US State Department until 2009 when it was placed on tier two (Dept. of State 2009b). A comprehensive trafficking law is lacking, but the government has launched a national task force on the issue and has begun mounting an information campaign.

Despite the lack of anti-trafficking law, several provisions in Botswana's penal code address the types of activities that usually accompany trafficking. For example, kidnapping, slavery, prostitution, running a brothel, profiting from prostitution, "procuration" (purchasing services from a prostitute), "detention for immoral purposes," certain forms of child labor, and so forth (Dept. of State 2009b). Using these laws, the government convicted three individuals in 2009 for trafficking-related crimes and deported nearly 600 children to Zimbabwe on the assumption that they were trafficked (Dept. of State 2010c). The government also provides services to people who have been trafficked.

Child labor is a more serious concern, and Botswana is working with ILO consultants and others to improve workplace inspections and overall enforcement (Dept. of State 2010c). Botswana is also working to enhance its border control with a new digital passport that can be machine-readable and will include the holder's fingerprint (Dept. of State 2009a; Keoreng 2010).

To what extent do our theories explain this behavior? Perhaps more so than we've encountered thus far, the liberal model offers a fairly impressive analysis. Botswana's policies on terrorism and trafficking, while somewhat muted, seem fairly appropriate for the circumstances and can be expected to have the support of the people as a whole. This likely explains why the domestic statutes in place were less than exacting – the problems they are designed to solve are less than urgent, after all. The government already had in place before 2005 a wide range of laws governing the ordinary crimes – money laundering, arms possession, assault, threatening behavior, and so forth – that are typically committed by terrorists, consistent with years of routine law-making. The same can be said for anti-trafficking regulations.

The government seems to have internalized the general concept of rule of law, making it easy for it to understand the arguments of international bodies. It is part of the "society of nations" discussed by Hedley Bull and others (see Chapter 1). Of course the internalization of democratic and legalistic approaches to policy is consistent with both the reputational and legitimacy schools. To put it succinctly, Botswana is a stable democracy that appreciates intrinsically the rule of law. It also values its reputation as a supporter of the rule of law internationally. When presented with an inconsistency between its domestic statutes and international norms, it strives to remedy the situation.

Botswana's economic openness does not seem related to the cases. Although traffickers and terrorists might have a somewhat easy time entering the country because of its relatively open borders, there seems to be relatively little interest in doing so. One can assume that they are calculating they aren't abusing the privilege.

The fact that Botswana generally has the capacity to implement these statutes means that there should be no fundamental break between adoption and behavior. Naturally, policing its very long border, much of which passes through difficult and isolated terrain, will be a challenge, but given the relatively few attacks on the border, the problem should be mostly manageable. The fact that the country happens to be sitting on diamond deposits that were not discovered until after the British had left was lucky. The real test will be whether the government can orchestrate a smooth transition to a post-diamond economy.

The cultural approach does not seem to offer much on first glance. It does not seem to explain in itself the adoption of laws in response to international pressure. On the other hand, the fact that the people of Botswana, including some minority groups, have chosen not to take up arms or resort to terrorism means that the government has more resources to address foreign threats. So a culture of compliance and self-restraint may in fact contribute a great deal to what the state can and can't do.

Finally, can Botswana's approach to these issues be explained in terms of purely rational calculations? We can say that compliance may stem from a cynical calculation that it should do what the international community wants. But it does not tell us why the government was in such a strong position to begin with, such that adopting new statutes was so easy. Its legal baseline stemmed far more from a clear set of intrinsic values and procedures rather than from international demands – something the rationalist approach cannot explain very well.

Rules designed to regulate the market: shipping and airline regulation and CFC control

Air transport is important to Botswana since many tourists travel to hard-to-reach natural wonders by air. Tourism brings in roughly half a billion dollars in total revenue each year – or around 5 percent of GDP (Europa 2010b).

Botswana's airline industry is in chaos at the moment, although plans are in place to improve the situation. The airport in the capital Gaborone has recently been expanded, although it is still very small and serves flights to only a handful of destinations. The safety record is poor, as indicated by the scores in Table 9.2. In 2008, Air Botswana, a small, state-owned company, was forced to withdraw from the International Air Transport Association because it was unable to meet the organization's basic safety standards (Mmegi 2009).

According to the American government, Botswana's airline safety and regulations are far below international standards. It scored the lowest possible grade (1 out of 10) in the area of technical personnel qualifications and training and a 2 on Civil Aviation System and Safety Oversight (ICAO 2010a). The head of the country's civil aviation board has been criticized. Air Botswana is a marginal operation with a half-dozen aircraft and a dubious record of safety. In 1999, a distraught pilot commandeered one of the fleet's planes and crashed it into two aircraft on the ground, temporarily leaving the airline without a fleet (FSN 1999). The Botswana Guardian exposed the seriousness of the problem:

> Botswana Guardian investigations have unearthed information showing that the Rescue and Fire Services (RFS) of CAAB have an acute staff shortage which compromises the safety measures standards (SMS) in all of Botswana's airports.
>
> Further, the sector suffers serious low staff morale, which also compromises SMS requirements. The RFS staff members at Maun and Sir Seretse Khama International Airport (SSKA) work in two shifts with only four people per shift. Under the current state of affairs, RFS operates at a staff deficit of at least 33 people, making it incompetent to deal with emergencies such as accidents. The normal procedure is three shifts with about 37 people in total.
>
> (Kentshitswe 2010)

Frank Ramsden, civil aviation head, responded to the criticism by agreeing that the situation was serious, but blamed the slow transition from one administrative

Table 9.2 Indicators of compliance with market regulating laws

1999–2001 ICAO non-compliance score	46.64 (on a scale of 0–100; 0=no deficiencies)
ICAO follow-up 2004	39.34
ali_standard air liberalization score	99 (0–183; high=liberal)
ICAO Conventions ratified 2010	24 (out of 43)
Endorsed 1988 SUA Convention	Yes
Endorsed 1988 SUA Convention Protocol (platforms)	Yes
Ozone-related conventions ratified	4 (out of 16)
Cumulative Montreal Protocol compliance score	12 (0–24; low=compliance)
Reported data to Ozone Commission 2002–2007	Failed to report
Found non-compliant 2002–2007	Yes
Broke existing program 2002–2007	Three times

arrangement to a new one – something the International Civil Aviation Organization (ICAO) has also noted (ICAO 2010b, 1).

The ICAO has expressed impatience with the slow progress being made in Botswana with respect to airline safety, personnel training, and airport safety, and has urged the government to increase staffing, provide training to bush pilots and other private services, disseminate safety information – especially problems – and in general take their obligations more seriously (ICAO 2010b, 3).

Botswana consumes very little in the way of ozone-depleting substances, although it consumes less today than in the past. Its baseline chlorofluorocarbon (CFC) consumption level is merely 6.9 ozone-depleting potential tons (ODP). Botswana was classified as a "developing country" and was given an extended timetable to reduce its CFC still further (UN 2002a, 24). Botswana reached the target (UNEP 2010a, 2).

Botswana has struggled to comply with the Montreal Protocol. To begin, Botswana has failed to submit its reports on a regular basis, meaning that the data are spotty and somewhat unreliable. Even though it was found in non-compliance in 2002, it reported no data for 2003 (UNEP 2009, 287). It delayed eliminating consumption of methyl bromide and continues to consume halons.

But there was considerable dissatisfaction with the country's performance with respect to ozone-depleting substances. The following is a list of concerns developed following a country-wide assessment:

> the technology dumping and procurement of environmentally sound technologies; future cost scenarios and projections; hazards and consequences of a depleted stratospheric ozone layer; capacity building to provide technical training to retrofit refrigerators with the new technologies and related handling requirements; ability to identify ODS, whether new or recycled; effective substitutes at reasonable costs; and the adoption of appropriate destruction technologies.
>
> (UN 2002a, 24)

The government was therefore required to do the following:

> provide information, annually, on the quantity of ozone depleting substances used in Botswana; develop a phase out of the use/consumption of ozone depleting substances; and promote awareness and exchange information on the availability of options and alternatives to controlled substances in certain products.
>
> (UN 2002a, 24)

This performance comes despite Botswana's commitment to a wide range of ozone-related international conventions and regulations (UN 2002a, 25; UNEP 2009, 523). It has also welcomed international experts to mount various training programs related to air pollution generally.

How do our theories perform? In the case of ozone protection, political liberalism does not seem to provide an explanation, but there is evidence that government officials are being held accountable for their failure to protect air travel. It is unclear whether the Batswana take seriously the need to convert the economy to non-CFC refrigerants and propellants – but there does seem to be sincere interest in making sure tourists feel safe when flying in the country. In this sense, though, economic liberalism seems to offer a more persuasive argument than political liberalism.

The managerial school seems to explain some of what we see. It is difficult to assess – as an outsider – whether Botswana's governing elite are sincere in their promises to comply. The performance record is mixed, although there is evidence that the government is taking steps to improve. The elimination of CFC imports is clearly the product of increased focus and training on the part of customs officials and other inspectors. Likewise, the government seems very aware of the problems with air safety, but the priority for now seems to be on increasing the capacity of the principal airport rather than improving the quality and numbers of air traffic control and air safety technicians. One problem may be that it is far easier to obtain overseas credits and grants to address capital investments rather than recurring budgetary expenditures.

Botswana seems concerned about its reputation, but it is difficult to say to what degree. One would think that it would be most responsive to concerns about air safety, but in fact it is complying somewhat more in the area of ozone-depleting substances. This observation relates to whether Botswana considers these rules legitimate. There is considerable ambivalence on the part of the government. Certainly laws have been passed, but funds have not been forthcoming to implement them even though the government does not lack financial resources. It appears that concerns over reputation and the legitimacy of the law are not enough to push policy through the obstacles.

It seems doubtful that Batswana culture is much of a factor in explaining either airline safety or ozone protection. In both cases, the decisions are being made and implemented by a relatively small cadre of elites. On the other hand, it appears that rational calculations are going into Botswana's policy on CFC consumption since it is clear that the timing of it stemmed largely from threats of sanctions from the Ozone Secretariat. Whether rational calculations drove airline safety policy isn't so clear, although it isn't always easy to determine the rationality of what appears to have been a mistake. The relatively small investment of a few dozen aircraft technicians and air traffic controllers seems a small price to pay to maintain Botswana's reputation as a safe place to fly, after all. It is difficult to conclude that the decision was based on a rational calculation of costs and benefits as a result.

Laws on human rights promotion: anti-slavery law and anti-discrimination against women

Botswana's human rights record is well regarded by the international community, although not without reservation. The government's policy on relocating the San people likely violates international norms regarding the treatment of indigenous peoples and has been criticized.

Table 9.3 provides some of the information about Botswana's compliance with anti-slavery and women's rights norms. The government has ratified a number of important conventions on these topics and has made efforts to codify them as domestic law. Observers in Botswana readily acknowledge that there are at least several thousand slaves and indentured servants. On the other hand, abuse of women is better known, prompting the very poor score from the WomanStats project.

As mentioned, Botswana has a number of laws on the books related to slavery. Kidnapping is punishable by up to ten years in prison, with enslaving someone five years (Botswana 2010). The law also prohibits child labor to a considerable extent. Only immediate family members may hire a child under thirteen, and this cannot involve work in industry (Dept. of State 2010a). Official reports indicate that as many as 38,000 children work in the formal sector of the economy. "Approximately half of those employed were younger than 14" (Dept. of State 2010a). Still more are employed informally as domestic servants and cattle herders.

With respect to adult worker rights, the record is mixed. Unions are permitted but strikes typically are not. Zimbabwean immigrants have reportedly been exploited by local farmers and other employers due to their economic vulnerability (Freedom House 2010a). Likewise the San have been exploited by ranchers in the central regions of the country and are trapped in "voluntary slavery" (Good 2008, 107). Some women are pressed into work as sexual servants in safari lodges (Dept. of State 2009b).

Women in Botswana face a curious split legal status. On the one hand, urban women enjoy essentially equal legal status to men. They have a wide range of Western-style civil rights, enjoy positions of responsibility in government and business, and are protected from harm by numerous laws and relatively effective police protection. Women in rural areas, however, generally live under a traditional legal code and are subject to considerable violence, poverty, disease, and insecurity.

Botswana has ratified and partially internalized the Convention on the Elimination of All Forms of Discrimination against Women. Consistent with the norms embodied in the Convention, Botswana has outlawed discrimination in the workplace, in marriage – at least those known as "out of common property"

Table 9.3 Indicators of Botswana's compliance with anti-slavery and women's security norms

Ratified ILO Conventions 29, 105, 182	Yes to all three
CEDAW Status	2 (ratified)
Share of women in parliament	11%
Average age of first marriage for a woman	26.5
WomanStat physical security of women 2007	4 (1 to 4; 1 is most secure)

marriages – and outlawed rape, domestic violence, polygamy, and so forth (Dept. of State 2010a). The courts in Botswana have accepted the principle that CEDAW, while not entirely codified, should influence rulings (UN CEDAW 2010a).

Botswana's laws are not adequate, however, according to the CEDAW Committee. It has pointed to the lack of statutes prohibiting marital rape and sexual harassment and the fact that exceptions are made to protect traditional marriages (UN CEDAW 2010a).

In traditional marriage, women's control of property is severely restricted and they must obtain their husband's approval before applying for credit, selling property, and entering into contract – much like a child.

> Customary law allows husbands to treat their wives in the same manner as minor children. Under customary law husbands may use corporal punishment to discipline their wives, which was common in rural areas.
>
> (Dept. of State 2010a)

According to CEDAW:

> The Committee is concerned about the persistence of patriarchal attitudes and deep-rooted stereotypes concerning women's roles and responsibilities that discriminate against women and perpetuate their subordination within the family and society. It notes that such discriminatory attitudes and stereotypes constitute serious obstacles to women's enjoyment of their human rights and the fulfillment of the rights enshrined in the Convention…
>
> The Committee is concerned about the prevalence of violence against women and girls, including domestic violence, which appears to be tolerated by society.
>
> (UN CEDAW 2010a)

The net effect is that roughly three out of five women in Botswana experience physical violence – most in the home (UNIS 2005). The causes may be more related to alcohol than just patriarchal attitudes (Phorano *et al.* 2005). Victims tend not to press charges against relatives and at any rate police officers generally lack the skills to investigate rape (Dept. of State 2010a).

Political liberalism explains much of what is taking place in Botswana with respect to slavery and the status of women. The notion that work should not be coerced seems to have accepted by the vast majority of Batswana. The laws are not controversial, nor are the efforts to enforce them. Likewise, the notion of gender equality is accepted by an overwhelming majority. At the same time, minority views on the subject are not dismissed out of hand and are in fact enshrined in a clause of the Constitution. Of course, the respect for the minority view on the status of women comes at the expense of women – especially those in rural areas.

Botswana's rather limited engagement with the world economy does not seem to explain the presence or lack of slave-like practices. It appears that slavery manifests itself mostly in the production of goods and services that are not traded internationally. Women generally participate in the competitive formal economy and often rise to prominence. At the same time, discrimination against women in agriculture increases profits for certain land-holders.

The managerial school's insights again seem to offer considerable traction in our cases. With respect to slavery, we can probably trust the government's intentions and blame shortcomings on lack of capacity. This does not apply to the issue of the right to strike, however. Strikes, the government may believe, are a luxury of wealthy economies. With respect to the status of women, it appears as though political will is somewhat more to blame. It is surprising that traditional marriages are still tolerated, given the country's commitment to women's equality. It is also curious that Botswana waited until 2008 to adopt a law against domestic violence and that marital rape is still considered legal.

Botswana's decision to adopt a domestic violence law seems to coincide with increased scrutiny and pressure from abroad. This, however, does not explain its willingness to endure criticism over its dual marriage laws. Likewise, although Botswana is willing to accept certain norms, it will not always internalize them – as we see with respect to CEDAW. Botswana, on the other hand, has embraced norms related to slavery. Ultimately, then, both the reputational and legitimacy theories offer just partial and incomplete explanations.

Culture is clearly a key factor in these areas. Treatment of workers and of women requires private individuals to decide how they will treat each other. The state's power to monitor conduct is limited at best. In the case of Botswana, it appears as though this personal internalization process is mixed. Slavery appears to be limited in part because of local norms and traditions against it. On the other hand, violence against women is widespread. It appears that many men allow themselves to abuse spouses and daughters. While the state has made an effort to reverse this mentality, it has not acted quickly or forcefully enough to change the culture. And with respect to dual marriages, it seems clear that the government has decided to sacrifice some of the key rights of rural women as a concession to rural tradition.

Finally, rationality seems to explain some of what we see with respect to the failure to protect women in the home and in rural areas. The government made a calculation that preserving the support of traditional tribal societies is necessary to preserve national unity. On the other hand, urban women have been allowed to play a role in the nation's economy and society and enjoy legal equality. Likewise, the state may have calculated that confronting violent men, given their vast numbers, is too politically risky.

Concluding remarks on Botswana and theories of international law compliance

Botswana offers some rather intriguing puzzles for analysts of international law compliance. While it is clear that democracy is alive and well, this does not necessarily mean that everyone's rights are protected. While people are free to express themselves by joining NGOs and trade unions, voting for opposition parties, and opening a newspaper, this does not mean they'll be able to strike, defeat incumbents, or compete with the government-run media.

Likewise, it is clear that Botswana cares deeply about its international reputation and has enough resources to ensure compliance with important norms. But this does not mean it respects international norms equally or that it is always willing to devote the resources that are necessary to ensure compliance.

Some compliance is over-determined, as in the case of anti-terror policy where internal domestic forces run parallel to and reinforce international norms. On the other hand, in some areas none of the theories work especially well, as in the case of airline safety. We are left to wonder whether the behavior is simply eccentric.

Looking at Table 9.4's rows, we find that only two theories – political liberalism and cultural factors – explain more than half of the cases well. On the other hand, economic liberalism and rationalism explain little. It seems overall that something other than calculations of interest tends to drive Batswana policy in most areas, and that much depends on the culture, beliefs, and decision-making procedures. It appears that Botswana is a country driven more by principle than calculation, with the result that sometimes this leads to outcomes that may not appear particularly rational – or even prudent.

Papua New Guinea

Overview

The six million people who occupy Papua New Guinea's 600 islands speak nearly 800 languages (CIA 2010). Most are spoken by only a few hundred people in isolated villages and islands (UNESCO 2008, 5). There are so many different ethnic groups, tribes, clans, and sub-cultures that it is impossible for any sort of unified opposition to the central government to emerge and threaten overall state viability (Reilly 2008). Such diversity, on the other hand, makes the country almost ungovernable (May 2008, 5).

Papua New Guinea has nonetheless managed something few developing nations can claim: forty-five years of continuous democratic government. It has done this despite economic growth that has been anything but steady, daunting topography, weak government service provision and police protection and elevated levels of official corruption, and alarming levels of violence and crime. To say that Papua New Guinea is dysfunctional would be an understatement – and yet it soldiers on as a relatively stable democracy with remarkable economic prospects. It has even managed to generate budget and balance of payments surpluses, despite thousands of "ghost employees" in state bureaucracies that drain millions (World Bank *et al.* 2007, 5).

Papua New Guinea enjoys a few advantages. To begin, it holds some of the world's most productive gold and copper mines as well as deposits of natural gas that could yield one billion dollars a year in export revenue beginning in 2014

Table 9.4 Competing theories of international law compliance and the case of Botswana

"To what degree does the theory explain outcomes?"

		Sovereignty defense		*Market control*		*Human rights*	
		Anti-terror	*Anti-trafficking*	*Air transport*	*Ozone depletion*	*Slavery*	*Protection of women*
Liberalism	Political	much	much	some	little	much	much
	Economic	little	little	some	little	little	some
	Managerial	much	much	some	some	much	some
	Reputational	much	much	some	much	some	some
	Cultural	much	much	little	little	much	much
	Legitimacy	much	much	some	much	some	some
	Rationalism	some	some	some	much	little	much

(*New York Times* 2010). It also has the support of Australia, both economically and politically. It enjoys a relatively peaceful relationship with its other neighbors. The factors have freed up the state to undertake a number of projects although most plans have failed to one degree or another. Failures stem mostly from the fragmented administrative and political institutions where devolution of power has given control to unscrupulous local rulers (World Bank *et al.* 2007, 21–22).

Papua New Guinea lacks ties to the outside world – except for Australia, its one-time administrator. It has signed only 136 multilateral treaties and hosts delegations from only Australia, China, and the European Union.

Liberalism

How democratic is Papua New Guinea? The story is mixed. Both Polity and Freedom House rank the government in the middle range; the World Bank places the ability of citizens to influence the government as above the norm.

Papua New Guinea has held regular elections at least every five years since its independence in 1975. Participation in elections is very high, and debate about politics is lively in print in the street. Each seat in the national assembly attracts around fifteen candidates (UN CEDAW 2009, 12) and half the incumbents are unseated at each election on average (Connell 1997, 275). The country has independent newspapers and electronic media, unlimited access to the Internet, and a steady influx of around 60,000 foreign tourists coming each year. Numerous NGOs bring important issues to the public eye and provide critical services.

The government has considerable checks and balances. The Ombudsman is especially active, challenging corruption and political abuses (Dept. of State 2010e). Likewise the judiciary – and especially the Supreme Court – has shown considerable independence, having convicted a number of senior officials on corruption charges.

This relatively happy image is offset by a general lack of accountability of elected officials. While there are four major parties, they avoid spelling out a legislative program or national vision but instead provide patronage. A large percentage of legislators are not members of any party at all (Europa 2010c). This led to extremely fragile governing coalitions. At the slightest offense, the legislature removes the Prime Minister with a vote of no confidence and forces a new election or formation of a new coalition (Dept. of State 2010d). All of this created instability and undermined the legitimacy of the ruling government:

> For some people, at least, this has raised questions about the extent of candidates' mandates: in 1999 … former prime minister Sir Michael Somare was reported as telling a seminar organized by the Constitutional Development Commission that, with reference to the 1997 elections, "We were rejected by 80.20 per cent of the population. The national figures do not mandate the current Members of Parliament to make decisions on their behalf" (*Post-Courier* 7 September 1999).
>
> (May 2004, 5)

In an effort to remedy these problems, the Constitution was revised to limit votes of no confidence (Connell 1997, 277). In 2003 an electoral reform introduced a modified system of proportional representation (May 2008, 19). The result was more strategic voting by those who support politicians who are known to be unpopular outside of a limited ethnic group. Political parties are growing larger and governments more stable. Sir Michael Somare (the country's first leader) was the first Prime Minister to complete his five-year term (2002–2007) and win reelection for another term. That said, in 2010, he threatened to kill an opposition MP who supported a motion of no confidence against him (Sydney Morning Herald 2010).

The second key problem is the extreme level of devolution of political authority across the country. Stemming in large part from the high levels of unrest in Bougainville, the central government eliminated the locally elected provincial governments while at the same time expanding the provinces' budgetary authority in 1995 (Europa 2010c). The result is that the budgeting process in the legislature is far more combative and national MPs dominate the distribution of funds at the provincial level. As explained by the World Bank:

> Behind the revised arrangements was a political concern at the national level that national parliamentary members (particularly those who were not ministers) were unable to influence the allocation of resources by the provincial and district governments for the main devolved functions – particularly primary education, health, and rural transport infrastructure. Unfortunately, the current devolution arrangements make it almost impossible for PNG to reap any significant benefits from decentralization because they are not organized on sound principles. As presently organized, devolution has led to waste due to ineffective deployment of resources and at times been the cause of perverse outcomes, as, for example, when provincial and district spending patterns have deviated significantly from nationally agreed policies.
>
> (World Bank *et al.* 2007, 198)

The last problem is endemic violence – particularly at election time. Campaigns for national office routinely pit ethnic groups against each other and passions run high. Inter-ethnic violence is designed to intimidate rivals in the hope that they will not turn out at the polls.

> Longstanding inter-group rivalries, briefly set aside during the colonial period, have been compounded by competition for the benefits provided by the modern state and by fighting over the distribution of returns from the several big mining and petroleum projects located within the province or impinging upon it.
>
> (Haley and May 2009, 1)

At the level of economic freedom, Papua New Guinea presents a mixed picture. At this point in time, the country's trade policies are quite restrictive.

Papua New Guinea reversed a very liberal trade policy in the 1980s by imposing a protective tariff for domestically manufactured goods. Tariffs are very high – around 100 percent on some products – which keep prices elevated (Chowdhury 2004, 42). Trade with Australia and New Zealand is more liberal. Foreign investment is permitted with few restrictions, but the lack of security has inhibited foreign operations. The copper mines in Bougainville continue to lie dormant while armed guerrillas patrol the area and litigation over land ownership is pursued outside the country. The more recent investments in natural gas by ExxonMobil in the Southern Highlands province have faced considerable opposition but are moving forward (*New York Times* 2010).

Australia is far and away Papua New Guinea's principal trading partner, buying more than a quarter of its exports and selling it more than two-fifths of its imports. That has begun to change as China has become an increasingly important part of the country's trade. Once the natural gas comes on-line, we will see an even greater East Asian presence in Papua New Guinea's current account.

The government's fiscal and monetary policies have whip-sawed over the years, but for the past ten years or so they have been relatively stable and cautious. The government enjoyed a sizable fiscal surplus during the 2000s, along with low levels of inflation, relatively stable exchange rates, and moderate levels of foreign debt (Europa 2010c). Its Economic Freedom score in 2010 was 53.5 (out of a range of 8.0–89.5) (Heritage Foundation 2010).

Managerial school

Papua New Guinea is not bereft of economically valuable resources, and its economy has grown in fits and starts over the years. The government is able to generate revenue (public spending accounts for roughly one-third of GDP) from both domestic and international sources. But there are vast areas of the territory and many policy arenas in which the government's presence is scarcely felt. Although a poor country (per capita GDP hovers around $1,000), it has made itself even poorer through mismanagement, fragmentation, and corruption.

Papua New Guinea is ranked below average on most governance scores produced by the World Bank and other organizations. Each ship in the country's navy is individually responsible for nearly 600 kilometers worth of coastline. Papua New Guinea enjoys the protection of Australia which has provided peacekeepers and advisors to assist in Bouganville and elsewhere.

The degree of corruption is profound. In relation to other countries, Papua New Guinea's corruption has gone from bad to worse. This is manifested across the spectrum of officialdom, from beat cops who demand bribes from ordinary citizens to jailers who brutalize and extort from prisoners; from politicians who offer voters "inducements" to cabinet members who skim millions from foreign loans and investments (Connell 1997, 274; Dept. of State 2010e).

> [T]he declining capacity of the state to assert its authority against *raskol* gangs, local "warlords" and corrupt politicians has undermined the state's

> legitimacy and fostered a downward spiral of weak governance, lawlessness and violent conflict.
>
> (Haley and May 2009, 17)

Corruption at the provincial level appears to be even more acute than in the capital. This serves to exacerbate the problem of fiscal accountability mentioned earlier. The result is considerable variation in service provision from one province to the next. Literacy rates vary dramatically across the country, standing at over 70 percent in the cities and below 30 percent in the highlands (UNESCO 2008, 10). The World Bank estimates that one-quarter of all nursing positions (1,000 total) and more than one-third of community health worker positions (1,700 total) positions are vacant but still funded, enabling local officials to pocket the surplus (World Bank *et al.* 2007, 5).

Some variance in service provision is to be expected. Many villages are surrounded by jungles or swamps which prevent travel and communication with the outside world (Chowdhury 2004, 21). Only two-thirds of Papua New Guineans have easy access to a road.

> The situation in the Lake Kopiago sub-district provides a snapshot of what life is like for Southern Highlanders living in the remote rural parts of the province. As one moves northwest from Tari, what little infrastructure there is in the province completely dissipates. For example, the reasonably well-maintained and graded roads and iron bridges of the Tari and Koraba areas give way to a 4WD track with log bridges, and thence to barely-defined walking tracks. There is no health extension officer at the sub-district health center, the last one having left in 1996; the local nurses and health workers posted to the area have since relocated to Mount Hagen, as have the school teachers. There are no police or village court magistrates. Health and immunization patrols have ceased, and formal education is at risk of being completely phased out.
>
> (Haley and May 2009, 8)

Not only are services not being adequately provided, the trend is generally flat or downward. Poverty rates across the country are rising dramatically, with more than half of the population now living in absolute poverty (under $1 a day). Infant and maternal mortality rates remain high and HIV/AIDS is spreading rapidly (World Bank *et al.* 2007, 21, 83).

Papua New Guinea resembles a failed state in some respects:

> I am concerned that the Royal Papua New Guinea Constabulary is not always in a position to enforce the rule of law due to insufficient human and financial resources, a high level of corruption and unprofessionalism, difficulties in accessing remote rural areas and a lack of political will. These deficiencies have led to private security companies carrying out some of the main duties of the police. The fact that there are far more private security

> officers than police officers in the country is a worrying sign of police weakness and a failure of the state to provide security and freedom from fear to its people. Particularly worrying is the Royal Papua New Guinea Constabulary's lack of capacity to prevent and to investigate crimes relating to domestic violence, tribal fighting and to victims of accusations of sorcery [often used to justify abuse against women].
>
> (UNHCHR 2010)

Reputational theory

While governance at home is clearly sub-standard, recent national leaders have undertaken to set their house in order with respect to international obligations. International credit-rating agencies have given Papua New Guinea relatively high marks, especially with respect to currency stability and international indebtedness. Naturally, paying one's bills is not necessarily enough to attract foreign investment, and the government's difficulties in providing basic security in more remote regions – where the natural resources happen to be located – could continue to stifle growth. The Panguna copper mine on Bougainville has sat idle for twenty years even though the owners are eager to return.

In general, Papua New Guinea seems to show some interest in maintaining a reputation as a reliable partner on a variety of issues, but it is not particularly consistent in the commitments it makes and is even less able to follow through.

Culture

As mentioned, Papua New Guinea is very diverse. It is also very rural, as roughly four out of five live outside of cities. Geography contributes to culture in that isolation intensifies the narrowing of identity. This in turn increases self-reliance (the majority of villagers are subsistence farmers) as well as distrust of outsiders.

Eighty percent of Papua New Guinean justice is handled by village courts, consisting of 4–6 local elders who rule on a wide range of issues, including criminal law. Generally, the principle governing these courts is to find an amicable settlement to the "dispute" – including criminal acts – with the result typically being payments of compensation and apologies rather than prison sentences (UN CEDAW 2009, 30–31; Dept. of State 2010f). Village court rulings may be overturned by formal appellate courts. For example, village court rulings that mandated using a girl as a form of debt payment have been reversed (Dept. of State 2010g).

We have already discussed the rise in inter-tribal and inter-village violence (Connell 1997, 279). The introduction of small arms has increased the scale of the damage to new heights. Violence against weaker members of society has also increased dramatically in recent years, with domestic violence, gang rapes, rape by policemen, and abuse of children becoming endemic (UNICEF/PNG 1996, 140). A majority of women have reported being raped and roughly 70 percent report having been attacked by a husband or boyfriend (World Bank *et al.* 2007).

There is a sense that the society is losing its traditions of strong families and peaceful conflict resolution, although it is difficult to know how deeply entrenched they were given the lack of information about village life. While the rights of families have generally prevailed over those of individuals, they are used as a pretext for harsh justice and violence against individuals (UN CEDAW 2009, 22).

Legitimacy

Papua New Guinea takes a somewhat selective approach to international norms. Its decisions to commit to particular international instruments are difficult to predict. It chose not to endorse some treaties with which it complies while supporting other treaties – such as CEDAW – which it violates. But overall the government is endeavoring to be a peaceful, cooperative state. It is not especially active or prominent in the United Nations, although a dozen UN specialized agencies and special programs have permanent offices in Port Moresby. It is a member of the ASEAN Regional Forum as well as several Pacific island regional groupings. In general, the government has internalized a number of international conventions through the traditional legislative processes. The difficulty lies in implementing the legislation.

Papua New Guineans tend to resent foreign interference – especially from Australia. The Australian government has volunteered its personnel to administer Papua New Guinea's domestic institutions. But since these officials answered to Canberra, local authorities eventually protested, prompting Australia to recall most of them (May 2008, 14).

Rationalism

Decision-making in Port Moresby involves competition between elites at various levels. Provincial leaders and members of parliament compete regularly over everything from budgets to international norms. In particular, provinces that object to the expenditure of resources to implement a particular norm will resist it – this, even when the Prime Minister is under pressure from international actors. Only when national and local interests coincide with international norms will we expect to see implementation of international norms.

Of particular concern will be the differential powers of the Center province and the capital area against the poorer provinces such as Bougainville and Southern Highlands. Issues that are of principal concern to the national elites, such as national security, do not always prevail if they come at the expense of provincial interests and needs.

Overall, we should expect to see a certain degree of collusion between the wealthier provinces and the national authorities. Highland provinces and poorer islands that might benefit from the adoption of a particular norm – such as minority rights – will likely be disappointed.

Performance across issue-areas

Rules governing territorial defense: anti-terrorism, anti-piracy, and anti-trafficking

The war on terror is a distant problem for Papua New Guinea. There is no evidence of terrorism – especially Al Qaeda-directed terrorism – anywhere in the country. As put by long-time Papua New Guinea scholar Ronald May:

> The probability of Papua New Guinea being used as a base for terrorists is perhaps exaggerated: not only does Papua New Guinea lack an obvious constituency for terrorism, but in a closely knit community like Papua New Guinea's the activities of foreigners (and unusual activities of locals) attract attention and subversive activities are unlikely to go undetected.
>
> (May 2008, 13)

With so many other issues on its agenda and the resource constraints we've discussed, it is perhaps understandable that Papua New Guinea has simply not addressed terrorism. This lack of engagement is illustrated by the figures we see in Table 9.5. As of 2005, the government had not fulfilled even the most basic level of compliance with the anti-terror measures adopted by the United Nations. Nonetheless, the country is under little pressure to remedy the situation (Dept. of State 2009c).

Piracy is also not a major concern, although attacks have occurred from time to time. Three attacks occurred during the 2000s, and in two cases the government responded as minimally required. This represents a fairly active anti-piracy regime. The most recent incident, in November 2007, and taking place near Milne Island to the north, is described as follows:

> The captain of a workboat, transporting workers and cargo, jumped overboard when pirates boarded his vessel. The pirates robbed the crew and injured them with sharp objects. Later the crew received medical treatment at a shore hospital. A search party was sent to locate the captain but he could not be found.
>
> (IMB 2007)

Table 9.5 Indicators of compliance with rules governing territorial defense

UN CTC total score	0 (7 possible)
UN CTC score, minus treaty ratifications	0 (5 possible)
Total pirate attacks 2000–2009	3
Pirate attack response rate	67%
SUA endorsement	No
SUA Protocol endorsement	No
US State Dept. TIP score (2006)	3 (1–3, with 1 signifying compliance)
2000 Trafficking Protocol signature	No
2000 Trafficking Protocol ratification	No

While profoundly tragic, it is important to note the relatively small scale of the attack. The port authorities in Papua New Guinea pride themselves on maintaining fairly tight security and they can point to a long history without incidents involving ships in the country's vicinity or at port (PNG Ports 2010). The government has received assistance from the Australian government which has provided several tens of thousands of dollars specifically to improve port security in the country's four largest ports, as well as from private security firms (Australian AID 2004). It also adopted a stricter set of regulations in the form of the Merchant Shipping (Maritime Security) Regulation of 2005 which now requires uniform digital identification cards for all visitors, workers, and seamen around the country's ports, among other things (PNG Ports 2010).

While benign neglect has not coincided with an increase in terrorism, the same cannot be said for the issue of trafficking. The US State Department has classified Papua New Guinea as a tier three country – something that in recent years has been reserved for America's enemies. Human trafficking to, from, and through the country is a common occurrence against which the government has made minimal efforts. In fact, there is evidence that many government officials collude with traffickers. Local tribal leaders also engage in selling young women into marriages and prostitution in exchange for political favors, weapons, and other benefits (Dept. of State 2010f).

Despite being prohibited by law, prostitution is widespread in Papua New Guinea, and many women elect to work in towns, mines, logging camps and so forth:

> In rural areas, commercial sex is available at markets, clubs, discos, bingo games, and even at government stations where male wage workers gather. One study that mapped risk zones along the Highlands Highway in 1995 found that women also exchanged sex for betel nuts at markets, for beer at small clubs, and for rides on trucks and buses.
>
> (World Bank *et al.* 2007, 89)

Many others are forced into prostitution by traffickers and pimps. Rural families sell their daughters into forced marriages to settle family debts, and those sold often become domestic servants for the husband's family. In urban areas, girls are sometimes sold to traffickers by relatives (Dept. of State 2010f). There is evidence of women arriving in Papua New Guinea from other countries in Southeast Asia and China, but data are scarce. The government does not monitor trafficking, electing instead to delegate the work to local NGOs, many of which lack capacity. Trafficking victims face imprisonment and/or deportation (Dept. of State 2010f). There are no laws specifically addressing adult trafficking, although there are statutes on the books against child trafficking and forced labor and prostitution, some of which carry long prison terms (Dept. of State 2010g). Even the laws on the books are generally not enforced, however. There have been no prosecutions of alleged traffickers or of government officials who have allegedly collaborated with traffickers (Dept. of State 2010f).

The most serious aspect of the problem is collusion by government officials.

> Government officials facilitate trafficking by accepting bribes to allow illegal migrants to enter the country or to ignore victims forced into prostitution or labor, by receiving female trafficking victims in return for political favors, and by providing female victims in return for votes.
>
> (Dept. of State 2010f)

Beginning in 2004, the government of Papua New Guinea began to take limited steps to address the problem. Australia offered to loan the country hundreds of officials and police to take over the tasks of administration in key ministries, including border control and law enforcement. Because these officials would enjoy diplomatic immunity, the PNG Supreme Court overturned the program and expelled the police contingent (ADB 2010). The International Organization for Migration was invited to establish a permanent office in Port Moresby with Australian funding. The program provided training for dozens of immigration and border control officers on the basics of immigrant identification and processing (IOM 2010b).

> While it does not attempt to cover all situations that immigration officers might face or encounter, the training package will give them insight into how they can best perform their functions under current legislative and policy frameworks," says IOM Port Moresby Chief of Mission Giuseppe Crocetti.
>
> (IOM 2010b)

The government has also established a task force on trafficking and child labor and initiated public education campaigns on the issue (IOM 2010a). But the government has not signed or ratified the 2000 Trafficking Protocol nor has it developed statutes on trafficking that meet international standards.

We will now turn to an assessment of our different theories of compliance with respect to this case. Considering political liberalism first, we can see that while Papua New Guinea has internalized principles relating to elections and elite turnover, this does not extend to the protection against abuse and exploitation. Policies to combat trafficking are not only inadequate, they are corrupt. The relatively limited actions with respect to terrorism and piracy seem prudent and popular. Likewise, the approach to port security seems generally consistent with what voters would support.

Economic liberalism helps to explain Papua New Guinea's policies on piracy and maritime security since there is a clear incentive to maintain the free flow of goods under a blanket of relative safety. One could argue that, if women are a commodity and sex trade a business, that economic liberalism also explains the prevalence of trafficking. But economic liberal theory does not privilege clandestine transactions over the rule of law. The theory has little to say about counter-terrorism in a country where there is no terror threat.

Papua New Guinea, as discussed earlier, lacks capacity – not only because of poverty but also because of mismanagement and corruption. In our three situations, the government seems to have been capable of prioritizing. On the other hand, anti-trafficking seems to have been encouraged by corrupt acts on the part of those who were expected to enforce the laws. Since much of the problem takes place in and around the capital where government capacity is at its strongest, much could be done to clean up Port Moresby at the very least. Lack of capacity, then, does not seem to explain what we are seeing.

Papua New Guinea, as predicted, seems largely uninterested in establishing a strong reputation for international law compliance across these issue-areas. It knows that it occupies a very peripheral place in the war on terror. On the other hand, its ability to address piracy stems from domestic rather than international concerns.

With respect to anti-trafficking measures, while the government has made a very conspicuous gesture to world opinion by inviting IOM experts to rebuild its immigration infrastructure, it has done nothing to disrupt the collaboration between traffickers and government officials. It is difficult to interpret these actions as anything but cynical. It was even willing to be placed on the State Department's tier three and suffer the consequence of automatic economic sanctions.

To what extent does Papua New Guinean culture explain the outcomes? As mentioned by May, the cultural make-up of the country may make it impervious to infiltration by foreign jihadist elements. Papua New Guineans are not famous for their maritime tradition, and the lack of pirates may reflect that (Connell 1997, 227). Trafficking, on the other hand, is clearly supported by village and tribal traditions, as well as customs and mores that have developed in recent years as family life has been disrupted and corruption and violence have spread. There are no doubt many who believe that trafficking is not problematic.

The legitimacy theory matches the outcomes on terror and trafficking. Where the government has not embraced the international norm, its domestic policies are weak. In the area of piracy there seems to be a disconnect, in that compliance is fairly strong even though commitment is rather weak.

Finally, to what extent are Papua New Guinea's policies a product of rational calculation of short-term material interests? The answer is: to a considerable extent. The lack of concern about terrorism seems proportional to the threat. On the other hand, the national government has addressed piracy, consistent with the priorities of coastal provinces that have the most to lose should shipping become too dangerous. Finally, the venality of public officials coincides with the interests of criminal organizations and affluent exploiters to make human trafficking a serious problem in the country. Families and tribal leaders have contributed to the problem, as has the police. Only a few NGOs seem to be reaching out to victims of trafficking, and they are underfunded and undertrained.

Rules designed to regulate the market: shipping and airline regulation and CFC control

Table 9.6 paints a picture of a government that struggles to regulate business. Papua New Guinea has ratified only a few of the international conventions on maritime safety. It has not ratified the SUA Convention and it has also declined to ratify the 1974 Safety of Life at Sea (SOLAS) Convention, as well as number of pollution control agreements and a key seafarer safety convention (Maritime Int'l Sec. 2009). The treaties it has ratified are of lesser significance.

The Papua New Guinea merchant fleet is middling, with twenty-one ships of significance and another hundred small vessels. While not considered a flag of convenience, six ships from the United Arab Emirates are flagged as Papua New Guinean (CIA 2010; Europa 2010d). Shipping is an important part of the national economy, although the priority is on protecting foreign shipping rather than the national fleet. The country has joined the Tokyo Memorandum of Understanding and participates actively having hosted the 2009 annual meetings and carried out numerous inspections of visiting ships (Tokyo MOU 2010).

This is not to say that Papua New Guinea exercises effective control over its own fleet. Many Papua New Guinean ships have been inspected, and a growing number have been detained for serious safety code violations (Tokyo MOU 2008, 2010). The country has spent some time on the Tokyo MOU "grey list," but in 2009 it was placed on the organization's "black list." The situation was not helped by the fact that the head of the National Maritime Safety Authority also owned a shipping company (Tubuans and Dukduks 2008). Prime Minister Somare and other provincial leaders also have a personal stake in a private firm that was responsible for inspecting merchant ships (Post-Courier 2008). The situation clearly involves a conflict of interest.

On the other hand, there are signs that the government is taking seriously these outcomes since it was scheduled to adopt new maritime safety regulations in 2008 and allowed the establishment of the new private Pacific Maritime Training College in 2009 (NMSA 2010). The government's airline safety legislation is considered strong – rating a nine on a ten-point scale developed by the US Federal Aviation Administration (ICAO 2010c).

Papua New Guinea's record of airline safety also leaves much to be desired. The country owns Air Niugini and its nineteen aircraft that fly across the country and to

Table 9.6 Indicators of compliance with market regulating laws

Ship detention rate, Tokyo MOU 2005–2009	12.3%
1999–2001 ICAO non-compliance score	44.96 (on a scale of 0–100; 0=no defects)
ICAO follow-up 2004	33.39
ali_standard air liberalization score	2 (0–183; high=liberal)
Cumulative Montreal Protocol compliance score	14 (0–24; low=compliance)
Reported data to Ozone Commission 2002–2007	Yes
Found non-compliant 2002–2007	Once
Broke existing program 2002–2007	Four times

regional destinations. The airline is joined by three other private services that carry cargo and passengers on a more limited schedule (Endres 2009). Air travel, while an important component of the tourism and cargo transport economy, is important as a lifeline to the 20 percent of Papua New Guineans who cannot be reached by road or river (Haley and May 2009, 7). It also enables logging companies to bring in workers and rescue teams to deploy medical and other specialists.

Air travel in Papua New Guinea faces numerous obstacles of which the inaccessible terrain is but one. Although the country boasts nearly 600 airports, nearly all are unpaved and only two are long enough to accommodate larger jet aircraft. There is discontent among the air traffic controllers who went on strike in 2008 over wages and working conditions (Freedom House 2010b). The level of training for technical personnel and licensing procedures are considerably below international averages and well below expectations (ICAO 2010c). The country has witnessed five airline accidents during the 2000s of which three involved casualties (Aviation Safety Network 2010). Table 9.6 shows that even after an audit from the ICAO, Papua New Guinea's airline safety regime was still considered one-third deficient. In January 2010, Australia banned flights to four major Papua New Guinean airports.

The situation was serious enough to attract the attention of the Western press. In 2008, ABC News reported that

> Papua New Guinea aviation insiders claim safety standards have plummeted in the last two decades. A senior PNG air crash investigator, says standards have "fallen over the edge" ... [Transport Minister Don Polye said] "There's been insufficient funding to upkeep the maintenance of airports and airstrips in Papua New Guinea not only in aviation but in other sectors as well."
>
> (Marshall 2008)

The government is taking steps to address the international criticism. This includes improving its accident investigation administration and investigating aircraft more systematically. In 2007, this effort resulted in findings that led to the grounding of Airlink over concerns about safety (Aviation Safety Network 2008; Marshall 2008).

Finally, to what extent is Papua New Guinea complying with regulations on ozone-depleting substances? Consumption of chlorofluorocarbons has always been relatively low. It was therefore classified as a low-volume consuming developing country from the outset and given extended deadlines for compliance with the Montreal Protocol (Multilateral Fund 2003).

The government of Papua New Guinea pled poverty and asked for international assistance to meet its target of zero CFC usage by 2010 (UNEP 2006, 538). Papua New Guinea struggled in the first half of the 1990s, rarely submitting required reports and often fell out of compliance (UNEP 2006, 362–363). However, beginning in 2002, CFC consumption declined dramatically, dropping well below the baseline and falling to zero by 2008. Papua's transition is likely attributable to halting imports of older refrigerators and aerosols.

Considering theoretical propositions, let us begin by asking whether Papua New Guinea's rough and tumble democratic institutions help explain its failure to comply fully with maritime and airline safety while complying better with ozone depletion norms. While maritime safety and ozone depletion issues do not affect large numbers in the country, almost everyone has an interest in airline safety, and so one would expect that a government that is responsive to public concerns would make this a priority. Instead government seems fairly insensitive to its own public. Concerns expressed internally do not seem to have made much of a difference, although once those concerns were articulated to foreigners they gained considerable traction. While we also do not have specific evidence of corruption in any of these cases, it seems that not enough is done until international pressures reach a certain level.

Likewise, it is not clear that liberal economic norms are driving the situation since Papua New Guinea has increased the safety of Port Moresby for foreign shipping while neglecting its ocean-going fleet. Likewise, while Papua New Guinea's aircraft are permitted to land at airports across the region, foreign carriers hesitate to land in Papua New Guinea. Were the economic liberal theory correct, we should not see these inconsistencies. And it does little to explain compliance with ozone norms.

The leaders of Papua New Guinea are quick to excuse themselves on capacity grounds. Certainly, the expense of building safe airports throughout the country and staffing them with trained technicians is considerable and probably beyond the reach of even the most conscientious government. But the fact that some resources are mobilized to address certain problems while others are left untouched indicates that the real question most likely has to do with political and regulatory discretion.

It is clear that the closer the international scrutiny, the more likely Papua New Guinean authorities will comply. This may stem in part from a desire to establish a reputation for compliance. Anticipating the rationalist arguments, it does not appear that Papua New Guinea pays much of a price for its deficiencies, but nonetheless seeks to limit their detection.

It is difficult to see how the culture of the country with its heterogeneity would explain these outcomes. Certainly there is probably less interest on the part of national elites to ensure that air links are made safe and cheap for every city in the Highlands, but this does not explain the lack of concern for the safety of the merchant fleet which no doubt affects affluent port cities more than the rest of the country.

The fact that Papua New Guinea has endorsed only a smattering of international conventions related to these issues, and has inconsistently codified them and implemented even more haphazardly is consistent with the legitimacy school. Of course, all of this begs the question why the country has chosen to be so selective.

The rationalists would argue that the behavior flows from the needs of the capital taking precedence over the needs of the periphery, which does seem to explain airline safety and strong ozone policies. It is clearly to the advantage of those in power to maintain the appearance of compliance. This is especially clear in the ozone area. And there is also evidence that individuals responsible for these issues are mostly concerned about job security. Likewise there is concern that the Prime Minister and maritime safety head may be profiting from lax ship inspections. It makes sense, then, that they would expend just enough resources to get by from year to year to keep the international wolves at bay while retaining their seats.

Laws on human rights promotion: anti-slavery law and anti-discrimination against women

Papua New Guinea's performance with respect to slavery and the treatment of women is related but significantly different. The government has made serious international commitments on both issues. Codification and enforcement of these provisions is incomplete, however, as indicated in the measures provided in Table 9.7.

Slavery and indentured servitude are not an important part of Papua New Guinean contemporary tradition, although some working arrangements deprive workers of the types of freedoms enshrined in international instruments (Dept. of State 2010g). Trade unions are active and generally free to bargain collectively and strike. The state has, however, intervened to alter or nullify contracts or arbitration awards that ran counter to government policy and has sometimes required arbitration prior to approving a strike (Dept. of State 2010g).

Government inspections of workplaces are infrequent and sometimes ineffective. In particular, health and safety inspections are performed only when requested by workers or trade union officials due to the small number of inspectors (Dept. of State 2010g).

Child labor is thought to be widespread, especially in subsistence farming. Children as young as 11 are permitted to work for a family business, and it is apparent from relatively low school enrollment levels that many children are thus employed (World Bank *et al.* 2007, 194). The state does little to monitor labor patterns in villages or in domestic situations.

With respect to the employment of children as domestic servants, we have already discussed the practice of selling or renting girls to families or into marriage where in either case they are often put to work in the home without the right to leave (UN CEDAW 2010b, para. 25). Such practices violate statutory law and when imposed as a penalty by a village court have been overturned at the district level (Dept. of State 2010g).

Table 9.7 Indicators of Papua New Guinea's compliance with anti-slavery and women's security norms

WomanStat physical security of women 2007	3 (1–4; 1 is most secure)
Share of women in parliament	0.5%
Commitment to CEDAW	Ratified
Ratification of ILO Conventions #29, 105, 182 on slavery	All three

In general, the statutory protections for women are reasonable, but insufficient (UN 2002b). There is no law against sexual harassment, which is widespread (Dept. of State 2010g). There is no specific law against violence against women or domestic abuse, although most acts of abuse are covered by laws against assault, rape, or other crimes (UN CEDAW 2009, 18–19, 27–28). Men cannot use the excuse that since the victim was a relative the penalty should be lighter. Sex acts by an adult male against a girl under sixteen are criminal and can never be considered consensual. Both incest and marital rape are thereby illegal (Dept. of State 2010g).

Furthermore, recent amendments to the Evidence Act protect the rights of victims of rape by providing for closed hearings, the inadmissibility of information on the victim's reputation or lifestyle and the end to the practice of cross-examination by the accused (UN CEDAW 2009, 29). This is a fairly progressive regime and consistent with the government's commitments under CEDAW (UN CEDAW 2009, 27).

What then explains the score of 3 from WomanStat and the following assessment?

> Papua New Guinea has a 2007/8 Gender-Related Development Index (GDI) of 124, giving it an equivalent ranking to its HDI and placing it once again at the lowest level for all Pacific Island Countries (PICs) and just above Haiti and Sudan.
>
> (UN CEDAW 2009, 17)

The simple answer is that the government has done relatively little to give effect to its commitments. It does not have specific action plans related to the various international instruments it has endorsed, has generally not codified them, and does not consistently submit reports to monitoring agencies (Talao 2009, 8). It lacks the staff and resources to consistently monitor implementation, and has turned over enforcement of most laws related to the safety and security of women to village courts that generally do not treat the cases as crimes but rather as "disputes" to be resolved with payments or apologies (UN CEDAW 2009, 30–31). The subservient status of women is welcomed and perpetuated by men in positions of power at all levels. As put by the CEDAW Committee in 2010:

> [T]he Committee expresses its serious concern about the persistence of harmful norms, practices and traditions, as well as patriarchal attitudes and deep-rooted stereotypes, regarding the roles, responsibilities and identities of women and men in all spheres of life. These include polygamy, bride price (dava), "good" woman stereotypes, the traditional view of "big man" leadership and the custom of including women as part of compensation payment.
>
> (UN CEDAW 2010b, para. 25)

Most serious is the degree of impunity enjoyed by members of the police and jailers. The CEDAW Committee again expressed its judgment:

> In addition, the Committee expresses its deep concern about reports of sexual abuse of women upon arrest and in police custody, perpetrated by both police officers and male detainees, and at times in the form of collective rape, and that such abuses are rarely documented and investigated and perpetrators not prosecuted and punished.
>
> (UN CEDAW 2010b, para. 29)

Police have been accused of raping girls as young as six without consequence (Human Rights Watch 2009). They have also been accused of beating and killing prostitutes in custody (Amnesty International 2010).

Mention has already been made of the widespread practice of gang rapes. To this has been added a new concern about sorcery and the actions taken to punish it. Women who in one way or another have offended males in a village are sometimes accused of sorcery as a way of justifying what in essence is a lynching. For example, there is a report of a woman who was attacked in her home. While fighting off the assailant, she bit off a piece of his tongue. The next day she was accused of sorcery, stripped in public, poked with hot iron rods, and set on fire (Human Rights Watch 2009). No consequences befell the lynch mob. In 2008, more than fifty such killings were reported (Amnesty International 2010).

In the midst of this violence and discrimination, women are ill-equipped to take advantage of the limited legal resources at their disposal. They are strongly discouraged by family members to accuse relatives of crimes. They lack the financial resources to travel to cities to go to court. They naturally don't trust the police to defend them (Dept. of State 2010f).

There are obvious differences in how workers in general and women in particular are treated in Papua New Guinea, which implies that our theories of international law compliance will not be equally effective in explaining outcomes. To begin, although the political liberalism we find in the country means that the progressive norms embodied in international legal instruments are generally accepted and incorporated in domestic law, they are not always implemented or internalized. There appears to be a clash between civil law and cultural traditions, and the latter often prevails. Economic liberalism does not explain the treatment of women, although it seems consistent with practices related to slavery. Economic liberals cannot explain wholesale discrimination, abusive practices, exclusion from the market, or other dysfunctional behaviors. On the other hand, the protection of some basic worker rights and the exclusion of children from the industrial work force seem consistent with the "fair play" notions of economic liberalism.

The managerial school helps to explain why government policy tends to be reactive rather than proactive with respect to worker rights. We've already discussed the considerable obstacles of travel and communication faced by government inspectors and regulators. The government's intentions with respect to ending slavery and promoting worker rights – at least for men – seem sincere. The problem lies in a lack of resources.

The same cannot be said for protecting women, where the government has failed to adopt, implement, and enforce most norms on the issue. What is most serious is that enforcement agents themselves commit acts of violence against women. Women are extremely vulnerable as a result of these systematic choices by government officials – none of which is the result of lack of resources.

While Papua New Guinea authorities seem happy to be seen internationally as opposed to exploitation of labor, the same is not the case where the rights of women are concerned. CEDAW, the US State Department, Amnesty International, and Human Rights Watch are in agreement that Papua New Guineans mistreat their women.

Culture seems to explain labor policy to a degree, and it goes far in explaining the treatment of women. In fact, the degree to which culture influences policies toward women is so high that we might be tempted to stop there. But mistreatment of women has varied over time – mostly deteriorating – while culture has remained relatively constant.

Legitimacy theory provides some insight where workers' rights and slavery are concerned, but none at all with respect to the treatment of women. Rational choice models also seem to provide limited insight. Anti-slavery norms seem to have been accepted and internalized – at least with respect to men and boys. Violence against women, on the other hand, seems designed almost entirely to protect and promote the high status of men in society. There appears to be a conspiracy of men against women that serves to perpetuate their oppression. While short-sighted, such behavior is at least understandable from a rational choice perspective.

Concluding remarks on Papua New Guinea and theories of international law compliance

We will now assess the utility of our theories of international law compliance with respect to Papua New Guinea. As we see in Table 9.8, two theories explain a great deal of the processes and outcomes we've observed. Specifically, the rationalist theory explains almost everything rather neatly, taking into account the interests of elites and other dominant actors against those who are weaker and more peripheral. It fails only to explain patterns of slavery – specifically male slavery – which seem to stem from the internalization of anti-slavery norms first and foremost. However, if we were to include patterns of female exploitation in the form of obligatory domestic service, the theory does a fair job.

Legitimacy theory also explains a great deal. In other words, where there was not a strong commitment to the international norm, there was little effort expended in its implementation. In other words, foreign and domestic pressures did not generally overcome ideational resistance.

The theories that fared the poorest were the reputational and cultural theory. Cultural theory seems to explain the fundamental direction of policy in more cases while the reputational theory clarifies what could be considered superficial actions. Reputational theory seems more adept at explaining a country's public face, while in this case cultural theory gets at the more

Table 9.8 Competing theories of international law compliance and the case of Papua New Guinea

"To what degree does the theory explain outcomes?"

		Sovereignty defense			*Market control*			*Human rights*	
		Anti-terror	*Anti-piracy*	*Anti-trafficking*	*Air transport*	*Ship safety*	*Ozone depletion*	*Slavery*	*Protection of women*
Liberalism	Political	much	much	little	little	some	some	much	little
	Economic	much	much	some	little	little	little	much	little
	Managerial	much	much	little	some	little	little	much	little
	Reputational	little	little	some	some	some	much	much	some
	Cultural	some	much	much	little	little	little	some	much
	Legitimacy	much	little	much	much	much	much	some	little
	Rationalism	much	much	much	much	much	much	little	much

essential motives driving conduct. It is not surprising that they are sometimes in conflict – note that cultural theory tends to best explain those cases reputational theory cannot. Reputational theory and cultural theory combine to expose hypocrisy.

The other three theories seem to work in tandem. In the cases of piracy and terror, where the threat is small, so is the energy devoted to addressing it. We might find similar patterns in areas such as space law, internet regulation, or other esoteric or high-tech problems that simply don't affect Papua New Guinea. The three theories break down on other issues, however, where the competence of the bureaucracy conspires with public corruption and ineptitude. Of course, they all run aground where liberal principles are simply non-existent as in the cases of trafficking and the overall security of women.

General conclusions

These two countries – Botswana and Papua New Guinea – offer an intriguing comparison. On the one hand, they are both democratic and somewhat isolated. They are both dependent on mineral exports and have large rural populations. The urban areas are somewhat more cosmopolitan and open to Western values and attitudes while in both cases large segments of the populations operate under traditional tribal and village rules and mores. In both cases the civil constitutional law has yielded considerable space to traditional law – typically at the expense of women's rights. Both are under-resourced.

The similarities end there, however. Botswana is clearly the more stable and Westernized of the two. The goals, procedures, and policy outcomes of each government are radically different in most respects as Botswana shows a capacity to formulate and implement high priority programs while Papua New Guinea struggles to keep governments intact and prevent the police from acting like criminals. In many respects, the central government in Port Moresby appears to have given up the effort to govern beyond the capital, while Botswana has demonstrated it can deploy effective border stations in the middle of deserts. Likewise, the traditional misogynistic culture of Papua New Guinea is given almost free rein while Botswana's civil law prevails in most facets of its citizens' lives.

After considering the findings in this chapter, we provide the following observations.

Democracy vs. traditionalism. These cases make it clear that far more thought needs to be given to our definitions of democracy and culture. Botswana's 2010 Freedom House score was seven while Papua New Guinea's was five, but the two countries are worlds apart when it comes to the operation of government and state-society relations. While it may be possible to describe some of this by adding or multiplying measures of governance along with measures of state permeability, it seems that more is needed to capture the phenomenon. A sort of "ground level democracy" measure is called for to capture what it is to live in these places. Further, there are few measures that adequately describe the cultural characteristics of a society. Knowing that 80 percent of court cases in Papua

New Guinea are handled by village tribunals, for example, and that these tribunals serve to perpetuate patriarchal dominance, tells a powerful story.

Ultimately, from what we have seen in our cases, civil law and traditionalism are caught in a dialectical dance. In most respects, they provide different perspectives on social problems, both with respect to defining appropriate relationships and how best to repair breaches. International norms generally enter the equation on the side of civil law, but this is not always enough to tip the balance in its favor. Much depends on the political strength and ideological commitment of the leadership, which in turn reflects the balance of power between traditionalists and modernizers in society as a whole – as well as the resources the central government can bring to bear.

Capacity revisited. While in other chapters we've explored the notion that capacity is malleable, these cases show the limits of that notion. Certainly Papua New Guinea could reallocate its resources away from enriching corrupt elites and more toward hiring and training enforcement officers, but the case of Botswana shows that even where governance is strong, capacity can impede compliance with international norms. Further, it is clear that governing capacity is not necessarily fungible across issue-areas. An air traffic controller cannot necessarily provide post-trauma counseling any more than a workplace inspector can inspect a ship. Likewise, the infrastructure required to prevent piracy is not useful in protecting children from exploitation in the fields. Some norms require their own tools.

The implication is that when government capacity is limited, some things are likely to be left undone. When the international community applies pressure in the hope of persuading governments to adjust policy priorities, we should understand that in many cases this will have a teeter-totter effect of removing resources from another area. We see this in the transportation areas where governments seem to weigh just how safe an airline and air traffic control system must be in order to minimize international censure so that resources can be devoted to other, more urgent issues. One wonders whether the pressure to minimize the importation of obsolete refrigerators or control the activities of non-existent terrorists made it more difficult for central governments to impede traffickers and slavers. International institutions rarely carry out the legal triage, however, and the nature of bureaucratic specialization leads to each agency placing the highest priority on its own particular set of issues. It's up to states to make these choices.

Dependency and compliance. Although we did not choose these cases for this reason, the fact that both are heavily dependent on a few consumers and creditors and yet behaved very differently provides us an opportunity to draw another insight. Specifically, we see that Papua New Guinea adopts a more recalcitrant demeanor vis-à-vis the West while Botswana seems far more pliant. It is particularly noteworthy that officials in Port Moresby seem especially willing to challenge Canberra. They demand respect for their status as an equally sovereign state, even when they cannot survive without Australian aid and commerce.

Botswana demonstrates a considerable willingness to comply even with hard rules. A reputation for compliance is very important to governing elites – and this seems to be what drives its public positions rather than any fear of sanction. Papua New Guinea on the other hand does not seem to mind being thought of as a bit obstreperous. It also seems to be counting on its location on the periphery of the planet as a protection against serious sanctions.

References

Afrobarometer (2004) "Afrobarometer Round II: Compendium of Comparative Results from a 15-Country Survey." Working Paper #34. March. Available at www.afrobarometer.org/papers/AfropaperNo34.pdf. Accessed November 10, 2010.

Afrobarometer (2009) "Popular Attitudes Toward Democracy in Botswana: A Summary of Afrobarometer Indicators, 1999–2008," August 5. Available at www.afrobarometer.org/Democracy%20Indicators/bot_dem.indicators_5aug09_final.pdf. Accessed November 10, 2010.

Amnesty International (2010) *Amnesty International Report 2010 – Papua New Guinea*, 28 May. Available at www.unhcr.org/refworld/docid/4c03a80bc.html. Accessed August 25, 2010.

Asian Development Bank (2010) "Asian Development Outlook 2006: II. Economic Trends and Prospects in Developing Asia." Available at www.adb.org/documents/books/ado/2006/png.asp. Accessed August 25, 2010.

Australian Agency for International Development (2004) "Strengthening Port Security in the Pacific," AA 04 031, May 10. Available at www.ausaid.gov.au/media/release.cfm?BC=Media&Id=8158_9412_7852_108_7057. Accessed November 16, 2010.

Aviation Safety Network (2008) "News." *Flight Safety Foundation*. Available at http://aviation-safety.net/news/news.php?var=200706%. Accessed August 24, 2010.

Aviation Safety Network (2010) "Operator Index for Papua New Guinea." *Flight Safety Foundation*. Available at http://aviation-safety.net/database/record.php?id=20050222–0. Accessed August 27, 2010.

BBC News Online (2002) "Botswana Bushmen's Last Stand," March 18. Available at http://news.bbc.co.uk/2/hi/africa/1879429.stm. Accessed November 9, 2010.

Botswana Central Statistics Office (2009) *Botswana AIDS Impact Survey III, Statistical Report*. November. Gaborone, Botswana. Available at www.cso.gov.bw/images/stories/HouseHold/baisiii_report.pdf. Accessed November 8, 2010.

Botswana, Government of (2010) Penal Code, Chapter 8, section 1. Available at www.laws.gov.bw/Docs/Principal/Volume2/Chapter8/Chpt8–01%20Penal%20Code.pdf. Accessed August 23, 2010.

Botswana official (2010) Interview with the author, September 3.

Central Intelligence Agency (2010) *CIA World Factbook – Papua New Guinea*. Available at www.cia.gov/library/publications/the-world-factbook/geos/pp.html. Accessed August 26, 2010.

Chowdhury, Mamta Banu (2004) *Resources Booms and Macroeconomic Adjustments in Developing Countries*. Aldershot, UK: Ashgate.

Connell, John (1997) *Papua New Guinea: The Struggle for Development*. London: Routledge.

Department of State, United States (2009a) *Country Reports on Terrorism 2008 – Botswana*. April 30. Available at www.unhcr.org/refworld/docid/49fac6bbc.html. Accessed August 24, 2010.

Department of State, United States (2009b) *Trafficking in Persons Report 2009 – Botswana*. June 16. Available at www.unhcr.org/refworld/docid/4a4214ccc.html. Accessed August 25, 2010.

Department of State, United States (2009c) *Country Reports on Terrorism 2008 – Papua New Guinea, Solomon Islands, Vanuatu*. April 30. Available at www.unhcr.org/refworld/docid/49fac686c.html. Accessed August 23, 2010.

Department of State, United States (2010a) *2009 Country Reports on Human Rights Practices – Botswana*. March 11. Available at www.unhcr.org/refworld/docid/4b9e530e82.html. Accessed August 4, 2010.

Department of State, United States (2010b) *2009 Country Reports on Terrorism – Botswana*. August 5. Available at www.unhcr.org/refworld/docid/4c63b6542.html. Accessed August 23, 2010.

Department of State, United States (2010c) *Trafficking in Persons Report 2010 – Botswana*. June 14. Available at www.unhcr.org/refworld/docid/4c188406c.html. Accessed August 23, 2010.

Department of State, United States (2010d) *2009 Country Reports on Human Rights Practices – Papua New Guinea*. March 11. Available at www.unhcr.org/refworld/docid/4b9e52cd2.html. Accessed August 24, 2010.

Department of State, United States (2010e) Interview by the author of the Papua New Guinea desk officer, September 3.

Department of State, United States (2010f) *Trafficking in Persons Report 2010 – Papua New Guinea*. June 14. Available at www.unhcr.org/refworld/docid/4c1883cf2d.html. Accessed August 24, 2010.

Department of State, United States (2010g) *2009 Country Reports on Human Rights Practices – Papua New Guinea*. March 11. Available at www.unhcr.org/refworld/docid/4b9e52cd2.html. Accessed August 24, 2010.

Endres, Gunter (2009) "World Airline Directory 2009." *Flight International* 175(5182). March 31–April 6.

Europa World (2010a) "Regional and International Co-operation (Botswana)," Europa World online. London: Routledge. Available at www.europaworld.com.erl.lib.byu.edu/entry/bw.is.25.1. Accessed August 3, 2010.

Europa World (2010b) "Tourism (Botswana)," in Europa World online. London: Routledge. Available at www.europaworld.com.erl.lib.byu.edu/entry/bw.ss.61. Accessed 25 August 2010.

Europa World (2010c) "Recent Developments: The Election of 2007 and Subsequent Events (Papua New Guinea)," in Europa World online. London: Routledge. Available at www.europaworld.com.erl.lib.byu.edu/entry/EE001602. Accessed August 25, 2010.

Europa World (2010d) "Transport (Papua New Guinea)," in Europa World online. London: Routledge. Available at www.europaworld.com.erl.lib.byu.edu/entry/pg.ss.66. Accessed August 25, 2010.

Flight Safety Network (1999) Criminal occurrence description. October 11. Available at http://aviation-safety.net/database/record.php?id=19991011–0. Accessed November 10, 2010.

Freedom House (2010a) *Botswana*. February 15. Available at www.freedomhouse.org/template.cfm?page=22&year=2009&country=7572. Accessed August 3, 2010.

Freedom House (2010b) *Papua New Guinea*. February 15. Available at www.freedomhouse.org/template.cfm?page=22&year=2009&country=7681. Accessed August 25, 2010.

Good, Kenneth (2008) *Diamonds, Dispossession & Democracy in Botswana*. Woodbridge, UK: Boydell & Brewer Ltd.

Haley, Nicole and Ronald J. May (2009) "Introduction: Roots of Conflict in the Southern Highlands," in Nicole Haley and Ronald J. May, eds., *Conflict and Resource Development in the Southern Highlands of Papua New Guinea.* Canberra: Australia National University Press, pp. 1–19.

Henk, Dan (2010) *Botswana Defense Forces*. Available at www.xairforces.com/history.asp?id=5. Accessed November 9, 2010.

Heritage Foundation (2010) *Economic Freedom Rankings*. Available at www.heritage.org/index/ranking. Accessed December 15, 2010.

Hope, Kempe Ronald and Gloria Somolekae (1998) *Public Administration and Policy in Botswana*. Juta: Kenwyn.

Human Rights Watch (2009) *Where Violence Against Women is Rampant*. January 27. Available at www.unhcr.org/refworld/docid/498178ad1e.html. Accessed August 28, 2010.

Integrated Regional Information Networks (2010) *Botswana: Technology to Catch Undocumented Migrants*, March 1. Available at www.unhcr.org/refworld/docid/4b960e3ec.html. Accessed August 3, 2010.

International Civil Aviation Organization (2010a) *Flight Safety Information Exchange* "USAOP Status for States Which Have Authorized the Release of Information Including Progress Validated by ICAO." Available at www.icao.int/fsix/AuditRep1_icvm.cfm. Accessed August 26, 2010.

International Civil Aviation Organization (2010b) *Table of Recommendations – Botswana*. Available at www2.icao.int/en/acip/Documents/Gap%20Analysis/SADC/Annex%20A1%20Table%20of%20Recommendations%20-%20Botswana.pdf. Accessed August 26, 2010.

International Civil Aviation Organization (2010c) *Flight Safety Information Exchange*. "USAOP Status for States which have Authorized the Release of Information Including Progress Validated by ICAO." Available at www.icao.int/fsix/AuditRep1_icvm.cfm. Accessed August 26, 2010.

International Maritime Bureau of the International Chamber of Commerce (2007) *Pirate Attack Map – 2007*. Available at www.icc-ccs.org/index.php?option=com_fabrik&c=form&view=details&Itemid=102&fabrik=25&rowid=182&tableid=23&fabrik_cursor=181. Accessed November 16, 2010.

International Organization for Migration (2010a) "Papua New Guinea," March. Available at www.iom.int/jahia/Jahia/papua-new-guinea. Accessed August 28, 2010.

International Organization for Migration (2010b) "IOM Trains Papua New Guinea's immigration Service Officers," July 9. Available at www.iom.int/jahia/Jahia/media/press-briefing-notes/pbnAS/cache/offonce?entryId=27970. Accessed August 28, 2010.

Kentshitswe, Livingstone (2010) "Botswana's Airport Security Lacking," *Botswana Guardian*. October 22. Available at www.botswanaguardian.co.bw/newsdetails.php?nid=709&cat=BG%20NEWS. Accessed November 10, 2010.

Keoreng, Ephraim (2010) "Immigration Officers Hail New Border Control System," *Mmegi*. April 22. Available at www.mmegi.bw/index.php?sid=1&aid=1811&dir=2010/April/Thursday22. Accessed August 24, 2010.

Maritime International Secretariat (2009) "Shipping Industry Flag State Performance Table: 2009 Update." London: Maritime International Secretariat Services Limited. Available at www.marisec.org/FlagStatePerformanceTable09.pdf. Accessed August 25, 2010.

Marshall, Steve (2008) "The Fatal Sky," *ABC News*. August 19. Available at www.abc.net.au/foreign/content/oldcontent/s2464246.htm. Accessed August 25, 2010.

May, Ronald (2004) *State and Society in Papua New Guinea: The First Twenty-five Years*. Canberra: The Australian National University.

May, Ronald (2008) "Improving Development and Respecting Sovereignty: Australia and Papua New Guinea," Australian Strategic Policy Institute's *Insights* #43 (September).

Mmegi (2009) "AB to Rejoin IATA-Ramsden," March 4. Available at www.mmegi.bw/index.php?sid=1&aid=2&dir=2009/March/Wednesday4. Accessed November 10, 2010.

Multilateral Fund for Implementation of the Montreal Protocol (2003) "Press Releases." Available at www.multilateralfund.org/press_releases.htm. Accessed August 26, 2010.

National Maritime Safety Authority (2010) "Maritime Regulations Made Under the Merchant Shipping Act." Available at www.nmsa.gov.pg/maritime_legislation.html. Accessed November 17, 2010.

New York Times (2010) "In One of World's Poorest Corners, a Flood of Wealth and Worry," by Norimitsu Onishi. October 26, A1.

Parsons, Neil (1999) *Botswana History Pages – Society*. Available at www.thuto.org/ubh/bw/bhp13.htm. Accessed November 9, 2010.

Phorano, Odireleng, Keitseope Nthomang, and Dolly Ntseane (2005) "Alcohol Abuse, Gender-based Violence and HIV/AIDS in Botswana: Establishing the Link Based on Empirical Evidence," *Journal of Social Aspects of HIV/AIDS* 2(1) (April): 188–202.

PNG Ports Corporation Ltd. (2010) "ISPS Code." Available at www.pngports.com.pg/isps_code.html. Accessed November 16, 2010.

Post-Courier (2008) "Somare Sails in Deep Waters," February 19, p. 3. Available at www.postcourier.com.pg/20080215/news.htm. Accessed November 18, 2010.

Reilly, Benjamin (2008) "Ethnic Conflict in Papua New Guinea," *Asia Pacific Viewpoint* 49(1) (April): 1–19.

Saunders, Christopher (2010) "Recent History (Botswana)," in Europa World online. London: Routledge. Available at www.europaworld.com.erl.lib.byu.edu/entry/bw.hi. Accessed August 25, 2010.

Skelemani, Phandu T.C. (2011) "Promoting Human Rights and the Rule of Law While Countering Terrorism," Statement by Hon. Phandu T.C. Skelemani, MP, Minister of Foreign Affairs and International Cooperation, Republic of Botswana, at UN Secretary General Symposium on International Counter-Terrorism Cooperation. September 19, New York.

Sydney Morning Herald (2010) "Somare Threatens to Kill Opposition MP," by Ilya Gridneff, July 22. Available at www.smh.com.au/world/somare-threatens-to-kill-opposition-mp-20100721–10l4i.html. Accessed November 15, 2010.

Talao, Freda (2009) "Papua New Guinea: Country Report on Human Rights," *Victoria University of Wellington Law Review* 40. Available at www.austlii.edu.au/nz/journals/VUWLawRw/2009/3.pdf. Accessed August 25, 2010.

Tokyo Memorandum of Understanding (2008) *2007 Annual Report of the Tokyo MOU on Port State Control in the Asia-Pacific Region*. April 16, Tokyo. Available at www.tokyo-mou.org/ANN07.pdf. Accessed November 17, 2010.

Tokyo Memorandum of Understanding (2010) *2009 Annual Report of the Tokyo MOU on Port State Control in the Asia-Pacific Region*. April 15, Tokyo. Available at www.tokyo-mou.org/ANN09.pdf. Accessed November 17, 2010.

Tubuans & Dukduks – blog (2008) "The Papua New Guinea National Maritime Safety Authority: A Ship with a Hole?" Available at http://garamut.wordpress.com/2008/08/26/the-papua-new-guinea-national-maritime-and-safety-authority-a-ship-with-a-hole/. Accessed November 18, 2010.

United Nations (2002a) "Johannesburg Summit 2002: Botswana Country Profile." Available at www.un.org/esa/agenda21/natlinfo/wssd/botswana.pdf. Accessed August 26, 2010.

United Nations (2002b) "Papua New Guinea Country Report on the Declaration of Commitment on HIV/AIDS (UNGASS)." Available at http://data.unaids.org/Topics/UNGASS2003/Asia-Pacific/papua_new_guinea_ungassreport_2003_en.pdf. Accessed August 25, 2010.

UN Committee on the Elimination of Discrimination Against Women (CEDAW) (2008) *Consideration of Reports Submitted by States Parties Under Article 18 of the Convention on the Elimination of All Forms of Discrimination against Women: Combined Initial, 2nd and 3rd Periodic Reports of States Parties: Botswana*, October 20, CEDAW/C/BOT/3. Available at www.unhcr.org/refworld/docid/4a1fa6e22.html. Accessed August 15, 2010.

UN Conference on Trade and Development (2006) "Botswana and the Multilateral Trading System: The Impact of WTO Agreements, Negotiations, and Implementation." UNCTAD/DITC/TNCD/2005/17. Available at www.unctad.org/en/docs/ditctncd200517_en.pdf. Accessed November 9, 2010.

UN Convention on the Elimination of Discrimination against Women (2009) *Consideration of Reports Submitted by States Parties Under Article 18 of the Convention on the Elimination of All Forms of Discrimination against Women: Combined Initial, 2nd and 3rd Periodic Reports of States Parties: Papua New Guinea*, May 22. CEDAW/C/PNG/3. Available at www.unhcr.org/refworld/docid/4a8be72b2.html. Accessed August 24, 2010.

UN Convention on the Elimination of Discrimination against Women (2010a) "Concluding Observations of the Committee on the Elimination of Discrimination against Women: Botswana," January 18–February 5, CEDAW/C/BOT/CO/3.

UN Convention on the Elimination of Discrimination against Women (2010b) "Concluding Observations of the Committee on the Elimination of Discrimination against Women: Papua New Guinea," July 13–20, 10–46605 (E), published July 30.

UN Educational, Scientific and Cultural Organization (2008) *National Report on the State-of-the-Art of Adult Learning and Education in Papua New Guinea: A Situation Analysis*. June 30. UNESCO: Paris.

UN Environmental Programme (2006) Ozone Secretariat "Declaration by the Pacific Island Countries Attending the 13th Meeting of the Parties to the Montreal Protocol." In *Handbook for the Montreal Protocol on Substances that Deplete the Ozone Layer*. 7th edn. Available at http://ozone.unep.org/Publications/MP_Handbook/Section_3.8_Annexes_Declarations/Declaration_by_the_Pacific.shtml. Accessed August 23, 2010.

UN Environment Programme (2009) Ozone Secretariat, *Handbook for the Montreal Protocol on Substances that Deplete the Ozone Layer*. 8th edn. Available at www.unep.ch/ozone/Publications/MP_Handbook/MP-Handbook-2009.pdf. Accessed August 27, 2010.

UN Environmental Programme (2010a) *Executive Committee of the Multilateral Fund for the Implementation of the Montreal Protocol*. Project Proposal: Botswana. UNEP/OzL.Pro/ExCom/60/22. April 12–15. Available at http://multilateralfund.virtual.vps-host.net/files/60/6022.pdf. Accessed November 10, 2010.

UN High Commissioner for Human Rights (2010) "UN Special Rapporteur on Torture Presents Preliminary Findings on his Mission to Papua New Guinea," May 25. New York: UN.

UN Human Rights Committee (2008) *Consideration of Reports Submitted by States Parties Under Article 40 of the Covenant: Concluding Observations of the Human Rights Committee*. CCPR/C/BWA/CO/1, April 24. New York.

UN Human Rights Council (2009) "Report of the Special Rapporteur on the Situation of Human Rights and Fundamental Freedoms of Indigenous People." September 23. A/HRC/12/34/Add.4.

UNICEF and the Government of Papua New Guinea (1996) *Children, Women and Families in Papua New Guinea: A Situation Analysis*. October. Port Moresby: UNICEF.

UN Information Service (2005) "Behind Closed Doors – Violence against Women," May 3. Available at www.unis.unvienna.org/pdf/violence.pdf. Accessed November 10, 2010.

United States Committee for Refugees and Immigrants (2009) *World Refugee Survey 2009 – Botswana*, June 17. Available at www.unhcr.org/refworld/docid/4a40d2a0c.html. Accessed August 3, 2010.

van Binsbergen, William (2002) *Botswana's Ethnic Structure: An Abortive Research Proposal*. Available at http://ethnicity.bravepages.com/ethnicity/botswana.htm. Accessed November 9, 2010.

Van Buren, Linda (2010) "Economy (Botswana)," in Europa World online. London: Routledge. Available at www.europaworld.com.erl.lib.byu.edu/entry/bw.ec. Accessed August 25, 2010.

Werbner, Richard (2004) *Reasonable Radicals and Citizenship in Botswana: The Public Anthropology of Kalanga Elites*. Bloomington: Indiana University Press.

World Bank (1999) *Botswana: A Case Study of Economic Policy Prudence and Growth*. August 31. Available at www-wds.worldbank.org/servlet/WDSContentServer/WDSP/IB/2000/02/03/000094946_00011405343417/Rendered/INDEX/multi_page.txt. Accessed August 4, 2010.

World Bank (2009) *Botswana – Country Brief*. September. Available at http://web.worldbank.org/WBSITE/EXTERNAL/COUNTRIES/AFRICAEXT/BOTSWANAEXTN/0,,menuPK:322821~pagePK:141132~piPK:141107~theSitePK:322804,00.html. Accessed August 3, 2010.

World Bank, Asian Development Bank, and the Agency for International Development of Australia (2007) *Strategic Directions for Human Development in Papua New Guinea*. Washington D.C.: World Bank.

10 Conclusions

Summary of findings: how did the theories fare?

The principal aim of this work has been the quest for the strongest explanation of international law compliance from among the existing theories. This has been done across a variety of issue-areas and a range of cases during the period from 1990 to 2008.

Using a variety of measures, we have found that most theories of law compliance can explain important developments in world affairs. For example, it was clear that the theory of political liberalism did the best job of explaining compliance with the protective provisions of the Convention on the Elimination of Discrimination against Women – so long as culture was not taken into account. On the other hand, knowing a state's culture – particularly with respect to adherence to Islam – can also explain compliance with CEDAW. A country's managerial capacity explained much of its degree of compliance with anti-trafficking norms as well as limited consumption of ozone-depleting chemicals as provided for under the Montreal Protocol. A country's reputation, as measured in terms of its international credit-worthiness, explained its policies on fighting terror and maintaining high standards of aircraft safety. And finally, legitimacy theory explained anti-terror policy.

There are sound theoretical reasons why each of these statistical patterns was observed. What is perhaps most surprising is that more of them did not occur. It was surprising that anti-piracy, anti-slavery, and ship safety rules seemed to defy explanation – at least in the aggregate. Further, it was surprising that in most cases only one theory emerged as the most promising explanation – but it was very difficult to predict which theory would emerge when moving from one issue-area to the next. Why does a country's administrative capacity explain compliance with the Montreal Protocol, but not with airline safety? Why does a country's level of democratization explain compliance with CEDAW, but not with anti-terror measures?

The lack of answers pointed to a need to adopt another research method. The likely explanation for these puzzling patterns lies in the possibility that causation involves subtle and dynamic processes which our statistics could not capture adequately. The solution was to undertake a series of country studies – holding constant the issue-areas and the time-frame. We selected the cases along three dimensions: wealth, democracy, and globalization. We also took geography and culture into account where feasible.

In this chapter we will review the findings from the case studies and relate them to the findings from Chapter 5.

Table 10.1 revisits the cases and their characteristics. Table 10.2 repeats the assessment of theories as presented at the close of each country study. We judge the utility of a theory on a three-point scale; a theory is judged to explain "little," "some," or "much" of the outcomes and processes. Table 10.2 shows that some theories performed better across the board than others. Later we will see whether this is contingent on issue-area. It is worth keeping in mind the country characteristics as presented in Table 10.1 as we consider Table 10.2.

The first observation is that, as could have been expected from the cross-national statistical findings, no one theory provides a strong explanation across cases and across issue-areas. Each theory fails to explain outcomes. Conversely, no theory is entirely useless, as each one provides a strong explanation of at least a few outcomes. Cultural theory, for example, offers a compelling explanation for human rights law compliance in many of the cases, while the legitimacy school and reputational theory explain outcomes in the area of market regulation.

Overall, however, the rationalist approach makes a reasonable starting point for any explanation of international law compliance across countries and across issue-areas. Out of sixty-seven total cells with results (excluding maritime policy for most of the landlocked countries), it explains "much" of the outcome in more than half (thirty-seven) and explains "some" of the results in a quarter of the possible cases (eighteen). This is a key finding that could not have been determined without the case studies since it is very difficult to test this theory through cross-national statistical analysis. Understanding a regime's interests – both at home and abroad – requires situational knowledge that is not easily quantified or generalized. As we have seen, however, other theoretical approaches can help us better understand a government's interests – particularly with respect to the place of reputation and the need to maintain power at home. Rationalism by itself – as is generally acknowledged by the theory's proponents – offers a template rather than a forecast. More will be said about this below.

Table 10.1 Characteristics of country cases

Democratic in bold	*Isolated in bold*	*Low GNP/cap in bold*
Peru	Peru	Peru
Bolivia	Bolivia	**Bolivia**
Tunisia	Tunisia	Tunisia
Pakistan	Pakistan	**Pakistan**
Belarus	**Belarus**	Belarus
Equatorial Guinea	**Equatorial Guinea**	**Equatorial Guinea**
Botswana	**Botswana**	Botswana
Papua New Guinea	**Papua New Guinea**	**Papua New Guinea**

The next clear finding is that understanding a nation's culture does little to explain its approach to international law generally and particularly with respect to laws governing market transactions (namely airliner and ship safety and ozone protection). This is perhaps not surprising, as we will see below, because these rules involve a more technocratic approach that applies international professional expertise. But the approach also does a poor job of explaining most nations' approach to combating terrorism and fending off pirates – issues where culture might have played a part.

All of the theories are remarkable for the similarity of their mixed records. Political liberalism and the legitimacy school each explains "much" of the outcome in twenty cases. Economic liberalism and reputation theory both explain nineteen cases well, and the managerial school explains "much" in eighteen cases. Reputational theory does better, overall, than the other five, failing to explain outcomes in only ten cases, while the managerial school fails to explain outcomes in twenty cases. If one were to rank the theories, then, rationalism would come out on top, followed by reputational theory. Cultural theory would be at the bottom, preceded by the managerial school. The other three theories – political and economic liberalism and legitimacy theory – would essentially tie for third place.

Looking closer, we can ask whether certain theories do a better job of explaining certain types of countries. In other words, do the causal dynamics hypothesized by political liberalism manifest themselves with states that are relatively more engaged in the international society? As it happens, the answer to this question is no, since political liberalism explains "much" of the result in only seven out of thirty-one relatively more globalized states (as opposed to thirteen times for relatively isolated states). On the other hand, economic liberalism accurately predicts outcomes for twelve of the globalized states – significantly better than for states with higher GNP per capita. In other words, with respect to our eight country studies, political liberalism better explains the behavior of isolated states while economic liberalism better explains outcomes for internationalized states. This implies that democratic regimes need not be exposed to foreign ideas and visitors to embrace international norms – that the impulse to comply may have domestic rather than international origins. On the other hand, economic liberalism almost always involves globalization – so in some ways the category measures the same dimensions at the theory itself.

Other findings include a distinct tendency for the managerial school to better explain outcomes where states are democratic, internationalized, and wealthy, while it does a relatively poor job explaining why the other states do not comply. This is not to say that poor, isolated, autocratic states do not have the resources to comply, but rather that their patterns of compliance are less tied to their capacity. As observed earlier, capacity seems to be malleable in these cases, as opposed to the wealthy, liberal states. Rationalism does a much better job of explaining policy in internationalized states, which likely ties in to the predictions of economic liberalism. Economically globalized states have more to lose from their policy choices.

Table 10.2 Assessing theory persuasiveness

	Sovereignty defense			*Market control*			*Human rights*	
	Anti-terror	*Anti-piracy*	*Anti-trafficking*	*Air transport*	*Ship safety*	*Ozone depletion*	*Slavery*	*Protection of women*
Political liberalism								
Peru	some	some	some	much	much	much	little	little
Bolivia	much		some	little	little	little	some	some
Tunisia	much	much	much	some	some	some	some	some
Pakistan	some	little	little	little	some	some	some	some
Belarus	little		little	little		little	some	some
Equatorial Guinea	much	much	some	much	much	some	much	much
Botswana	much		much	some		little	much	much
Papua New Guinea	much	much	little	little	some	some	much	little
Economic liberalism								
Peru	little	some	much	much	much	some	much	some
Bolivia	little		much	much	some	some	much	some
Tunisia	some	some	some	much	some	some	much	some
Pakistan	little	much	much	some	some	some	much	some
Belarus	little		little	some		some	much	some
Equatorial Guinea	some	much	some	some	much	much	some	some
Botswana	little		little	some		little	little	some
Papua New Guinea	much	much	some	little	little	little	much	little

continued

Table 10.2 Continued

	Sovereignty defense			*Market control*			*Human rights*	
	Anti-terror	*Anti-piracy*	*Anti-trafficking*	*Air transport*	*Ship safety*	*Ozone depletion*	*Slavery*	*Protection of women*
Managerial								
Peru	much	much	much	much	much	much	little	little
Bolivia	much		much	some	some	some	some	some
Tunisia	much	much	little	some	much	some	some	some
Pakistan	some	much	some	little	some	little	little	little
Belarus	much		much	little		little	little	little
Equatorial Guinea	little	some	little	little	some	some	little	little
Botswana	much		much	some		some	much	some
Papua New Guinea	much	much	little	some	little	little	much	little
Reputational								
Peru	some	little	little	much	some	much	some	some
Bolivia	some		some	much	little	much	some	some
Tunisia	some	some	little	much	some	much	some	some
Pakistan	much	much	some	much	much	much	little	little
Belarus	little		little	some		some	some	some
Equatorial Guinea	some	some	much	some	some	some	much	much
Botswana	much		much	some		much	some	some
Papua New Guinea	little	little	some	some	some	much	much	some
Cultural								
Peru	some	some	some	little	little	little	much	much
Bolivia	little		some	littler	little	little	much	some
Tunisia	little	little	some	little	little	little	some	some

Pakistan	much	little	much	little	little	little	some	much
Belarus	some		some	little		little	much	much
Equatorial Guinea	little	little	much	little	some	little	some	some
Botswana	much		much	little		little	much	much
Papua New Guinea	some	much	much	little	little	little	some	much
Legitimacy								
Peru	little	little	little	much	much	some	some	some
Bolivia	some		some	much	little	much	some	some
Tunisia	some	some	little	much	some	much	some	much
Pakistan	some	much	little	some	some	much	little	little
Belarus	little		some	some		some	some	some
Equatorial Guinea	little	little	little	some	some	much	much	much
Botswana	much		much	some		much	some	some
Papua New Guinea	much	little	much	much	much	much	some	little
Rationalism								
Peru	much	much	much	much	some	much	much	little
Bolivia	some		some	much	some	much	some	little
Tunisia	much	much	much	much	some	much	much	much
Pakistan	much	much	some	much	much	much	much	some
Belarus	much		some	much		much	much	some
Equatorial Guinea	some	much	some	some	some	some	much	much
Botswana	some		some	some		much	little	much
Papua New Guinea	much	much	much	much	much	much	little	much

The legitimacy school's predictions seem to apply better to democratic states and relatively poor societies – something which may stem from a statistical artifact: legitimacy theory does not explain any of the policies of Belarus especially well. Likewise the reputational theory explains poor country behavior better than rich country behavior, but this may stem from the fact that it explains policies on ozone depletion so well across the board. Cultural theory seems to fit somewhat better in democratic states, but the difference is not large.

Context and interaction: the next generation of theory

All of these findings point to a need to look more closely at how the various factors highlighted by the theories interact. Starting from a rationalist perspective, we need to ask which factors seem to loom the largest, when do they matter, and how do they interact. It is to this task that we now turn.

To begin, reputation matters, but not always in the way the international community hopes. To begin, there are always two reputations at stake: the reputation a government has in the minds of the international community and the reputation it has in the minds of its citizenry at home. While each of these audiences is diverse, it useful to assume each is internally homogenous for the time being. It is essential to understand that these two reputations are not always – or even often – in harmony. We have seen that it is extremely dangerous for some governments to develop a reputation for selling out to the international community. We have seen this in the cases of Bolivia and Pakistan. Conversely, citizens may grow weary of an always-defiant head of state. This may be true in Belarus, although it is impossible to know at this point. It was certainly true in Serbia where Slobodan Milosevic was concerned. Thus heads of state must often walk a fine line between embracing and resisting international norms for the sake of their political survival. Even where a regime has made an internal commitment to improving its international reputation – that is for appearing to be a team player – it may often feel compelled to fine-tune its rhetoric for the sake of the domestic audience. The reverse is also true. Thus we find states that embrace international norms, but do not present them as such to their domestic audiences. Rather, they "indigenize" the norms and present them as home-spun (see Botswana's approach to the status of women). Conversely, we find states that publicly attack the international community while simultaneously accepting norms behind closed doors. See, for example, Pakistan's criticism – and continued acceptance – of American drone attacks within the country's borders. Even more troubling from an international law perspective is the possibility that governments will simply switch back and forth from compliant to non-compliant policies.

None of this is to imply that reputation does not matter. It simply means it is very difficult to measure. We have seen that understanding a government's basic orientation to the international community helps us predict compliance and non-compliance. It helps us predict whether resources will be mobilized and whether domestic opposition will be resisted. In general, states that seek a good reputation will make a concerted effort to comply. Whether they succeed will depend on yet other factors.

The initial decision to establish a good relationship with the international community may derive from the embrace of certain norms, the calculation of certain interests, or yet other factors. From a rationalist point of view, it is important to consider how engagement with the international community might benefit the regime in power. Again, we must consider both international and domestic factors more or less simultaneously since they will likely interact. Autocratic regimes will find that they must make a choice with respect to compliance with international norms, since it is unlikely that they will be able to embrace all of them and remain in power. As we have seen, human rights norms are generally ignored in favor of more technical market-regulation norms and sovereignty-protecting norms – especially where the latter happen to coincide with the international community's priorities. Such regimes may offer the international community an implicit "trade": compliance with anti-terror measures in exchange for violation of democratic election norms. In the case of Tunisia the choice is rather explicit since the repression of Islamist political parties is part and parcel of its anti-terror strategy. Whether the international community will accept this bargain is not always easy to predict, and will be discussed further below.

Autocratic regimes have a further advantage in that they are better able to resist domestic pressures to change the state's policies. Generally speaking, the regime is in a stronger position to impose its views regarding international law compliance by imprisoning critics, censoring the press, concealing its actions, and so forth. Even where opposition may be widespread, these regimes may be able to maintain control of policy implementation. The result will likely be the internalization of whichever international norms the regime chooses. Further, it is likely that either compliance or non-compliance will persist for some time. While autocrats are not likely to comply with all international norms, they are at least more reliable when they do and predictable when they don't. Even their hypocrisy and foot-dragging are likely to be predictable (testing the minimum standard for "free and "fair" elections, providing minimum press freedoms, etc.).

Democratic regimes may be able to comply with all rules across the board, but they are far more vulnerable to changes in their domestic reputations. Institutional constraints may lead to unpredictable outcomes. As we have seen, legislatures often fail to adopt bills proposed by the executive, supreme courts often overturn laws once they have been adopted, and the electorate routinely replaces whole governments. Each of these events may lead to the repeal of a particular pattern of compliance or non-compliance. This implies that democratic regimes – especially those with a tenuous hold on power – may be utterly unreliable treaty partners. It is worth recalling that democratic regimes are no more compliant with international law than autocratic regimes, despite their basic hope to establish a reputation for cooperation with the international community. The situation is all the more complicated by the fact that international lawyers care about different dimensions of "democracy" than most political scientists. What matters to them is who can block or overturn a treaty commitment, not whether the public's will is expressed in public policy. The opinion of Pakistan's Supreme Court Chief is of far greater import in international law than the country's public opinion polls. Likewise, the Papua New Guinea Supreme Court has far more capacity to reverse a treaty commitment (say – to Australia) than the many disparate and disorganized political parties. In some respects, then, it is the somewhat "undemocratic" aspects of democracy that matter most in international law.

Returning to our basic argument that rationalism offers a useful framework for explaining compliance, we can already see that while a country's reputation – and the type of reputation is seeks – is very important, knowing this alone will not allow us to predict compliance across issue-areas. Not only do we also need to know what type of domestic reputation the government seeks, but also the institutional and political powers at the disposal of the regime to resist domestic opposition to its policies.

Related to the question of domestic reputation is the question of "executive tenacity," as mentioned in previous chapters. Note at the outset that this is not equivalent either to autocracy or to executive survival. It refers instead to the degree to which the head of state wishes to stay in power. Both Franklin D. Roosevelt and Josef Stalin had high levels of executive tenacity, although this is where the similarity ends. Laurent Gbagbo of Ivory Cost epitomizes executive tenacity in that he tried to remain the country's president despite losing an internationally verified election and facing an onslaught from a considerable opposition army. In some cases tenacity refers to just one individual's hold on power, such as Obiang or Lukashenka, while in others it may relate to that person's legacy or party – as in Botswana. Of course, all depends on the degree of domestic opposition to the executive. Pervez Musharraf had high executive tenacity, which simply precipitated a crisis when the public's opposition was able to manifest itself. The same may be true of Evo Morales, although it is too early to tell. Ben Ali of Tunisia, on the other hand, surprised everyone when he abruptly fled his country following what in retrospect were relatively limited anti-government protests. One thing is clear: it is very difficult to measure a leader's executive tenacity in the abstract.

One of the observations that can be gleaned from the case studies and which is not apparent from the statistical analysis is that executive tenacity has a direct effect on international law compliance. In particular, it tends to generate considerable consistency of policy over time – something that is of paramount importance in international law. As mentioned, the shadow of the future looms large to those with high executive tenacity, which in turn leads them to weigh carefully the decision to commit to a norm and also increases the likelihood that they will internalize it and comply. On the other hand, these are also the leaders that are most likely to twist and bend constitutional constraints to the breaking point, which generally results in non-compliance with some international norms and may result in a sudden change of government. But executive tenacity and longevity in office are not necessarily autocratic and may be consistent with high levels of compliance across many international legal issues.

An issue that emerged at several junctures in the work is the role of capacity as a constraint or opportunity for governments. The managerial school assumes that most states want to comply with most laws. We have seen that this premise is likely too optimistic. Further, the approach infers that non-compliance is largely the result of lack of capacity rather than lack of will. We have seen that capacity itself is remarkably malleable, with the implication that lack of capacity is often a reflection of lack of will. Time and again we have seen instances of governments choosing to withhold resources to enforce international norms to which they are not politically committed. The example of Equatorial Guinea's hoarding of cash is certainly the most egregious, but almost none of the autocratic regimes invested funds in the creation of independent election monitors, for example. States with strong levels of cultural traditionalism were reluctant to invest heavily in changing attitudes toward women and the poor. This was particularly true for several democratic regimes (see Peru, Botswana, and Papua New Guinea), which recalls our point that democracy and international norm compliance need not dovetail with each other. Even Tunisia was reluctant to challenge tribal law in the southern desert and instead devoted its attention to enforcing women's rights in the cities and along the coasts.

Not only did states pick and choose which local traditions to challenge, they clearly were selective about which laws would be enforced. We can look back on our cases and take note of the fact that almost all states had clearly formulated statutes on a wide range of international norms, from protection of women to the banning of slaves and prevention of human trafficking. But in most cases the resources needed to enforce these laws – even when it was clear the resources were available – were not deployed. This was all the more apparent when states were able to mobilize considerable resources to enforce rules that ran parallel to international norms. Thus some states were able to halt terrorists and weapons at the border, but not children on their way to servitude. Still others were perfectly capable of organizing a national campaign against AIDS but not change attitudes about trafficked persons. Still others were able to significantly increase their naval patrols to prevent smuggling but ignored piracy. And still others simply pocket the foreign aid.

Overall, the managerial school underestimates the importance of political will. But the situation is even more complex in that decisions to deploy resources are not only dependent on political priorities, the possession of those resources often reflects a train of previous decisions that were inherently political. These include decisions to open or close one's economy, to rely entirely on a single export, to join or resist regional trade agreements, to fund or starve education and research, and so forth. While much depends on history, geography, and luck (Botswana will never be a major oil exporter, just as Equatorial Guinea will never be the breadbasket of the world), the cases reveal that even a poorly dealt hand can be well-played. It is easy to predict where both Botswana and Equatorial Guinea will be ten years from now – and it is very unlikely to be the same place.

Not only is capacity a question of generating resources, it is also a question of manipulating what needs there are. Governments tend to be unimaginative about their needs, seeing them as exogenous, but the fact remains that radical steps can change the capacity/needs ratio. Ending apartheid freed up South Africa's security apparatus to focus on real crime rather than the political opposition. Likewise, the dismemberment of the Soviet Union and the ending of the Cold War radically altered the resource/needs calculus in Moscow. The dismemberment of Pakistan may be no more costly than its preservation – especially where Kashmir is concerned. Allowing an open media and free and fair elections in Belarus will probably still culminate in Lukashenka's reelection, but would free up the police to focus on trafficking (after substantial retraining, of course). In many cases, these dramatic shifts would lead to increased international support and resources as well.

Taken together, we need to pay attention to a government's overall orientation to the international legal sphere, the executive's tenacity, to its capacity to control public opinion, and its control over implementation of treaty commitments, as well as its resources, the public's sentiment (including, of course, elite attitudes and capacity), and to its place in the world economy.

Conclusions

The most obvious implication of this work is primarily negative: when it comes to explaining why states follow the rules, there is no single theoretical silver bullet. This in turn implies that all theorists should downplay the significance of their findings, whatever they are. Although some have found that ratifying treaties does not improve human rights performance (Hathaway 2002), we have found that ratification is a strong predictor of compliance with CFC regulation and safe air transport systems. Although some have found that stable democracies and long-lasting autocracies are least likely to improve human rights performance in conjunction with human right treaties, we have found that these types of regimes do very well in virtually every other area of law. Although realists will tell us that culture shouldn't matter, we have found that culture goes far in explaining whether a country abuses its women and allows trafficking in humans and slavery.

Part of the reason why each theory seems to have something to say stems from the finding that when it comes to rule compliance, government policies are selective, calculated, situational, and driven by often intangible factors. Rationalism is clearly the best starting point for explaining all of this. We have found – especially in the case studies that allowed us to unpack local factors and decision-making processes – that governments do not automatically comply with rules simply because they feel they are appropriate. Appropriateness matters little when rules conflict, the regime's survival is at stake, or when the costs are formidable. Rather, regimes will strive to enhance their security and status – both at home and abroad. This ultimately requires considerable information on the part of the scholar who would predict behavior.

Where a regime cares deeply about its reputation as an upstanding member of the international community, then the appropriateness of a rule matters a great deal. This is particularly true where the head of government is bound by constitutional restrictions and has little desire to flout them. On the other hand, where the regime prides itself on deviating from what is expected – and where the leader hopes to remain in office until death – the greater the rule's appropriateness, the less likely it is to constrain behavior. After all, unless you know the rules, you don't know how to be a deviant. In some cases, the creation of a rule spawns its own scofflaws.

Where a regime has the resources to live apart from the international community – or is willing to deprive its citizens of the benefits of cosmopolitanism – we should expect compliance with rules to be purely situational. Where compliance provides important benefits – as we see when states receive more tourists because they have safe aircraft – then compliance will be high. Conversely, where penalties are harsh, non-compliance will be more rare.

But we should not assume that states would all comply if only they had the resources. We have seen – especially from the case studies – that almost all states have almost all the resources they need to comply with almost all rules. What they nearly all seem to lack, however, is the political will to mobilize these resources. Corruption – whether systemic or isolated – is always a choice, as is a national budget that deprives the authorities from having the resources and training they need to enforce basic laws. Sympathizing with governments that plead poverty is a form of enabling.

What does this mean for the next generation of compliance scholars? To begin, we have shown that these insights were possible only by adopting a variety of research methods, and so we urge future scholars to do likewise (recent work by Tomz [2007] provides a model). Beyond cross-national statistical analysis and comparative case studies, we recommend careful historical work and process-tracing in order to more specifically identify turning points in policy formulation. Participant observation and extensive review of internal policy documents (including minutes of meetings and legislative debates) will help clarify which issues are raised and why and by whom. This will clearly not be feasible in autocratic regimes, but will at least help us understand how democracies make decisions about law compliance. Statistical analysis that covers a variety of issues and employs more sophisticated factor analysis and additive or multiplicative approaches would also be promising. At any rate, the detailed analysis of a single issue or a single country is unlikely to yield new insights.

More work should be done on the tipping points for different factors. We have begun the process of showing that reputation, tenacity, domestic power, and so forth are important, but we cannot at this point specify how much of one will precipitate particular outcomes. It seems plausible that such an exercise could be undertaken. Recent work by Grieco *et al.* (2009) merits closer examination. We would especially encourage more effort at measuring "desire to please" and "executive tenacity" with the expectation that these two variables will interact in predictable ways. Likewise, it should be feasible to create economic models on some of the more quantifiable norms (especially market regulation norms) in order to predict how the degree of capacity, the cost of implementation, the risk of non-compliance, and so forth all interact to produce policy outcomes. Finally, clarifying the domestic/international trade-offs would be of considerable value to policy-makers as they weigh the adoption of new norms and decisions about enforcement.

In the final analysis, this study has shown that states address international norms differently, and a familiarity with the domestic resources, institutions, preferences, and even personalities is essential to predicting compliance. These interact in important and often predictable ways to produce outcomes that are significant to both the citizens at home and the world as a whole.

Broader implications

While the nature of man may not have been resolved in this study, it is worth noting that the nature of society has been clarified, as well as man's place in it. We can see that society exists – virtually as an exogenous phenomenon from the perspective of heads of state. In fact, two societies exist simultaneously and heads of state are faced with important choices with respect to their participation in them. On the one hand, there is clearly an international society – as predicted by the English School and Kant – and world leaders understand what is required to be in good standing. States interact in predictable and constructive ways, offering inclusion and privileges to those who follow along and ostracism and penalties to those that do not. The international regimes and legal structures that have been developed over the years are often remarkably coherent and effective, comparable in many respects to domestic policy initiatives. Interactions between state actors are frequent and on-going, offering numerous points of contact and opportunities for socialization and learning. Note that this society is not at all identical to the liberal "zone of peace" in that many autocratic regimes belong to it (Tunisia) while some democratic regimes do not (Papua New Guinea) (Doyle 1986).

In some respects, the pariah states help to delineate the parameters of this international society. Belarus, for example, helps to clarify what is unacceptable to the international community by virtue of its open resistance to most international norms. Equatorial Guinea, on the other hand, does not serve this purpose since its attitude about international norms is more ambivalent.

At any rate, it is clear that state elites face a choice with respect to membership in the international society, as is the case with private individuals. They may opt to be "loners" or "curmudgeons" – although the costs may be prohibitive. These choices do not diminish the reality of the society, however, and in general the members of international society continue to reach out to those on the fringes. It seems clear that to those on the inside, persuading outsiders to join is the most efficient means of ensuring their participation in a whole range of constructive activities.

The other "society" to which heads of state elites must choose to belong is the domestic society. As we have seen, national leaders have the option of insulating themselves from national society and treating citizens as means rather than ends.

Leaders' attitudes toward Kant's second formulation of the categorical imperative seems to be a relatively clear dividing line that explains policies on civil liberties, citizen empowerment and participation, welfare policy, and even official corruption (1993[1785], 30). The symbolism of the deposed dictator fleeing the country is potent: he is acknowledging his disassociation with the nation he ruled. The dictator's return must be forced and can be expected to result in his incarceration – yet another symbol of disassociation from his countrymen. This has already happened with Alberto Fujimori and may yet happen with Ben Ali of Tunisia.

On the other hand, some leaders appear to accept the notion that power is a trust and are willing to concede the need to accommodate the interests of the majority along with important segments of the population. This is most apparent in the case of Botswana, but is also evident at different times in Peru and Bolivia. It is reflected in a low degree of "executive tenacity" and a willingness to tolerate a free press, opposition parties, independent judges, a full airing of views and public comment on legislation, and fiscal transparency.

A head of state's engagement with the national society often dovetails with engagement with the international society – consistent with liberal theory. This need not always be the case, however, as leaders may sometimes find themselves forced to choose between the two, as in the case of raising tariffs to protect domestic jobs during a financial crisis or protecting Islamic terrorists from Christian courts. Even Western state elites sometimes find themselves torn between the demands of international and domestic society, as we see with respect to the internalization of European civil rights norms in British law (Stiles 2006).

Much in this work has addressed the relationships between state elites and international society on the one hand and between state elites and domestic society. Many have also discussed the links between domestic and international society, although it is far less understood than the other two relationships (Klotz 1995; Keck and Sikkink 1998; Simmons 2009). But these links play an important part in decisions by state elites to comply with international law – particularly where compliance requires substantial changes at the societal level. Compliance with anti-trafficking, anti-terror, anti-slavery, and women's rights laws requires far more than mere adoption of appropriate statutes, but rather the participation of ordinary citizens: husbands, fathers, brothers, plantation owners, mine operators, toy manufacturers, pimps, madams, johns, imams, and so forth. As we have seen, where these types of individuals are somehow "converted" to international norms state compliance is at least facilitated if not guaranteed. How this conversion occurs may take many forms – including advocacy and education by non-state actors and peers. This in turn is facilitated by political openness and multiple contacts to the outside – particularly Western – world. But liberalism and globalization can naturally backfire as well (Stiles 2002). They can deepen commitment to traditional social structures and norms and where the state is unwilling to advance international norms, practices and attitudes may never change (see Botswana with respect to women's rights).

Policy implications

That previous comment leads to some observations about increasing compliance, assuming this is generally a good thing. To begin, we should not assume that compliance is always a function of precision, obligation, or delegation. While it is often difficult to measure compliance with soft law, it is also the case that defiance is rare where those types of standards are concerned. However, as laws become increasingly precise, where the expectation of compliance increases, and where third parties have been asked to monitor and/or enforce them, compliance necessarily drops to a degree. At the very least, non-compliance is exposed and must therefore be addressed.

This is not to say that laws should remain soft – but that our expectations of full compliance should be tempered. As in the case of domestic law, partial compliance is often sufficient to achieve the desired results. Relatively few issue-areas involve a collective good of the "weakest link" variety in which all must contribute or all is lost (Sandler 2004). Even international terrorism can be largely inhibited if 80 or 90 percent of the world's governments are stable and have effective anti-terror policies in place (see Chapter 2). The same is true for human trafficking and ozone depletion. In most cases, what we are looking at is a "best shot" scenario in which compliance on the part of a critical mass of states – often a very few great powers – is enough to remedy the problem at hand. This is certainly true for such issues as global warming, ozone depletion, nuclear arms control, and international monetary stability. The goal of 100 percent compliance with every rule is not only unwarranted, it is also wasteful. It is far better to expend the world's energies on achieving sufficiency rather than perfection.

Next, it is better to understand the states with which we are dealing than to always adopt the role of schoolmaster. On the one hand, for instruction to be effective, the pupil must be ready to learn. The international community – particularly NGOs and IGOs – often assume that repeated chastisement ("naming and shaming") will wear down a state into submissive compliance. But doing so may have two very negative effects. As mentioned, it might embolden an anti-social government. But it might also breed contempt in the pliant one. The good news is that state sovereignty requires that laws obtain the consent of the governed before they can be considered binding. In most cases states will attempt to shield themselves from laws that they do not wish to implement. But not always. We should resist the temptation to put pressure on governments to endorse rules they will not soon internalize – particularly in the case of rules that are precise and binding. Although compliance may occur with respect to vulnerable and otherwise accommodating regimes, it will not happen with the rest. And it does not take a prophetic gift to anticipate that a time will come when those states that were pressured into compliance will take note of the fact that their more recalcitrant counterparts have been able to get away with something. The seeds of contemporary Latin American neo-mercantilism were sewn in the failure of American sanctions against Cuba. Rules must be "ripe" or they will simply turn sour. Specifically, since there is no connection between compliance on the one hand and a state's military dependence on the United States, it is perhaps best for the world's only superpower to restrain its efforts to pressure states to comply with international law. The danger that such efforts will backfire is great (Chomsky 2001), even if successful. Better to serve as a role model – a task that is difficult enough.

Taken together, liberal society at both the domestic and international levels is a key starting point for compliance with international law. World leaders should have reasons – both material and social – to wish to comply. Inclusion in global orders that are both just and profitable will create a potentially irresistible incentive to follow the rules. We have seen some evidence of this with respect to international trade regimes as well as European regionalism – despite their many flaws and the ulterior motives of many members. Invitations to participate ought to be cast far and wide, as recommended by Rawls (1999). Even "barbarians" and "criminals" may become part of this broad network of states. Selective sanction – particularly ostracism – should be applied selectively and consistently to punish anti-social behavior. But reformers should be exonerated quickly. After all, the difference between a pariah and a good citizen may be how the leader responds to a few thousand protesters in the streets.

References

Chomsky, Noam (2001) *Blowback: The Costs and Consequences of American Empire*. New York: Henry Holt & Co.

Doyle, Michael (1986) "Liberalism and World Politics," *The American Political Science Review* 80(4) (December): 1151–1169.

Grieco, Joseph M., Christopher F. Gelpi, and T. Camber Warren (2009) "When Preferences and Commitments Collide: The Effect of Relative Partisan Shifts on International Treaty Compliance," *International Organization* 63 (Spring): 341–355.

Hathaway, Oona (2002) "Do Human Rights Treaties Make a Difference?" *Yale Law Journal* 111: 1935–2041.

Kant, Immanuel (1993[1785]) *Grounding for the Metaphysics of Morals*. 3rd edn. translated by James W. Ellington. Indianapolis: Hackett.

Keck, Margaret and Kathryn Sikkink (1998) *Activists Beyond Borders*. Ithaca: Cornell University Press.

Klotz, Audie (1995) *Norms in International Relations: The Struggle against Apartheid*. Ithaca: Cornell University Press.

Rawls, John (1999) *The Law of Peoples*. Cambridge, London: Harvard University Press.

Sandler, Todd (2004) *Global Collective Action*. Cambridge: Cambridge University Press.

Simmons, Beth (2009) *Mobilizing for Human Rights: International Law in Domestic Politics*. New York: Cambridge University Press.

Stiles, Kendall (2002) *Civil Society by Design: Donors, NGOs and Intermestic Development Circles in Bangladesh*. Westport, CT: Praeger Publishers.

Stiles, Kendall (2006) "Transnational Norms, International Institutions and Attitude Shifts: The Case of the ECHR and the UK," *Canadian Journal of Political Science* 39(1) (March): 1–24.

Tomz, Michael (2007) *Reputation and International Cooperation: Sovereign Debt across Three Centuries*. Princeton: Princeton University Press.

Index

For Product Safety Concerns and Information please contact our EU representative GPSR@taylorandfrancis.com
Taylor & Francis Verlag GmbH, Kaufingerstraße 24, 80331 München, Germany

www.ingramcontent.com/pod-product-compliance
Ingram Content Group UK Ltd.
Pitfield, Milton Keynes, MK11 3LW, UK
UKHW020017200926
475702UK00014B/1927
9780415791090